Cultural Complexity in Organizations

Cultural Complexity
in Organizations

Inherent Contrasts and Contradictions

Sonja A. Sackmann

Editor

SAGE Publications
International Educational and Professional Publisher
Thousand Oaks   London   New Delhi

For information:

SAGE Publications, Inc.
2455 Teller Road
Thousand Oaks, California 91320
E-mail: order@sagepub.com

SAGE Publications Ltd.
6 Bonhill Street
London EC2A 4PU
United Kingdom

SAGE Publications India Pvt. Ltd.
M-32 Market
Greater Kailash I
New Delhi 110 048 India

Printed in the United States of America

Library of Congress Cataloging-in-Publication Data

Sackmann, Sonja, 1955-
    Cultural complexity in organizations/Sonja A. Sackmann.
      p. cm.
    Includes bibliographical references and index.
    ISBN 0-7619-0574-X.—ISBN 0-7619-0575-8 (pbk.)
    1. Corporate culture. 2. Multiculturalism. I. Title.
HD58.7.S228 1997
302.3'5—dc20   96-35691

This book is printed on acid-free paper.

97 98 99 00 01 02 03 10 9 8 7 6 5 4 3 2

Acquiring Editor:	Marquita Flemming
Editorial Assistant:	Frances Borghi
Production Editor:	Diana E. Axelsen
Production Assistant:	Denise Santoyo
Typesetter/Designer:	Marion Warren
Cover Designer:	Ravi Balasuriya
Print Buyer:	Anna Chin

Contents

Part I:
Culture With a Focus on the National Level

Part II:
Culture With a Focus on
the Organizational Level 105

Acknowledgments

Many people have contributed to this book—directly and indirectly. First of all, I thank all authors in this volume for their willingness to continue to polish their ideas and manuscripts up to this stage and bear with my faxes, phone calls, and some of the streamlining I needed to do for the sake of the flow of the book. I also thank those who participated in our heated and stimulating discussions during the three days of the EGOS Colloquium in Istanbul and those whose work is not included in this volume because of a different focus or the stage of the research. I hope that some of the spirit of our stimulating discussions in Istanbul is present in this book.

Maggi, many thanks to you as my dear friend and critical colleague. I could always count on your emotional as well as professional support and your advice from the "M.O.M." (Mothers in Management) voice. Without that and all those years of intense intellectual discussions regarding the issues of culture and cultural multiplicity in organizational settings, the idea for this book would not have been born.

Many thanks to Marquita Flemming from Sage, who took an immediate interest in publishing this book, and her helpers at Sage, Frances Borghi, Diana Axelsen, Denise Santoyo, Marion Warren, and Anna Chin, who brought the manuscript into its final book version. I am also indebted to Katrina Burrus, who corrected the English in several of the manuscripts. Silke Agricola, my secretary at the University BW Munich, has done a tremendous job with integrating all my editing into the final manuscript and converting all contributions to the same format. In addition to Silke, Michaela Birus, Sandra Kienleitner, Thomas Dettling, and my colleagues at the Department of Management and Organizational Sciences (Fakultät für Wirtschafts- und Organisationswissenschaften) have managed to keep my duties at the university to a minimum during my sabbatical, which I used to prepare this book.

Finally, I am grateful for your emotional and technical support, Wolfi, and I hope, Julia and Angela, the time will come when you understand why I could not let you sit on my lap and play with my computer or play with you as often as the two of you wanted. This is why I dedicate the book to the two of you.

Chapter 1

Introduction

Sonja A. Sackmann

The concept of culture as it applies to organizations has gone through various stages since its rediscovery in the early 1980s. The initial phase of infatuation was followed by disenchantment. Many organizational scholars and practitioners wrote and talked about the importance of culture for an enhanced understanding of organizational life and about its relevance for organizational performance. Little rigor and less consensus, however, existed regarding the use of the term *culture* (Sackmann, 1991, pp. 7-32). The few empirical studies that were performed were too spotty to contribute to a better understanding, and culture change programs seemed more likely to produce frustration than to improve corporate performance.

This picture has changed. Interest in the concept of culture has become more serious and more differentiated. Attempts have been made toward more rigorous conceptualizations both of the concept (Sackmann, 1991) and of the field (Frost, Moore, Reis Louis, Lundberg, & Martin, 1991; Martin, 1992; Sackmann & Phillips, 1992). Research on the failure of reengineering projects has revealed that cultural issues deserve more serious attention and attention of a different kind (Scott-Morgan, 1994).

Most of the conceptualizations of, as well as the research on, culture, however, give a "cleaner" or more rational picture than the nature of the concept and its manifestations in organizational life may deserve. For example, as Frost et al.

(1991) and Martin (1992) point out, understandings of culture and its study have been primarily framed within one of their advocated perspectives. Culture in organizational settings is treated as a homogenous or integrated entity, as a differentiated entity composed of several subcultures, or as a fragmented entity characterized by ambiguity.

The results of my research on the formation and location of subcultures in a conglomerate, however, indicated that culture within an organizational setting may be both integrated and differentiated at the same time (Sackmann, 1991, 1992). To be able to surface both, however, requires a sufficiently fine-grained perspective of culture and its operationalization. The framework of cultural knowledge that I developed in this research proved to have this fine granulation. This framework identified various types of commonly held knowledge—for example, directory knowledge (the "how"—how things are done) and dictionary knowledge (the "what"—the labels people use to denominate things and events). With regard to directory knowledge, a homogenous culture existed across different divisions, locations, and industries of the conglomerate. With regard to dictionary knowledge, several differentiated subcultures could be found. If I reanalyzed my data across all four kinds of cultural knowledge, I probably would find evidence of fragmentation as well. In addition, real-life experiences and the combination of research conducted at different organizational levels suggested that multiple cultures are carried to organizations by individuals and may influence organizational life. This led to what Maggi Phillips and I (Phillips, Goodman, & Sackmann, 1992; Sackmann & Phillips, 1992; Multiple Cultures, Chapter 2, this volume) labeled the "multiple cultures perspective."

The concept of cultural complexity advocated in this book encompasses both ideas: simultaneously existing multiple cultures that may contribute to a homogenous, differentiated, and/or fragmented cultural context. Hence, the cultural complexity perspective suggests that culture in organizational settings is much more complex, pluralistic, diverse, contradictory, or inherently paradoxical than previously assumed, conceptualized, or acknowledged. Members of an organization are unlikely to be restricted in their membership to one single culture or subculture, because people may identify with their gender, ethnic background, parent and spouse roles, sports club, city, the university from which they hold a degree, profession, department, division, work organization, geographical region, industry, nation, or greater region such as Europe, America, or Asia. All these potential cultural identities may simultaneously influence the cultural context of an organization, as illustrated in Figure 1.1.

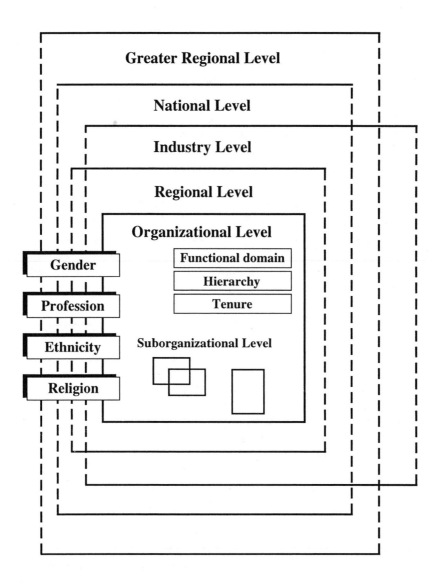

Figure 1.1. The Cultural Context of an Organization

In addition to the multiple cultural levels that may be reflected in simultaneously existing multiple cultural identities, aspects of cultural homogeneity may characterize an organization in combination with the existence of several subcultures. The resulting picture of cultural life in organizational settings may thus be full of contrasts and contradictions, showing aspects of harmony next to differentiation with or without dissent and a multiplicity of cultural identities that may be in a constant flux depending on the issues at hand. Hence, the concept of cultural complexity goes beyond existing conceptualizations and overcomes Western *either-or* logic by replacing it with a *both-and* logic.

Because this perspective is a rather new and difficult framework for empirical research, few studies have been conducted from this perspective of cultural complexity. This was the reason I chose to use this perspective as a framework for a conference track that I was asked to develop for the 12th European Group of Organization Studies Colloquium held in Istanbul in July 1995. This perspective served as a subtheme around which I coordinated a working group during the three days of the colloquium. The "best" contributions to the working group, which were revised on the basis of the working group's feedback, are included in the book along with several other chapters of like quality and focus. Here, the word *best* implies that each chapter makes a valuable contribution to an enhanced understanding of cultural complexity in organizations as defined previously in that

1. each chapter is based on original empirical research (except the first one, which is conceptual);
2. included chapters focus on different levels of culture and their dynamic interplay;
3. the chosen research settings represent a wide spread across industries, most of which have been infrequently studied or not at all;
4. methodologies employed are appropriate for the research question, innovative, and show a wide range of possible ways to uncover cultural complexity, including quantitative and qualitative approaches;
5. authors go beyond description and make recommendations regarding how to better deal with different aspects of this cultural complexity in organizational settings; and
6. authors themselves represent a wide range of cultural backgrounds and bring with them different lenses and perspectives to tackle cultural complexity.

Hence, this book is designed to represent a microcosmos of the cultural complexity perspective. The selection of chapters is based on variety, difference, nontraditional research, and their authors' commitment to contribute to a better understanding of cultural complexity as well as some of its implications for management, research, or both. Authors demonstrate imaginative research approaches that go beyond mainstream methodologies. Much of the research required a longitudinal perspective, implying dedication, focus, and commitment to a single stream of research. Some of the research is based on several years of data collection at the research site, including participant observations and, at times, interventions. Most of the authors go beyond pure description in that they address relevant issues for management.

The style of writing and reasoning of some of the contributions may be somewhat unusual for a native North American trained in the United States university system. Although we tried to "Westernize," "Americanize," or Anglicize some of the chapters with my suggestions to the contributors and with the help of a native English speaker, the difference or otherness still shines through, especially in contributors' style of reasoning and, at times, in their advocacy of value-based stands in their research process.

The contributors address culture at various levels, including different national, industry, organizational, and suborganizational contexts. The issues that are addressed include implicit managerial understandings and overt practices; in-depth case studies of the growth and decline of organizations with a focus on culture; managerial control strategies and the dynamics of subcultural formation; change and temporary reconciliation; factors that influence homogeneity and heterogeneity and that contribute to the maintenance of a "strong" corporate culture even in recessionary times; and issues of gender, ethnicity, and social and organizational identity as concepts that may foster a better understanding of the complexities inherent in handling multiple cultural identities.

A variety of different and nontraditional research settings are represented in this book, such as the Korean company Samsung, a car plant in Slovenia, a U.S. software developer, a Dutch amusement park, Hewlett-Packard's (HP) British operation, the shop floor of a Japanese transplant in Great Britain, a company in the Finnish paper industry, Dutch supermarket stores, a Swiss bank, an airline (Scandinavian Airlines System [SAS]), Philips plants in Austria, and Shell operating in Curaçao. Examples are also drawn from the not-for-profit sector, such as a Swiss reading society, the Dutch police force, and Norwegian hospitals. Only a few of these settings —HP, banks, and airlines—have been extensively researched. Even in these cases, however, the focus of research is different—revealing HP's bureaucratic side, listening to a woman's voice in a male banking setting, or focusing on a strike among employees of SAS, which is usually cited for its "great" and homogenous culture.

The perspectives from which the contributions of the book are researched and written are also rooted in multicultural backgrounds. The authors are from Denmark, Finland, France, Germany, Great Britain, Korea, The Netherlands, Norway, Switzerland, Turkey, and the United States. Their professional background is mostly interdisciplinary, including management, organization studies, psychology, sociology, and anthropology. They conducted their research from different professional roles, such as doctoral student; assembly-line worker; and professor, manager, or consultant.

Despite all this diversity, there is a common bond that all contributors share; it is the cultural diversity among the contributors, their interest in cultural complexity, and their willingness to look beyond their various cultural boundaries—especially their professional ones. All the chapters, written from the authors' cultural perspectives, make a valuable contribution to a better and enhanced understanding of the impact of cultural complexity on organizational life. In that respect, this book represents work in progress. I hope that more researchers will be encouraged to investigate the messiness of culture in organizations and do not shy away from such research for practical reasons or career issues.

Overview of the Book

The book is organized into five parts on the basis of the cultural context of organizations. Figure 1.1 serves as a map for the reader to locate the various issues addressed in the different studies. The second chapter presents an overview of research and perspectives in international cross-cultural management research. This chapter's last section provides a detailed description of the multiple cultures perspective. This discussion frames for the reader the issues and levels of culture addressed in the chapters that follow. It helps the reader understand the grouping of the contributions into specific parts of the book. Although most of the chapters address several levels of culture, they are grouped according to the following major research foci:

- Part I focuses on the national level combined with ideological and industry foci.
- Part II focuses on the organizational level.
- Part III focuses on the suborganizational level.
- Part IV explores the cross-cutting issue of ethnicity.
- Part V provides some answers regarding the handling of multiple cultural identities.

Chapter 2, "Single and Multiple Cultures in International Cross-Cultural Management Research: Overview," provides an overview of the evolution of research and perspectives of treating culture in management research. Authors Sonja A. Sackmann, Margaret E. Phillips, M. Jill Kleinberg, and Nakiye A. Boyacigiller classify approaches into three groups: cross-national comparison, intercultural interaction, and multiple cultures. Each perspective is discussed in terms of its framing context, underlying assumptions and frameworks, and insights gained. This book utilizes the multiple cultures perspective in that the chapters provide data for a number of the issues raised within this perspective. The authors are from the United States, Germany, and Turkey. They all teach, research, and consult in the area of management but have different specializations such as strategy, organizational behavior, human resource management, and anthropology.

The major focus of the chapters in Part I is on the national, ideological, and industry level. In Chapter 3, Seungkwon Jang and Myung-Ho Chung use discourse analysis to explore the ideological differences between Eastern ("Confucian capitalism") discourses and Western ("Protestant capitalism") discourses and discuss the implications for Korean management practices, which embrace the contradictions of tradition and modernity. Using Samsung's management renewal program, they illustrate how Korean management practices have succeeded in combining these discursive contradictions based on the Korean tradition of social responsibilities for both people and organizations. They argue that this "skill" of combining paradoxes and managing them successfully is the major factor for Korean management's success and may be more generally for firms in the future.

Chapter 4, by Tatjana Globokar, takes us from Asia to Eastern Europe. Commissioned by French Management, Globokar carried out an action research study in the plant of a French company's automobile factory in Slovenia. This factory had been taken over by a French car producer in 1989, and this takeover created problems for French management. Her participant observations and in-depth interviews conducted with 40 informants across hierarchical levels and functions over a period of four years revealed major culture clashes in daily work and in their interpretation of management concepts such as total quality. These culture clashes were predominantly based on national differences. In addition, Globokar discusses the role of the researcher, which went beyond gathering data and became that of a translator and mediator between the two factions. She was able to fill this role because of her specific background as a native of that region, a specialist of the economies of Eastern Europe and their cultural management models, and a person who had worked and lived in both Germany and France.

The last chapter of Part I, by Yasemin Arbak, Ceyhan Aldemir, Ömür Timur-canday Özmen, Alev Ergenç Katrinli, Gülem Atabay Ishakoglu, and Jülide Kesken, investigates the nature of Turkish managers by comparing perceptions of Turkish managers in the private and public sectors. Strictly speaking, their questionnaire study focuses on the industry level (private vs. public). The study and discussion, however, also reveal interesting issues at the national level. Hofstede's (1980) characterization of Turkey as having high power distance, strong uncertainty avoidance, femininity, and collectivism seems to apply today predominantly to the public sector, with its roots in the Ottoman Empire, but no longer to today's private sector. The private sector is relatively young in Turkey and seems to be much more closely related to Western entrepreneurship with its youth, dynamism, risk taking, entrepreneurship, openness to change, innovation, and ambition. When Hofstede collected his data in the late 1960s and early 1970s, the private sector was virtually nonexistent in Turkey.

The four chapters included in Part II focus primarily on the organizational level. Terry Schumacher tells the story of the rise and decline of the culture of a 10-year-old software engineering corporation in the United States, basing his account on an ethnography that he conducted during a five-year period. He first describes the constructivist approach that he used to surface knowledge domains. His study explores issues of culture development, including culture-building activities; culture change, including contrasts and contradictions; and subculture formation and factors that contributed to its decline. The change process was associated with the company's rapid growth from "9 guys in the garage" to nearly 3,000 employees with $400 million in annual revenues. Interestingly, a major factor in the cultural decline process was that a highly valued culture characteristic (working long hours) based on voluntary "buying in and making a contribution" was turned into an explicit demand by management. Schumacher concludes with some propositions about cultural dynamics in organizations.

Thomas S. Eberle's study takes us from Schumacher's high-tech, for-profit organization and Silicon Valley to a nonprofit reading society of a small town in Switzerland. The reader is introduced to the organization of reading societies as carriers of the modernization process and as products of the Age of Enlightenment with their characteristics of voluntary membership, self-determined objectives, structures, and processes. On the basis of documentary analysis, he reconstructs some essentials of the society's cultural life from its beginnings until its death, including an analysis of external factors, inherent contrasts, contradictions of goals and objectives, and how these were handled by different management. Interest-ingly, the very purpose that fostered the society's growth also contributed to its decline, both because the changes in the external environment were not sufficiently considered by management and because management could not successfully manage the cultural paradoxes. The reader also learns more about the dynamics of change, or rather of preventing change, in a democratic society through a success-fully staged process by a minority.

The third contribution in Part II takes the reader to an amusement park in The Netherlands. Although Sierk Ybema addresses subcultures, the main focus of the study is at the organizational level. He integrates quantitative and qualitative data in his study to investigate subculture formation and culture change. The results illustrate the messiness of cultural life and thus support the complex culture perspective. The results reveal different subcultures between shop floor service workers and white-collar office workers and between the "old guard" and the "new guard," and cultural conflicts between formal and informal authority. They also show how people can manage to reconcile and live with cultural paradoxes. With regard to culture change, his findings are closely related to Schumacher's. In Ybema's case, however, the gradual growth of the amusement park and its professionalization changed the park's core ideology of a fairy-tale amusement park into a commercially managed and successful operation selling fun to as many people as possible.

Chapter 9, by Patrick McGovern and Veronica Hope-Hailey, examines the use of corporate culture as a management tool in organizations in postrecessionary times. The authors studied Hewlett-Packard's U.K. operations with two foci: what happened to HP's core philosophy of lifetime employment when confronted with a major downsizing program and the role of HP's managerial control strategies. The methods for data collection included quantitative and qualitative approaches (semistructured and unstructured interviews as well as a questionnaire survey). Despite the negative impacts of downsizing that contradicted or even violated "The HP Way," the authors describe how employees managed to retain a high level of organizational commitment through the flexible interpretation of a symbolic creed across business units and countries. In addition, they found a highly developed form of bureaucratic control to be an integral part of the HP culture. Paradoxically, this close attention to detailed measurement is supposed to promote employees' individual freedom, innovation, and entrepreneurial spirit.

Part III contains four chapters that explore culture with a focus on the suborganizational level. Katrina Burrus invites the reader to journey into the conference room of one of Switzerland's three big universal banks to explore a decision-making situation of the top executive group from the perspective of a professional woman and U.S. national. Her experiential narrative sheds light on the inherent contrasts and contradictions of gender issues and culture clashes at the national and regional levels in that bank, which is a good representative of Swiss national culture. The narrative is even more striking when the reader learns that the issue of decision making is the funding ($7,000) that the president of the Women Managers' Association is asking for their program. The narrative characterizes and typifies quite well the organizational life in that country, region, and industry.

Diana Rosemary Sharpe takes the reader to the shop floor of a Japanese transplant in the United Kingdom and explores managerial control strategies and subcultural processes. Her work is based on an ethnography and participant observation in which she worked on one of the assembly lines for an extended period of time. Her detailed description and analysis of the social processes and social relations on the shop floor focus on the cultural dynamics, how people coped with conflicting issues, and the nature and dynamics of managerial control systems utilized within a manufacturing system characterized by "just-in-time," total quality management, and lean production. She identified several subcultures in a complex interplay: the imposed Japanese best practices imported by the expatriates; the adaptation of these practices to the national and regional culture by local managers; and the interpretation of these practices and their enactment at the firm's model assembly line where task, authority, and age subcultures conflicted with each other, both influencing and being influenced by the evolving managerial control strategies. It is interesting to see how old and young assembly-line workers developed quite different ways of coping with managerial demands and control strategies.

Juha Laurila's case study of managerial subcultures of a Finnish paper industry company explores how conflicting managerial subcultures become mobilized and reconcile temporarily when faced with discontinuous technological change. His data included a combination of oral history, different kinds of interview, documentary, and survey data collected during several years, partly in real time using the situation of discontinuous technological change as a means to expose existing subcultures. Despite their common background (same industry, all managers, the same gender, and sharing a technical background), subcultures existed between company and mill management and between old-timers and newcomers. These subcultures are characterized in terms of their typical representatives. Nevertheless, the members of all subcultures bought into a major change project as long as the outlook was successful—but for quite different reasons. As such, the same overt behavior was spurred by very different reasons, hopes, expectations, and ideologies. When it became clear that some of the objectives could not be reached or that the project might even fail, however, the old subcultures became reinforced, and the managers blamed each other. Hence, the reader learns more about the staging and managing of a change process in a situation of conflicting subcultures.

The study by Bas A. Koene, Christophe A. J. J. Boone, and Joseph L. Soeters uses an empirically derived data set to investigate the variation in cultural agreement among employees in 50 supermarket stores of a Dutch retail chain and the impact of social and organizational factors on cultural homogeneity (operationalized as agreement within the stores). Methodologically, the authors try to bridge the gap between a comparative quantitative focus on cultural diversity and a qualitative in-depth focus. Among other things, the results of the quantitative analyses show that store size and level of agreement are negatively related, but, surprisingly, that the number of departments within a store as well as demographic diversity are positively related to cultural homogeneity. The authors suggest that extra efforts may be spent by store supervisors toward integrating a larger number of departments and, in the case of demographic diversity, in communicating more explicitly "the way we work here." They also found that a climate of innovation is related to a low level of agreement at the task level. Although some may argue that quantitatively measuring perceptions of organizational climate and leadership is not the best way to operationalize cultural diversity, the study provides some valuable insights regarding both methodology and the interplay of cultural homogeneity and heterogeneity based on quantitative data.

Part IV contains two chapters that explore ethnicity as cross-cutting organizational, industrial, regional, and national boundaries. Both chapters, especially Chapter 15, also explore how ethnicity can be used as a "strategic tool."

The contribution by Sjiera de Vries investigates ethnic diversity in the context of multiethnic teams within the Dutch police force, with a focus on issues of discrimination, solo role, and affirmative action. The findings provide insight into the complexity of perceptions and problems related to multiethnic teams. They are based on the content analysis of 90 interviews that were always conducted with a triad of people: minority officers, their majority colleagues, and their supervisor. The term *multicultural* was immediately interpreted as creating a problem of discrimination for the minority who did not want to be approached as a minority. Situations of discrimination were perceived quite differently by the majority colleague and the minority person. After having overcome initial problems, all three groups of respondents saw several benefits in working in a multicultural group, including the loss of their prejudices.

Willem C. J. Koot argues that ethnicity is a strong organizing principle and a good vehicle for social mobility because it rallies people of all ranks and ages. He questions the basic assumptions as well as the feasibility of the view of cultural synergy in which the positive aspects of all cultures involved are combined. Instead, he advocates ethnic rivalry as a means to produce energy and power. He describes two cases of ethnic rivalry that he studied from an anthropological and ethnographic perspective. One is between two Philips plants located in two different regions of Austria and the other between Curaçaoans and Venezuelans in a former Shell refinery on Curaçao. In the Philips case, a fighting spirit emerged in the newer "country" plant that resulted in excellent productivity and their takeover of the older Viennese plant. The refinery case tells a story of the rise, fall, and resurrection of European, Dutch, and Shell cultures in the Curaçao refinery environment with their complex dynamics involved. After exploring potential answers regarding how to deal with ethnocentrism and ethnic rivalry on the basis of the theory of intercultural management, Koot suggests that ethnicity should be used strategically to tap this source of energy and power in dealing with issues of increasing ethnic and national segmentation, identification, and rivalry in the age of globalization.

The two chapters in Part V suggest that organizational and social identity may be a critical concept in understanding human behavior when dealing with complex cultural settings. Helge Hernes explores the issue of salience or magnitude of cultural identification and how people deal with multiple and conflicting identities. He presents a framework for understanding multigroup memberships and their cognitive and behavioral consequences. This framework is based on social identity and self-categorization theory. He applied the framework in his questionnaire study of intergroup relations in 145 departments of 48 Norwegian hospitals, with a focus on profession (comparing doctors and nurses). His results indicate that the concept of social identification is much more complex and multifaceted than previously conceptualized. Furthermore, profession seems to be the prominent explanatory variable for the direction of prosocial behavior.

Peter Dahler-Larsen explores organizational identity, or, rather, "we typifications," as key to organizational identity. These are defined as "what is essentially distinct and relatively stable over time for those who identify with it." He uses two strikes at SAS—the first among Danish cabin attendants and the second in which the attendants were joined by thousands of employees in Copenhagen to shed light on how people handle different cultural identifications that may come into conflict with each other. In his in-depth interviews with key informants, he explored "who are we," "who are they," and how boundaries between "us" and "them" should be managed. His case description, results, and discussion provide a rich understanding of how the cabin attendants handled their simultaneously existing identities at the national level (Danes), the organizational level (SAS), the professional level (cabin attendants), and the suborganizational level (employee function) and how the salience of these identities shifted during the nine-day strike as events unfolded.

While reading the different chapters, the reader is encouraged to use Figure 1.1 for reference and orientation. This figure can be used to locate the various issues that are addressed in the chapters, the answers that are given from a certain cultural perspective, and the additional questions that are raised with regard to cultural complexity. Readers may ask themselves what they learn from each chapter about

- multiple cultures and multiple cultural identities and their dynamic interplay;
- ways to handle and manage simultaneously existing multiple cultures;
- creative ways to research multiple cultures; and
- the specific cultural perspectives that authors take in their research and in their writing.

The mix of readings may lead to an increasingly differentiated picture and even new understandings about cultural complexity in organizations including its inherent contrasts and apparent contradictions. The readers may feel invited and are encouraged to assess personal experiences of cultural complexity in prior and current organizational engagement. The new frame may include inconsistencies or paradoxes that were previously rationalized away or overlooked. Furthermore, new ideas may arise in the reading process about critical research questions that need to be pursued in the future.

References

Frost, P. J., Moore, L. F., Reis Louis, M., Lundberg, C. C., & Martin, J. (Eds.). (1991). *Reframing organizational culture*. Newbury Park, CA: Sage.

Hofstede, J. (1980). *Culture's consequences: International differences in work-related values*. Beverly Hills, CA: Sage.

Martin, J. (1992). *Cultures in organizations: Three perspectives*. New York: Oxford University Press.

Phillips, M. E., Goodman, R. A., & Sackmann, S. A. (1992). Exploring the complex cultural milieu of project teams. *pmNETwork—Professional Magazine of the Project Management Institute, 7*(8), 20-26.

Sackmann, S. A. (1991). *Cultural knowledge in organizations: Exploring the collective mind*. Newbury Park, CA: Sage.

Sackmann, S. A. (1992). Cultures and subcultures: An analysis of organizational knowledge. *Administrative Science Quarterly, 37*(1), 140-161.

Sackmann, S. A., & Phillips, M. E. (1992). *Mapping the cultural terrain in organizational settings: Current boundaries and future directions for empirical research* (CIBER Working Paper No. 92-05). Los Angeles: University of California at Los Angeles, Anderson Graduate School of Management, Center for International Business.

Scott-Morgan, (1994). *The unwritten rules of the game*. New York: McGraw-Hill.

Chapter 2

Single and Multiple Cultures in International Cross-Cultural Management Research

Overview

Sonja A. Sackmann
Margaret E. Phillips
M. Jill Kleinberg
Nakiye A. Boyacigiller

Globalization is causing researchers engaged in cross-cultural organizational re-search to reconsider the notion of "cultural identity" and to question traditional ways of viewing its antecedent, the construct "culture." As our organizational contexts become more complex, and simultaneously more culturally diverse, what is the most efficacious way to consider cultural identity and to conceptualize culture? Embedded in this question are assumptions about the nature and mandate of scientific inquiry. What is it that we seek to learn from cross-cultural research? What are productive ways to deal with the concept of culture in research designs? Does the rapid globalization of business make different demands on the type of cross-cultural management research that should be done? How does the nature and mandate of cross-cultural management research reflect the social, political, and economic context of the time?

In this chapter, we review and interpret international cross-cultural management research (ICCM)[1] with regard to the conceptualization of culture. Our perspective is historical and largely North American.

In our review of the international cross-cultural management literature, we find evidence of three streams of research, each with a relatively distinct interpretation of the culture construct. We find the central characteristic of each stream to be the degree to which cultural identity is seen as having a single or multiple nature. These three streams of research are found to grow out of different social, economic, political, and intellectual contexts. We see the direct reflection of these variations in context in the conceptualization of culture employed by each stream. This is further evidenced by differences in the theoretical and assumptional underpinnings of each perspective; distinctions in the character, manner, and content of research questions posed; diversity in the frameworks or methodologies employed or both; and, consequently, variations in the knowledge and understanding we have acquired or could glean from each perspective. We tentatively identify these streams as

1. studies with a focus on cross-national comparison;
2. studies with an intercultural interaction focus; and
3. studies from a multiple cultures perspective.

For each stream of research, we address the following issues:

a. the context that framed and encouraged the stream of research;
b. assumptions and frameworks underlying the perspective and research methods typically employed; and
c. insights gleaned from the research stream.

Our larger quest is to ascertain what we have learned from international cross-cultural management research that has employed different conceptualizations of culture and has viewed cultural identity as single or multiple in nature. Directions for future research in cross-cultural organization and management are drawn.

Cross-National Comparison

Historical Context of Cross-National Comparative Research

Just as organizations are imprinted during their early years and carry that influence permanently, so too is social inquiry (Stinchcombe, 1965). Even today, the field of ICCM appears to bear the imprint of its early years. Interest in cross-cultural management research first arose in the United States during the late 1950s and mid-1960s, led by the pioneering work of Harbison and Myers (1959), Farmer and Richman (1965), and Haire, Ghiselli, and Porter (1966). The imprint of this era and of these intellectual foundations of the field continues to be reflected in the dominant stream of ICCM research—cross-national comparison—and in its unique and implicit conceptualization of culture as a nation-based independent variable.

World War II had left most of the industrialized economies of the world decimated. Thus, following the war, the United States accounted for 75% of the world's gross national product (Thurow, 1988). The 1960s were characterized by continued American economic dominance (Servan-Schreiber, 1968; Thurow, 1988), most dramatically symbolized by the international reach of U.S. corporations. As they moved into ever-expanding markets around the globe (Vernon, 1971), the growing importance of multinational corporations and the reality of operating in different economic and political environments created a need to understand different national contexts and the implications of these contexts for the management of organizations.

At the same time, academic management research was primarily a Western and, to a large degree, a U.S. enterprise (Boyacigiller & Adler, 1991). In addition to the interest in U.S. management practices bred by the economic success of the United States, institutional forces, such as the leadership of key journal editorial boards and academic professional organizations and the minimal international content of doctoral programs, encouraged a parochial approach to management inquiry. Furthermore, few researchers explicitly addressed the influence of American cultural values on the largely U.S.-based organization science (Adler, 1991; Adler & Jelinek, 1986; Boyacigiller & Adler, 1991; Burrell & Morgan, 1979; Hofstede, 1980a, 1980b; Newman, 1972). These contextual, institutional, and cultural factors led to an implicit universalism in much of organization science.

The political context of the time, complemented and encouraged by the economic expansion of the United States, promoted a great concern with development. Because the defining political agenda for the post-World War II period in the United States was the ideological and real war against communism, this interest in development was natural. From the U.S. perspective, the countries most at risk of communism were the developing countries of Asia, Africa, and Latin America. If mechanisms could be found to bolster development, it was less likely that communism would take hold. The comparative study of management became important because management was viewed as "the single most critical social activity in connection with economic progress" (Farmer & Richman, 1965, p. 1).

Assumptions, Frameworks, and Methods of Cross-National Comparative Research

Because the economic and political context encouraged attention to cross-national differences, the early movers in ICCM adopted the nation-state as the logical unit of analysis. "Nation-state" became a surrogate for culture. Because national origin was considered a given, single, and permanent characteristic of an individual, cultural identity was also assumed to be given, single, and permanent.

A particular set of circumstances fostered the acceptance of these assumptions. From a practical standpoint, cross-cultural management research was initially undertaken to better understand how to conduct business in and with other nations. Data collection for such international research, however, was found to present very real logistical difficulties. Also, many researchers in the field at the time believed that no universal definition of culture existed (Kroeber & Kluckhohn as cited in Farmer & Richman, 1965). Given these circumstances, it is understandable that researchers were attracted by the relative ease of assuming cultural and national borders to be synonymous in the conduct of their work.

Two differing sets of interests emerged from the pioneering work in the field of ICCM, each with differing implications for the conceptualization of culture in subsequent cross-national comparative research. Harbison and Myers (1959) and Farmer and Richman (1965) were the precursors to an interest in the relationship between management and economic development and the interest in comparative management (Nath, 1986). Culture per se was not of interest.[2] These works were also strongly multidisciplinary in their orientation, especially the work of Farmer and Richman (1965), who included educational-cultural, sociological-cultural, political-legal, and economic variables in their model. Both works were premised on the convergence hypothesis, which predicts the "convergence of cultures [toward a single, homogeneous, and pervasive global culture] as well as [the development of a common set of] applicable management principles and practices, throughout the industrial world" even if "this type of universal convergence is likely to take decades, generations, and even centuries in some extreme cases" (Farmer & Richman, 1965, p. 394). Although no longer articulated with the same optimism or force, the convergence thesis hypothesizing the emergence of a single culture continues to maintain an important philosophical place in cross-national comparative research (Kerr, 1983).

Haire et al.'s (1966) *Managerial Thinking: An International Study,* with its explicit focus on managerial attitudes, can be more closely seen as the precursor to later studies aimed at understanding the link between cultural values and managerial attitudes and behaviors. Haire et al. sought to determine whether managers around the world hold similar attitudes.

They also sought to understand if certain country clusters exist. Theirs was the first large-scale empirical study in international cross-cultural management. As such, *Managerial Thinking* reflects many of the assumptions about cross-cultural research that were prevalent at the time. Of central importance in their thesis were the assumptions that

- cultural boundaries coincide with national boundaries,[3] and
- national, and hence cultural, identity was a given, single, and permanent characteristic of an individual.

Other critical cultural assumptions of Haire et al. (1966) included the following:

- The dependent variable of interest was managerial attitudes and not culture—in fact, culture was not defined a priori.
- Culture was considered an independent variable.
- If significant differences could be found across nations, holding other factors constant, then these differences were attributed to cultural differences; culture, however, (again), was not explicitly measured.

The lack of explicit attention to culture continued unabated with most of the cross-national research of the 1970s. Ajiferuke and Boddewyn (1970) found that, of 22 studies they reviewed that had culture as an independent variable, only 2 attempted to define it. Roberts and Boyacigiller (1984) found an overwhelming majority of studies employing culture as an independent variable and used it as a categorical variable—that is, as a pseudonym for "nation" (Nath, 1986, p. 252).

A significant exception to this trend was the work of Triandis (1972). Triandis offered the notion of subjective culture as "a cultural group's characteristic way of perceiving the man-made part of its environment" (p. 4). His model of culture includes distal antecedents (physical and environmental resources and historical events), proximal antecedents (such as occupation, language, and religion), basic psychological processes (cognitive learning and conditioning), subjective culture (a complex interplay of roles, norms, tasks, affect, cognitive structures, and behavioral intentions), and consequences (patterns of actions). Triandis's work influenced that of many subsequent authors of cross-national comparative studies (England, 1975; England & Harpaz, 1983; Erez & Earley, 1993). The utility of his framework, however, remains limited by the absence of middle-range theories specifying "how particular variables subsumed under each of these concepts are related to variables subsumed under adjacent concepts" (Triandis, 1972, p. 24).

Culture's Consequences (Hofstede, 1980a) filled an important vacuum in the field as cross-national comparative researchers gained a parsimonious, readily accessible set of universal dimensions from which measures of culture could be derived. On the basis of Clyde Kluckhohn's (1951) and Kroeber and Parsons's (1958) work, Hofstede (1980a) defined culture as "the collective programming of the mind which distinguishes members of one human group from another" (p. 25). Grounded in an extensive literature review and one of the largest databases ever analyzed (attitude surveys of 116,000 IBM employees), Hofstede found four "universal categories of culture":

- individualism-collectivism, which "describes the relationship between the individual and the collectivity which prevails in a given society" (Hofstede, 1980a, p. 213)—that is, whether individuals define themselves as, for example, independent of a group, part of a loosely knit social framework, or strongly interdependent;
- power distance, which describes the extent to which hierarchies and the unequal distribution of power are accepted among members of a culture;
- uncertainty avoidance, which is the extent to which members of a culture are more or less risk averse and reflects the emphasis on ritual behavior, rules, and labor mobility within a group (Erez & Earley, 1993, p. 54); and
- masculinity-femininity, which reflects the extent to which individuals are materialistic, competitive, and assertive as opposed to nurturing, service oriented, and concerned with the quality of life.

In research based in China, Hofstede and Bond (1988) found a fifth category, Confucian dynamism, which measures employee devotion to the work ethic and respect for tradition (Chinese Culture Connection, 1987).

Hofstede (1980a) asserted that these universal categories "describe basic problems of humanity with which every society has to cope; and the variation of country scores along these dimensions shows that different societies do cope with these problems in different ways" (p. 313). In his argument, we again see the equating of nation-state ("country") with culture (societal cultures in this instance). Hofstede's research and arguments were compelling, however, undoubtedly in part because, even before empirical testing, strong links were seen between his four dimensions and many aspects of international organizational behavior, such as leadership, authority relations (power distance), decision making, political risk (uncertainty avoidance), importance of work goals, interpersonal relations (masculinity-femininity), and motivation and compensation systems (individualism). In fact, Søndergaard (1994) argues that Hofstede's framework became employed as a paradigm "where the questions and the dimensions are used as taken-for-granted assumptions" (p. 453). Moreover, Hofstede's dimensions were a boon to cross-national comparative researchers who sought to incorporate culture as an independent variable into their work. A plethora of studies using Hofstede's various dimensions have arisen, including studies focusing on individualism and collectivism (Albanese & van Fleet, 1985; Earley, 1989, 1993; Morris, Davis, & Allen, 1994), power distance (Kanungo & Wright, 1983), uncertainty avoidance (Schneider & de Meyer, 1991), individualism and masculinity (Kim, Park, & Suzuki, 1990), power distance and uncertainty avoidance (Birnbaum & Wong, 1985), or a cultural distance measure derived from all four dimensions (e.g., Benito & Gripsrud, 1992; Kogut & Singh, 1988; Li & Guisinger, 1991; Shenkar & Zeira, 1992). These studies all reflect the underpinnings of the basic assumptions of Haire et al. (1966) outlined previously, with the exception of elaborating culture in terms of a standardized, universally applicable set of dimensions.

In disciplines outside the growing field of cross-national comparative ICCM, conceptualizations of culture employing standardized, universally applicable sets of dimensions existed before Hofstede (i.e., Hall, 1959; Kluckhohn & Strodtbeck, 1961). A citation analysis of 24 English-language journals that publish ICCM research identified in the Social Science Citation Index, however, found that these authors were minimally cited in cross-national comparative ICCM literature prior to 1980. Although some academic texts in the field of ICCM have expanded our understanding of both the Hall and the Kluckhohn and Strodtbeck dimensions of culture (i.e., Adler, 1991; Lane & DiStefano, 1991; Ronen, 1986), no empirical work from a cross-national comparative perspective based on these frameworks (beyond that of the original authors) appears to have been conducted.[4]

Parallel to the development of cross-national comparative research, the scientific norms of the physical sciences were becoming the norms for the social sciences (Redding, 1994; Sullivan, 1994). ICCM researchers could not avoid this trend. As such, cross-national comparative research followed a natural science model from a positivist perspective. The natural science model "presents scientific knowledge and truth as though they were transcendent, independent of any society or historical period" (Sampson, 1978, p. 1332). Large-scale quantitative studies became the normative form of research, despite the attendant difficulties of functional equivalence, instrumentation, sampling, measurement, and analysis.[5] With a focus on large-scale, multivariate, empirical research, culture as a variable, simply and singly defined as nation-state, became one of but many independent variables considered.

Insights Gleaned From Cross-National Comparative Research

Research in the cross-national comparative stream has provided us with great momentum and allowed us to make initial steps toward understanding cultural differences. It has motivated the development of various typologies of culture (Hofstede, 1980a; Triandis, 1983) for understanding these differences. In addition, the cultural clusters approach (Ronen & Shenkar, 1985), an outcropping of the focus on national culture, has provided both researchers and practitioners alike with a sense that culture is tractable—that we can make certain generalizations at cultural levels of analysis beyond nation-state. Thus, the empirical evidence of commonalities between countries within the Anglo, Germanic, Nordic, Latin European, and Latin American clusters that have strong support (Ronen, 1986) have influenced our sense that one can "learn culture" and that certain lessons can be used on a regional basis.

The focus on a finite set of dimensions of culture has allowed other management disciplines—for example, strategy (e.g., Kogut & Singh, 1988; Li & Guisinger, 1991), marketing (Eramilli, 1991), and accounting (Gray, Radebaugh, & Roberts, 1990)—a relatively straightforward means to include cultural variables in cross-national research. In addition, the use of quantitative measures of culture has allowed computation of "cultural distance," an important construct for many topics in international human resource management in which the difficulty of adjusting to the foreign culture is seen as a function of the host culture's distance from one's own culture (Black & Mendenhall, 1992; Boyacigiller, 1990).

Erez and Earley's (1993) self-representation model exemplifies one type of theoretical development from the cross-national comparative perspective that may lead to a clearer understanding of how culture influences work behavior. Their model consists of the following four major factors:

[National] *culture* and *management practices* as macro- and meso-level factors; the *self* as the link between the macro-meso levels and employees' behavior, whereby the self serves as an interpreter of managerial practices in line with [national] cultural values and with respect to their contributions to the satisfaction of self-derived needs; and *employees' behavior.* [italics added] (p. 233)

For Erez and Earley (1993),

The self seems to be the link between culture and employees' work behavior. On the one hand, it is shaped by cultural values and norms; on the other, it directs employees' behavior toward self-enhancement. Therefore, it captures the cultural characteristics which are most relevant for work behavior. [italics added] (p. 21)

This new direction offered by Erez & Earley (1993) is a compelling attempt to build bridges between traditional parochial conceptions of behavior in organizational settings and developing understandings of behavior in cross-national contexts.

Progress has also been made in testing organizational theories cross-culturally. Although limited to national contexts, we now know more about how leadership (Doktor, 1990; Smith & Peterson, 1988), motivation (Redding & Wong, 1986; Triandis, 1993), and job satisfaction (Lincoln & Kalleberg, 1990; Redding, Norman, & Schlander, 1993) can differ in different cultures.

Finally, some of the most conceptually revealing findings of the cross-national comparative approach have been self-reflective in nature. These have included an increased understanding of U.S. cultural characteristics (the country of origin of a large percentage of the research), an appreciation of the parochialism of American organization theory (so widely used internationally), and increased attentiveness to the difficulty, and often futility, of transferring American management techniques to other nations (Adler, 1991; Hofstede, 1980b; Jaeger, 1986; Shenkar & von Glinow, 1994).

Intercultural Interaction

Historical Context of Intercultural Interaction Research

"Interaction, not merely comparison, is the essence of most managerial action." These words were addressed to cross-national comparative researchers by Adler, Doktor, and Redding (1986). They express a felt need to refocus some of the attention of those working in the dominant stream of ICCM research toward certain issues of escalating significance in the increasingly globalized business environment. Of immediate concern was the interaction of persons from different nations in organizational contexts—specifically, what impact does the meeting of national cultures have on an organization and its members? Growing out of this concern is the question of the cultural identity of salience when individuals of varying national origins interact within an organizational context.

Three interrelated trends prompted unprecedented interest among management scholars and practitioners in the interaction of national cultures and its consequences. One was the changing balance of global economic power. As the locus of energy shifted from the United States toward Japan and the newly developing Asian countries, attention focused on the issue of competitiveness. In the United States, this meant a preoccupation with Japan. The assumption that a unique Japanese culture contributes to the success of Japanese businesses underlaid this preoccupation (Drucker, 1971; Ouchi, 1981; Pascale & Athos, 1981).

A second global trend was the dramatic increase in direct foreign investment in the form of joint ventures, foreign-owned subsidiaries, or multinational corporations. Whether in the realm of business negotiation or organizational operation, we began to be interested in the impact of national culture on successful outcomes. Again, from the U.S. perspective, Japan loomed large. A host of articles and books examined how to negotiate with the Japanese (Black & Mendenhall, 1993; Graham & Sano, 1984). The proliferating Japanese "transplant" firms also were scrutinized. Initial optimism about the smooth transfer of Japanese ideologies and organizational practices from expatriate Japanese managers to American employees (Johnson & Ouchi, 1974) gave way to recognition that intercultural processes are exceedingly complex (Kleinberg, 1989).

The global movement of people from their country of origin, independent of firm-sponsored transfers, was the third significant trend, contributing to an increasingly multicultural workforce. Heightening awareness of a variety of national cultures in the workplace joined with growing attention to differences in ethnicity, gender, age, and sexual preference. Issues of intercultural interaction thus began to engage the attention of a wider array of U.S. scholars and practitioners.

Assumptions, Frameworks, and Methods of Intercultural Interaction Research

The historical context predisposed early intercultural interaction research in ICCM toward a cross-national focus. Several concurrent and, to some degree, intersecting developments in various fields of study, however, contributed to the emerging framework for conceptualizing interaction between persons in these multinational organizational settings, modifying this focus to some degree. These developments include (a) a general trend in organizational theory toward interpretive research, (b) a growing body of work generated on "organizational culture," (c) developments regarding intercultural communication in the workplace, and (d) current debates on anthropological theory and methodology. Assumptions, frameworks, methods, or all three from each of these developments have been absorbed and integrated by the stream of intercultural interaction research. These are summarized in the following sections to reveal the underpinnings of the emerging framework for this stream of ICCM research.

The Interpretive Perspective

Organizational scholars interested in interpretive research basically ask how organizational participants make sense of their social world (Jones, 1988; Pondy, Frost, Morgan, & Dandridge, 1983; Putnam & Pacanowsky, 1983). Interpretive studies fall within a naturalistic research paradigm (Lincoln & Guba, 1985). According to the paradigm, reality not only is socially constructed but also is multiple—that is, different sets of actors within an organization may define their reality differently. Furthermore, reality cannot be fragmented into independent variables and processes that enable direct cause-and-effect relationships to be posited. Instead, all entities are "in a state of mutual and simultaneous shaping" (Lincoln & Guba, 1985). Thus, in place of generalization and prediction, naturalistic inquiry emphasizes the transferability of research findings—specifically, under similar conditions, similar outcomes can be anticipated.

Not all researchers of an interpretive bent use the term *culture* to refer to their reconstruction of their subjects' system of meaning. For anthropologist Clifford Geertz (1973), however, whose ethnographic writing has greatly influenced interpretive research, the "webs of significance" that are revealed by these researchers are indeed cultural. Furthermore, interpretive researchers generally describe their approach as *ethnographic* (a term implying attention to cultural phenomena) as they adopt the methods of anthropological ethnography—that is, intensive, open-ended interviews and participant observation.

Organizational Culture Research

The organizational culture literature exhibits considerable variation in focus and methods (Martin, 1992). Conceptualizations of culture range from viewing it as an independent variable that managers can manipulate for desired ends (Davis,

1984)—that is, something an organization "has"—to viewing it as something an organization "is" (Smircich, 1983). The latter viewpoint carries the interpretive approach to its logical conclusion. Among organizational researchers, those concerned with the phenomenon of organizational culture have gone farthest toward offering clear definitions of culture, a way of representing culture as a social construct, and a basis for examining the implications of culture for organization.

Interactional research discussed here has emerged along with a developing view in organizational culture research that organizations encompass a multiplicity of cultures, with national culture being only one possible cultural grouping (Martin, 1992; Sackmann & Phillips, 1992).[6] The way in which cultures may intersect or otherwise influence one another—the central issue in intercultural interaction research—remains a recognized but still relatively unexplored question among organizational culture researchers.

Basic commonalities in the definition of culture are shared by a growing number of scholars working on organizational culture, the cross-national, intercultural interaction framework, and the multiple cultures perspective. As a minimal definition, we shall use the following:

> The core of culture is composed of explicit and tacit assumptions or understandings commonly held by a group of people; a particular configuration of assumptions and understandings is distinctive to the group; these assumptions and understandings serve as guides to acceptable and unacceptable perceptions, thoughts, feelings, and behaviors; they are learned and passed on to new members of the group through social interaction; and culture is dynamic—it changes over time, although the tacit assumptions that are the core of culture are most resistant to change. (Adapted from Kleinberg, 1989; Louis, 1983; Phillips, 1990; Sackmann, 1992b; Schein, 1985)

This definition stresses the ideational or cognitive aspect of culture and, therefore, is sensitive to the various foci around which cultural groupings in and across organizations may emerge.

Intercultural Communication in the Workplace

An intercultural communication model (Samovar & Porter, 1991) underpins a theory of culture widely accepted in the field of comparative and cross-cultural management (Adler, 1991) but often only implicitly integrated into research design (Kleinberg, 1989). That theory states that members of a bounded nation are seen as bearers of a common culture that influences the behavior in and of organizations. Thus, people from different national backgrounds acquire different expectations about the formal structures of firms and the informal patterns by which work is accomplished. These expectations then color the way people respond to unfamiliar or unexpected behaviors when they work with, negotiate with, or generally do business with counterparts from another society. The implication is that, all too often, cross-national, cross-cultural encounters result in misperception, misinterpretation, and a negative evaluation of the cultural other's intentions and abilities.

A cultural synergy model of interaction, which builds on the intercultural communication model, currently attracts organizational scholars dealing with either international or domestic cultural diversity (Adler, 1991; Moran & Harris, 1981). This model assumes that successful intercultural communication and, therefore, successful task accomplishment hinges on conscious management of both differences and similarities. Organizational members learn to "create new forms of management and organization that transcend the individual cultures of their members" (Adler, 1991, p. 108). The concept of cultural synergy essentially concerns the conscious construction of new cultural understandings at the work group or organizationwide level.

Anthropological Theory and Methods

To anthropologists, ethnography "is the science—and art—of cultural description" (Frake, 1983, p. 60). The goal of cultural description is to sort out, represent, and contextually explain the meanings that humans create for themselves through social interaction (Geertz, 1973). Despite broad agreement on what ethnography is, several currents of thought coexist with regard to representing culture. Organizational scholars doing interpretive research have clearly entered the dialogue (Smircich, 1983; Smircich & Calas, 1987; Van Maanen, 1988).

Many researchers have adopted a concept of culture drawn from cognitive anthropology (Frake, 1983; Goodenough, 1981; Spradley, 1980). Gregory (1983) introduced this approach to organizational studies in an early article on mapping "native-view paradigms." The researcher's task is to discover the shared "cultural knowledge," both explicit and tacit, that reflects the way members of a culture make sense of their social setting. The assumptions that comprise cultural knowledge are inferred from the "doings and sayings" (Frake, 1983) of organizational participants, normally through some kind of content analysis (Spradley, 1980). The assumptions that surface are sometimes represented as broad, encompassing categories of cultural knowledge (termed "cultural themes" by Spradley, 1980) that organize into constituent subcategories of cultural knowledge (Gregory, 1983; Sackmann, 1992b). Sometimes member assumptions or understandings are represented merely in terms of cultural themes, without the emphasis on taxonomy

(Martin, 1992). Cognitive anthropologists typically do not presume a priori cultural dimensions such as those proposed by Kluckhohn and Strodtbeck (1961) or Hofstede (1980a). Some organizational culture researchers, however, surface culture constructs through similar content analysis but organize the revealed cultural knowledge around Kluckhohn and Strodtbeck's universal dimensions of culture (Dyer, 1985; Phillips, 1994).

Among anthropologists, cognitive anthropology has been criticized on two counts: for imposing on culture a coherence and an inflexibility of a set of "rules" or "grammar" that it does not really exhibit and for leaving critical contextual analysis out of the cultural description. For example, Geertz (1973) argues that

> to set forth symmetrical crystals of significance, purified of the material complexity in which they were located, and then attribute their existence to autogenous principles of order . . . is to pretend a science that does not exist and imagine a reality that cannot be found. (p. 20)

These criticisms may be true of cognitive anthropology in its most formalized form. Frake's (1977; quoted in Spradley, 1980, p. 7) metaphor of culture as cognitive "sketch maps" indicates that not all cognitive anthropologists have such a coherent vision. Moreover, many scholars who borrow methods of discovering and representing culture from cognitive anthropology share with critics an emphasis on contextuality.

As an alternative mode of cultural representation, Geertz (1973) offers what he labels "thick description." Through finely detailed, multilayered description of people, events, and actions, the ethnographer arrives at an interpretation of the "interworked systems of construable signs" (p. 14)—that is, the meanings that are culture. Rohlen's (1974) ethnography of a Japanese bank provides a contemporary organizational example of thick description, one that vividly illustrates the interplay between national culture and behavior in and of an organization.

Geertzian thick description, in turn, has been criticized for being too local in its conceptualization of history and, consequently, presenting too self-contained and unified a representation of culture (Roseberry, 1989). An alternative view sees the cultural other as a product of a history that itself is connected to a larger set of economic, political, social, and cultural processes (Appadurai, 1991; Clifford, 1986; Marcus, 1986; Roseberry, 1989; Wolf, 1982). Within a broad political economy framework, culture "shifts from being some sort of inert, local substance to being a rather more volatile form of difference" (Appadurai, 1991, p. 205). Indeed, culture may be viewed as actively negotiated (Giddens, 1979). Clifford (1986) stated,

If "culture" is not an object to be described, neither is it a unified corpus of symbols and meanings that can be definitively interpreted. Culture is contested, temporal, and emergent. *Representation and explanation—both by insiders and outsiders—is implicated in this emergence* [italics added]. (p. 19)

In the organizational culture literature, the cultural fragmentation perspective that Meyerson and Martin (1987) propose reflects the view of culture in today's complex organizations as being ambiguous, incongruent, and actively negotiated.

Emerging Framework for Cross-National Intercultural Interaction

Due to these many and sometimes contradictory theoretical influences, the emerging framework for considering cross-national, intercultural interaction in organizations is loosely constructed. Nevertheless, some common threads connect the existing research. The research in large part concerns Japanese-owned and -managed firms in the United States, and the researchers are persons whose disciplinary training is wholly or partially in sociocultural anthropology (Brannen, 1992; Kleinberg, 1989, 1992, 1994a, 1994b; Sumihara, 1992).[7]

A number of assumptions about culture and its consequences underlie the cross-national, intercultural framework. Researchers generally conceptualize culture as a group-level phenomenon—a social construct that encompasses shared understandings. Moreover, national culture is considered not only salient but also of critical importance. Researchers assume that national cultural identity remains separate and distinct throughout the process of interaction (while recognizing that an individual's thinking and behavior may be temporarily or enduringly altered by intercultural experiences). In addition, researchers assume that national culture is reflected in a work-related cultural subset that members of each nation bring to the binational setting. Along with national culture, the original organizational culture of a binational firm's employees may be relevant—a set of understandings different from national culture or a nation-specific work culture but still theoretically (Enz, 1986) connected to the wider national culture.

Finally, researchers believe that cultural differences may affect communication processes much in the same way as described by the intercultural communication model, with misperception, misinterpretation, and misunderstanding evident. They assume as well, however, that the binational organization is a context for the construction of new understandings as participants interactively make sense of an extraordinary, unfamiliar organizational terrain. Therefore, the focal question for this stream of ICCM research—"What is it that representatives of different national cultures create through their interaction?"—anticipates the development of a new organizational culture (or cultures). In addition to the content and form of emergent organizational culture(s), of key concern is the process of culture formation.

Researchers arrive at different but not inconsistent models of process. For example, Brannen (1992) presents a model of "negotiated culture" based on her study of the Japanese takeover of an American firm. According to the model, a "bicultural" organizational culture evolves as particular issues trigger cultural negotiations among individuals. An individual, however, may be "marginally normal," "cultural(ly) norm(al)," or "hyper-normal" with regard to any specific cultural foci—nation, organization of origin, or bicultural organization. In contrast, Kleinberg's (1992, 1994a, 1994b) model, derived from her study of a U.S.-based Japanese subsidiary, focuses on emergent organizational cultures at various levels: organizationwide culture, Japanese (expatriate) and American subgroup cultures, and individual work group cultures. The assumptions of each cultural grouping are shown to largely reflect enhanced awareness of national cultural differences in expectations about work resulting from cross-national interaction. Nevertheless, analysis of one particular work group (Kleinberg, 1994a) shows that, despite the understanding at the organizationwide level that "we are a company divided," spontaneously created intercultural harmony and synergy are possible.

With roots in sociocultural anthropology, researchers in this stream of ICCM research employ the traditional inductive methods of their discipline. Long-term participant observation is undertaken in conjunction with an extensive series of ethnographic interviews conducted with a wide range of informants. Researchers arrive at a cultural interpretation primarily through qualitative data analysis, often including content analysis described previously. Cultural description may involve a representation of cognitive structures underpinned by thick description (e.g., "nation-specific work sketch maps" [Kleinberg, 1989]) or thick description alone (e.g., Brannen, 1992).

Insights Gleaned From Intercultural Interaction Research

As a result of the variety of theoretical and methodological influences, intercultural interaction research focuses initially on the cross-national nature of the interaction but recognizes that the organization provides a cultural context for this exchange. Therefore, researchers in this area expand their focus to include organizational culture as a critical contextual element in the interaction. Furthermore, they recognize that new cultural forms may emerge and evolve from a set of individuals of varying national origins interacting within a unique organizational context. Thus, the intercultural interaction perspective offers to ICCM research the insight that cultural identity must be assumed to be broader than the "single, given, permanent" national culture of the cross-national comparative perspective. Intercultural interactionists view national culture, organizational culture, and the emergent and evolving cultural forms as all relevant to the identity of the individual acting within the setting of the multinational organization.

In addition, the research on cross-national, intercultural interaction has made considerable progress in making culture a visible construct and showing how formal and informal organizational processes are mediated by national culture. Detailed cultural description provides insight into how individuals interactively construct shared understandings. Cultural description also helps illuminate the interplay of cultural factors and noncultural contextual variables. For example, in the cases described in this chapter, the relative power held by Japanese and Americans and relations between the U.S. operation and the Japanese headquarters are important contextual factors, as are external environmental variables relating to industry, labor markets, and national and international politics.

This area of ICCM research has also drawn attention to issues of "writing culture" when culture is viewed as contested, temporal, and emergent (Clifford, 1986). For example, Brannen's (1992) notion of negotiated culture seeks to capture the volatility of the culture construct. Furthermore, she reminds us that any interpretation of a culture necessarily reflects the background and values of the ethnographer (Lincoln & Guba, 1985) and is interactively negotiated between ethnographer and members of the culture (Dwyer, 1982). In writing culture, we must strive to empower those being studied to voice the incongruencies and contradictions of their subjective world (Abu-Lughod, 1991).

Multiple Cultures

Historical Context of Research From a
Multiple Cultures Perspective

During the past decade, many changes in all spheres of life have been introduced, turning commonly accepted rules and assumptions upside down.

Recent developments in world economies, as well as within societies, question the central importance of nations and of national cultures. Economic questions are increasingly discussed with regard to regions or continents, such as Europe or the European Union, North America or the North American Free Trade Agreement, Japan or the Pacific Rim, the Four Tiger (Singapore, Hong Kong, Taiwan, and South Korea), or the newly industrialized countries. If firms want to be successful in these new economies, they have to reach beyond the national level and span the globe. Being global, however, does not suffice for success unless it is complemented by a sensitivity for the special needs of local markets.

Radical developments in communication technology have led to a global economy in which companies are no longer restricted to the market in which they are geographically located. The entire globe has become the potential marketplace. If a firm wants to become a major business player, it needs to have global presence. This has been predominantly established by starting operations in foreign locations and thus creating a multinational firm, by acquiring or merging with firms already established in a desirable market, by forming strategic alliances, or all three (Hamel, Doz, & Prahalad, 1989; for examples, see De la Torre, 1990; Strenger, 1990). As a result, interdependencies have grown dramatically around the globe (De la Torre, 1990; Dunning, 1988).

The number of joint ventures and strategic alliances has rapidly increased during the past few years, providing smaller companies from smaller nations the opportunity to stay competitive and the possibility to participate in resource-intensive, long-term projects. The resulting workforces are diverse in interests, backgrounds, training, and nationalities—even within the same firm and the same geographic location. For example, at Asea Brown Boveri, the Swiss-Swedish merger, it is not uncommon for 125 employees of a department (or "profit center") to share among themselves 25 passports. Such culturally diverse contexts force attention far beyond the binational research contexts of cross-national intercultural interactionists.

In the political sphere, established national boundaries have been questioned or even destroyed. Vivid examples are evident in Central and Eastern Europe—the former USSR, the former Yugoslavia, the former Czechoslovakia. Once solid national boundaries have melted away as ethnic identities have grown stronger. Thus, we are forced to reconsider the assumption of nation-state as sole, or even central, determining boundary for cultural identity.

In summary, these different contextual conditions require that an intensive effort be made to complement our national and binational understandings from ICCM cross-national comparison and cross-national intercultural interaction research with studies of culture that take into account the multiplicity of cultures experienced in organizational settings and in individual lives.

Assumptions, Frameworks, and Methods of Research From a Multiple Cultures Perspective

It has long been recognized that multiple cultures exist within larger societies and organizations, and research into their source and nature has been conducted (Bochner, 1982; Sackmann, 1992b). Their study, however, was predominantly bound to preselected subcultures—groups with minority representation and identification specified a priori as they seemed relevant in the existing context. In the cross-national intercultural interaction research previously reviewed, there is a broadening in scope of the definition of cultural identity in conjunction with developing attention to emergent cultures at the organizational, in addition to the suborganizational, level. With current rapid changes in the global business context, other cultural groupings also emerge as critical and, therefore, need to be studied simultaneously. Growing outside the dominant stream of ICCM research, from organization theorists' research into organization-based culture, is a widening current with a focus on the multiple cultural identities brought to and the multiple cultures developed within organizations.

The multiple cultures perspective in organization studies derived its recent momentum from a countercurrent in the developing field of organization culture. As interest in this new area of organization theory was rising in the late 1970s and early 1980s, leading researchers in the organization culture field conceptualized an organization as the carrier of a single, unique, and monolithic culture (e.g., Deal & Kennedy, 1982; Ouchi, 1981; Pascale & Athos, 1981; Peters & Waterman, 1982; Pettigrew, 1979; Schein, 1983). In borrowing the term *culture* from the field of anthropology, this dominant group of organization culture theorists also incorporated what they assumed was an anthropological presupposition of "one culture to a society" (Phillips, 1990, p. 21).

In contrast, a second conception of cultural groupings in organizational settings was emerging that was fed by the findings of a small group of organization researchers largely engaged in inductive research (e.g., Gregory, 1983; Louis, 1983; Martin & Siehl, 1983; Martin, Sitkin, & Boehm, 1985; Sackmann, 1986; Van Maanen & Barley, 1985). These researchers observed that an organization is not a simple, primitive society, as was the traditional field site of anthropological research; rather, it is a heterogeneous, pluralistic system whose members live within a larger, complex society. Therefore, they recognized that organization members may develop shared sets of assumptions within the organization setting, but they can also bring with them the various sets of assumptions that they acquire outside of the organization. Thus, the organization is viewed as the potential carrier of a multiplicity of separate, overlapping, superimposed, or nested cultures, with the organization's participants maintaining simultaneous membership in any number of these cultural groups. For example, the membership body of any particular group may be nested within the organization, forming a suborganizational culture (e.g., functional, hierarchical, departmental, site specific, divisional, countermovement, union, clique, or tenure-based association); it may coincide precisely with the organization's membership, producing an organizational culture; it may cross-cut a number of organizations as does a transorganizational culture—for example, profession and guild, joint venture, problem- or project-focused group such as a project team or a "directed interorganizational system" (Lawless, 1981), religion, race, gender, age, and sexual preference; or it may be overlaid on that and other organizations as is a supraorganizational culture, geographically based (e.g., global, continental, national, or regional), ideological (communist, socialist, capitalist, Eastern or Western, or religion), or industrial (Sackmann & Phillips, 1992).

Organizational culture researchers with this conceptual perspective believe that any and all of these types of cultural groupings may exist and coexist within an organizational setting. That is, an organization, like the people who compose it, does not simply carry one specific type of culture (e.g., national culture or organizational culture); instead, it is embedded in a pluralistic cultural context (Kopper, 1992; Louis, 1983; Phillips, Goodman, & Sackmann, 1992). The actual existence of any particular cultural grouping within, coincidental with, cross-cutting, or overlaid on the organization (specifically, the identification of the culture[s] affecting the organization at any given time, around any specific issue, in any particular circumstance, and to any certain degree), however, is an empirical question and not an a priori assumption. This precludes the strong and purposeful focus on national culture as the cultural grouping of certain relevance to the organization (as assumed in cross-national intercultural interaction ICCM research) and as a culture of permanent identity for the individual (as assumed in cross-national comparative ICCM research).

Underpinning the multiple cultures conception of cultural groupings in organization settings is a definition of the key construct—culture—that accounts for potential cultural diversity and is sensitive to emerging cultural groupings at various levels. This definition, shared by cross-national intercultural interaction researchers and previously elucidated in the section titled "Organizational Culture Research," has several implications for theory, research, and the carriers of culture—organizations and individuals.

Of theoretical importance is the definitional implication that culture is a collective social phenomenon that is created, rather than inherited, by group members. Once in existence, these assumptions subtly influence perceiving, thinking, acting, and feeling in ways that are consistent with the cultural reality of that group. As guidelines for "map making and navigation" (Frake, 1977), these basic assumptions guide selection, interpretation, and communication of information in ways that are meaningful to the group. They channel the choices of actions in ways considered appropriate by the group.

The previous definition implies that the essence or core of culture is cognitive rather than factual or symbolic in nature (Sackmann, 1983). Values, norms, symbolic events (e.g., rites, rituals, and ceremonies), and artifacts are at a more accessible level of culture (Schein, 1985) and can be considered part of the cultural network (Sackmann, 1983). Although several organization theorists suggest the importance of symbols with regard to culture (e.g., Trice, 1985), their specific meanings need to be inferred in a given cultural context because the same symbols or artifacts may be attributed with different meanings in different cultural contexts (e.g., Bochner, 1982; Sackmann, 1992b). This deciphering process is possible only by understanding the underlying basic assumptions of the group.

The previous definition further implies that a culture may exist or emerge whenever a set of basic assumptions is commonly held by a group of people. This has led multiple cultures researchers to focus on identifying commonalities in assumptions as the precursor to drawing boundaries around the cultural group. Tentative boundaries are sometimes drawn around anticipated or hypothesized groups, and then cultural commonalities are found to support maintaining or reconfiguring those boundaries of shared understandings (e.g., Gregory, 1983; Grinyer & Spender, 1979; Martin et al., 1985; Phillips, 1990; Sackmann, 1986; Van Maanen & Barley, 1984). Consequently, unanticipated groupings, as well as emergent cultures (a product in common with cross-national intercultural interaction research), can be identified.[8]

An individual's cultural nature is also addressed by this definition. Individuals are seen as simultaneous carriers of several cultural identities because they are assumed to belong to various cultural groups at any given moment. It is hypothesized that, depending on the issue at hand, a different cultural identity may become salient at a given moment. When, how, and to what extent are, again, empirical questions and not a priori assumptions. The business reality of the resulting multiple cultural identities and their potential impact has been illustrated for an individual practicing manager (Phillips, Boyacigiller, Sackmann, & Bolton, 1992) and for an international project team (Phillips, Sackmann, & Goodman, 1992).

A wide variety of methods for data collection, analysis, and representation is employed by multiple cultures researchers, reflecting the newness of the field and the absence of strong roots in any single academic discipline. Because this area of research flows from organization theory, a hybrid field composed of sociologists, psychologists, anthropologists, economists, and industrial engineers, no single methodology predominates, in contrast with the dominance of state-of-the-art social anthropological methods used in cross-national intercultural interaction research. Also, the relatively recent development of a critical mass of researchers exploring multiple cultures in organization settings has not allowed sufficient time for broader commonalities in methodology to evolve.

In seeking to identify the boundaries of commonly held assumption sets in order to reveal the extant cultural groupings within organization settings, however, the definitional notion that the "particular configuration of assumptions is distinctive to the group" implies an "emic" approach (Sackmann, 1991). To decipher the specific meaning of a given cultural group in context requires in-depth probing to gain an insider's view rather than imposing an outsider's perspective. Consequently, multiple cultures researchers generally tend to advocate, although not necessarily purely employ, empirical investigations involving inductive methodologies and field data collection. Similar to the manner in which cross-national intercultural interactionists have tailored research methodologies to their organizational settings and research interests, researchers in this area of ICCM research have employed specifically tailored combinations of ethnographic and quasi-ethnographic methods such as participant observation (Gregory, 1983; Sapienza, 1985), in-depth interviews (e.g., Phillips, 1990, 1994; Sackmann, 1991; Schein, 1985; Vinton, 1983), group discussions (Schein, 1985), assumptional analysis (Kilmann, 1983), and cognitive mapping methods such as causal mapping (Axelrod, 1976; Narayanan & Fahey, 1990), the repertory grid technique (Reger, 1990), argument mapping (Fletcher & Huff, 1990), or narrative semiotics (Fiol, 1990).

These different data collection techniques involve different degrees of "engagement" with the research subjects and produce different depths of understanding with regard to the research setting. Choices of technique appear to be related to the researcher's long-term interest in theory building versus practical application. The more extensive and intensive the ethnographic nature of the engagement, the more detailed view of the cultural assumptions is attained (Martin, 1992).[9]

To condense, systematize, and report the collected data, researchers have applied the categories of a priori developed frameworks and delineated the cultural assumptions in terms of the framework's dimensions, or typology (Handy, 1978; Pümpin, 1984; Sackmann & Phillips, 1992).

Others have used the categories of empirically derived frameworks (e.g., Hofstede, Neuijen, Ohayv, & Sanders, 1990; Phillips, 1990; Sackmann, 1991; Schein, 1985). A third approach, employed in cross-national intercultural interaction research, is to let the relevant dimensions of a given culture emerge from the research and to use these in the organization and presentation of the findings (Kleinberg, 1989; Van Maanen, 1979). Choices in this regard also tend to be related to the researcher's interest in theory building or practical application.

Insights Gleaned From Research From a Multiple Cultures Perspective

Researchers using the multiple cultures perspective have identified and delineated the cultural assumptions of a variety of different groups existing and coexisting within organization settings. At the suborganizational level, Van Maanen and Barley (1984, 1985) found the origins for the cultural differentiation process in organizational segmentation and acquired or emerging diversity regarding skills, technology, ideas, or interests. Resulting suborganizational cultures have been shown to develop according to function or functional domains (Handy, 1978; Sackmann, 1991, 1992b), tenure and hierarchy (Martin et al., 1985; Sarnin, 1989), ethnicity (Gregory, 1983), gender (Blackhurst, 1986; Symons, 1986), role (Rusted, 1986), plant site (Bushe, 1988), and countermovement (Dent, 1986). At the organizational level, cultural boundaries have been drawn around a single business (Pacanowsky, 1987; Pederson, 1987; Rosen, 1986; Rusted, 1986; Schein, 1985), a global enterprise (Garsten, 1990), a conglomerate (Pettigrew, 1985; Sackmann, 1991; Tunstall, 1985), and a family firm (Dyer, 1986). Professions or guilds, as a form of transorganizational culture, have been found to exist in research by Barley (1984), Dubinskas (1988), Geist and Hardesty (1987), and Gregory (1983). At the supraorganizational level, cultural boundaries have been drawn around nation (Hofstede et al., 1990; Kleinberg, 1989; Meek & Song, 1990), geographical region within a country (Weiss & Delbecq, 1987), economic region (Hickson, 1993), industry (Grinyer & Spender, 1979; Kreiner & Schultz, 1990; Pederson, 1987; Phillips, 1990, 1994), and ideologies such as religion (Aktouf, 1988) and differences between Eastern and Western civilizations (Westwood & Kirkbride, 1989).

This perspective has heightened awareness of the inherent complexity of cultures in organizational settings. First, the salience of a particular cultural group is no longer a given. Researchers have to make a conscious choice about the focal cultural context to be used in their study, to determine not only whether the focal culture exists within the context but also whether it is salient to the circumstance, and to be aware of the other cultural contexts most likely to interact with the one of central concern.

What have we gained from this perspective besides complexity? The major advantage seems to be the acknowledgment of the very complexity that the new social, political, and economic realities have created. Even if it is important, the mere distinction between nations is no longer sufficient in understanding today's cross-cultural issues.

Although largely comparative and descriptive in orientation heretofore, this perspective invites investigations of the multiple interactions between multiple cultural contexts and thus reinforces the necessity of the more dynamic approach of intercultural interaction to cross-cultural studies. It also provides a way of exploring issues of synergy that are raised in the cross-national comparison perspective (Adler, 1991; Moran & Harris, 1981) and encouraged in the intercultural interaction perspective. Rather than finding ways to bridge differences of national cultures, the question becomes how to build on similarities engendered in other commonly held cultures for creative solutions.

Directions for Future Research

From the multiple cultures perspective, we can see that an emphasis on national culture obscures other cultural foci that may impinge on organizations and distracts from other cultural identities that individuals may carry. National culture may not be as salient a factor in all situations. Comparison, therefore, should extend to cross-cultural interaction that does not exclusively involve national differences. Such inclusion works toward a broader theory of cultures in organizations.

Because the multiple cultures perspective illustrates that organizations do not simply operate within one specific cultural context, the critical issues for investigation become "When and under what conditions do certain cultures become salient and more relevant than others?" and "How do the various cultures interact in different circumstances?"

Cross-cultural research in social psychology suggests that major differences exist regarding within-society and between-society cross-cultural contacts, with territoriality being the most important factor. In within-society contacts, members are less likely to differentiate between hosts and visitors, which is the case in between-society contacts. Additional dimensions suggested to be relevant in cross-cultural contact are the time span of interaction; its purpose; the type of involvement; the frequency of contact; and the degree of intimacy, relative status and power, numerical balance, and distinguishable characteristics of the people involved (Bochner, 1982). The differences that separate interacting people tend to become salient (e.g., Bochner & Ohsako, 1977), with the most important differentiating characteristics apparently being the highly visible ones, such as race, skin color, language, and religion (Klineberg, 1971). More exploration is needed regarding the circumstances and validity of attributing a certain cultural identity to an individual based on highly visible characteristics, with special attention to the effect of organizational settings on these attributions.

It is further suggested that the larger the differences between interacting groups, regardless of whether these differences are real or imagined, the more likely individuals are to distinguish between "we" and "them," or in-group and out-group membership. Although known to ICCM researchers, these findings have not yet been applied to investigations to determine their applicability in ICCM settings or their transferability to the individual level. Future studies need to determine the usefulness of these findings in resolving individual cultural identity issues, such as which cultural identity will become most important and how the various cultural identities are "managed" by an individual, as well as the larger group salience issues. Heightened attention is needed to the psychological facilitation of and constraints on the carrying and use of multiple cultural identities by a single individual. The work by Dahler-Larsen (Chapter 17, this volume) shows a promising direction.

Appropriate research methods need to be selected to tap the cultural multiplicity from the culture carrier's perspective. Also, the methodology of choice needs to be sensitive to potentially existing intercultural dynamics. Logistical obstacles (i.e., linguistic and cultural fluency and ethnographic time frames) are also methodological issues that must be addressed and overcome by the researcher.

Finally, on a practical level, the multiple cultures perspective suggests that people who live in the new global business reality need to develop an appreciation for multiple cultures that exist simultaneously. This requires that practitioners develop special skills to help them deal with this culturally diverse context and use it in synergistic ways, rather than considering cultural differences as a problem that must be coped with. The field of ICCM has always exhibited an acute sensitivity to and sense of responsibility for practical application. Therefore, future research in cross-cultural organization and management growing out of this field might be partially geared to clarifying and developing those necessary skills for reading the multiple cultural context and managing it in sensitive ways (Sackmann, 1992a).

Notes

1. This pedantic description is necessary because cross-cultural research need not be international and international management is not always cross-cultural.

2. Harbison and Myers (1959), who first studied cross-national management, did not even have culture in their index. Rather, they focused on national demographic and economic variables.

3. The bicultural nature of Belgium was an exception that was recognized with questionnaire instruments in French and Flemish and with the resultant grouping of the two regions into two different clusters.

4. In fact, John Daniels (1991), in his Presidential Address to the Academy of International Business, cited Hall's (1959) research as an example of literature that has endured within the field without much empirical testing.

5. In addition to many critiques of the methodology of this area of research noting these difficulties (Adler, 1984; Bhagat & McQuaid, 1982; Roberts, 1970; Ronen, 1986; Sekaran, 1983), methodological concerns unique to cross-national comparative research have also been raised. Specifically, Triandis (1972) cites concern about "pseudo-etic" research in which "instruments based on American theories, using items reflecting American conditions, are simply translated and used in other cultures" (Bhagat & McQuaid, 1982, p. 662), and Kelley, Whatley, and Worthley (1987) raise a crucial concern regarding the ability to isolate the impact of culture from other explanatory variables.

6. Our discussion of the third area of ICCM research elaborates on this multiple cultures perspective and its link to the research on organizational cultures.

7. Previous discussion of contextual factors influencing and encouraging intercultural interaction research helps explain why more research effort revolves around the U.S.-based Japanese firm than other possible foci of cross-national interaction.

8. Unlike that second area of ICCM research, which focuses on the nature and the product of the interaction between two cultural groups within an organization, the focus of the multiple cultures perspective heretofore has been primarily on identification of extant cultural groupings and the description of their assumptions.

9. The skills of interpreting culture in a particular setting come only through prolonged engagement (Lincoln & Guba, 1985; Van Maanen, 1988). Moreover, cultural interpretation is best accomplished if the researcher has linguistic and cultural fluency in the national cultures of the participating informants. The time it takes to acquire such fluency, and the ethnographic time frame itself, discourages many researchers. Data gathering, data analysis, and writing culture involve more investment than generally is allowed by the timetables of either management-related academic careers or the practice of management.

References

Abu-Lughod, L. (1991). Writing against culture. In R. G. Fox (Ed.), *Recapturing anthropology: Working in the present* (pp. 137-162). Santa Fe, NM: School of American Research Press.
Adler, N. J. (1991). *International dimensions of organizational behavior.* Boston: Kent.

Adler, N. J., Doktor, R., & Redding, S. G. (1986). From the Atlantic to the Pacific century: Cross-cultural management reviewed. *Journal of Management, 12*(2), 295-318.

Adler, N. J., & Jelinek, M. S. (1986). Is "organization culture" culture bound? *Human Resource Management, 25*(1), 73-90.

Ajiferuke, M., & Boddewyn, J. (1970). Culture and other explanatory variables in comparative management studies. *Academy of Management Journal, 35,* 153-164.

Aktouf, O. (1988, July). *Corporate culture, the Catholic ethic, and the spirit of capitalism.* Paper presented at the Istanbul Workshop on Organizational Culture in Different Civilizations, Standing Conference on Organizational Symbolism, Istanbul, Turkey.

Albanese, R., & van Fleet, D. D. (1985). Rational behavior in groups: The free-riding tendency. *Academy of Management Review, 10*(2), 244-255.

Appadurai, A. (1991). Global ethnoscapes: Notes and queries for a transnational anthropology. In R. G. Fox (Ed.), *Recapturing anthropology: Working in the present* (pp. 191-210). Santa Fe, NM: School of American Research Press.

Axelrod, R. (1976). *Structure of decision.* Princeton, NJ: Princeton University Press.

Barley, S. R. (1984). *The professional, the semi-professional, and the machine: The social ramifications of computer-based imaging in radiology.* Unpublished doctoral dissertation, Massachusetts Institute of Technology, Sloan School of Management, Cambridge.

Benito, G. R. G., & Gripsrud, G. (1992). The expansion of foreign direct investments: Discrete rational location choices or a cultural learning process? *Journal of International Business Studies, 23*(3), 461-476.

Bhagat, R. S., & McQuaid, S. J. (1982). Role of subjective culture in organizations: A review and direction for future research. *Journal of Applied Psychology Monograph, 67*(5), 653-685.

Birnbaum, P. H., & Wong, G. Y. Y. (1985). Organizational structure of multinational banks in Hong Kong from a culture-free perspective. *Administrative Science Quarterly, 30*(2), 262-277.

Black, J., & Mendenhall, M. (1992). The u-curve adjustment hypothesis revised: A review and theoretical framework. *Journal of International Business Studies, 22*(2), 225-248.

Black, J. S., & Mendenhall, M. (1993, Spring). Resolving conflicts with the Japanese: Mission impossible? *Sloan Management Review,* 49-59.

Blackhurst, M. (1986, June). *The role of culture in affirmative action strategy.* Paper presented at the International Conference on Organizational Symbolism and Corporate Culture, Montreal, Quebec, Canada.

Bochner, S. (1982). The social psychology of cross-cultural relations. In S. Bochner (Ed.), *Cultures in contact* (pp. 5-44). Elmsford, NY: Pergamon.

Bochner, S., & Ohsako, T. (1977). Ethnic role salience in racially homogenous and heterogenous societies. *Journal of Cross-Cultural Psychology, 8,* 477-492.

Boyacigiller, N. A. (1990). The role of expatriates in the management of interdependence, risk and complexity in multinational corporations. *Journal of International Business Studies, 21*(3), 357-382.

Boyacigiller, N. A., & Adler, N. J. (1991). The parochial dinosaur: Organizational science in a global context. *Academy of Management Review, 16*(2), 262-290.

Brannen, M. Y. (1992). *Your next boss is Japanese: Negotiating cultural change at a Western Massachusetts paper plant.* Unpublished doctoral dissertation, University of Massachusetts, Amherst.

Burrell, G., & Morgan, G. (1979). *Sociological paradigms and organizational analysis.* London: Heinemann.

Bushe, G. R. (1988). Cultural contradictions of statistical process control in American manufacturing organizations. *Journal of Management, 14*(1), 19-31.

Chinese Culture Connection. (1987). Chinese values and the search for culture-free dimensions of culture. *Journal of Cross-Cultural Psychology, 18*(2), 143-164.

Clifford, J. (1986). Introduction: Partial truths. In J. Clifford & G. E. Marcus (Eds.), *Writing culture: The poetics and politics of ethnography* (pp. 1-26). Berkeley: University of California Press.

Daniels, J. D. (1991). Relevance in international business research: A need for more linkages. *Journal of International Business Studies, 22*(2), 177-186.

Davis, S. M. (1984). *Managing corporate culture.* Cambridge, MA: Ballinger.

Deal, T. E., & Kennedy, A. A. (1982). *Corporate cultures.* Reading, MA: Addison-Wesley.

De la Torre, J. (1990, July). *Managing in a changing global economy.* Lecture given at the Advanced Executive Program, University of California at Los Angeles, John E. Anderson Graduate School of Management, Los Angeles.

Dent, J. F. (1986, June). *A case study of the emergence of a new organizational rationality.* Paper presented at the International Conference on Organizational Symbolism and Corporate Culture, Montreal, Quebec, Canada.

Doktor, R. H. (1990). Asian and American CEO's: A comparative study. *Organizational Dynamics, 18*(3), 46-56.

Drucker, P. F. (1971). *Men, ideas, and politics: Essays* (pp. 704-711). New York: Harper & Row.

Dubinskas, F. A. (1988). Janus organizations: Scientists and managers in genetic engineering firms. In F. A. Dubinskas (Ed.), *Making time: Ethnographies of high-technology organizations* (pp. 170-232). Philadelphia: Temple University Press.

Dunning, J. H. (1988). The future of the multinational enterprise. In J. C. Baker, J. K. Ryans, Jr., & D. G. Howard (Eds.), *International business classics* (pp. 55-71). Lexington, MA: D. C. Heath.

Dwyer, K. (1982). *Moroccan dialogues.* Baltimore, MD: Johns Hopkins University Press.

Dyer, W. G., Jr. (1985). The cycle of cultural evolution in organizations. In R. H. Kilmann, M. J. Saxton, & R. Serpa (Eds.), *Gaining control of the corporate culture* (pp. 200-229). San Francisco: Jossey-Bass.

Dyer, W. G., Jr. (1986). *Cultural change in family firms.* San Francisco: Jossey-Bass.

Earley, P. C. (1989). Social loafing and collectivism: A comparison of the United States and the People's Republic of China. *Administrative Science Quarterly, 34*(4), 565-581.

Earley, P. C. (1993). East meets West meets Mideast: Further explorations of collectivistic and individualistic work groups. *Academy of Management Journal, 36*(2), 317-348.

England, G., & Harpaz, I. (1983). Some methodological and analytic considerations in cross-national comparative research. *Journal of International Business Studies, 14*(2), 49-59.

England, G. W. (1975). *The manager and his values: An international perspective.* Cambridge, MA: Ballinger.

Enz, C. A. (1986). New directions for cross-cultural studies: Linking organizational and societal cultures. In R. N. Farmer (Ed.), *Advances in international comparative management* (Vol. 2, pp. 173-189). Greenwich, CT: JAI.

Eramilli, M. K. (1991). The experience factor in foreign market entry behavior of service firms. *Journal of International Business Studies, 22*(3), 479-501.

Erez, M., & Earley, P. C. (1993). *Culture, self-identity, and work.* New York: Oxford University Press.

Farmer, R. N., & Richman, B. N. (1965). *Comparative management and economic progress.* Homewood, IL: Irwin.

Fiol, M. C. (1990). Narrative semiotics: Theory, procedures and illustration. In A. S. Huff (Ed.), *Mapping strategic thought.* New York: John Wiley.

Fletcher, K. E., & Huff, A. S. (1990). Argument mapping. In A. S. Huff (Ed.), *Mapping strategic thought.* New York: John Wiley.

Frake, C. O. (1977). Plying frames can be dangerous: Some reflections on methodology in cognitive anthropology. In *Quarterly newsletter of the Institute for Comparative Human Development* (Vol. 3, pp. 1-7). New York: Rockefeller University.

Frake, C. O. (1983). Ethnography. In R. E. Emerson (Ed.), *Contemporary field research* (pp. 60-67). Prospect Heights, IL: Waveland.

Garsten, C. (1990, June). *The fluidity of space and time: The amorphous culture of global high-technology companies.* Paper presented at the Seventh International Conference on Organizational Symbolism and Corporate Culture, Saarbrucken, West Germany.

Geertz, C. (1973). *The interpretation of cultures.* New York: Basic Books.

Geist, P., & Hardesty, M. (1987, June). *The symbolics of quality care: The intangible product of the hospital organization.* Paper presented at the Third International Conference on Organizational Symbolism and Corporate Culture, Milan, Italy.

Giddens, A. (1979). *Central problems in social theory: Action, structure and contradiction in social analysis.* Berkeley: University of California Press.

Goodenough, W. H. (1981). *Culture, language, and society.* Menlo Park, CA: Benjamin-Cummings.

Graham, J. L., & Sano, Y. (1984). *Smart bargaining: Doing business with the Japanese.* Cambridge, MA: Ballinger.

Gray, S. J., Radebaugh, L. H., & Roberts, C. B. (1990). International perceptions of cost constraints on voluntary information disclosures: A comparative study of U.K. & U.S. multinationals. *Journal of International Business, 21*(4), 597-622.

Gregory, K. (1983). Native-view paradigms: Multiple cultures and culture conflicts in organizations. *Administrative Science Quarterly, 28,* 359-376.

Grinyer, P. H., & Spender, J. C. (1979). Recipes, crises, and adaptation in mature businesses. *International Studies of Management and Organization, 9*(3), 113-133.

Haire, M., Ghiselli, E. E., & Porter, L. (1966). *Managerial thinking: An international study.* New York: John Wiley.

Hall, E. T. (1959). *The silent language.* New York: Doubleday.

Hamel, G., Doz, Y. L., & Prahalad, C. K. (1989, January-February). Collaborate with your competitors—and win. *Harvard Business Review,* 133-139.

Handy, C. B. (1978). Zur Entwicklung der Organisations-kultur durch Management Development Methoden [Developing organizational culture through management development]. *Zeitschrift fuer Organisation, 7,* 404-410.

Harbison, F., & Myers, C. A. (1959). *Management in the industrial world: An international analysis.* New York: McGraw.

Hickson, D. J. (Ed.). (1993). *Management in Western Europe.* New York: de Gruyter.

Hofstede, G. (1980a). *Culture's consequences: International differences in work-related values.* Beverly Hills, CA: Sage.

Hofstede, G. (1980b, Summer). Motivation, leadership and organization: Do American theories apply abroad? *Organizational Dynamics,* 42-63.

Hofstede, G., & Bond, M. (1988). The Confucious connection: From cultural roots to economic growth. *Organizational Dynamics, 16*(4), 4-21.

Hofstede, G., Neuijen, B., Ohayv, D. D., & Sanders, G. (1990). Measuring organizational cultures: A qualitative and quantitative study across twenty cases. *Administrative Science Quarterly, 35*(2), 286-316.

Jaeger, A. M. (1986). Organizational development and national culture: Where's the fit? *Academy of Management Review, 11*(1), 178-190.

Johnson, R. T., & Ouchi, W. G. (1974). Made in America (under Japanese management). *Harvard Business Review, 5,* 61-69.

Jones, M. O. (1988). In search of meaning: Using qualitative methods in research and application. In M. O. Jones, J. D. Moore, & R. C. Snyder (Eds.), *Inside organizations: Understanding the human dimension* (pp. 31-47). Newbury Park, CA: Sage.

Kanungo, R. N., & Wright, R. W. (1983, Fall). A cross-cultural comparative study of managerial job attitudes. *Journal of International Business Studies, 14*(2), 115-129.

Kelley, L., Whatley, A., & Worthley, R. (1987). Assessing the effects of culture on managerial attitudes: A three-culture test. *Journal of International Business Studies, 13*(2), 17-31.

Kerr, C. (1983). *The future of industrial societies.* Cambridge, MA: Harvard University Press.

Kilmann, R. H. (1983). A dialectical approach to formulating and testing social science theories: Assumptional analysis. *Human Relations, 36*(1), 1-22.

Kim, K. I., Park, H., & Suzuki, N. (1990). Reward allocations in the United States, Japan, and Korea: A comparison of individualistic and collectivistic cultures. *Academy of Management Journal, 33*(1), 188-198.

Kleinberg, J. (1989). Cultural clash between managers: America's Japanese firms. In S. B. Prasad (Ed.), *Advances in international comparative management* (Vol. 4, pp. 221-244). Greenwich, CT: JAI.

Kleinberg, J. (1992). *Organizational cultures in a bi-national setting.* Unpublished manuscript, University of Kansas, School of Business, Lawrence.

Kleinberg, J. (1994a). "The crazy group": Emergent culture in a Japanese-American bi-national work group. In S. Beechler & A. Bird (Eds.), *Research in international business and international relations* [Special issue] (Vol. 6, pp. 1-45). Greenwich, CT: JAI.

Kleinberg, J. (1994b). Practical implications of organizational culture where Americans and Japanese work together. In *National Association for the Practice of Anthropology bulletin* (Vol. 14, pp. 48-65). Washington, DC: American Anthropological Association.

Klineberg, O. (1971). Black and white in international perspective. *American Psychologist, 26,* 119-128.

Kluckhohn, C. (1951). Values and value-orientation in the theory of action: An exploration in definition and classification. In T. Parsons & E. A. Shils (Eds.), *Toward a general theory of action* (pp. 388-433). Cambridge, MA: Harvard University Press.

Kluckhohn, F. R., & Strodtbeck, F. L. (1961). *Variations in value orientations.* Evanston, IL: Row, Peterson.

Kogut, B., & Singh, H. (1988). The effect of national culture on the choice of entry mode. *Journal of International Business Studies, 19*(3), 411-432.

Kopper, E. (1992). Multicultural workgroups and project teams. In N. Bergemann & A. L. J. Sourisseaux (Eds.), *Interkulturelles management* [Intercultural management] (pp. 229-251). Heidelberg: Physica-Verlag.

Kreiner, K., & Schultz, M. (1990, June). *Cultures in collaboration—The genetic code of conduct in biotechnology.* Paper presented at the Seventh International Conference on Organizational Symbolism and Corporate Culture, Saarbrucken, West Germany.

Kroeber, A. L., & Parsons, T. (1958). The concepts of culture and of social system. *American Sociological Review, 23,* 582-583.

Lane, H., & DiStefano, J. (1991). *International management behavior.* Boston: PWS-Kent.

Lawless, M. W. (1981, June). Toward a theory of policy making for directed interorganizational systems. *Dissertation Abstracts International, 41*(12, Pt. 1), 5226A. (University Microfilms No. 8111245)

Li, J., & Guisinger, S. (1991). Comparative business failures of foreign-controlled firms in the United States. *Journal of International Business Studies, 22*(2), 209-224.

Lincoln, J. R., & Kalleberg, A. L. (1990). *Culture, control, and commitment: A study of work organization and work attitudes in the United States and Japan.* Cambridge, UK: Cambridge University Press.

Lincoln, Y. S., & Guba, E. G. (1985). *Naturalistic inquiry.* Beverly Hills, CA: Sage.

Louis, M. R. (1983). Organizations as culture-bearing milieux. In L. R. Pondy, P. J. Frost, G. Morgan, & T. C. Dandridge (Eds.), *Organizational symbolism* (pp. 39-54). Greenwich, CT: JAI.

Marcus, G. E. (1986). Contemporary problems of ethnography in the modern world system. In J. Clifford & G. E. Marcus (Eds.), *Writing culture: The poetics and politics of ethnography* (pp. 165-193). Berkeley: University of California Press.

Martin, J. (1992). *Cultures in organizations: Three perspectives.* New York: Oxford University Press.

Martin, J., & Siehl, C. (1983). Organizational culture and counter-culture: An uneasy symbiosis. *Organizational Dynamics, 12*(2), 52-64.

Martin, J., Sitkin, S. B., & Boehm, M. (1985). Founders and the elusiveness of a cultural legacy. In P. J. Frost, L. F. Moore, M. R. Louis, C. C. Lundberg, & J. Martin (Eds.), *Organizational culture* (pp. 99-124). Beverly Hills, CA: Sage.

Meek, C. B., & Song, Y. H. (1990, August). *The impact of national culture on management and organization: Lessons from the land of the morning calm.* Paper presented at the annual meeting of the Academy of Management, San Francisco.

Meyerson, D. E., & Martin, J. (1987). Cultural change: An integration of three different views. *Journal of Management Studies, 24,* 623-647.

Moran, R. T., & Harris, P. R. (1981). *Managing cultural synergy.* Houston, TX: Gulf.

Morris, M. H., Davis, D. L., & Allen, J. W. (1994). Fostering corporate entrepreneurship: Cross-cultural comparisons of the importance of individualism versus collectivism. *Journal of International Business, 25*(1), 65-89.

Narayanan, V. K., & Fahey, L. (1990). Evolution of revealed causal maps during decline: A case study of Admiral. In A. S. Huff (Ed.), *Mapping strategic thought* (pp. 109-133). New York: John Wiley.

Nath, R. (1986). The role of culture in cross-cultural and organizational research. In R. N. Farmer (Ed.), *Advances in international comparative management* (Vol. 2, pp. 249-267). Greenwich, CT: JAI.

Newman, W. H. (1972). Cultural assumptions underlying U.S. management concepts. In J. L. Massie & S. Laytie (Eds.), *Management in an international context* (pp. 327-352). New York: Harper & Row.

Ouchi, W. G. (1981). *Theory Z: How American business can meet the Japanese challenge.* Reading, MA: Addison-Wesley.

Pacanowsky, M. (1987). Communication in the empowering organization. In J. A. Anderson (Ed.), *ICA Yearbook 11.* Newbury Park, CA: Sage.

Pascale, R. T., & Athos, A. G. (1981). *The art of Japanese management.* New York: Warner.

Pederson, J. S. (1987, June). *Organizational cultures within computer firms.* Paper presented at the Third International Conference on Organizational Symbolism and Corporate Culture, Milan, Italy.

Peters, T. J., & Waterman, R. J., Jr. (1982). *In search of excellence: Lessons from America's best-run companies.* New York: Harper & Row.

Pettigrew, A. M. (1979). On studying organizational cultures. *Administrative Science Quarterly, 23*(4), 570-581.

Pettigrew, A. M. (1985). *The awakening giant.* Oxford, UK: Basil Blackwell.

Phillips, M. E. (1990, August 15). Industry as a cultural grouping. *Dissertation Abstracts International,* 5102A. (University Microfilms No. DA 9017663)

Phillips, M. E. (1994, August). Industry mindsets: Exploring the cultures of two macro-organizational settings. *Organization Science, 5*(3), 384-402.

Phillips, M. E., Boyacigiller, N. A., Sackmann, S. A., & Bolton, M. K. (1992, June). *Multiple cultural mindsets as a normal state: A cultural perspective on European organizational life.* Symposium conducted at the Second International Conference of the Western Academy of Business, Leuven, Belgium.

Phillips, M. E., Goodman, R. A., & Sackmann, S. A. (1992). Exploring the complex cultural milieu of project teams. *pmNETwork—Professional Magazine of the Project Management Institute, 7*(8), 20-26.

Phillips, M. E., Sackmann, S. A., & Goodman, R. A. (1992, November). *The cultural environment of project teams: An expanded view of their complex nature.* Paper presented at the EIASM Workshop on Managing in Different Cultures, Cergy-Pontoise, France.

Pondy, L. R., Frost, P. J., Morgan, G., & Dandridge, T. C. (Eds.). (1983). *Organizational symbolism.* Greenwich, CT: JAI.

Pümpin, C. (1984). *Unternehmenskultur, Unternehmensstrategie und Unternehmenserfolg* [Corporate culture, corporate strategy and corporate performance]. Paper presented at the ATAG Conference "Die Bedeutung der Unternehmenskultur für den künftigen Erfolg Ihres Unternehmens" [The importance of corporate culture for the future success of your firm], Zurich.

Putnam, L. L., & Pacanowski, M. E. (1983). *Communication and organizations: An interpretive approach.* Beverly Hills, CA: Sage.

Redding, S. G. (1994). The comparative management theory zoo: Getting the elephants and ostriches and even dinosaurs from the jungle into the iron cages. In B. Toyne & D. Nigh (Eds.), *International business inquiry: An emerging vision.* Columbia: University of South Carolina Press.

Redding, S. G., Norman, A., & Schlander, A. (1993). The nature of individual attachment to the organization: A review of East Asian variations. In M. D. Dunnette (Ed.), *Handbook of industrial and organizational psychology* (Vol. 4, pp. 647-688). Palo Alto, CA: Consulting Psychologists Press.

Redding, S. G., & Wong, G. Y. Y. (1986). The psychology of Chinese organizational behavior. In M. H. Bond (Ed.), *The psychology of the Chinese people* (pp. 267-295). Hong Kong: Oxford University Press.

Reger, R. K. (1990). The repertory grid technique for eliciting the content and structure of cognitive constructive systems. In A. S. Huff (Ed.), *Mapping strategic thought* (pp. 71-88). New York: John Wiley.

Roberts, K. H. (1970). On looking at an elephant: An evaluation of cross-cultural research related to organizations. *Psychological Bulletin, 74*(5), 327-350.

Roberts, K. H., & Boyacigiller, N. A. (1984). Cross-national organizational research: The grasp of the blind men. In B. M. Staw & L. L. Cummings (Eds.), *Research in organizational behavior* (Vol. 6, pp. 423-475). Greenwich, CT: JAI.

Rohlen, T. P. (1974). *For harmony and strength: Japanese white-collar organization in anthropological perspective.* Berkeley: University of California Press.

Ronen, S. (1986). *Comparative management and multinational management.* New York: John Wiley.

Ronen, S., & Shenkar, O. (1985). Clustering countries on attitudinal dimensions: A review and synthesis. *Academy of Management Review, 10*(3), 435-454.

Roseberry, W. (1989). *Anthropologies and histories: Essays in culture, history, and political economy.* New Brunswick, NJ: Rutgers University Press.

Rosen, M. (1986, June). *Christmas time and control: An exploration in the social structure of formal organizations.* Paper presented at the International Conference on Organizational Symbolism and Corporate Culture, Montreal, Quebec, Canada.

Rusted, B. (1986, June). *Corporate entertainment as social action: The case of a service organization.* Paper presented at the International Conference on Organizational Symbolism and Corporate Culture, Montreal, Quebec, Canada.

Sackmann, S. A. (1983). Organisationskultur—Die unsichtbare einflussgrösse [Organizational culture—The invisible influence]. *Gruppendynamik, 14,* 393-406.

Sackmann, S. A. (1986, March). Cultural knowledge in organizations: The link between strategy and organizational processes. *Dissertation Abstracts International, 46*(9), 2748-A. (University Microfilms No. DA 8525878)

Sackmann, S. A. (1991). *Cultural knowledge in organizations: Exploring the collective mind.* Newbury Park, CA: Sage.

Sackmann, S. A (1992a). Culture and management development in a global economy. In R. M. Schwarz (Ed.), *Managing organizational transitions in a global economy* [Monograph and Research Series, Vol. 57, pp. 31-56]. Los Angeles: University of California at Los Angeles, Institute of Industrial Relations.

Sackmann, S. A. (1992b). Cultures and subcultures: An analysis of organizational knowledge. *Administrative Science Quarterly, 37*(1), 140-161.

Sackmann, S. A., & Phillips, M. E. (1992). *Mapping the cultural terrain in organizational settings: Current boundaries and future directions for empirical research* (CIBER Working Paper No. 92-05). Los Angeles: University of California at Los Angeles, Center for International Business, Anderson Graduate School of Management.

Samovar, L. A., & Porter, R. E. (Eds.). (1991). *Intercultural communication: A reader.* Belmont, CA: Wadsworth.

Sampson, E. E. (1978). Scientific paradigms and social values: Wanted a scientific revolution. *Journal of Personality and Social Psychology, 36*(11), 1332-1343.

Sapienza, A. M. (1985). Believing is seeing: How organizational culture influences the decisions top managers make. In R. H. Kilmann, M. J. Saxton, & R. Serpa (Eds.), *Gaining control of the corporate culture* (pp. 66-83). San Francisco: Jossey-Bass.

Sarnin, P. (1989, June). *Stability of leader's cognitions in the firm and the need for strategic change: The role of socio-cognitive conflict in a service company.* Paper presented at the Fourth International Conference on Organizational Symbolism and Corporate Culture, INSEAD, Fontainebleau, France.

Schein, E. (1983). The role of the founder in creating organizational culture. *Organizational Dynamics, 12*(1), 13-28.

Schein, E. (1985). *Organizational culture and leadership.* San Francisco: Jossey-Bass.

Schneider, S. C., & de Meyer, A. (1991). Interpreting and responding to strategic issues: The impact of national culture. *Strategic Management Journal, 12,* 307-320.

Sekaran, U. (1983, Fall). Methodological and theoretical issues and advancements in cross-cultural research. *Journal of International Business Studies,* 61-72.

Servan-Schreiber, J. J. (1968). *The American challenge* (R. Steel, Trans.). New York: Atheneum.

Shenkar, O., & von Glinow, M. A. (1994). Paradoxes of organizational theory and research: Using the case of China to illustrate national contingency. *Management Science, 40*(1), 56-71.

Shenkar, O., & Zeira, Y. (1992). Role conflict and role ambiguity of chief executive officers in international joint ventures. *Journal of International Business, 23*(1), 55-75.

Smircich, L. (1983, September). Concepts of culture and organizational analysis. *Administrative Science Quarterly, 28*(3), 339-358.

Smircich, L., & Calas, M. B. (1987). Organizational culture: A critical assessment. In F. M. Jablin, L. L. Putnam, K. H. Roberts, & L. W. Porter (Eds.), *Handbook of organizational communication* (pp. 228-263). Newbury Park, CA: Sage.

Smith, P. B., & Peterson, M. (1988). *Leadership in context.* London: Sage.

Søndergaard, M. (1994). Research note: Hofstede's consequences: A study of reviews, citations, and replications [Special issue]. *Organization Studies, 15*(3), 447-456.

Spradley, J. P. (1980). *Participant observation.* New York: Holt, Rinehart & Winston.

Stinchcombe, A. L. (1965). Social structure and organizations. In J. G. March (Ed.), *Handbook of organizations* (pp. 142-193). Chicago: Rand McNally.

Strenger, H. J. (1990). Bayer: Bestens gerüstet für die 90er Jahre [Bayer: Well prepared for the 90's]. *Handelsblatt, 116*(20), 6-43.

Sullivan, J. (1994). Theory development in international business research: The decline of culture. In B. Toyne & D. Nigh (Eds.), *International business inquiry: An emerging vision.* Columbia: University of South Carolina Press.

Sumihara, N. (1992). *A case study of structuration in a bicultural work organization: A study of a Japanese-owned and -managed corporation in the U.S.A.* Ann Arbor, MI: UMI Dissertation Services.

Symons, G. L. (1986, June). *Corporate culture, managerial women, and organizational change.* Paper presented at the International Conference on Organizational Symbolism and Corporate Culture, Montreal, Quebec, Canada.

Thurow, L. (1988). Keynote address. Big Sky, MT: Western Academy of Management.

Triandis, H. C. (1972). *The analysis of subjective culture.* New York: John Wiley.

Triandis, H. C. (1983). Some dimensions of intercultural variation and their implications for community psychology. *Journal of Community Psychology, 11,* 285-302.

Triandis, H. C. (1993). Cross-cultural industrial and organizational psychology. In M. D. Dunnette (Ed.), *Handbook of industrial and organizational psychology* (Vol. 4). Palo Alto, CA: Consulting Psychologists Press.

Trice, H. (1985). Rites and ceremonials in organizational cultures. *Research in the Sociology of Organizations, 4,* 221-279.

Tunstall, W. B. (1985). Breakup of the Bell System: A case study in cultural transformation. In R. H. Kilmann, M. J. Saxton, & R. Serpa (Eds.), *Gaining control of the corporate culture* (pp. 44-65). San Francisco: Jossey-Bass.

Van Maanen, J. (1979). The fact of fiction in organizational ethnography. *Administrative Science Quarterly, 24,* 539-550.

Van Maanen, J. (1988). *Tales of the field: On writing ethnography.* Chicago: University of Chicago Press.

Van Maanen, J., & Barley, S. (1984). Occupational communities: Culture and control in organizations. In B. M. Staw & L. L. Cummings (Eds.), *Research in organizational behavior* (Vol. 6, pp. 287-365). Greenwich, CT: JAI.

Van Maanen, J., & Barley, S. (1985). Cultural organization: Fragments of a theory. In P. J. Frost, L. F. Moore, M. R. Louis, C. C. Lundberg, & J. Martin, J. (Eds.), *Organizational culture* (pp. 27-53). Beverly Hills, CA: Sage.

Vernon, R. (1971). *Sovereignty at bay: The multinational spread of U.S. enterprises.* New York: Basic Books.

Vinton, K. (1983, March). *Humor in the work-place: It's more than telling jokes.* Paper presented at the Western Academy of Management Meeting, Santa Barbara, CA.

Weiss, J., & Delbecq, A. (1987, March). High-technology cultures and management: Silicon Valley and Route 128. *Group and Organization Studies, 12*(1), 39-54.

Westwood, R. I., & Kirkbride, P. S. (1989, June). *Jonathan Livingston Seagull is alive and well and living in Hong Kong: Cultural disjuncture in the symbolization of corporate leadership.* Paper presented at the Fourth International Conference on Organizational Symbolism and Corporate Culture, INSEAD, Fontainebleau, France.

Wolf, E. R. (1982). *Europe and the people without history.* Berkeley: University of California Press.

Part I

Culture With a Focus on
the National Level

All three contributions in Part I share a research focus on the national level but include other levels of culture as well. In addition, the studies were conducted in different cultural contexts regarding nation, industry, and region.

The chapter by Seungkwon Jang and Myung-Ho Chung examines the specific characteristics of Korean management practices at the national level. These are rooted in the ideology of Confucian capitalism, which the authors compare to the ideology of Protestant capitalism. This ideological base can be located at the "greater regional level" of Figure 1.1. In addition, the authors explore the specifics of Samsung's management renewal program and how people manage to deal with the program's inherent contradictions. These issues are located at the organizational level with their specific enactment being influenced by culture at the ideological level. The uniqueness of culture at the national level seems to be influenced by their ideological base, which allows them to integrate apparent paradoxes.

The chapter by Tatjana Globokar focuses on the differences between French and Slovenian management in a Slovenian car plant that was taken over by a French automobile producer. Globokar explores managerial issues predominantly at the national level of culture within the automobile industry and within a certain region. The discussion indicates that different interpretations of managerial issues are strongly influenced by national culture, especially ethnicity on the Slovenian side, with some regional influences. Globokar also shows how these differences can be overcome by fostering mutual understanding and appreciation for the otherness.

The chapter by Yasemin Arbak, Ceyhan Aldemir, Ömür Timurcanday Özmen, Alev Ergenç Katrinli, Gülem Atabay Ishakoglu, and Jülide Kesken explores the nature and differences of Turkish managers within the private and public sector. Their major research focus addresses issues at the industry level of culture (public vs. private) within the managerial profession of Turkey. Because of this national research context, the study and discussion sheds light on the specifics of the Turkish managerial context. Thus, the reader learns more about attributes of modern Turkish managers that have changed or rather emerged since Hofstede conducted his study of cultural differences a quarter century ago.

Chapter 3

Discursive Contradiction of Tradition and Modernity in Korean Management Practices

A Case Study of Samsung's New Management

Seungkwon Jang
Myung-Ho Chung

Recently, discussion on the Korean economy and management has increased. Amsden (1989) calls the thriving Korean economy "Asia's Next Giant." The coming 21st century is widely viewed as the era of East Asia and Pacific Rim, where China, Japan, and Korea will become the major players (Kennedy, 1993; Naisbitt, 1996). These perspectives more or less underscore the important role of Confucianism and the traditional systems in creating such economic success.

It is maintained that affinities exist between emerging East Asian capitalism and Confucian values—that is, work ethics and family values. For instance, a weekly magazine, *The Economist* ("New Fashion," 1995), reports that the Singaporean government, among the most successful newly industrializing economies (NIEs), promotes the "teaching of Confucian values in schools."[1] This chapter positively correlates East Asian tradition (including Confucianism) as serving as a driving force behind the success of East Asian economies; thus, Confucian ethics become "old wisdom." In this respect, East Asian capitalism can be called "Confucian capitalism" parallel to the Western concept of Protestant capitalism.

Weber and Traditional Discourses of East Asian Capitalism

Two widely known perspectives in social theory address the relationship between economic systems (including management practices) and religious (or cultural and value) systems. One is the Weberian theory of capitalism and religions, and the other is the theory of organizational culture. Both perspectives are discussed in the light of the emerging East Asian capitalism.

The processes of Western capitalism have long been articulated in Weberian and Marxian language. Weberian theory of rationalization and religion addresses the relationship between religions and economic systems, specifically Protestant ethics and capitalism. According to Weber (1951), latent backward characteristics in Chinese religions, especially in Taoism and Confucianism, were the main reason why East Asian countries could not develop capitalist social and economic systems.

The Weberian thesis on Chinese religions should be criticized on many counts. First, Weber (1951) could not foresee the possible selective affinities between capitalism and Chinese religions and philosophy, especially Confucianism (and the Confucian ethics such as self-discipline, education, etc.). The Weberian sociologist, Bellah (1957), reveals the affinities between Japanese religion and the capitalist economic system of Japan. Second, Weberian theory stresses the ideological side of religion and not the formative, active, dynamic, and changing features of religious systems. Third, the Weberian idea of the rationalization process and notions of rationality are very limited to "formal" or "instrumental" perspectives that often aim to reduce cost and enhance efficiency.

Organizational Culture of East Asian Management

Some theorists positively discuss the ways in which Confucianism has been a key factor for economic development and business success in East Asia. This line of argument has been supported by East Asian success stories such as that of Japan.

For instance, in organization theory the success of East Asian management practices (especially Japanese) is attributed to aspects of their culture (e.g., Ouchi, 1981). Following this line of argument, Confucianism as a foundation of East Asian culture has played a very significant role. In the cases of Korean and Japanese management, Confucianism has been taken seriously as a dominant ideology. Even if there are differences in the transformation process of Confucianism in the two countries,[2] Confucian value systems are undoubtedly key to understanding the two countries.

In this context, Korean management is often compared with Japanese management. It has been said that Korean management styles are simply a duplicate of Japanese models. Surely, there are similarities between these two countries when compared to other countries. Nevertheless, many reports also point out the differences (Lie, 1990; Oh, 1991). Each country has its own history, with different social and political backgrounds.

This kind of approach has been aligned with "corporate culture theory." In this way, organizational culture theory has recently emerged as a very popular theme of management practitioners and scholars. Most arguments on organizational culture, however, are based on empiricism, which reduces cultural aspects (such as value systems) to measurable instrumental factors. Survey methods to measure operational concepts in culture are widely used (e.g., Hampden-Turner & Trompenaars, 1993).

In summary, Weber (1951) considers that certain elements of East Asian tradition work as negative forces that hamper capitalism. Conversely, there are other opinions arguing that East Asian tradition plays a positive role in forming a successful Confucian capitalism. Both are basically cultural explanations, however. These perspectives do not illuminate dynamic processes of East Asian tradition.

Empirical and linear comparisons of some organizational measures and factors, such as leadership patterns and group dynamics, are very simplistic and limited approaches in terms of theoretical and even practical values. This is also the case with organizational culture. For these reasons, a new language is necessary to explain Korean management practices.

In this chapter, we introduce a new way (language) of explaining Korean management practices—that is, "discourse." We discuss the differences between Korean discourses and Western discourses in light of logic and illuminate underlying discursive contradictions in Korean management practices through the case of Samsung. This chapter is organized as follows: The first part is about discourse and discursive transformation; the second part is about the different logic behind these discourses; and the last part of this chapter presents a case study of Samsung in which we argue that discursive contradictions are shown in the management renewal program.

Discourse as a New Language for Korean Management Practices

The two contrasting perspectives about Confucianism mentioned previously do not seem to reconcile with each other easily. In fact, the influence of Confucianism in the East Asian economy still remains a controversial issue. Thus, we wonder if there are other ways of grasping the nature of Korean management. In fact, we have many reservations and questions on these two contrasting approaches to East Asian traditions, especially Confucianism.

First, the positive viewpoint of traditional discourses of Korean management (e.g., organizational culture) simply stresses the harmonious work practices and the Korean work ethic that values hard work. This viewpoint, however, is fairly problematic in that the ordinary docility in the Korean workplace is overestimated (Chang, 1994; Kim, 1992). Korean workers simply want to show their willingness to follow their supervisors' control and corporate ideology to avoid conflict.

Furthermore, there is a lack of recognition that Western modernity, often represented by management principles and techniques such as Taylorism, has not been suppressed but rather well received in Japan (Warner, 1994). Taylorism in Japan has been modified and localized with great enthusiasm.

Second, the negative viewpoints about East Asian traditions, notably in the Weberian thesis, also miss the dynamic aspect of East Asian discourses and affinities between Western modernity and East Asian tradition. They simply highlight the role of traditions that hinder the development of East Asian countries. Along such a line of argument, only Western modernity can fit into modern management practices.

In conclusion, we contend that both positive and negative viewpoints of the East Asian tradition are equally insufficient. We argue that East Asian tradition and Western modernity are two contrasting systems that come together with a creative tension. Our discussion will focus on the contradictions of these contrasting systems.

Discursive Practices

Our new language derives from Foucault's (1977) work, especially the notions of *formative discourse* and *discursive transformation*. In its ordinary sense, *discourse* refers to speech and writing or, more specifically, to a coherent body of speech or written statements. Foucault's (1972) analysis uses the term *discourse* as a group of statements that give us a language for talking about a specific topic. For instance, when we talk about the West, the East, and their relationship, these are called *discourses* (Hall, 1992). We usually use *the West* as a neutral term. These discourses, however, are not simple and neutral ways of speaking and writing. Rather, a particular discourse (such as the West) influences us to think in a particular way. Discourses actually construct our ways of thinking and looking at the world.

Discourse in this sense is expressed and formed by practice or action. Discourse is not simply a linguistic or semiotic structure but also is an enacted (i.e., practiced) form of knowledge in which language is not separated from action and vice versa. This approach to discourse is called *discursive practice*. All social practices are said to have discursive aspects: "discourse enters into and influences all social practices" (Hall, 1992, p. 291). Foucault (1977, p. 200) himself illustrates that discursive practices (discursive transformation) are "embodied in technical processes, in institutions, in patterns for general behavior, in forms for transmission and diffusion, and in pedagogical forms which, at once, impose and maintain them."

Foucault's (as cited in Hall, 1992, p. 292) elaboration of the notion of discursive formation rests on the following points:

1. Although a discourse is formed by many individuals in different institutional settings, it is fundamentally independent of each individual's position. Nevertheless, anyone using a discourse and placing themselves in a discourse is normally compelled to act as the "subject of the discourse."

2. Because "discourses are not closed systems," normally many elements of other discourse are adopted by a particular discourse through the processes of altering, translating, and binding other discourses into its own "network of meaning."

3. "The relationships and differences between discourses must be regular and systematic, not random," although it does not necessarily mean that the statements within a discursive formation should be the same.

Discourse and Ideology

As Hall (1992) points out, a discourse seems to be similar to an ideology. There are differences between the two, however. An ideology is logically based on the true and the false, although we cannot easily distinguish the true from the false in the social, political, and moral world. Ideology offers no ground for compromising between the true and the false; communism as an ideology does not allow itself to compromise with capitalism, which it categorizes as the false.

Discourse that particularly expresses itself in language, however, has impact on human and social practices. Thus, descriptions by a specific discourse (e.g., the West) become "true." Nevertheless, this can also be changed with regard to discursive transformation. This process necessarily involves an agonistic contestation for the "truth" or, more accurately, the dominant discourse. In fact, most everyday discourses (e.g., politician's statements) are really discursive practices that compete for this status. They are motivated by the desire to win the coveted status of truth. Following Nietzsche, Foucault (1977, p. 202) maintains that "knowledge (discourse) is an 'invention.' " Moreover, knowledge is produced on the stage of "struggle against each other": The production of discourses is "not the effect of their harmony or joyful equilibrium, but of their hatred, of their questionable and provisional compromise, and of the fragile truce" (Foucault, 1977, p. 203). In this regard, discursive transformation can represent the will to power.

In this chapter, we consider management disciplines such as management science (or operations research) as discourse because management science as a discipline is implemented in the forms of technical processes in factories and training processes. Furthermore, these become control mechanisms of Korean business organizations so that the word *science* is a quite widely applied term in management practices, which consists of discursive practices.

As Foucault (1977) mentions, discursive practices such as management disciplines are transformed in a specific mode. For instance, the quality control movement in Japan originally came from the United States, but it has been transformed in a very specific manner (Warner, 1994). The collective control of people and group decision-making processes have been well located in traditional Japanese ways of management.

Logic and Contradiction

The term *contradiction* should be defined clearly. Following Western philosophy, contradiction means a mutually exclusive entity derived from Aristotelian logic. In this sense, however, contradiction has hardly existed in Chinese
logic, which has led East Asian philosophy although paradoxical logic has
long been recognized by East Asians as well as westerners. For instance,
Zeno's paradox was also known by Chinese scholars, notably Kung-sun lung
and Hui hsui, who were named "School of Name." These scholars, however,
have been ignored and undervalued in that their concerns were trivialized as
simply a "name" or "logic." Logical abstraction could not be a main concern
for the Chinese. There was no such intellectual tradition as Aristotelian formal
logic in China.

Two Contrasting Logics:
Identification and Differentiation

The Korean philosopher Park (1993) contends that there are two strategies of
logic: identification and differentiation. The strategy of identification in logic can
be widely seen in the Western world. This logic is based on the sameness that
reduces the different things to the same things. According to this logic, A should
be A; thus, A should not be non-A. This logic is called syllogism. The important
point in this logic is to try to find reality in substance (A and non-A) and not in
relation (Needham, 1956). For instance, even Mill's induction logic and Hegel's
dialectical logic can be said to have restored the identification strategy of deductionism, while they have criticized the deductionism of classical logic (Park, 1993,
p. 78).

Considering the different paths of Eastern and Western civilization, the old
question—"Why wasn't there a scientific revolution in China?"—is still valid
when discussing different types of logic in the East and the West. Many prominent
scholars on the history of science, including Needham (1956, p. 343), highlight
the significance of material foundation. Unlike this line of understanding, Park
(1993) accounts for the reason why a scientific revolution never happened in China
by suggesting that answers should be viewed in terms of different types of "logic."

Western rationality and logic can be represented by the Ancient Greeks,
notably the Pythagorean school (Park, 1993, pp. 196-199). Because the Greeks

believed in number atomism, they could not tolerate the logical inconsistency that marginal phenomena (such as irrational numbers) should be solved by the explanatory systems. The notions of "number" could be expanded and reconstructed toward a general system of numbers (which contains irrational number)—that is, "real number." Thus, geometric algebra can be possible in Greek mathematics, unlike in Chinese mathematics.

This obsession to achieve pure logical consistency (or to avoid contradiction) ignores practical effectiveness, which was the main motive of Chinese mathematics. Therefore, westerners' effort to avoid contradiction has been relentlessly made until their logical thinking meets a dead end. At this point, westerners reluctantly reconstruct the basic premises of their logic. In their pursuit for consistent deductive logic, westerners are able to reach a limit that cannot be overcome by means of the established (existent) premises and axioms or commensurable concepts and criteria. In this regard, Park (1993, p. 199) calls deductive (i.e., identifying) logic the "periphery-leading" logic.

In contrast, East Asian logic (mainly derived from China) is called differentiating logic, which is based not on sameness but rather on difference. It can be both A and non-A; likewise, neither A nor non-A. For Chinese, logic is simply a name. For them, logic is inevitably nonidentifiable. There are always differences and gaps between the real and the name. They underline only the significance of relationship between the real and the name. Chinese logic tries to escape from the limit point at which we can meet the crisis and failure of extremity and want to stay within the eclectic center. This is called the "center-leading" logic (Park, 1993, p. 204). In this sense, Chinese logic is different from Western logic.

Yin-Yang Logic

Differentiating logic is easily seen in yin and yang dynamism, which is a cyclic logic: both yin and yang or neither yin nor yang. Throughout the history of Chinese philosophy, the terms *yin* and *yang* have been pervasive in every perspective of Chinese ideas. Yin and yang are normally regarded as the two fundamentally opposite terms that explain natural and social phenomena throughout Chinese thinking. These two fundamental forces are generally contrasted by the series of meanings shown in Figure 3.1 (Needham, 1956).

These two oppositions, however, are not clearly separated from each other. Rather, they complement each other toward a harmony of two oppositions, which is understood as the cyclical patterns in the motion between yin and yang (Wang

Yin	Yang
Darkness	Light
Shady side of a mountain	Sunny side of a mountain
Female	Male
Receptive power	Creative power
Maternal element	Paternal element
Earth	Heaven

Figure 3.1

Ch'ung; Needham, 1962, p. 7): The Yang having reached its climax retreats in favour of Yin; the Yin having reached its climax retreats in favor of Yang.

Thus, it is said that yin and yang constitute eminent Chinese thinking and are constituted by each other. The relationship between yin and yang is complementary. Yin-yang is not a hierarchical notion.[3] With respect to Chinese thinking, yin can be grasped by means of yang. Chinese conceptual polarity is complementary, as Hall and Ames (1987, p.17) state: "Yin does not transcend Yang, nor vice versa. Yin is always 'becoming Yang' and Yang is always 'becoming Yin,' night is always 'becoming day' and day is always 'becoming night.' "

Relational Logic

As the yin-yang dynamism shows, Chinese thinking (and Taoism in particular) is concerned with "relation." As Needham (1956, p. 478) states, "while European philosophy tended to find reality in substance, Chinese philosophy tended to find it in relation."

Western metaphysical ideas based on substance regard identity as a basic principle of thought. In most European thinking, the fundamental logic (especially formal logic such as syllogism) derives from the question format of "either X or non-X" (Park, 1993). Thus, we should perceive a thing as either X or non-X; a thing can never be both X and non-X at the same time because this formalistic logic is based on simultaneous time span and not on a moving and changing time dimension.

Unlike Western thinking, relational thinking of Chinese thought leads to a radically different perspective that a thing is always becoming. Thus, a thing can be both X and non-X. Because Chinese thinking is not concerned with identifying logic and substance, this contradictory rule of formal logic (i.e., Aristotelian syllogism) does not matter at all. Rather, Chinese is concerned with differentiation of relationship between substance. For this reason, Chinese avoid the questions about being and metaphysics. Although westerners ask the question "What essentially is it?" Chinese ask "How is it related in its beginnings, functions, and endings with everything else, and how ought we to react to it?" (Needham, 1956, p. 199).

Discursive Contradictions of Tradition and Modernity in Korean Management Practices

Our research questions are concerned with the following: whether traditional discourses (e.g., Confucianism and Taoism) and modern discourses (Western management disciplines, Taylorism, engineering, and sciences) are working together toward an effective management discourse; whether traditional discourses and modern discourses of management disciplines in Korea are contradictory; how traditional discourses and modern discourses can work together or coexist; and why these contradictory discourses cannot be problematic in the Korean management context.

To answer these questions, we use the Samsung case as representative of a creative tension in practical management; Samsung shows both the contradictions between discourses and how to resolve these contradictions. Samsung's new initiative for a corporate renewal program, called New Management, consists of traditional discourses and modern discourses. This recipe of mixing the two is becoming one of the characteristics of Korean management practices.

Contradiction of Tradition and Modernity in Korean Management

Western management disciplines as scientific (i.e., rational) knowledge and representative of scientific practice have been highly regarded as bringing about modernization. Here, we have to bear in mind the significance of science and scientific approaches in modern Korea. This is all related to Western power and hegemony, namely, Western political and economic power and Western cultural hegemony of mass media. Thus, discourses of science, especially Western natural science, have meant for Koreans the triumph of human rationality against the threat of Nature. In management practices, scientific management attains very high status as a source of materialistic power (engineering), as a source of capitalism, and as a source of Western political power. Western power is equated to Western discourses of science and knowledge.

Therefore, Korean management and organizations have faced overwhelming pressure from the West. Western management disciplines have been posited as the "rational" (and inevitable) option toward better management. This has implications on Korean history and culture. For Korean managers, it is inevitable to accept Western discourses as the "ideal" alternative. Thus, scientific management has been a dominant discourse in Korea.

Even if we can observe this kind of change in management practices, we cannot assert that management practices in Korea are dominated by Western discourses. In his ethnographic study of a Korean company, Kim (1992) points out the coexistence of traditional and Western discourses in Korean management practices. His study shows that Korean industrial relations and management styles share both tradition (Confucianism) and modernity (Western management disciplines). Although the basic organizational principles of the Korean company are the same as those characteristics of Weberian formal and rational organizations, traditional cultural traits (such as managerial paternalism, authoritarianism, rigid formality, and hierarchy) can be seen in Korean companies (Kim, 1992, p. 209).

As we have argued, the meaning of contradiction is the key factor for understanding Korean management discourses and practices. For Koreans, the notion of contradiction is not the same as the Western perception of contradiction. Koreans do not take seriously the Western-style logic of syllogism (e.g., the rule of contradiction), at least when they consider management discourses and practices. Furthermore, Koreans feel comfortable in the coexistence of A and non-A in the same place. This kind of "generous" acceptance of contradiction comes from the Korean (or East Asian) perception of contradiction.

Familism in Korean Management Practices

Recently, research on the organizational culture of Korean Chaebol shows that middle managers in Korean Chaebol have very strong patterns of behaviors and value systems, such as collectivity and innovation (Cho, 1995). According to this survey, 83.7% responded that they have tendencies toward collectivity; at the same time, 89.3% were in favor of innovation. They are following old values, such as collectivism, while supporting social reform, automation, and increased female workers' participation.

In this case, the term *collectivism* actually means familism, which is often translated into courtesy to the elders and harmonious relations with colleagues. For Koreans, familism also indicates various other traits and characteristics of Korean people such as heartwarming emotion, hierarchy, and so on. In this regard, familism has very much the same meaning as tradition in Korea. It is said that most significant principles of Korean management practices in general can be seen in the Confucian ethics that are embedded in Korean business organizations. It is often called familism (collectivism) and paternalism. Familism of Korean management practices is also supported by top management succession. A survey shows that the eldest sons dominate in management succession (80%) among the 30 largest companies in Korea ("The management succession," 1996).

Paternalism and authoritarian leadership are said to be rooted in Confucius doctrine such as the five cardinal relations. These are filial piety (father and son), faithfulness (husband and wife), brotherhood (elder brother and younger brother), loyalty (monarch and subject), and sincerity (friend and friend) (Oh, 1991). Among these five cardinal relations, harmonious family relationships are paramount. This principle permeates every aspect of Korean management practices.

Family-like relationships are widely seen in Korean companies. Slogans use family metaphors such as "the company as my home, the colleagues as my family" (Kim, 1992). In fact, this emphasis on family-like relationships within the company is not simply metaphorical but a serious and real phenomena. For instance, employees are expected to behave like sons and daughters in front of top management so as to bow to the elder people and senior managers.

With regard to selection and recruiting processes, family connections are often used by managers because family connections can serve to prevent strike actions of trade unions (Kim, 1992). Ordinary Korean managers, especially in small-sized companies, believe that strong family commitment never allows employees to act like unknown people in the street. Therefore, managers want to build family-connected relationships and even use their community networks preferentially hiring people from the same family (the same surname) and hometown.

For this reason, it is very difficult to break the old tradition of seniority-based rules and regulations in organizational control mechanism due to deep-rooted familism. Also, in Samsung, familism is an underlined assumption in their organization logic. For instance, in the Samsung Electronic Company, implementation of specialist personnel development programs has failed because of a strong tendency for promotion based on seniority in organizations.

Filial Piety (Hyo) and Patriarchal Leadership

Hyo not only is a family matter but also is used by Korean management practices. The Samsung Life Insurance Company utilizes images of hyo in an advertising campaign that has been featured by mass media and has been well received by consumers ("Samsung's ad," 1995). Hyundai, a Korean Chaebol, encourages new employees to come along with their parents for the entrance ceremony, just as parents escort their children at the beginning of primary school. Through this ceremonial happening, the company seeks to control employees by means of family ties ("Hyundai construction," 1995). Another case shows the different ways of familism as represented by an emphasis on filial piety ("Hankuk Dojaki group's," 1995). That company awards a "King of Hyof" (king of filial piety for the parent) for encouraging filial piety.

In this familism, fatherhood is most important in the organization. Leadership of Korean companies becomes patriarchal authoritarian such that "some Korean chairmen still behave like emperors" (Kraar, 1993). The role model for a leader is to be a strict and stubborn but gentle and generous father. The notion that fathers should keep their families in order is implemented in a wider context. Patriotism and paternalism come together in Confucius teaching. In this sense, the ideal model for leadership is also seen in entrepreneurship. Kim (1992, p. 19) uses the term *entrepreneurial patriotism* to refer to serving the country by running a useful and successful business. In this sense, business is not conducted for the profit and money but for patriotic nation building; profit is simply an outcome of this patriotic activity.

With regard to the view that profit is not the ultimate goal for business, work ethics and motivation of Korean workers arise from sincerity, which is a highly valued quality of human beings. In case of failures in business or any other activity, managers may allow workers to have another chance if they did their best. If one does not do one's best, however, he or she does not provide a good impression to managers, even if he or she achieves the goal(s). In Korea, sincerity and hard work are considered to be among the most important Confucian values.

In this sense, motivation in Korean companies is not derived from incentive or some extrinsic rewards; rather, Korean workers are scared of being labeled as lazy and insincere people. It is said that the main organizational source of motivation is fear or "strict and thorough control" of employees or both (Oh, 1991, p. 50). This is again related to authoritarian leadership. Together with patriarchal leadership, paternalism in Korean companies is ubiquitous in every aspect of working life. Moreover, this seems to be very similar to the "total institutions" of military camps and the all-embracing institutionalism of military life (Kearney, 1991).

Samsung's New
Management

Since 1993, Samsung, the largest Chaebol in Korea, has initiated a management renewal program called New Management (Samsung, 1994). It is called "Chairman Lee Kun-Hee's cultural revolution" in the sense that it strives to change the focal point of Samsung employees' minds from quantity to quality (Burton, 1993). In addition to quality management, however, New Management has features that are designated as "moral management" or "social management." According to the schema of Samsung's New Management (Samsung, 1994), moralistic principles can promote quality management, which could make Samsung a first-class company in the 21st century.

The moralistic principles of Samsung's New Management are called Samsung's Constitution. They consist of four elements: morality, etiquette, *Inkanmi* (literally, personal beauty: kindness and heartwarming personality), and *Yeui* (literally, manner and righteousness: good manner, polite behavior, and courtesy). These principles of New Management, however, are built on basically rather contradictory discourses. The most efficient and competitive company (which is the ideal mission of the best company in light of the management goal to achieve the best performance) is posited as opposite to companies and people who are morally responsible according to traditional Confucian teaching (Figure 3.2).

What, then, are the contradictions within the discourse? The principle of Inkanmi (morality) stresses how important harmonious human relationships are in Korean organizations. It states that the basic principle of Korean organization is not efficiency but relationships. Samsung's Chairman Lee, however, also maintains "Be Professionals with Inkanmi," which is a typical example of a contradictory slogan in the New Management. Another principle of New Management teaches Samsung's employees to behave with Yeui (etiquette). Yeui in organizational life means that the principle of seniority comes first. Thus, it stands in contrast with innovative ideas and people in organizations.

Samsung's effort to foster Inkanmi is persistent. Recently, the Office of the Executive Staff where New Management has been steered has developed a measurement of Inkanmi that consists of the appropriate attitude and behavior to parents, spouses, supervisors, subordinates, neighbors, the nation, and even mankind. The questionnaire is not only used to measure the level of Inkanmi of employees but also may be used as "relevant" data for selection, promotion, and other personnel practices, in the same way that the personality assessment tools

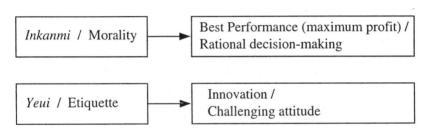

| Inkanmi / Morality | → | Best Performance (maximum profit) / Rational decision-making |
| Yeui / Etiquette | → | Innovation / Challenging attitude |

Figure 3.2

such as the Myers-Briggs Type Indicator have been adopted for the same purpose in Western companies.

The New Management is distinctive in the sense that culturally latent characteristics of Korean companies have attempted to set up guiding principles and use them as building blocks for organizational change. Samsung's New Management aims to build businesses that are driven by these principles.

Interestingly, Western viewpoints of Samsung's New Management may be different from this. For instance, New Management has reported that radical Western management practices introduced into the Korean Chaebol were most influenced by Japanese corporate culture (Burton, 1993). From this perspective, because Japanese corporate culture represents East Asian management practices, Samsung's New Management was an attempt to introduce Western management practices. For some Samsung watchers, Chairman Lee's effort is interpreted as "grafting modern Western management practices onto the group's Confucian hierarchy" (Paisley, 1993). It is more complex than this, however. Here, we can see the contradiction between tradition and modernity in New Management. Because two discourses come together, people may take one aspect or another as they like.

The guiding principle is prone to contradiction in that it triggers the dispute between East Asian discourse and Western discourse. In other words, New Management reveals a hidden dimension of discourse. This unconscious and well covered level of East Asian discourse is often called culture. Practices of the New Management Constitution in organizations push familism and Confucianism up to the conscious level of discourse.

It may be said that while management practices in Korean companies are one thing, guiding principles are another. This is the case even in joint venture companies.[4] Westerners and Koreans (or their ways of practice), however, usually compete against each other when faced with conflict in management practices. They cannot understand each other due to their own management principles.

We have interviewed Samsung's middle managers (about 70 managers and general managers) regarding contradictions within the New Management principles.[5] In these interviews, we found that most of the managers are not conscious of whether the stated principles of New Management are contradictory. After the contradictions were pointed out, however, most seemed to agree reluctantly with the argument. Thus, we conclude that people in Samsung could not take this kind of contradiction seriously even if a few managers (notably, production managers and sales managers) insist that the aims of a business corporation should be making money.[6] Such attitudes may arise from the beliefs that New Management is simply a buzzword and that their viewpoint of contradiction and attitude differs from that of Westerners. In conclusion, Korean workers are not conscious of this contradiction in everyday life, which may produce a considerable amount of confusion for westerners.

Different Styles of Korean Management Practices

We suggest three management processes in Korean management practices: lines A, B, and C (Figure 3.3). With regard to New Management, these are the three benchmarks for comparison with other styles of management practices.

Line A in Figure 3.3 represents the ordinary Korean company's pattern and shows the duality of tradition and modernity, or Western-style management and Confucianism. Line B shows the characteristics of transformation in Samsung's own effort to build their New Management style. In line A, we cannot see the features of Korean management in which, on the surface level, Western management is dominant over East Asian tradition. This is because it is natural for Koreans to live together with tradition and modernity. They do not differentiate between the traditional and modern aspects in everyday practices, or they are not interested in these differences.

Confucian teaching is the traditional discourse that is dominant in the Korean society and culture. Confucianism used to endow rulers hundreds of years ago with moral superiority. Now, management is maintaining a sense of similar moral superiority of the company, based on Confucian decrees. This also serves to reinforce the legitimacy of management. In contrast, modern discourses from the Western world—that is, scientific management, Taylorism, or management

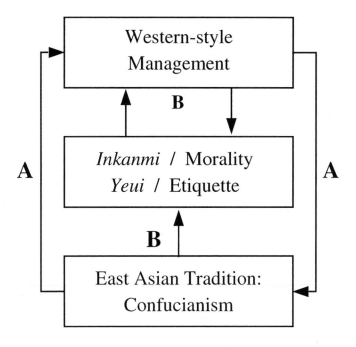

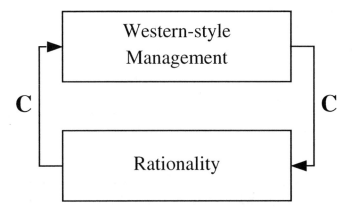

Figure 3.3

disciplines based on science and engineering—make claims of legitimate management based on notions of technological efficacy and efficiency.

Line C in Figure 3.3 represents Western-style management. It is possible, however, for Western-style management to be combined with other cultural bases. In Western countries, Western management styles are founded on principles of rationality. In Asian countries, however, Western management styles conflict and often contradict with Confucian traditions.

By referring to Western-style management, we are speaking primarily of rationality-driven management. Using structuralist terminology (Althusser & Balibar, 1970), the correspondence between productive forces and relations of production (or superstructure and infrastructure)—this process being based on rationality—is constructed to be a complete management model. From this Western-based context and from a Weberian perspective, East Asian infrastructure seems irrational. East Asian cultural bases, however, are beyond the continuum of rationality-irrationality and can be called "arationality." Culture in East Asian countries consists of various roots, such as familism and yin-yang, so that East Asian management appears to be a multilayered form. In the last instance, tradition determines the characteristic of East Asian management.

Western-style management and East Asian management may be contradictory in that East Asian management's cultural base is not one of rationality. It is also difficult to say, however, that the characteristics and effectiveness of East Asian management have nothing to do with rationality. Rather, their rationality seems to be of a different kind.

Conclusion

We have argued that traditional discourse is neither the sole nor the major factor in accounting for the success of the Korean economy. Rather, the combination of Confucianism and Western management disciplines has given rise to thriving Korean business corporations. Confucianism as a driving force of East Asian economies (NIEs) toward Confucian capitalism might be the counterargument to the Weberian thesis that has maintained that traditional discourses, such as Confucianism and Taoism, have played a negative role in East Asian backwardness. Naive cultural explanations for the phenomena of the NIEs have also been problematic because Warner (1994) contends that Taylorism in Japan has been well received, modified, and localized.

How, then, will business corporations look in the future? It might be an important question with regard to the future of Samsung's New Management. One answer could be that, in the future, business corporations will no longer simply be wealth-generating organizations. Rather, we have to take seriously some of the roles of business corporations such as the relationship between business and society, the necessity of social responsibility of business organization to society, and the business organization as a society itself. Business organizations in the future will appear as community leaders, preservation-driven organizations, and even ethical organizations (Maynard & Mehrtens, 1993). Toward this vision, business organizations should be transformed into team-based, participatory organizations founded on moral voluntarism (Galbraith & Lawler, 1993; Pinchot & Pinchot, 1993). The raison d'être of business corporations should not be pure economic interest but one of responsibility defined by its many stakeholders—from economic entity to social institution (Bartlett & Ghoshal, 1994). In this regard, the core ideology or guiding principles of a business company should be proactive to society.

The principles of Samsung's New Management as core ideology are probably more effective than the ideology of companies in Western countries in terms of proactiveness to society, because the cultural base of Samsung (namely, Confucianism) originally underlines the social responsibilities of human beings and organizations. Western business corporations' so-called moral management, such as Merck's core ideologies and Johnson & Johnson's CREDO, seem to be similar to Samsung's New Management. Morality in Western-style management, however, is based on an individualistic and contractual relationship often labeled rationality, whereas Samsung's core principles of the New Management do not stem from rational behavior but from a deep-rooted sense of tradition—an arationality-based morality (beyond rationality).

Some scholars pay attention to contradiction (and paradox) as a source of excellence. For instance, Collins and Porras (1994) argue that successful habits of visionary companies thrive by going through a contradictory phrase: preserve the core, stimulate progress. According to them, successful and long-lasting companies, such as 3M, Boeing, and IBM, have overcome the "tyranny of the OR" (management by either-or choices between volume and quality, efficiency and innovation, etc.) and become the "genius of the AND" (management by both-and thinking).

Thus, we maintain that the contradiction of modernity and tradition in Korean firms might work positively in the age of paradox (Handy, 1994). Will Korean companies be able to prosper in the future under the favor of their capabilities to manage paradox? This is another question. In our point of view, however, Korean management practices can be called the "management beyond rationality."

Notes

1. In the same context, President Kim Young-Sam of Korea declared "moral nation" in his inaugural address in 1993.

2. For instance, one can argue that "Confucian influence appears stronger and more visible in Korea than in Japan" (Ching, 1993, p. 165). Moreover, "the earliest Japanese 'modernisers' were usually from the samurai class, which had a Confucian classical and literary education" (Ching, 1993, p. 169), whereas in Korea Confucian ethics and philosophy were promoted mainly by yang-ban (similar to Chinese Literati). Thus, "the influence of Confucianism in Japan is limited to the warrior ethic (Samurai)" (Oh, 1991, p. 47). These differences should be regarded when studying these two management styles.

3. Thus, yin-yang logic is different from the Hegelian dialectical logic—that is, the "unity of the opposite"—in that the former is fundamentally circular logic, whereas the latter is progressive.

4. One of us (Dr. Chung) has observed this in one Korean-American joint-venture company.

5. In the workshop of Samsung's corporate cultures (May, 1995).

6. One of the interviewees resolutely said, "New Management Constitution is a fairy tale. But business is not a fairy tale. 'To make a good product and to earn much' is the rule of the game even in New Management."

References

Althusser, L., & Balibar, E. (1970). *Reading capital.* London: Verso.

Amsden, A. H. (1989). *Asia's next giant: South Korea and late industrialization.* New York: Oxford University Press.

Bartlett, C. A., & Ghoshal, S. (1994, November-December). Changing the role of top management beyond strategy to purpose. *Harvard Business Review, 79-88.*

Bellah, R. N. (1957). *Tokugawa religion: The values of pre-industrial Japan.* Glencoe, IL: Free Press.

Burton, J. (1993, December 30). Samsung engages in a higher quality revolution. *Financial Times,* p. 16.

Chang, J. A. (1994). *Kiyeup inyum youpowa suyong yangsange kwanhan yonku* [A study on the dissemination and accommodation of corporate ideology]. Unpublished doctoral dissertation, Seoul National University, Department of Anthropology, Seoul, South Korea.

Ching, J. (1993). *Chinese religions.* London: Macmillan.

Cho, Y.-H. (1995, May). *Hankuk Daikiupui Kiupmumwha Tuksung* [The characteristics of corporate culture in Korean companies]. *Personnel Management,* 54-55.

Collins, J. C., & Porras, J. I. (1994). *Built to last: Successful habits of visionary companies.* New York: Harpers Business.

Foucault, M. (1972). *The archaeology of knowledge.* London: Tavistock.

Foucault, M. (1977). *Language, counter-memory, practice: Selected essays and interviews* (D. F. Buchard, Ed. & Trans.). Ithaca, NY: Cornell University Press.

Galbraith, L., & Lawler, E. E., III. (1993). *Organizing for the future.* San Francisco: Jossey-Bass.

Hall, D. L., & Ames, R. T. (1987). *Thinking through Confucius.* New York: State University of New York Press.

Hall, S. (1992). The West and the rest: Discourse and power. In S. Hall & B. Gieben (Eds.), *Formations of modernity.* Cambridge, MA: Polity.

Hampden-Turner, C., & Trompenaars, A. (1993). *The seven cultures of capitalism.* New York: Currency.

Handy, C. (1994). *The age of paradox.* Cambridge, MA: Harvard Business School Press.

Hankuk Dojaki group's new corporate vision. (1995, March 24). *The Korean Economic Daily,* p. 39.

Hyundai construction company: Invitation for new employees' families. (1995, April 4). *The Chosun Ilbo,* p. 39.

Kearney, R. P. (1991). Managing Mr. Kim. *Across the Board, 28*(4), 40-46.

Kennedy, P. M. (1993). *Preparing for the 21st century.* New York: Random House.

Kim, C. S. (1992). *The culture of Korean industry: An ethnography of Poongsan Corporation.* Tucson, AZ: University of Arizona Press.

Kraar, L. (1993, May 3). How Samsung grows so fast. *Fortune,* pp. 16-21.

Lie, J. (1990). Is Korean management just like Japanese management? *Management International Review, 30*(2), 113-118.

The management succession of Korean Chaebol. (1996, January 18). *Hangyerae 21,* No. 92, p. 19.

Maynard, H. B., & Mehrtens, S. E. (1993). *The fourth wave.* San Francisco: Berrett-Koehler.

Naisbitt, J. (1996). *Megatrends Asia: Eight Asian megatrends that are reshaping our world.* New York: Simon & Schuster.

Needham, J. (1956). Mathematics and science in China and the West. *Science and Society, 20*(4), 320-343.

Needham, J. (1962). *Science and civilisation in China: Vol. 4: Physics and physical technology.* Cambridge, UK: Cambridge University Press.

New fashion for old wisdom. (1995, January 21). *The Economist,* pp. 38-39.

Oh, T. K. (1991). Understanding managerial values and behaviour among the Gang of Four: South Korea, Taiwan, Singapore and Hong Kong. *Journal of Management Development, 10*(2), 46-56.

Ouchi, W. G. (1981). *Theory Z: How American business can meet the Japanese challenge.* Reading, MA: Addison-Wesley.

Paisley, E. (1993, May 13). Innovate, not imitate, Far Eastern. *Economic Review,* 64-68.

Park, D. (1993). *Tongyangui nollinun oduie itnunka* [The oriental logic]. Seoul, Korea: Koryowon.

Pinchot, G., & Pinchot, E. (1993). *The end of bureaucracy and the rise of the intelligent organization.* San Francisco: Berrett-Koehler.

Samsung. (1994). *Samsung's new management.* Seoul, Korea: Author.

Samsung's ad using the images of Hyo. (1995, May 27). *The Chosun Ilbo,* p. 15.

Warner, M. (1994). Japanese culture, Western management: Taylorism and human resources in Japan. *Organization Studies, 15*(4), 509-533.

Weber, M. (1951). *The religion of China: Confucianism and Taoism* (H. H. Gerth, Trans.). New York: Free Press.

Chapter 4

Eastern Europe Meets West

An Empirical Study on French Management in a Slovenian Plant

Tatjana Globokar

In 1989, an automobile factory in Slovenia was taken over by a large French company. Being the major capital holder of the plant, the French partner put French managers at the head of 3,000 Slovenians who were supposed to produce French cars for Western markets. The Slovenian plant had to be quickly adjusted to Western quality standards, and because the French company worked with global quality procedures transposed from Japanese working methods, Slovenian workers had to adopt new working methods and behavior. A large number of French-training and human resources personnel invaded the Slovenian plant.

The newcomers were extremely keen to modernize the Slovenian company but found it difficult to be understood and fully accepted by Slovenian staff. Despite the fact that they had brought modern technology and financial resources to the young Slovenian republic in times of a very difficult economical and political situation, the Slovenians did not seem to appreciate their help. The Slovenian staff members certainly made an effort to follow French instructions for change, but they remained suspicious toward the French and even felt humiliated to a certain extent. A French audit team sent from the Paris headquarters in mid-1991 made observations concerning the workers' inefficiency on the shop floor, the lack of authority at the supervisory level, and the poor interdepartmental communication.

In fact, inefficiency in the workplace and lack of responsibility of the workers corresponded to the stereotyped image held by Western businessmen of the planned economy in former Eastern European countries. In the Slovenian factory, French managers found that it was not possible to make such generalizations. Some units in the production department achieved very good quality results. An explanation for the diverging results within the plant was needed. To obtain a deeper understanding of the Slovenian behavior at work, a sociological study was ordered by headquarters to be carried out inside the plant in 1992 and 1993.

The research study had to answer the following questions:

▓ What are the values, rules, and traditions of the Slovenian people that influence their work behavior and organization?

▓ How can the quality difference between production units be explained?

▓ Can the French firm's Total Quality Methods match the Slovenian management culture or do other reengineering procedures have to be invented?

The study also aimed to improve the mutual understanding of two cultures. Therefore, a constant comparison of French and Slovenian management cultures had to be undertaken. Existing analyses of French management (d'Iribarne, 1989) were of great help in showing the differences or similarities between French and Slovenian behavior at work.

Theoretical Basis of the Study

In this case study, the emphasis on national culture seemed essential. Furthermore, the study showed the usefulness of an approach based on qualitative analyses that enabled detailed observations and helped to build a national management model. This meant defining a set of logics that, within a specific cultural context, gave sense to the action of the individuals concerned. The conceptual background of such a procedure was based on several arguments combining sociological and modern anthropological approaches.

Since E. B. Tylor (as cited in Seger, 1970) first published his definition of culture in 1871, a number of definitions have been used by anthropologists and sociologists. One of the latest versions that is quite exhaustive is proposed by Phillips (1994):

> At the core of cultural knowledge is a set of assumptions shared by a group of people. The set is distinctive to the group. The assumptions serve as guides to acceptable perception, thought, feeling, and behavior, and they are manifested in the group's values, norms, and artefacts. The assumptions are tacit among members and are learned by and passed on to each new member of the group. (p. 384)

In our case study, the group was born and educated with the nation over generations. In its historical development, a nation develops actions to which people adhered or to which they were supposed to adhere in order to preserve their national identity. Such actions could be ideological, giving new moral values, or social and political, providing for the physical survival of the nation. The phenomena linked to such events were, for instance, religions, wars, revolutions, and social orders and their corresponding institutions.

Parsons and Shils (1951) analyzed how such projects can become cultural systems that produce values, beliefs, and symbols. They showed how these became institutionalized in a social system and internalized by individuals. They argued that culture means not only "symbols for communication" but also "norms for action." Parsons and Shils concentrated their work on isolated periods, however, without taking into account the impact of previous cultural systems.

Modern anthropology provides answers regarding the continuity of cultural references in time. Levi-Strauss (1958) introduced the notion of "structural elements," which he considers "this something that maintains and what a historical observation helps to free progressively" (p. 30). Claiming that the anthropological analysis is interpretative and in search of meaning, Geertz (1973) focuses on the role of references that cultural systems play throughout the history of nations. In his works, d'Iribarne (1991) combines the previous mentioned arguments by claiming the existence of referential elements within each national culture that persist over time and participate in the construction of an individual's identity, thus creating an appropriate universe of meaning.

To capture the important moments in the history of nations, the studies of Reynaud (1991) are useful. He developed a theory about the rules produced when groups of people adhere to important projects. These rules are based on values and norms. The term *project* embraces the idea of action introduced previously. By defining through historical observation which projects were of great importance for the survival of a nation and to which the majority of people adhere, the origin and nature of fundamental references that give meaning to social relationships are defined.

Thus, in our case, the meanings and significance of relationships at work had to be defined within the Slovenian context and linked to the historical references of the nation.

Data Collection

The data collection included observations on the shop floor and a series of interviews of one hour or more. Three production units were studied during a four-year period, and some personnel from the maintenance, methods, and quality departments were interviewed. Our experience indicated that in qualitative research, the choice of the sample of informants and the time spent interviewing them are more important than the number of interviews. About 40 interviews were conducted at all hierarchical levels. These included

- heads of different departments and different units to understand their ways of communicating with their superiors and their subordinates as well as to understand the level of communication between the departments;
- supervisors to understand the work behavior; and
- workers to see how they manage to cooperate at a horizontal level and how they respond to their superiors.

The descriptions given by informants of their daily work, their difficulties at work, and their problems with superiors and subordinates were compared to analyze the same situation from several points of view. Combining and contrasting information on specific situations enabled us to interpret corresponding behaviors in connection with fundamental cultural references to define the parameters and dimensions with which to build the cultural model.

Preliminary Hypotheses

Even a very superficial look at the history of France and Slovenia indicates that their populations experienced a very different social evolution. The resulting cultural references are therefore likely to be quite different, if not opposed.

French history provided enough opportunities to maintain strong hierarchical social structures, which even the French Revolution could not abolish completely. New social classes and elites appeared as other forms of "nobles" and "commoners," the most fundamental opposition of French society in history. Furthermore, the division of three social stratas—the nobles, the clergy, and the third state (commercials, manufacturers, etc.)—as it existed before the French Revolution is still indirectly present in the French society of today. As d'Iribarne (1989) claims in his work, they correspond to the authority differentiation inside French organizations in which these three levels can be identified by engineers, supervisors, and workers.

On the basis of socialization processes, such attitudes became a part of culture in France. Respecting hierarchical distances within an organization was therefore a given and natural behavior for a French citizens. As we were to discover, however, it was not at all natural for a Slovenian. The importance of social position in French society legitimized competition as a means of upward mobility. The individual struggle to distinguish oneself through one's own qualities is the motor of success. The distinction is a permanent visual and individual affirmation.

In Slovenian society, the need for distinction is based on the principle of equality inside the community. The only way to distinguish oneself from others is by developing particular skills, not by aspiring material fortune and social position. Furthermore, survival in the Slovenian village community was possible only if its members helped each other at work, in the field, or in building houses. This need for and tradition of helping each other made the collective exchange of skills and work one of the most important values to be respected in Slovenian society.

Dominated for several centuries by foreigners, Slovenians never had their own aristocracy or any other leading social class. Their social structure was based on the village community in which hierarchy was particularly flat. The most important people of the village were the mayor and the priest, but even their hierarchical position was not out of reach of the community members. A rich peasant could become a mayor and any poor peasant's son a priest. In the towns and the better-off villages, the social difference was very small between the rising Slovenian middle class, and the bourgeoisie was mostly foreign.

Contrary to the French notion of "grandeur" and nobility, the Slovenian identity has been forged within the village community, in which the members would share their misery and poor conditions and watch carefully to see that members did not distinguish themselves through a privileged position. To preserve their political force against the foreign master, the feeling of all being equal, trustworthy, and helping each other was of great importance.

Thus, the first hypothesis was that the marked hierarchical distances that are typical of French management will not be found in Slovenian work relations, which are characterized by a flat hierarchical structure.

The second hypothesis on differences between French and Slovenian cultural and social references was that social distinctions are essential for the French social structure but very badly accepted by Slovenians for whom the principle of equality presents an important symbol of social equilibrium. This notion of equality influences relationships and behavior at work in Slovenian plants.

The third hypothesis was that within the plant, the French with their individualistic attitudes will be unable to understand the Slovenian collective behavior and spontaneous mutual help at work.

Strong Hierarchical Structures
Versus Need for Equality

The research process started in two workshops: the panel shop and the paint shop. I was told by the French that

> the panel shop is a disaster. The workers are fine but they don't seem to be achieving anything. The paint shop has outstanding results. We'd be delighted if they did as well at French plants. We don't understand why they should be so different.

I carried out my interviews first in the panel shop and discovered that the (French) head of this shop was trying to reestablish a hierarchical structure and kept a distance from his subordinates. The workers seemed to be unhappy and told me,

> If the person I'm working for doesn't convince me that he knows as much as I, if not more, how can he pass on information and tell me what to do? If I can't share my own knowledge I have no role here. I feel excluded. I have no professional dignity.

They were ready to accept the authority of their superiors only if the superior possessed at least the same degree of knowledge if not more: "For me, the

boss has to be able to say how to do it. If I do not know how to do it, he has
to be able to show me."

In the paint shop, however, the head of the shop told me,

> Well, you know, I'm not really one for hierarchy. We all work together here, we
> talk to each other all the time, we pool our knowledge and we have meetings
> where everyone can say what he or she likes. I let people talk so that they feel
> part of things.

He practiced a dynamic teamwork approach in his group including brain-
storming activities, and he saw his role not as a boss but as a motivator. He
met with his supervisors frequently and the workers talked to their superiors
more often. One of the foremen stated, "I see my boss every day. He comes
to the shop floor to give us information to discuss a problem, or whenever we
need to talk to him."

A comparison of the responses of the informants in the panel shop and in the
paint shop made it become clear that the hierarchical distance and the sharing of
professional knowledge played an important role in the relationships within the
working groups and hence in their productivity. The fact that in the panel shop the
superior preferred to keep a distance and strictly respected the hierarchical structure
gave the impression to his subordinates that he did not want to share his knowledge
with them. To them, not wanting to share meant not having enough to share.

Two consequences derived from this situation. On the one hand, the workers
could not trust the professionalism of their superior. As they repeated on several
occasions, they were ready to take orders from their superior only if they felt his
professional superiority. If this was not the case, they refused to follow him. For
that reason, the authority of the superior in the panel shop was very weak. On the
other hand, it was important for the workers to share their knowledge with their
superior so that a relationship of mutual trust could be developed. Such exchanges
gave the workers a feeling of dignity on a professional level. The fact that the
superior did not want to take into account the professional knowledge of his
subordinates created an atmosphere in which they did not feel stimulated to work.

In a Slovenian context, the demand for professionalism at work comes from
the workers themselves. They accept the authority based on professional knowledge and know-how and refuse authority derived from an administrative position.
A permanent professional exchange with the superior also functions as a guarantee
for his superiority. In this case, they were ready to follow as well as to participate
in the work process in the same way as a sports team follows its coach. The

relationship with the leader is respectful but also has to be friendly so that the subordinates can have the feeling of being treated as equals.

In the paint shop, management was based on trust between the superior and the subordinates—together focusing on production problems as their main interest. Priority was given to a very flexible hierarchical system in which only one kind of authority was respected: that of professionalism—knowing and doing one's own task to the best of one's ability. In this mode of functioning, the need for equality was fully integrated. The superior did not look for respect by creating distances; he was automatically respected for his professionalism. His know-how strengthened his position but consequently it also strengthened the feeling of mutual respect and solidarity within his working group. Such behavior could be observed at different hierarchical levels. It reflected at the same time a mixture of autonomy as well as a collective spirit.

The superior who does not know how to approach his subordinate in a friendly way, or whose professional skills do not seem good enough, will have trouble obtaining the quality of work he wants from Slovenian workers. Whereas in French management authority is legitimized by the hierarchical position itself, in Slovenian management authority belongs to the person who has the expertise.

A true understanding of the relationships in the plant can be achieved only by analyzing each situation from the point of view of its cultural significance. Thus, from the French point of view, it would be important to respond to the lack of authority with strengthened hierarchical positions, making it clear who is the boss and even making the authority visible by different uniforms for responsible people. From the Slovenian point of view, such action would totally disintegrate the working group, disappoint the professional ambition of the workers, and reinforce their inertia.

Another example of different cultural significance is the use of professional knowledge and experience. In the Slovenian cultural context, the need for equality and mutual aid favors a permanent exchange of work solutions within the working group. From the French point of view, such exchange disturbs everybody's individualistic approach to his or her work task and represents an interference with the competencies and responsibilities of the individual.

Cultural Interpretations of the Total Quality Concept

The village symbolizes quite well the form of organization that best suits Slovenians at work. Further analyses confirmed that Slovenian workers could develop their skills only if they were placed in an atmosphere of mutual help. The strong concern for equality that guides their relationships with each other gives them a feeling of dignity and trust. When this is the case, they are innovative and cooperative workers. They find it normal to help their colleagues if there is time left after they have completed their own task.

I was able to study such behavior in the coach building department in which intensive quality control in the form of so-called self-control had just been introduced. This was part of the Total Quality procedure introduced by the French company in all its factories worldwide. The procedure was a transposition of *Kaizen,* the Japanese quality approach. It requires an individual commitment to the group work and is based on individual responsibility as well as spontaneous cooperation within the group, whose only goal is the final quality of the product. This implies precise execution of tasks for everyone concerned, good knowledge of work procedures, flexibility in the frequent change of work posts, intensive and permanent cooperation with other members of the working group, and, finally, constant improvement in the work organization and execution.

Although this Total Quality Method was quite new to the Slovenians, the groups worked very well. The emphasis of the procedure was on the group's identity, the quality of the result, and the responsibility of the individual in his or her work. Collective work was something they understood and cooperation functioned throughout the process at all levels. For workers, providing spontaneous aid to their colleagues on the assembly line was something totally natural: "As soon as I see that something is going wrong on the assembly line, I immediately go to help so that the line can get moving again as soon as possible." The absence of such behavior means a lack of a certain working maturity, as one foreman complained, "Young workers have not yet developed the awareness of mutual aid. They don't have the reflex to intervene."

The frequent contacts between the workers and their team leader in the coach building shop further stimulated collective and individual efforts for good overall results. As soon as an operator had a problem, the team leader came and worked with him or her or gave information. One young female worker confirmed this: "I can tell the head of the group what I want. I call him over and I tell him what is wrong." The retouching specialist, who was supposed to be at the end of the line and concentrate on retouching, told us, "As soon as I see that somebody else has a problem, I go and help them." Although the quality checker was from the quality department and not from the production department and was only supposed to be checking, he also helped the team leader, advised him, helped the retouching specialist, handed parts to the worker beside him, and so on.

Such work behaviors were quite different from the quality control methods envisaged by French management. The French transcription of the Japanese quality control method was based on the individualistic French way of working. In French organizations, working tasks are not prescribed and therefore are determined in a very personal way by each individual. He or she defines his or her working territory as *selon la coutume* (according to custom) and defends its boundaries. In such a situation, there is little or no place for cooperation and exchange with other working partners. Therefore, with the French quality control method, workers are to concentrate solely on their own tasks and be aware of the quality of their own work. This method also envisaged teamwork, but in the French cultural sense—not as actual cooperation but as individual efforts to contribute to collective results.

Thus, although the French interpretation of quality control was introduced into the Slovenian cultural context, it was transformed again. It became the collective ambition of "one for all and all for one," and in so doing it came closer to its Japanese origins by giving emphasis to teamwork. Individual know-how became part of the collective struggle for quality of the product on the assembly line. Everybody was committed and there were no boundaries to people's work tasks at each post. This working behavior was strikingly different to the French approach in which the emphasis was on the individual task and its control, without any reference to, or interest in, what people on either side were doing. Here also lay the answer to why this factory quickly became one of the French firm's best quality factories (viz., since 1993).

Observing the behavior of the Slovenians at the assembly line, the French missed the reactions of the Slovenian workers due to their cultural blinders. They thought that the Slovenian workers would care only for their own actions and the quality of their personal work by which they would be controlled and criticized as the procedure of self-control required. Thus, limited by their culture-bound understanding of *Kaizen,* the French almost condemned the most important part of this Japanese method—teamwork. Not surprisingly, this aspect is difficult to introduce into the French cultural context and, thus, into French factories.

A Search for Balance

The search for mutual understanding of different working cultures in international cooperation is inextricably linked to these problems of domination. Domination occurs according to the traditional images of the partners involved as well as an appreciation of their economic power. In the case of the French firm in Slovenia, the relationship was established at the beginning to the advantage of the French. The amount of money invested, and the know-how they were bringing to the country, placed them automatically in a position of command. In another cultural context, one might have expected respect, admiration, and the feeling of being honored to work with such a partner worthy of esteem. Slovenian history, however, provided a very ambiguous attitude toward foreigners in general and toward the Latin or French in particular.

In the past, Slovenians were used to being commanded by foreigners, mostly the German, Austrian, or Italian aristocracies or their high-class bourgeoisie. At the same time, any other foreigners with less important social status who wanted to settle and make a new home had to change their names and religions to be accepted by local Slovenian communities. This meant that the foreigner as such was accepted only in the role of a dominator.

When the French came to Slovenia with their modern technology for automobile production, the Slovenians did not have a favorable opinion on the matter. They had become used to referring to the German culture and its economic and technical superiority. The image of the French was associated with a Latin type of person whose promises and technical product quality are to be considered with mistrust. For the Slovenians, being French is a symbol for good living (*bon vivant*) rather than a symbol for good engineering. In their minds, excellence in this profession was reserved for the Germans.

When the French company came to settle at the Slovenian plant, Slovenia had just become an independent state for the first time in its history. The employees of the plant seeing the French arriving to occupy the leading management positions had spontaneous negative reactions: "Did we work for our independence to be under foreign authority again?"

Tensions emerged, and a feeling of inferiority developed on the Slovenian side. Although the French tried to respect the abilities of their new partners, they were not always successful. Misunderstandings and misinterpretations of words, behaviors, and actions through a lack of knowledge about each other's national culture differences were endless at the beginning of the cooperation. The partners could neither accept each other nor work together. The fact that nobody analyzed or explained their perspectives produced an even wider gap between the two partners. The poor situation in which the French audit team found Slovenian personnel in 1991 was the consequence of such disorientated beginnings.

The subsequent opportunity to receive feedback on their work behavior and a chance to explain it had positive impacts for their mutual understanding. First, the two main characteristics of Slovenian management described previously—the need for equality and mutual aid as a way to highlight skills—were taken into account seriously by French management. French executives listened with great interest to the results of the study and made a significant effort at integrating them. For the Slovenians, such attention represented a kind of respect on the behalf of the foreign investor, to which they were not accustomed. The study had even more importance for them, however. Being a nation with a modest history and small cultural heritage in comparison with the French, the Slovenians felt inferior to their partner and had nothing but their skills to show as a counterpart. The fact that their culture was studied in detail and results were presented to both French and Slovenian executives helped to reinforce a Slovenian identity and they became quite aware of it.

The French learned several important facts from the study. First, they discovered that varying management styles in different countries are linked to each country's culture. Second, they found that these management styles should be respected and not abolished as a consequence of underdevelopment. Third, they understood that defining the fundamental cultural references of a nation helps to anticipate the work behavior and reactions of individuals with regard to new management procedures. The more these procedures can correspond to such fundamental cultural references, the better the work results.

Mediating Between Two Cultures

During this research process, we also learned valuable lessons concerning the researcher's role. The experience showed that the researcher's job in such a situation goes far beyond collecting and analyzing data, and, indeed, goes beyond that of a mediator.

The study of national culture cannot be successful without knowing the languages concerned. Certainly, an interpreter can help, but the quality of the analysis might suffer because of the lack of detailed interpretation of an informant's discourse. For example, we had to avoid the paradox of cultural misinterpretation regarding the Slovenian workers' interpretation of the French's quality control procedure. At this point, the role of the researcher became crucial and went far beyond the classical search for and interpretation of knowledge. It was necessary to make the French, the dominant partner, understand that the working methods of the dominated Slovenian partner had to be accepted and respected if positive results were to be the goal of the partnership.

Furthermore, the relationship of trust between the informants and the researcher is of great importance. In dominant and dominated situations as described previously, the researcher is not seen by informants as a neutral person. He or she has to constantly prove their neutrality to gain trust from both partners. In this case, a French-only speaking researcher would have been seen by the Slovenian informants as an outsider in service of the French partner. They probably would not have openly shared what was really happening in the organization. The fact that the researcher came from France and that the research work was ordered by Paris headquarters created suspicion among Slovenians. Informants were asking themselves constantly, "Is the person who is asking questions with us or against us?" Speaking only Slovenian could have resulted in a lack of trust on the French side. French management wanted to be sure that there was no interpretation of the data collected in favor of the Slovenian partner.

Gaining the trust of both parties to collect appropriate information automatically puts the researcher in the position of a mediator. His or her approach has to ensure that the informants can express their opinions freely and spontaneously. With some knowledge of the culture, the researcher may establish a meaningful exchange with the informant that implies that he or she is able to approach informants in ways that are familiar to them so that they feel comfortable to participate and clarify different work situations. While listening to the answers and descriptions of work problems and situations, the researcher has to explain the cultural reasons for the behavior of the other partner and address the cultural references of the informants themselves. It is necessary to keep in mind that the aim of the whole research process is to help the two partners understand both national cultures involved and their differences. Such explanations are needed to ensure that a process of mutual understanding can develop.

The most important step in the explanation procedure was the final session in which the results of the study were presented to both partners. In the plant, approximately 30 Slovenian and French managers attended this final presentation. For the sake of the continuous search for balance, the written and spoken reports, as well as the transparencies used, were presented in both languages. Similarly, languages were alternated in descriptions of new topics.

This final presentation turned out to be a crucial moment of self-identification for the dominated partner in front of the dominant partner. The fact that the Slovenian history and Slovenian management model were exposed in front of

French managers in equivalent terms as the French history and French management model represented for Slovenian managers a unique opportunity to feel as important as the French in terms of social prestige. It was the moment when an external person valued their national and social existence and identified Slovenian culture in front of the French partner thus creating some basic elements for mutual respect.

Certainly, the researcher could have also just collected and analyzed the data, passed on the report to those who ordered it, and discussed the results in the scientific environment once the confidentiality would have been lifted. In doing so, however, the true logic underlying the continuous exchanges between the two partners would have been missed.

Conclusion

After four years tracking the evolution of relationships between the two partners in the plant, two kinds of questions remain unanswered. The first deal with the problem of distinguishing between the dimensions or behaviors that are "lasting" and others that are "changeable." The lasting behaviors are directly related to fundamental cultural references. They can be transposed into new forms, but they never change in their content. The changeable behaviors refer to manners and habits that can be replaced with new manners and habits. This distinction is quite important for cultural analyses of management practices because it would allow the conception of management models in which only lasting behaviors are taken into account.

The second kind of unanswered question concerns the attitudes of plant managers and their understanding of the changing or lasting behaviors of their employees and workers. Even if intercultural studies point out the main characteristics of national managerial cultures, it is not enough for the partners concerned to hear and read about the results of a study. Understanding cultural differences and their effects in the daily functioning of the organization to adapt managerial and working procedures is a very difficult task for managers.

Opinions of researchers and managers on the matter are getting closer and closer. In one discussion organized by the Ecole de Paris (1994), the following answers were given by two scholars and one chief executive officer (CEO) with regard to the question of whether national models really exist. The first scholar maintained that the best way to get people to work together depends largely on the norms and customs that they share. The second scholar found that talking about national management models can hide cultural differences that exist between different companies. Finally, the CEO claimed that understanding national management models helps to avoid making mistakes. For him, it was necessary to bring traditions closer together without melting them all together in a single mold.

This is what happens in joint ventures and multinational companies—the process of bringing traditions closer together. Only systematic analyses and observations of confronted cultures can make this process happen. Each case, however, is different and depends on the similarities or differences between norms and customs to be shared. This process is not geared toward a melting pot but rather toward developing a higher degree of mutual understanding and adaptation.

References

Ecole de Paris of management. (1994). Do national management models really exist? *Les Invités de l'Ecole de Paris* (No. 4). Paris. Conference report.

Geertz, C. (1973). *The interpretation of cultures.* New York: Basic Books.

d'Iribarne, P. (1989). *La logique de l'honneur* [The logic of honor]. Paris: Seuil.

d'Iribarne, P. (1991). Culture et "effet sociétal" [Culture versus societal effect]. *Revue française de sociologie, 32,* 599-614.

Lévi-Strauss, C. (1958). *Anthropologie structurale* [Structural anthropology]. Paris: Plon.

Parsons, T., & Shils, E. (1951). Values, motives and systems of actions. In T. Parsons & E. Shils (Eds.), *Towards a general theory of action.* Cambridge, MA: Harvard University Press.

Phillips, M. E. (1994). Industry mindsets: Exploring the cultures of two macro-organizational settings. *Organizational Science, 5*(3), 384-402.

Reynaud, J.-D. (1989). *Les règles du jeu* [The rules of the game]. Paris: Armand Colin.

Seger, I. (1970). *Knaurs Buch der modernen Soziologie* [Knaur's book of modern sociology] (p. 79). München: Droemersche Verlagsanstalt.

Chapter 5

Perceptual Study of Turkish Managers' and Organizations' Characteristics

Contrasts and Contradictions

Yasemin Arbak
Ceyhan Aldemir
Ömür Timurcanday Özmen
Alev Ergenç Katrinli
Gülem Atabay Ishakoglu
Jülide Kesken

While searching for answers to the questions, "How is a Turkish manager perceived?" and "Are there any commonalities or differences or both between the perceptions of working people?" we came across very little literature. Thus, to answer these questions and to explore the general characteristics of Turkish managers, we felt rather forced to think in terms of the Turkish managerial context. For this reason, although all the authors of this chapter have been educated in Western-style institutions, we tried to minimize the impact of Western values and teachings in our research. Thus, very little Western literature is cited in this study. In addition, we tried to avoid using any Western models or paradigms. One of the

87

main Western studies about national managerial values and perceptions is Hofstede's (1984) study.

Hofstede (1984) attempted to discover national values concerning management of 39 countries using data collected at two points in time: 1967 to 1969 and 1971 to 1973. Depending on his research, values concerning Turkish management can be identified as high power distance, strong uncertainty avoidance, feminine, and collective work values. Hofstede's study shows that with regard to power distance and uncertainty avoidance dimension Turkey seems to have similar practices as France, Colombia, and Chile. Also, Turkey is similar to France, Spain, Peru, and Israel when the dimensions of femininity and uncertainty avoidance are taken into consideration. From Hofstede's point of view, we can expect Turkish managers to be mostly autocratic or paternalistic leaders, strictly obeying rules, and their dependence on the organization is a result of the importance they give to the use of skills, physical conditions, training, advancement, recognition, and earnings.

Does this really provide a true picture of Turkish management values? We doubt it very much. In our opinion, Hofstede's (1984) research is very limited because of its sample. It is difficult to deduct a nation's managerial cultural values from the answers of a very few individuals (especially individuals working in the same organization). In addition, only a few studies exist in the Turkish management literature. These studies have centered on the style of managers in Turkey (Aldemir, 1985; Ataol, Özmen, Katrinli, & Arbak, 1992; Dilber, 1981). Aldemir (1979, 1985) found that there is almost no delegation of authority in Turkish private organizations. A similar result was obtained by Dilber (1981) and Kozan (1993). Dilber found that Turkish private sector managers and entrepreneurs were very reluctant to delegate authority. Kozan's finding also supports our expectation that Turkish managers show mostly autocratic and paternalistic leadership behavior.

Dilber (1981) also studied motivational aspects of managerial behavior. In his 1966 research, Dilber indicated that the need for esteem was the most important need of managers, whereas self-actualization, independence, security, and affiliation followed. In his 1977 study, however, he found that the order of these needs had changed. According to Dilber's results, the most important need perceived by managers was self-actualization followed by independence, affiliation, esteem, and security needs.

Ataol et al. (1992) tried to draw a profile of private Turkish managers by using a sample of 460 managers. In their study, they found that Turkish managers show mostly type A and type AB behavior. Type A personality is characterized by feeling a chronic sense of struggle to achieve more and more in less and less time, which results in high standards of productivity (Friedman & Rosenman, 1974). Type B is exactly the opposite of type A; the person never suffers from a sense of time urgency (Robbins, 1991). Type AB is a mixture of type A and type B. This personality type does not exhibit any clear pattern (Ivancevich & Matteson, 1980). In addition, type AB people are leaders that mostly criticize their subordinates and show typical autocratic behavior.

Although these few studies provided us with some hints with regard to our question, "How is a typical Turkish manager perceived?", they neglect an important distinction: the difference between Turkish private and public sector managers. When a Turk is asked to identify a typical Turkish manager, he or she will answer immediately by asking another question: "Who? Private or public?" Which one represents Turkish managers? We believe that both represent "the Turkish manager" and any study attempting to identify Turkish managers' characteristics must distinguish the managers of these two sectors (private and public). Our own daily observations, newspaper information, as well as articles of all kinds support the assumption that there are two different types of managers in Turkey, mainly public and private. Any observation and historical analysis will demonstrate the differences between the managers of the two sectors.

Public sector managers in Turkey are influenced by deep-rooted historical traditions and exhibit the respective behavior. Many of these are inherited from the Ottoman Empire, which was highly influenced by Central Asian, Arabian, Iranian, and Byzantinian managerial cultures. Typical characteristics of the Ottoman administrative culture are old, conservative, authoritarian with centralized decision making, strict obedience to the rules, dependence on superiors, limited creativeness, little freedom of action (initiative), introvert, and high resistance to change and to uncertainty (Güvenç, 1993; Hoca, 1992; Timur, 1985).

The Turkish private sector, however, is quite young. The private sector in Turkey started to boom in the 1960s. Typical characteristics of private sector managers, especially after 1980, include young, dynamic, risk taking, entrepreneurial, open to changes, innovative, ambitious, loyal to brand, social, liberal, capable of adapting themselves easily not only to the local markets but also to the international markets (thus flexible), pragmatic, little observance of rules, and less centralized in decision making when compared to the public sector. In this manner, Turkish private sector managers' major characteristics are tolerance and openness toward team work ("Profile," 1995).

Based on the previous discussion, the objectives of this study are to identify perceptions about Turkish managers and to see if these perceptions differ for private and public managers.

Research Design

Sample

Individuals who are working in public or private sector enterprises are the best and the most knowledgeable sources of information about the characteristics of Turkish managers and management. Thus, we decided to contact the largest 500 public and private sector industrial organizations because these organizations play leading roles in Turkish management life. In this respect, our population consists of managers working in the largest 500 organizations of Turkey in 1994. The list of these organizations, published in the yearbook of the Istanbul Chamber of Industry, was used as an initial sampling framework. The list consists of 65 public sector and 435 private sector organizations. Fifty-nine percent (293) of these organizations are located in the Marmora region of Turkey, 18% (92) in the Aegean region, 13% (65) in central Anatolia, 6% (30) in Mediterranean Anatolia, 2% (10) in the Black Sea region, and 1% (5) respectively in the East Anatolia and southern East Anatolia regions.

In this list, 25 of the private organizations did not give permission for their organization names to be published in the yearbook of the Istanbul Chamber of Industry. Thus, we did not have a chance to reach this group. The addresses of the organizations were provided from the chamber of commerce of each city. Although we tried our best, we could not find addresses of 35 private sector organizations. As a result, our study population consists of 440 organizations, 375 (85%) of which are private and 65 (15%) of which are public sector organizations.

Considering the recommendations of Krejcie and Morgan (1970), we decided to select a sample of 205 organizations. We used a proportionate stratified sampling design with two strata based on type of organization (public or private). For each strata, a sampling frame was defined and elements from these sampling frames were selected using a simple random sampling procedure. As a result of this sampling procedure, we selected 31 public sector and 174 private sector organizations (Table 5.1).

Data Collection Method

Questionnaires were used to collect data. The questionnaires designed for the study were sent to all the companies in the sample and included a cover letter indicating the purpose of the study, assurance of confidentiality of responses, and the deadline of the study in February 1995. The questionnaires were addressed to

Table 5.1 Distribution of Companies and Respondents in Study Population and Sample

Type of Organization	Study Population (%)	Sample (%)	Response Rate (%)	Respondents (%)
Private	375 (85)	174 (85)	48 (28)	138 (70)
Public	65 (15)	31 (15)	9 (29)	96 (30)
Total	440 (100)	205 (100)	57 (29)	234 (100)

NOTE: The numbers in Columns 2, 3, and 4 indicate companies, whereas the numbers in Column 5 indicate managers who have returned the questionnaires from these companies.

the presidents of the organizations. They were asked to duplicate and randomly distribute the questionnaire to at least five managers at any level in their organizations and ask the managers to mail back the questionnaires personally.

We received a total of 234 questionnaires from 9 public and 57 private sector companies with a 28% response rate from private sector and a 29% response rate from public sector organizations. Of the 234 respondents, 70% (138) were private and 30% (96) were public sector managers as shown in Table 5.1. Although most of the public sector organizations distributed the questionnaires to more than five managers in their companies, in several private sector organizations the questionnaire was distributed to less than five managers in the respective company or, if distributed, managers in these organizations did not return the questionnaire. One main reason for this difference could be that public sector organizations employ more managers than private sector organizations.

The mean age for our sample is 39 with the youngest manager being 21 years old and the oldest being 58 years old. The sample consisted of 21.7% female and 77.3% male managers. Of all managers, 2.3% have work experience of less than 1 year, 11.5% have 1 to 5 years, 14.7% have 6 to 10 years, 15.1% have 11 to 15 years, and 56.4% have more than 15 years of work experience. A high school degree only is held by 15.4% of the managers, whereas 70.7% hold a university degree, 12.1% a master's degree, and 1.9% a doctoral degree. Of the managers, 3.7% are members of the board of directors, 21.0% are general managers (presidents or general directors or both), 41.1% are department managers, 31.3% are chiefs of sections, and 2.8% are coordinators.

Measurement

Two simple open-ended questions were asked in the questionnaire in addition to questions about demographics. These open-ended questions asked the respondents to define general characteristics of Turkish private and public managers using a maximum of five positive and five negative adjectives (see Appendix). Before mailing the questionnaire, it was pretested with 10 managers—5 public and 5 private sector managers—to see if the questions led the respondents into areas that we did not want to measure. As a result of this test, we did not need to make any adjustments.

The major reason why we asked the respondents to identify five positive and five negative adjectives is because of the semantic difficulties related with the use of adjectives. In Turkish, some adjectives may have both positive and negative meanings depending on the context. For example, rule obedience might be regarded as positive by someone, whereas it might be regarded as negative by someone else. Because we did not have the chance to interview people, we decided that it was necessary to force respondents to categorize the adjectives they used.

Data Analysis

The adjectives were analyzed by using a technique proposed by Moles (1990) in the area of psychology. The aim of this technique is to graph attributes associated with any central concept. In this method, frequency curves are used.

During the analysis procedure, the attributes used by $\frac{1}{32}$ of the sample are placed on the outer circle, the attributes used by $\frac{1}{1}$ of the sample are placed on the inner circle. For placement, a distance score is computed for each attribute:

$$\text{Log distance} = 1/\log (1 + F_i/N),$$

where F_i is the frequency obtained for the ith attribute and N is the sample size.

Findings

Findings of the study are presented in Table 5.2 and Figures 5.1 through 5.4. Figures 5.1 and 5.2 show positive attributes describing Turkish private and public sector managers; Figures 5.3 and 5.4 contain negative attributes cited for these managers. These figures and Table 5.2 show that private sector managers are defined by 23 positive and 16 negative attributes, whereas there are 16 positive and 21 negative attributes describing public sector managers. These initial findings indicate that private sector managers are known to have

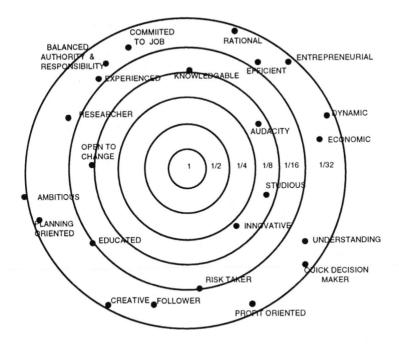

Figure 5.1. Positive Attributes of Private Sector Managers

more positive attributes than public sector managers and negative characteristics are more dominant in public sector managers.

The most commonly cited positive attributes for private sector managers are being innovative ($\frac{1}{8}$, 41), studious ($\frac{1}{8}$, 37), and audacious ($\frac{1}{16}$, 31). All these adjectives connote typical business codes. The most frequently cited positive attributes for public sector managers are patriotism ($\frac{1}{16}$, 21), being studious ($\frac{1}{16}$, 19), and being knowledgeable ($\frac{1}{16}$, 16). Patriotism has nothing to do with business codes. Being knowledgeable and studious are both cited for private and public sector managers. Although private sector managers are claimed to be more studious ($\frac{1}{8}$, 37) and knowledgeable ($\frac{1}{16}$, 19), our sample has also used the same attributes for public sector managers. Being knowledgeable is an attribute that on the circle represents $\frac{1}{16}$ of the sample for both private and public sector managers.

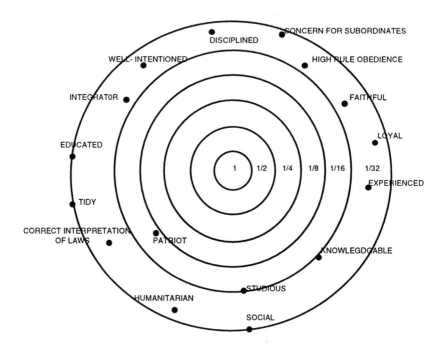

Figure 5.2. Positive Attributes of Public Sector Managers

The other most commonly cited positive attributes defining private sector managers are being open to change ($\frac{1}{16}$, 24), educated ($\frac{1}{16}$, 16), and a risk taker ($\frac{1}{16}$, 16). The most commonly cited negative attributes defining private sector managers are being materialistic ($\frac{1}{8}$, 39), selfish ($\frac{1}{16}$, 30), an exploiter ($\frac{1}{16}$, 21), and pompous ($\frac{1}{16}$, 19). Being selfish is also an attribute that is cited more frequently for public sector managers ($\frac{1}{8}$, 36).

Sixty-five respondents ($\frac{1}{4}$, 65) agree that public sector managers are politicized, which is considered to be a negative characteristic. This is because public sector organizations are mostly used for political purposes. Being conservative (33) and selfish (36) are negative characteristics of public sector managers and $\frac{1}{8}$ of them agree on it. Being narrow-minded ($\frac{1}{16}$, 31), a coward ($\frac{1}{16}$, 22), a dodger ($\frac{1}{16}$, 22), a nepotist ($\frac{1}{16}$, 20), uneducated ($\frac{1}{16}$, 19), not knowledgeable ($\frac{1}{16}$, 19), statutory ($\frac{1}{16}$, 16), reluctant in taking initiative ($\frac{1}{16}$, 27), having high obedience

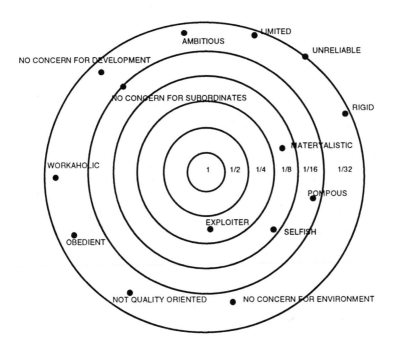

Figure 5.3. Negative Attributes of Private Sector Managers

of rules ($\frac{1}{16}$, 23), and not being job oriented ($\frac{1}{16}$, 22) are the other negative characteristics describing public sector managers.

Discussion and Conclusion

It is not surprising to see that private sector managers are defined as knowledgeable and educated and public sector managers are considered relatively uneducated and unknowledgeable. This is a result of the way promotion decisions are made in the public sector. They are based on either political preferences or seniority (Kalkandelen, 1985). This rules out employees having professional qualifications from becoming managers in the public sector. In addition, great wage differences exist between private and public sector

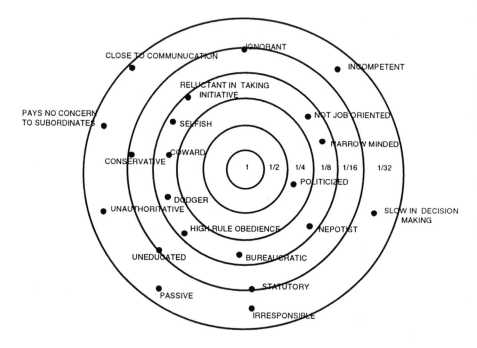

Figure 5.4. Negative Attributes of Public Sector Managers

organizations (Kalkandelen, 1985). This may also be one of the reasons why the ones who are more knowledgeable and educated prefer to work for the private sector. When compared, job security in the private sector is much lower than in the public sector. This means that there is also high competition among private sector managers. This causes them to continuously improve themselves.

Returning to the starting point, the reader may wonder whether we have been able to answer the questions, "How is a Turkish manager perceived?" and "Are there any commonalities or differences or both between the perceptions of working people?" Although we were not able to find clear-cut answers to these questions, we can make some suggestions based on the results of our study.

First, private sector managers tend to be more pragmatic, emphasizing values such as profitability, efficacy, and rationality (Luthans, 1989). Other attributes of this group of managers, such as balancing authority and responsibility, quick decision making, and being entrepreneurial, planning oriented, decisive, and efficient, are related to professional behavior (Khandwalla, 1977).

When we look at the negative attributes associated with private sector managers, attributes such as being materialistic, selfish, an exploiter, having no concern for subordinates, not being quality oriented, and having no concern for development and the environment indicate that private sector managers are perceived to exhibit more of a selfish, individualistic type of work behavior. When we consider the attributes of being statutory, having no concern for subordinates, high rule obedience, and correct interpretive abilities of rules and regulations we can infer that public sector managers are seen to show a more task-oriented type of managerial behavior (Luthans, 1989).

Attributes such as faithfulness, patriotism, loyalty, and being humanitarian, however, indicate that public sector managers are perceived to employ rather collectivist behavior. One may say that these managers tend to be seen as more moralistic when attributes such as patriotism, being integrators, humanitarianism, and having good intentions are taken into account. These attributes emphasize equity and social welfare (Luthans, 1989; Robbins, 1986).

When we compare our results with Hofstede's (1984), public sector managers resemble Hofstede's Turkish managerial culture, whereas private sector managers do not. The contrast, in our opinion, is due to changes that took place due to the time between Hofstede's study and when our study was conducted. Hofstede collected his data in the early 1970s. During those years, the Turkish economy was a closed economy and almost 85% of the economic activity was initiated, operated, and controlled by the state. Thus, it was quite natural that public sector managers were influenced by public sector practices. During those years, many of the private sector managers were transferred from public sector enterprises. Thus, they carried over their managerial experiences and understanding to the private sector.

Beginning in the 1980s, however, a series of economic reforms triggered drastic changes. One major change with a big impact was the opening of internal markets to foreign competition and the abandonment of the state-controlled economy on the behalf of the private sector. The opening to foreign markets and foreign competition forced private sector managers to adapt themselves to novelties. This, of course, required a change, which meant that they needed to understand Western managerial philosophy and practices. Having close contact with foreign individuals and organizations altered the approach of Turkish private sector managers to management. They have rapidly departed from the Ottoman-rooted classical and traditional management understanding and replaced it with a more

Table 5.2 Attributes Cited for Turkish Private and Public Managers ($N = 234$)

Private Sector Managers				Public Sector Managers			
Attribute	n	Portion Cited	Log	Attribute	n	Portion Cited	Log
Positive				**Positive**			
Innovative	41	1/8	14.42	Patriotic	21	1/16	26.13
Studious	37	1/8	16.77	Studious	19	1/16	30.69
Audacious	31	1/16	18.86	Knowledgeable	16	1/16	34.38
Open to change	24	1/16	25.31	Faithful	15	1/32	36.60
Knowledgeable	22	1/16	25.31	Integrator	15	1/32	36.60
Educated	16	1/16	34.38	Experienced	14	1/32	39.13
Risk taker	16	1/16	34.38	High rule obedience	14	1/32	39.13
Balanced authority and responsibility	14	1/32	39.13	Disciplined	12	1/32	45.47
Efficiency oriented	14	1/32	39.13	Well intentioned	11	1/32	49.50
Experienced	14	1/32	39.13	Local	11	1/32	49.50
Researcher	14	1/32	39.13	Interpretory abilities of rules and regulations	10	1/32	54.33
Understanding	12	1/32	45.47	Humanitarian	10	1/32	54.33
Entrepreneurial	11	1/32	49.40	Educated	9	1/32	60.24
Follower	11	1/32	49.50	Pays concern for subordinates	9	1/32	60.24
Profit oriented	11	1/32	49.50	Social	9	1/32	60.24
Committed to job	10	1/32	54.33	Tidy	9	1/32	60.24
Economic	10	1/32	54.33				
Dynamic	10	1/32	54.33				
Ambitious	9	1/32	60.24				
Creative	9	1/32	60.24				
Planning oriented	9	1/32	60.24				
Rational	9	1/32	60.24				
Quick in decision making	9	1/32	60.24				

Negative

Materialistic	39	$\frac{1}{8}$	14.76
Selfish	30	$\frac{1}{16}$	19.47
Exploiter	21	$\frac{1}{16}$	26.46
Pompous	19	$\frac{1}{16}$	29.13
No concern for subordinates	15	$\frac{1}{32}$	36.60
No concern for environment	12	$\frac{1}{32}$	36.60
Ambitious	11	$\frac{1}{32}$	49.50
Obedient	11	$\frac{1}{32}$	49.50
Not quality oriented	10	$\frac{1}{32}$	54.33
No concern for development	10	$\frac{1}{32}$	54.33
Rigid	10	$\frac{1}{32}$	54.33
Workaholic	10	$\frac{1}{32}$	54.33
Creative	9	$\frac{1}{32}$	60.24
Decisive	9	$\frac{1}{32}$	60.24
Stressful	9	$\frac{1}{32}$	60.24
Unreliable	9	$\frac{1}{32}$	60.24

Negative

Politicized	65	$\frac{1}{4}$	9.42
Selfish	36	$\frac{1}{8}$	15.90
Conservative	33	$\frac{1}{8}$	17.45
Narrow-minded	31	$\frac{1}{16}$	18.86
Coward	22	$\frac{1}{16}$	25.31
High rule obedience	23	$\frac{1}{16}$	24.46
Dodger	22	$\frac{1}{16}$	25.31
Not job oriented	23	$\frac{1}{16}$	25.31
Nepotism	20	$\frac{1}{16}$	27.73
Uneducated	19	$\frac{1}{16}$	30.69
Unknowledgeable	19	$\frac{1}{16}$	30.69
Reluctant to take initiative	17	$\frac{1}{16}$	32.43
Statutory	16	$\frac{1}{16}$	34.38
Irresponsible	14	$\frac{1}{32}$	39.13
Bureaucratic	12	$\frac{1}{32}$	45.47
Pays no concern for subordinates	12	$\frac{1}{32}$	45.47
Slow in decision making	12	$\frac{1}{32}$	45.47
Incompetent	11	$\frac{1}{32}$	45.50
Unauthoritative	11	$\frac{1}{32}$	49.50
Closed to communication	.10	$\frac{1}{32}$	54.33
Passive	10	$\frac{1}{32}$	54.33

Western and professional management style. The number of positive and negative adjectives used to describe private sector managers' characteristics typify this change.

These characteristics resemble not only Western professional business codes; they also seem to describe a management style for conducting business in global markets. The trend in Turkey today is a move toward the previously characterized private sector type of management understanding.

This study also has limitations, such as its reliance on mailed questionnaires. Using open-ended questions helped us to avoid statistical controls to ensure reliability of responses. The work presented here was the first study of its kind in Turkey. Additional investigations using a more structured instrument in a second stage will lead to more reliable and detailed results. In such a study, managerial characteristics may be defined by using several dimensions and then correlating these dimensions with organizational and cultural characteristics.

In addition, it may be interesting to conduct cross-cultural studies, especially using managers from countries that we found that showed similar organizational cultural characteristics to Turkey, such as France (Hofstede, 1984). Cross-cultural studies that include countries from the European market will be very informative for Turkish organizations that are in the stage of integration with the European market.

Appendix

Measurement Instrument

1. In your opinion what are the general characteristics of a typical Turkish Public Sector Manager? Please define these characteristics by listing maximum 5 positive and 5 negative adjectives

   Positive Adjectives   *Negative Adjectives*

   _____   _____
   _____   _____
   _____   _____
   _____   _____
   _____   _____

2. In your opinion what are the general characteristics of a typical Turkish Private Sector Manager? Please define these characteristics by listing maximum 5 positive and 5 negative adjectives

   Positive Adjectives   *Negative Adjectives*

   _____   _____
   _____   _____
   _____   _____
   _____   _____
   _____   _____

3. Your Age _____

4. Your Sex: (1) Female   (2) Male

5. Your Tenure
   (1) Less Than a Year   (2) 1-5 Years   (3) 6-10 Years
   (4) 11-15 Years   (5) More Than 15 Years

6. Your Job Title
   (1) Top Executive   (2) General Manager   (3) Department Manager
   (4) Chief   (5) Coordinator

7. Your Education
   (1) Primary School   (2) Junior High School   (3) High School
   (4) University   (5) Master's   (6) Doctoral

Letter Sent to Managers

Dear Manager,

The objective of this questionnaire is to determine cultural values of Turkish organizations and managers which will contribute to the organizational culture literature in Turkey.

Your company was chosen as part of a sample which is representative of the 500 largest firms in Turkey. Your answers are important, since the accuracy of the study heavily depends on your response. Please be assured that your responses will be held in strict confidence and used only for academic purposes.

Please duplicate the attached questionnaire and this cover letter and distribute it to at least five of your company managers at any level. The questionnaires should be sent back to our address given below personally by each manager for assuring more reliable answers.

Thanking for your contribution to our study in advance, we are looking forward to hearing from you until 12 of April 1995.

References

Aldemir, C. (1985). *Örgütler ve Yönetimi: Makro bir Yaklasim* [Organizations and management: A macro perspective]. Izmir, Turkey: Bilgehan Yayinevi.

Aldemir, M. C. (1979). *The relationship between organizational structure and managerial styles: A contingency approach.* Unpublished doctoral dissertation, Aegean University, Izmir, Turkey.

Ataol, A., Özmen, Ö., Katrinli, A., & Arbak, Y. (1992). *Türk Özel Kesim Endüstrisinde Yönetici Profili* [Profile of Turkish private sector managers] (No. 235, AYDB:22]. Izmir, Turkey: Association of Turkish Chambers and Bourses.

Dilber, M. (1966). *Management in Turkish private sector industry.* Unpublished doctoral dissertation, University of Minnesota, Minneapolis/St. Paul.

Dilber, M. (1977). *Türk Özel Kesim Endüstrisinde Yönetsel Davranis.* Istanbul, Turkey: B. Ü. Yayini.

Dilber, M. (1981). *Managerial behavior.* Istanbul, Turkey: Bosphorus University.

Friedman, M., & Rosenman, R. H. (1974). *Type A behavior and your heart.* New York: Knopf.

Güvenç, B. (1993). *Türk Kimligi* [Identity of Turks]. Ankara, Turkey: Kültür Bakanligi Yayinlari.

Hoca, S. (1992). *Tacü't ül Tevarih* [Crown of the history]. Eskisehir, Turkey: Kültür Bakanligi Yayini.

Hofstede, G. (1984). *Culture's consequences international differences in work related values* (Cross Cultural Research and Methodology Series, Vol. 5). London: Sage.

Ivancevich, J., & Matteson, M. T. (1980). *Stress and work: A managerial perspective.* Glenview, IL: Scott, Foresman.

Kalkandelen, A. H. (1985). Yöneticilerin Yetistirilmesi-Gelistirilmesi [Training and development of managers]. *Amme Idaresi Dergisi, Türkiye Ortadogu Amme Idaresi Enstitüsü, 18*(2), 83-112.

Khandwalla, P. N. (1977). *The design of organizations.* New York: Harcourt Brace Jovanovich.

Kozan, M. K. (1993). Cultural and industrialization level influences on leadership attitudes for Turkish managers. *International Studies of Management and Organizations, 23*(3), 7-17.

Krejcie, R., & Morgan, D. (1970). Determining sample size for research activities. *Educational and Psychological Measurement, 30,* 607-610.

Luthans, F. (1989). *Organizational behavior* (5th ed.). New York: McGraw-Hill.

Moles, A. (1990). *Deux methodes d'appreciation des valeurs connotatives: Constellation d'attributs* [Two methods for evaluating value concepts: Classifying symbols]. Paris: Institut De Psychologie Sociale Des Communications.

Profile of new business man. (1995, May 5). *Capital,* pp. 40-44.

Robbins, S. P. (1986). *Organizational behavior: Concepts, controversies, and applications* (4th ed.). Englewood Cliffs, NJ: Prentice Hall.

Robbins, S. P. (1991). *Organizational behavior: Concepts, controversies and applications* (5th ed.). Englewood Cliffs, NJ: Prentice Hall.

Timur, T. (1985). *Osmanl Kimligi* [Identity of Ottomans]. Istanbul, Turkey: Hil Yayinlari.

Part **II**

Culture With a Focus on the Organizational Level

The four chapters included in this section share a research focus predominantly at the organizational level, but they were all conducted in different culture contexts including different nations, industries, and regions.

Terry Schumacher investigates the evolution of the rise and fall of a once cherished organizational culture and focuses on the cultural dynamics within the boundaries of a software engineering corporation located in the Silicon Valley. As such, the major research focus stays at the organizational level, but the exploration of the evolving cultural dynamics includes the formation of various subcultures at the suborganizational level of culture.

Thomas S. Eberle's study addresses the same issues of cultural evolution and decline but in a rather different culture context. He introduces the reader to today's somewhat unusual organization or industry of reading societies and explores in-depth the cultural contrasts and contradictions within the boundaries of one particular reading society located in the eastern (most traditional) part of Switzerland. In his exploration over the life span of this organization, he investigates managerial issues as well as issues of subculture formation, clashes, and change at the suborganizational level.

The chapter by Sierk B. Ybema also explores the same issues of cultural evolution and change (although not decline)—again, in a different culture context. With his in-depth exploration of one specific Dutch amusement park, he takes us to a different nation, industry, and region, but some of the underlying issues and problems remain the same at the organizational and suborganizational level of culture. As in Schumacher's case, organizational growth leads to increasing professionalization that triggers a change in the organizations' core ideology. This exact lack of such a change contributed to the decline of the nonprofit reading society studied by Eberle.

The last chapter in Part II changes perspectives in that the authors deliberately chose a situation of external change (recession) to investigate its impact on a so-called strong culture. Patrick McGovern and Veronica Hope-Hailey take the reader to Great Britain's Hewlett-Packard division and explore how employees manage to reconcile new managerial messages and actions that apparently contradict their core philosophy. This exploration is predominantly at the organizational level of culture, but it also includes the suborganizational level. In contrast to Eberle's reading society, the results of this study illustrate how widely shared organizational beliefs can be maintained even in times of adversative change.

6

West Coast Camelot

The Rise and Fall of an Organizational Culture

Terry Schumacher

West Coast Camelot

Remember Camelot? It was an idyllic place. There was magic in the beginning as young Arthur pulled a sword from a stone to become king. There was a vision for the kingdom and hard work to attain it. The young king was concerned about ideals. "It's not might makes right, Guinevere, it's might for right! That's it! I will ask my knights to take an oath to fight for justice." The reputation of Camelot spread and knights came from distant lands to join Arthur at his "round table." (Recall that the table shape was consciously selected for its impact on group dynamics.)

The tale concludes with darker events. The magic was lost and Arthur was compelled to fight a battle he did not want. The movie ends with him waiting for dawn on the day of the battle. King Arthur, overtaken by events he did not fully understand, wonders where he went wrong.

Arthur talks with a boy near his tent who seems too young to fight in battle. The boy describes Camelot's ideals as his reasons for being there. Arthur finds new hope that all his work may not be lost if the story of his kingdom survives. He orders the boy to run away from the battle, to live long, and tell everyone he meets about the vision of Camelot. "Tell them how glorious a place Camelot was, tell them how well our ideals served us."

I was that boy. Not literally, of course. I was a doctoral student who wanted to apply ethnographic methods in a corporate setting. A rapidly growing software engineering firm agreed to let me study their culture. The results would be used in their training courses. I observed the company over a period of nearly 5 years. I arrived too late to witness the original magic, but I spoke with many who had seen it. There was rapid growth and considerable attention to their ideals during the period in which I did intensive interviewing. Many victories were won and the reputation of this "West Coast Camelot" spread. Gradually, however, the magic diminished. Many new citizens did not understand Camelot's ideals. Some of the founders forgot those ideals or stopped working to achieve them. The leaders responded to an external threat with actions they thought would strengthen the culture. Instead, they drowned the last of the magic. "Finger pointing" emerged as the standard response to growing problems. Then came big layoffs. Many of Camelot's knights who survived these voluntarily left the company during the final year of my observations. A few years later, I wandered into Camelot's booth at a trade show. When I mentioned to an employee the date of my study, he said, "Oh, you were here during Camelot's Golden Years."

Business Overview

In one decade, Camelot grew from "9 guys in a garage" to nearly 3,000 employees with $400 million in annual revenues (Table 6.1). Camelot became the world leader in a very competitive, very technologically sophisticated market—electronic design automation.[1] The company developed software used in designing integrated circuits and printed circuit boards. Their customers, companies such as Apple, Boeing, and Intel, raced to get new products to market within tight deadlines. Their customers loved them. In Japan, where many American firms complain that unfair trade practices exclude U.S. products, Camelot had over 60% of the market in 1989. Senior management frequently mentioned Camelot's culture as a key contributor to their success.

Study Methodology

I approached Camelot with a proposal that involved studying their culture and designing a "cultural simulation" for use in corporate training courses. Data

Table 6.1 Camelot's Rapid Growth

	Camelot's Growth Period Year									
	1	*2*	*3*	*4*	*5*	*6*	*7*	*8*	*9*	*10*
Employees	9	36	192	528	777	909	1,213	1,709	2,116	2,747
Sales ($ millions)	—	2	25	88	137	174	222	300	380	435
Earnings ($ millions)	—	(2)	0	8	8	11	20	34	45	24

on the effectiveness of the simulation in producing attitude change would form the core of a doctoral dissertation.[2] Interviewing and participant observation were the primary methods of gathering information about Camelot's culture. The ethnoscience approach (Spradley, 1979, 1980) was used as a guide. I conducted more than 200 interviews and observed more than 100 events (e.g., department meetings, training classes, customer demos, "mixers," strategic off-site planning sessions, etc.). A questionnaire developed from statements made during the interviews was completed by more than 100 employees. A substantial effort was made to read documents the organization produced (e.g., annual reports, employee newspaper, and product literature). A 90-minute videotape of conversations about Camelot's culture between senior managers and selected employees was created. I wrote a summary of these observations (Schumacher 1992a).

Constructivist Approach to Organizational Culture

Organizational culture began to receive widespread attention more than a decade ago (Deal & Kennedy, 1982; Peters & Waterman, 1982; Schein, 1985; Swartz & Davis, 1981). Reichers and Schneider (1990) review the evolution of the organizational culture construct. One of their conclusions is that no consensus has yet emerged on its definition. Another conclusion they reach is that "there is a paucity of any kind of empirical research on culture" (p. 22). This chapter is a small step toward filling that void.

A philosophic model labeled *constructivism*[3] was adopted in the work reported here. At the core of this model is the assumption that each person categorizes their experience and in doing so creates their own "subjective reality." The term *subjective reality* is used to stress that individuals, to varying degrees, are influenced by and respond to the categories they use to construe experience rather than to any "objective reality." At the same time, it indicates that for each individual, constructed reality is often viewed as an absolute reality and not simply as their categories of experience. Language is the most commonly used system for this categorization of experience. For this reason, ethnographic methods focus on language, collecting verbatim reports, and recording the nuances of usage to create an understanding of the shared definitions and interpretations that constitute a social reality. A group that shares a common language could constitute a culture in the constructivist framework.

The uniqueness of each individual's experience and the creativity he or she brings to the construction of categories for that experience results in each individual having a unique reality. This point is stressed by some constructivist authors (Bennett, 1977; Kelly, 1955). Furthermore, individuals have new experiences and thus their category systems evolve. Together, the factors of uniqueness and evolution imply that any socially shared category system is continually becoming outdated. The constructivist model therefore implies that cultures must be continually built through communication that renegotiates the categories for, and interpretations of, shared experience.[4] The quantity and quality of these building processes that are adopted by various organizations, and their effectiveness in building cultures, are of central interest to students of organizational change processes.

The constructivist model leads to expectations in organizational analysis. One is the uniqueness of each culture due to both the uniqueness of the contributing individual's realities and the ongoing dynamic evolution of shared category systems. This is not a universally held expectation. For example, Migliore and Martin (1994) present a questionnaire for assessing strategic planning across organizations. Their implicit (logical positivist) assumption is that the categories of experience included in the questionnaire language have the same meaning in different organizations. In contrast, the constructivist model suggests that researchers need to develop culturally unique instruments (such as those advocated by Morey & Luthans, 1984, 1985). The choice between a constructivist and a positivist approach raises serious philosophical and methodological questions for those wishing to make cross-organizational comparisons of culture. Answers to those questions are beyond the scope of this chapter.

A secondary expectation that can be derived from the constructivist model is that subcultures may often have greater strength, coherence, or richness than that of an organizationwide culture. This is because energy must be continually expended to build up and maintain a culture. Furthermore, the effort required for this building increases with the number of individuals involved, whereas time available for the communication that builds culture is limited. When an organization grows beyond a size in which its members can regularly communicate, then smaller intraorganizational groups may have advantages in building and maintaining subcultures. Examples of circumstances that support the interaction and communication that produce a shared definition of experience include the sharing of a professional language (in the legal department), shared tasks that require the development of specific linguistic categories (workers from various departments involved in the Compute Engine project), personal interests that lead to shared experience (the company volleyball team), or regular interaction that follows simply from geographic placement (the group on the third floor who frequently eat lunch together).

Knowledge and Membership
Dimensions of Culture

Two dimensions that could be used for describing a culture are the people who are "members" and the "knowledge domains" that they share. The domain is the primary unit of analysis in Spradley's (1979, 1980) ethnoscience approach. Any category for experience can be a domain. A single word or phrase is often used as a label for a domain. For example "taking risks" was a phrase that Camelot employees used to describe certain behaviors. The use of that phrase conveyed a particular meaning for members of the culture. Of course, in another culture the phrase "taking risks" may convey a different meaning or none at all.

Figure 6.1 provides some example categories for each of these dimensions. There is an infinite number of possible knowledge domains. The sum of the shared knowledge is one approach to defining culture and central to the ethnoscience approach. Knowledge domains differ in scope and detail as well as content. That is, the categories of experience used in a culture are not of uniform size or resolution. Researchers (e.g., Bem 1970; Spradley 1980; Taylor & Crocker, 1978) have concluded that cultural knowledge domains are hierarchically structured (a feature not portrayed in Figure 6.1). The ease with which people create and apply categories for experience that convey different granularity complicates the analysis of culture because different authors may focus on different levels in their analysis. For example, Deal and Kennedy (1982) used "degree of risk" and "speed of feedback" as two dimensions of a matrix in proposing a four-category system of culture types. "Risk," however, may be a central and broadly used construct in one

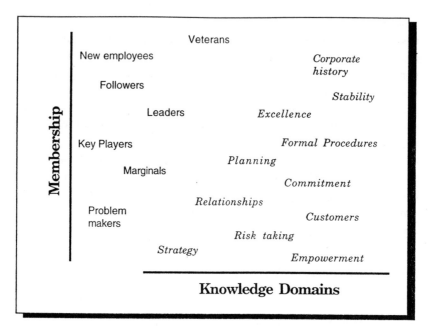

Figure 6.1. Example of Knowledge and Membership Dimensions of Culture

culture (giving it the status of "cultural theme" in Spradley's [1979, 1980] framework), whereas in another culture it may be peripheral. In the Camelot culture, people spoke of taking risks and (sometimes) distinguished between the organization's taking risks and risk taking by individual people. Camelot would probably have been described as a "work hard, play hard" culture in the Deal and Kennedy matrix, although it may be difficult to define whether degree of risk was high or low.

The membership dimension is more bounded, usually being approximately equal to "employees" (although new hires may not yet be members of the culture and some nonemployees, such as students, may be considered members). Of course, not all members share all domains. For example, employees in the accounting department may be unaware of how the products are made or who buys them, domains that are central to employees in the engineering and sales departments, respectively. Conversely, engineers and salespersons may not know about the changing capital structure or a project to secure new financing, which could be critical elements of the shared knowledge in the accounting department. If culture is defined as only that knowledge that is shared by all members, then organizations would appear to be dominated by many subcultures (e.g., engineers, salespersons, and accountants) because so much knowledge is task specific. The study reported here adopted a much broader definition of culture—knowledge shared among any subset of members. That is, culture is seen as a union of all knowledge that is shared among any members (rather than the intersection of every employee's knowledge).

Conceptualizing Culture Change and Subculture Formation

The membership and knowledge domain dimensions can be used in describing categories of culture change. The knowledge domain dimension can be defined as the number of domains that change and the membership dimension as the number of people for whom those domains change, as shown in Figure 6.2. Here, the membership dimension indicates only the number of members, although such an ordering is a considerable simplification that fails to represent qualitative differences between individuals (i.e., this representation ignores that the president probably has a greater impact on the culture than the new parking lot attendant). The knowledge domain dimension is likewise simplified to be only a listing of all domains in the culture, ignoring the fact that some are central and essential, whereas others are peripheral and of less consequence. This representation, however, provides a description of broad categories of organizational culture change. It is possible that only after defining types of culture change, and examining the factors that influence each, will we be able to speak with some confidence about the what and how of influencing organizational culture. If there are different types of culture change processes, then it may be difficult to distinguish the factors by examining a pool of examples drawn from the different types. Figure 6.2 offers categories that fit examples of change observed at Camelot.

Here, *drift* is considered to be gradual change in few domains for few members of the culture. This type of change is always occurring in all cultures, although of course the rate of change and the centrality of affected domains varies. This type of change is fragmented in nature, being more common for peripheral knowledge (because central knowledge is resilient due to its many cross-linkages). As an example of drift, Camelot adopted the C++ programming language in Year 7. Prior to this, all programming was done in Pascal. This change had little impact outside of the engineering groups and although it required considerable individual learning (often shared among team members) and new procedures (codified corporate

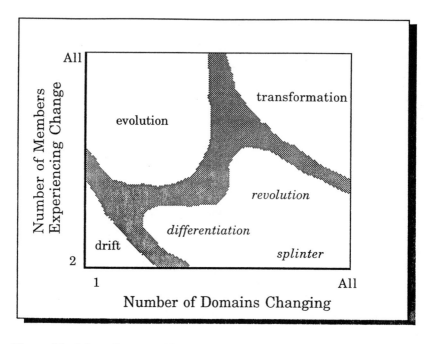

Figure 6.2. Culture Change and Subculture Formation Processes

knowledge), it had little impact on broader cultural themes such as risk taking or the open door policy. Changes that begin as drift may become integrated with other issues and processes and eventually lead to culture change that would be placed in the other categories. Reger, Mullane, Gustafson, and DeMarie (1994) use the term *incremental* in their discussion of culture change to describe a similar category of change. Here, drift is used to suggest the absence of any teleological considerations, whereas Reger et al. are considering directed change.

Evolution is used in Figure 6.2 to describe change in several significant domains for the majority of culture members. Teleology is again not specified in defining this category, but it is here that directed interventions leading to substantial productivity improvements are possible. Fully adopting total quality management or BPR or the responses to a shift in strategy (adding or dropping major product lines) are examples of culture change that might be described as evolution (although such changes may be broad enough to be labeled "transformation"). Most or all employees are aware of evolutionary change and many experience substantial impact. For example, after a successful company begins to decline or a struggling company returns to regular profitability, employee beliefs may change in a few key domains. One example of cultural evolution observed at Camelot was the termination of the hardware development group following the end of the Compute Engine project (described under "Example Contrasts and Contradictions").

Transformation is described here as change in many significant domains for the majority of the members of the culture. The change magnitude here is so great that the identity of the culture is at least questioned, perhaps redefined. More than a few central beliefs and cultural themes are changed in such a situation and therefore a longer time frame is usually required. Transformation is uncommon and is associated with extreme events such as major acquisitions that lead to integration of dissimilar cultures, substantial layoffs, or the successful effort over time of strong leadership. The adoption of many new products and markets or customer types can lead to transformation. An example of transformation in Camelot's culture was the loss of the "magic" of their "small company atmosphere" during the 8.0 project (described below).

The final area shown in Figure 6.2 has several labels but no distinguishing boundaries, indicating both the speculative nature of the figure and a perception that additional dimensions (e.g., teleology, domain significance, and time frame) may need to be considered to precisely describe these types of change. Differentiation, splinter, and revolution are offered as descriptors for change in few to many significant domains for a significant minority of culture members. The result in these cases is identifiable subcultures. When these remain coherent for most central domains, there is differentiation because the subculture members still see themselves as members in the broader organizational culture. Camelot examples include the contrasts between engineering and human resource departments along the innovation domain (see "Example Contrasts and Contradictions"). Early in the Compute Engine project, the "hardware versus software" conflict was only differentiation; each side accepted that the other was different and considered this appropriate.

When the domain differences are more extreme, and especially when conflict emerges, splinter becomes a more appropriate label. When a subculture begins to see itself as isolated, when a "we-they" boundary becomes central to perceptions, or when a group actively pursues goals knowing they are in conflict with, or detrimental to, other groups, then the change is beyond differentiation. Such change may not be well represented by a simple counting of the domains but may require consideration of qualitative differences among domains. The Compute Engine group had become a splinter group before it left its parent and spun off in a hostile act to form a separate company a year before it was acquired by Camelot. When analyzing examples of differentiation, splinter, and revolution, examination of the effect of culture-building activities at both culture and subculture levels, and an analysis of the specific domains involved, is probably necessary.

The previous discussion introduced a constructivist model of culture and culture change processes that can be useful in describing organizational change. The following sections complement this with discussions of concrete examples of culture-building activities and the knowledge domains of a specific organizational culture—Camelot.

Camelot's Culture-Building Activities

Employees and outside observers (competitors and industry analysts) remarked that Camelot had an unusually strong culture. The leaders paid attention to "the type of company we want to build" from its founding. This "vision of the kind of company we want to be" influenced many management practices. These were conducted so as to create a culture with the values and practices they believed would make Camelot successful. The culture-building behaviors discussed here include reference to organizational role models, telling stories that stressed ideals, regular communication from the leaders, public rewards and recognition, and attention to employee selection.

Identification of Organizations as Role Models

Camelot's leaders identified and often referred to two other organizations as role models. The more commonly referenced was a negative example and the second a positive one. Many early Camelot employees came from Company A and several stories explained how Camelot did not want to be like Company A. (In fact, Camelot had many things in common with Company A, but the stories always stressed how Camelot was different.) Several employees described Camelot as having a "Mayflower" culture: It was similar to that of the pilgrims who came to America on the *Mayflower,* and who, when they got to the new land, adopted values that were in contrast to the lands from which they came (e.g., establishing freedom of religion after fleeing religious persecution). Hard work and the goal of winning were central attributes of Camelot's culture and Camelot's leaders identified contrasts with Company A in these and other domains (Table 6.2). During Years 3 through 6 (Table 6.1), Camelot had a very intense rivalry with another start-up,

Company X. Camelot employees sometimes wore pins that said "Beat Company X" and that company was discussed frequently. Camelot's founders believed that having such an intense competitor strengthened their own culture and after they surpassed Company X and no equally strong competitor emerged, some regret was expressed that Camelot's culture was weakened with the absence of an identifiable external threat.

Telling Stories That Stressed Ideals

The themes "hard work" and "the desire to win" were found in comparisons to the company role models and were also highlighted in stories that were frequently repeated by the leaders. One often-told story was about an engineer who complained that when he went home at night the lights in the parking lot were turned off. He really disliked going to his car every night in the dark and wondered if someone could talk to the landlord about this. Well, they did. It seems the lights were on timers and were set to turn off at 3:00 a.m. The fish tank story (Table 6.2) implied a similar theme—that the employee spent more time in the office than at home. These stories and other references to the cultural ideal of working long hours were frequently mentioned at public events.[5] The image of being in a race with competitors was often used and working long hours was seen as a way to win the race. The interpretation given to races was that races are exciting, races are fun, and that races have winners. (You can be a winner if you work long hours.) The belief that working long hours leads to winning was an early ideal that helped Camelot distinguish itself from another organization and certainly helped the company succeed. It later played a key role in the culture's decline.

One story told of how the first significant decision in the company was delegated to an engineer. This person was not one of the founders and was not in a management position. The decision concerned what hardware platform to select, and it was seen as so crucial that it could make or break the young company. The engineer was the person with the most technical knowledge relating to this issue and the more senior people agreed he should be the one to make it. The story demonstrates the ideal of delegation. It was also one example of the leaders conveying that individual employees had a direct, substantial influence on the company (related to locus of control).

Another commonly repeated story was the "first facilities" story. When the company had only nine employees, they had an office that contained toilets for men and women. Because all nine employees were men, the women's room was never used. It was soon converted into a shower room that the men could use after

Table 6.2 Contrasts Between Camelot and Its Primary Role Model

Company A	Camelot ("Mayflower")
Satisfied to be "in the race." Top two or three is OK	Wants to win. "Finishing 2nd is worst than last"
In an interview, when asked "How many employees work at Company A?" the CEO answered, "About half of them"	Story of an employee who moved his 50-gallon fish tank to the office lobby "because I'll see them more often here"
Minimal negative feedback. "We're family"	Explicit goal for minimal employee turnover. Realized the need to face up to performance problems
Cramped work spaces, many partitions	Each professional has an office with a door
"Terminal room" approach	A workstation in each engineer's office
"Loser" projects fed for years. Slow response to markets	Port project killed after 3 months. "Execute." Get it done now
No showers for employees	Showers from Day 1. Jacuzzi and weight rooms in building No. 1
Elaborate planning process	"Vision" important. No planning staff. "Plans are always wrong, it's better to be able to turn on a dime"
Hardware	Software

jogging during breaks. Some employees repeated this story and offered the interpretation that "the company really cares about its employees, they had exercise facilities from day one." Another interpretation offered was that "things aren't done here only because of tradition, we are willing to change things when it helps us reach our goals." A willingness to change was a common attitude at Camelot. People often proudly stated that Camelot was doubling in size every year (even during Years 7 and 8 when the doubling time had slowed). Change was generally seen as positive (even exciting) and necessary. An implicit interpretation in this story is the internal locus of control of employees (discussed further below).

Regular Communication From the Leaders

The leaders at Camelot made extensive efforts to communicate with all employees about the vision of the company, its goals, and the issues it faced. This was accomplished using a number of methods including describing the vision, the company newspaper, mixers, and quarterly meetings. Several early employees (who were in the company when there were only 50 employees), told how King Arthur and Lancelot created a vision of the success of the company that was so compelling, it pulled them forward, urging them to succeed when there was considerable doubt about Camelot's future. "They painted such a vivid picture of the future, and how our tasks fit into that future, that they actually created that future." Camelot's leaders frequently expressed confidence that their employees could overcome difficult challenges and succeed. In the early years, this vision building was done mostly in one-on-one or very small group discussions. The vision addressed both the business issues (products, markets, and competition) and the people issues (the kind of employees we want and the types of behavior that will lead to success, e.g., the importance of "pushing back").

Camelot's leaders continually stated the goal of staying a "flat organization" and an egalitarian atmosphere was fostered. This style supported regular, informal communication throughout the company. There was only a single cafeteria, and senior management frequently ate lunch there. This provided opportunities for employees to communicate. Scheduling meetings (and interviews) was often difficult because of people's very busy schedules. The cafeteria and hallway meetings were often the scene for feedback, requests, and decision making. E-mail was also heavily used in engineering. Other indicators of the flat organization included no reserved parking, an open door policy (see description of pushing back under "Other Major Themes of Camelot's Culture"), and the use of a minimal amount of secretarial support. Employees typically made their own photocopies, coffee, popcorn, and so on.

When the company was approximately 4 years old, they began to publish a monthly newspaper, *Voices.*[6] It was described as "employee written"—that is, each story listed the name of the employee who wrote it and the newspaper coordinator's role was that of encouraging people to write stories about their experiences, a limited amount of editing, and the coordination with the printers. He described how this was far better than the typical approach of paying a staff person to write the newspaper. That would lead to "faceless bureaucrats . . . and no feeling of ownership among employees." A employee-written newspaper, in contrast, was believed to produce a greater feeling of the small company atmosphere.

There were many contributions from senior managers (15%- 20% of the total newspaper volume) and King Arthur wrote a column that appeared on the front page of every issue. Camelot's leaders sought to influence the culture through their articles. For example, in one story President Lancelot told of an unnamed employee who was invited to visit a customer (which would have required a plane flight).

Because he was unable to get a signature on a travel request (most of management was off-site), the employee did not travel. The president wrote, "That was a mistake. Knowing our commitment to customers, he should have gone even without a signature." This was consistent with an often repeated saying at Camelot, "It is easier to get forgiveness than permission." Several employees mentioned this article to me as "part of our culture." The story was consistent with the leaders urging employees to step up to new challenges and take initiative. Other articles often described a presentation (to a customer or at a conference) or "congratulations" along with a photo of a team who had completed a project. King Arthur insisted that the newspaper be mailed to employee's homes (despite greater expense) because he felt that it was important that employees and their families know about the issues facing the company.

Another communication activity was the holding of regular mixers, social events at which food and music were provided for employees. Often, there was a theme for a mixer, such as an interdepartment volleyball tournament, Valentine's Day, best costume contest on Halloween, or a day of skiing followed by dinner and dancing. Mixers occurred about once a month during the period of my interviews. They typically began about 4 p.m. on a Thursday or Friday and lasted until 10 or 11 p.m. The leaders said these events were held to contribute to the goal of making Camelot a fun place to work. They also provided important opportunities for interacting across departments. Usually, there was a small cluster of employees around each of Camelot's leaders during the mixers because many wanted to hear their opinions on the issues and events influencing the company. Attendance at mixers was voluntary. Some leaders attended regularly, whereas some never did (e.g., Arthur was always present and usually got up on stage for a few comments, whereas Lancelot never attended). During a period of several years, mixers became less frequent and fewer senior managers attended them.

As the company grew to the point that regular face-to-face interaction could no longer meet the need for communication, quarterly meetings were introduced. On the day before Camelot's financial performance was reported in the press, senior management held an end-of-the-quarter meeting in the cafeteria for all employees. They presented the results in more detail than the press release and answered questions. Sometimes donuts and beverages were provided, and these 1- or 2-hour meetings were well attended with many questions asked. A few years later, it was no longer possible for all employees to fit into the cafeteria at one time. The leaders then began to hold morning and afternoon sessions with a subset of departments invited to each. Other events that affected Camelot (e.g., acquisitions, new product release, etc.) also triggered these meetings, so they actually occurred approximately eight times per year.

A final example of the regular communication the leaders made is the values statement, which was displayed on posters in all company buildings, in new employee orientation materials, at company training classes, on coffee mugs, and so on and was mentioned frequently by the leaders in the newspaper, at mixers, and by other communication methods.

Public Rewards and Recognition

Another culture-building activity was giving rewards and recognition. Newspaper articles, and even the annual report, showed people working hard and succeeding in Camelot's tasks. The quarterly meetings included a segment in which team awards were given for things such as biggest market share, best new feature, or best customer reaction.[7] Plaques with the team members' names were presented and these "golden floppy awards" were later displayed on the walls. Each year, there was a selection of the "top ten employees of the year" who were honored at a dinner. Their pictures were in the newspaper and they received a significant cash award. The 3-day sales kick-off meeting each year included 10- to 15-minute employee presentations of how they obtained some victory. The senior managers thanked and commended the presenters. All employees received many small gifts (e.g., coffee mugs, Frisbees, hats, and T-shirts) that displayed the corporate logo and sometimes the company's values statement. These were given to new employees, given out at mixers, or given to various departments (when department or division managers took the initiative to give their employees such rewards). During an interview, one vice president said, "I have given away every conceivable article of clothing as a reward at one time or another to employees at Camelot." He believed it was critical for Camelot to continually reward people for their contributions. My questioning other employees about this statement drew both laughter and agreement.

Considerable Attention to Employee Selection

Camelot's people believed that the selection of new employees was strongly influencing their culture because of the company's rapid growth. They believed there was a large cost associated with poor hiring decisions and invested considerable time in screening potential employees. For an engineering position, a group of 5 to 10 employees met to prepare for candidates who would be interviewed (these were the best from those that passed resumé checks and telephone screening). The group would discuss the characteristics of the position, technical ability required, and team member roles. They agreed on who would probe which topics with the interviewee (school, specific projects in the work history, commitment, and personal interests). Usually, the interviewee would be flown in the day before and be met for breakfast by one member of the group. During the day, the interviewee would be taken around and spend time with each member of the interview group. The group would conduct a post-interview meeting to discuss their observations and prepare a recommendation. Camelot's people were proud that they had an acceptance rate of over 85%.

They also recognized that mistakes would be made and set an explicit goal for a minimum turnover level to encourage them to face up to employee problems (unlike Company A). One senior position was filled after pursuing an individual in another company for more than a year and offering a very high salary. He was fired within 5 weeks when he acted "politically," behavior that was in violation of Camelot's norms. Such a reversal may not occur in some cultures in which the hiring person may have been seen as "losing face" by acknowledging such a mistake. It was unusual that people were fired at Camelot, but it was not unusual that people changed their minds or reversed their actions when that was warranted.

This section has presented the major activities used at Camelot to build a strong, organizationwide culture. The leaders were very successful in establishing the type of culture they wanted and developing an organizational culture that dominated all subcultures. The following section describes a few additional themes (content) in that culture.

Other Major Themes of Camelot's Culture

People at Camelot were very busy, but they were empowered and excited. There was considerable pressure to perform. Individuals worked hard to achieve the "high mark on the wall" they set for themselves. Several made statements such as "This is the place where I have had my greatest achievements." Also, they usually seemed to be smiling, joking, and having fun in working on those tasks. They took great pride in their work and in their company. Many employees wanted to take time from their busy schedules to tell me about their unique culture. It was a wonderfully productive culture in which ordinary people did extraordinary things. It was Camelot.

Winning was an important goal and people often talked about it ("How was the presentation to the customer?" "We had a big win"). The corporate values statement was developed by the top 20 managers during a 2-day off-site meeting when the company was approximately 5 years old. Winning was placed first and it is described by more subpoints than the other values. Employees uniformly believed that Camelot was a winner and this was part of their obvious pride in their organization.

Another of the obvious themes in Camelot's culture I described as internal locus of control (Leftcourt, 1982).[8] Employees frequently mentioned the importance of "feeling in control of your own destiny" during interviews. This was a central element in what they described as their small company atmosphere and it was mentioned by managers as crucial to getting top performance. Camelot's top "coach" considered this feeling of control the key to effective coaching. He never told an employee how much he or she should do but rather tried "to avoid overcontrolling," asking them how much they could do, and even having them fill in the "X's" on the progress charts because he felt this helped them "feel more in control of their own destiny."

Employees expressed considerable confidence that they would succeed in the face of difficult technical, market, and competitive challenges. When adopting the C++ language as the platform for all future product development (always conducted under pressing deadlines), someone mentioned that the C++ compiler was not yet finished. The response was "well, we may have to write some of the compiler ourselves." As Camelot's markets grew and Hewlett-Packard and IBM began to consider those markets desirable, the response (from someone who had worked for years at IBM) was "they won't be serious competitors, we can run rings around IBM." When the stock market crashed during negotiations for a major acquisition (involving stock swaps), people said, "Let's ignore the crazy behavior on Wall Street and just focus on running our business well. When they come to their senses we can deal with them again." When Camelot's workstation supplier continued to deliver irregular and unacceptable quality, Camelot set up an elaborate process and tested every workstation[9] while joking that they were the quality control department for their workstation supplier. These responses were strong examples of a "we can do it" (internal locus of control) attitude.

Practices that encouraged an internal locus of control included the public rewards and recognition, the telling of stories about how employee actions influenced the company, the communication of a strong vision that included content about how individuals would succeed, and the coaching style. One specific example was a party celebrating Camelot's sixth birthday. An entertainment company was hired that filled the cafeteria with roulette and blackjack tables. All employees were given play money and there were prizes they could "buy" with this money at the end of the evening. The odds used to determine winners in the games were slightly modified so that, on average, employees and not "the house" would win, although this was not initially obvious to employees. The leaders' idea was to design the situation to reward employees for risk taking and to give them the feeling of being successful. Similar to other companies, quotas for the sales force were set so that about 85% of salespersons were able to be successful.

Many employees mentioned Camelot's open door policy and in the early years most used or knew someone who used it. The phrase "pushing back" was used by many employees and was an aggressive use of the open door. "Pushing back" meant to question a decision or procedure, to take on extra effort and work to improve processes, and to constructively work to change things. During the videotaping sessions, employees repeatedly referred to the importance of pushing back. Lancelot said in the video, "[to employees] if you don't push back, we die. No one has all the answers. If you see something that needs changing, go for it." From a perspective of exploring balance in a social system, pushing back was an important negative feedback. Unfortunately, as Camelot grew, employees pushed back less and less often. It was part of the strong, early vision of "the type of company we want to be," but the vision changed.

From one perspective, the vision had to change as the challenges changed. It evolved from "start a company" (achieved), to "develop the products" (achieved), to "beat 'Company X'" (achieved), to "become a Fortune 500 company" (achieved), to "become the world leader in EDA" (achieved). During those victories, however, less attention was paid to "the type of company we want to be," and the leaders started focusing on "becoming a billion dollar company." This goal suggested to many a conflict with the small company atmosphere that gave Camelot its magic.

Tom Peters (1987) notes,

> Inspiring visions rarely (I'm tempted to say never) include numbers. Earnings per share targets, however inspiring to the chief's pocketbook and stockholders, are seldom uplifting to 10 or 10,000 people. While the numbers are important . . . they are a by-product of spirited performance, not its cause. (p. 487)

The goal of becoming a billion dollar company was to elude King Arthur.

Example Contrasts and Contradictions

The following four examples of contrasts and contradictions observed at Camelot provide further understanding of Camelot's culture and offer examples of the types of culture change presented in Figure 6.2.

Example 1: Change Without Training

The company stressed the need for learning and for continual substantial changes, such as exemplified by their "10x improvement" goal. This was a corporatewide program in which they sought to improve productivity by a factor of 10 during a 2-year period. This is but one example of the setting of difficult goals for individuals and projects that the leaders had made a core element of the culture.

In contrast, the organization provided relatively little training and far too little coaching. Numerous employees stated during the interviews that there was a large need for coaching, and they regularly described a situation in which job responsibilities grew faster than an employee. This usually resulted in poor performance for a group, and then a somewhat painful reassignment for an individual. People were expected to "step up to new challenges," and that usually included finding the necessary resources to overcome those challenges. There was often insufficient support for the corequisite personal and technical skills growth that many employees needed to accomplish those challenges. For example, during the 8.0 project, the decision was made to adopt the C++ programming language.[10] Several employees commented that the project schedules remained unchanged, making no allowance for an (employee expected) drop in productivity while they learned a new computer programming paradigm.

Example 2: Only Some Departments
Sought to Be Innovators

The goals of innovation and being a leader (both in technology and in market share) were regular themes of conferences, corporate advertising, logos, and so on. Many employees made statements about Camelot's status as a leader and innovator. During interviews with engineers, some commented that Camelot was not really a technology leader but was slightly behind the "cutting edge." Still, the engineering and sales groups considered innovation an important part of competing in the design automation industry.

In contrast, the employees in the finance and human resource (HR) functions frequently stated that their role was not to innovate or take risks. Instead, they were conservative in selecting vendors, developing programs, and so on. Engineers and salespersons held a low opinion of these groups (especially HR, which was usually ranked at the bottom during Q-sort exercises). They asked the interviewer, who was seen as associated with HR, "why don't they hire better people and provide their internal services at the same level of excellence that we adopt as our goal?" Repeating these comments to people in HR was answered with, "They don't understand our mission." No attempt to communicate that mission was apparent, however. The low regard expressed for the HR group by others was very uncharacteristic for anyone at Camelot. Instead, employees nearly always expressed confidence, even admiration, for others in the company ("Gerry is the best possible person to head marketing," "Fred is a great coach," and "Al can sell anything" were more typical of statements Camelot employees made).

This "conflict of perceptions" remained unresolved throughout my 5 years of observation. Leaving these differences unresolved led to differentiation that defined subgroups at Camelot. Although this was not a major conflict, overall organizational effectiveness was reduced. The contrasts in innovative stance were partly determined by the personal styles of the vice presidents of the respective groups.

Example 3: Subgroup Formation in the Compute Engine Project

The Compute Engine (CE) project was an extreme example of subgroup development at Camelot. It was a major issue in the company during its 3-year life and was the central feature in one of Camelot's annual reports. An early strategic decision by Camelot founders had been not to build hardware;[11] instead, they developed only software and had an original equipment manufacturer relationship with a workstation company. In Year 4, a start-up company with about 25 people approached Camelot about buying the parallel computer they were designing. Camelot's leaders decided to acquire this start-up and it became the CE division.

The core CE group had spun off from another company less than a year before Camelot acquired them. The acquisition was seen as very positive for both sides; the CE group needed funding to complete their computer, and Camelot would be happy with the higher margins found in hardware and a broader product line. The CE group shared the values of high commitment and achievement of exceptional goals that were central to Camelot's culture. They were hardware engineers, however, who used certain design practices and specialized language that contrasted with those of the software engineers in the other Camelot divisions. A considerable we-they mentality developed between the hardware and software groups during the project. One founder said, "It was like two different cultures; even though they were separated by only a few hundred feet [building 1 and building 3], they didn't communicate." Before this project, a strong shared vision had united Camelot. The CE people came in with their own strong vision, but only very late in the project, and only after considerable internal selling efforts, did other groups get on board. The CE hardware was designed using Camelot's software tools and was finished on schedule. The software for it was given low priority by another division, was late, and the performance of the combination was so far below expectations it could not be sold without additional, extended rewriting of the compilers. New competitor products came to the market by the time acceptable performance was achieved. The window of market opportunity in which the CE could have "won" was missed. The decision was made to disband the CE group and exit the hardware business. Most of the employees in the group left the company.

Several factors acted together in the development of this corporate schism. The acquisition of a group that already had a strong vision may have slowed normal socialization processes. The new group had a different technical background (hardware vs. software—a difference that is widely recognized in the industry). The different linguistic and design practices hindered communication between groups. The tasks of the CE group were isolated from the other engineers, which further contributed to the building of separate perspectives about the project.

Example 4: Working "Eight-Dot-Oh" Days a Week at Camelot

The final conflict example describes the slow and painful unfolding of an issue that resulted in a dramatic, unintended transformation in Camelot's culture. Several of the most commonly told corporate stories[12] of the early days stressed working long hours as a key to success. Implicit in those stories was another core theme of the culture, internal locus of control for the employees of Camelot. The long hours that the founders worked were efforts that they freely chose to undertake. Employees whom I interviewed were excited about their work tasks and all that I observed worked extended hours to accomplish the high goals they set. Many of the leaders acknowledged the importance of having employees "feel in control of their own destiny." During the "8.0" project (pronounced "8 dot oh"), however, they focused on the long hours and acted in direct conflict with the feeling-in-control theme. The result was a divided kingdom, unwanted battles, and the loss of the magic that had made Camelot so special.

Over the years, Camelot's software followed the normal practice of numbered versions (e.g., version 1.0 in Year 2, version 5.4 in Year 6). At approximately Year 6, a small group began working on a new generation of products. This would not be simply another release with added features, bug fixes, and so on. It would be a major rewrite of much of the existing 3 million lines of code; the human interface would be redesigned, the database would be restructured, and it would add new functionality and intelligence that would put Camelot years ahead of its competitors. The acquisition of Camelot's workstation vendor, their only hardware supplier, by a competitor in Year 8 led to the decision that the company needed to bring this next generation to market soon. It was code named "Falcon"; customers would see it as version 8.0.

The memo that announced the 8.0 project internally carried a tone that the vice president of HR later described as "batten down the hatches, full speed ahead." It stated that employee vacations would be canceled and corporate training classes would be suspended until the project was complete—then estimated to be another year of effort. One senior manager commented that this would be an opportunity to rebuild some of the excitement and high-level commitment of Camelot's early days (when working long hours was a more common practice). The goal of working long hours was certainly heard loud and clear. At the project kick-off mixer, employees were given hats, bumper stickers, and other small gifts with the phrase, "I'm working 8.0 days a week at Camelot." The company cafeteria began serving lunches on Saturdays and Sundays for the many employees who were working weekends. Some employees were reassigned to different departments or tasks in a process that was more authoritative and allowed individual employees far less freedom to choose than had been typical at Camelot. Those reassigned began to refer to themselves as "draftees," a term that clearly indicated the change in their perception to one of an external locus of control.

Five months into the project, deadlines were being missed and the general manager who had written the batten-down-the-hatches memo was fired for "cultural reasons." Management pushed to complete the project, violating their own cultural theme of allowing others to feel in control of their destiny. "Work long hours" was imposed from above. The previous high level of commitment declined. Employees who had given much to the organization when it was voluntary reacted very differently when they were ordered to do so. Stress and frustration levels soared. Employee turnover increased and remained high after the project was completed. "Hundreds of resumés are going out," I was told.

As awareness grew that employees were becoming unhappy, there were attempts at "damage control." Seven months into the project, King Arthur and Lancelot began to make "spontaneous" appearances, poking their heads into employee offices to say, "How is it going? I appreciate your extra efforts." (They had often done this in the early days but the practice had been extinguished over the years.) These visits were soon stopped because employees, unaccustomed to seeing the leaders visit their offices and under considerable pressure to complete tasks, interpreted this as "management checking up on me." Some employees responded by leaving lights on and their jackets in their offices to give the appearance they were near and working hard. During one interview at this time, an employee showed me a flyer describing a stress reduction class that would soon be offered by the company. The flyer stated "class size will be limited to 25 so sign up early." The interviewee wadded up the announcement, threw it against the wall, and yelled, "That's a fucking joke! There are 25 *hundred* people in this company who need stress reduction!" Negative reactions to Camelot's events were extremely uncommon and nothing approaching this outburst was observed during the 3 years of interviewing before the 8.0 project began.

In the 8.0 example, two strongly held beliefs came into conflict. Senior management placed great emphasis on working long hours—as they always had. Apparently, however, they did not fully realize the crucial importance of each employee choosing to work those hours. The struggle of the 8.0 project lasted approximately 2 years. During that time, Camelot's magic—the very high levels of commitment seen in virtually all employees and the enjoyment they expressed in their work—was crushed. During the last 6 months of my observations, nearly all the senior management left Camelot for positions in other companies. King Arthur wondered what had gone wrong.

Some Reflections on Intraorganization Cultural Dynamics

The following comments are offered as speculative answers to questions regarding subculture formation and cultural identity. By speculative, it is meant that observations at Camelot support these answers but the sample size is very limited and the contextual nature of organizational culture implies that any conclusions require interpretation.

What external conditions influence the balance between homogeneity or diversity in cultural settings?

■ Strong competition can lead to stronger self-identity because the perceived boundary between self and other is accentuated. Individuals may then focus on intraorganizational similarities, downplaying differences, thus leading to greater homogeneity (or at least its appearance). In the case of Camelot, strong competition contributed to a stronger culture, but there was tolerance for diversity on many issues.

▨ Rapid industry growth would lead to greater cultural diversity when it results in the rapid addition of employees. (This effect is counterbalanced by organizational selection and socialization efforts.) When new employees are added at a rate faster than socialization processes act to establish homogeneity, the depth of the organizationwide culture declines. This is especially true when the growth is via acquisitions because preexisting subgroups are being brought into the organization. These would typically require greater time to undergo socialization into the new culture.

▨ Acquisitions are not limited to conditions of rapid market growth (see previous point). Other industry changes, such as the consolidation of a mature industry, lead to mergers and acquisitions and these are perhaps the largest source of cultural diversity in some industries.

▨ The presence of other organizations identified as role models can promote a more homogeneous culture. This is because an explicit model is easier to consistently emulate (or avoid). Camelot had two such organizations in its environment—one that it wanted to be like and one that it wanted to be different from.

Which internal environment factors contribute to differentiation into subcultures?

▨ Adherence to different functions or goals, different technical backgrounds (different in linguistic categories and work style), geographic differences (that reduce communication), and differences in leadership style and goals were all observed to be related to subculture formation at Camelot.

What are the critical dimensions of subculture formation and change?

▨ Membership and knowledge domains are suggested as two primary dimensions for describing subculture formation and change (Figure 6.2). Other dimensions that are probably relevant include teleology, domain significance (here content and structural dimensions blend), time frame, and leadership.

What triggers a given cultural identity and makes it more influential compared to another?

▨ The communication processes used to build up a shared reality at Camelot were described previously. These included reference to organizational role models, telling stories that stressed ideals, regular communication from the leaders, public rewards and recognition, and attention to employee selection. These all made a substantial contribution to the strong culture of Camelot.

▨ At a more abstract level, it was the vision of the founders (in particular King Arthur) to have a certain culture, and their willingness to continually apply the previously mentioned practices to achieve that vision, that led to the creation of this wonderfully successful kingdom. After observing Camelot, I feel I have really seen leadership, and for that I am grateful.

Notes

1. The electronic design automation (EDA) market was segmented by engineering function—for example, computer-aided engineering (the upstream functions of schematic capture and the logical layout and testing of circuits) and computer-aided design (the downstream functions of optimal physical placement and routing of components on integrated circuits or printed circuit boards).

2. Only the first portion of that study is reported here. Schumacher (1992b, 1996) describes other aspects of the study.

3. Examples of the constructivist literature include Bennett (1986), Kelly (1955), Kenny (1988), Maturana (1988), Watzlawick (1984), and, of course, the widely referenced Berger and Luckman (1966). The ethnoscience methodology of Spradley (1980) adopts a constructivist philosophy. The constructivism paradigm has contrasts with many of the tenets of logical positivism. (See Morgan & Smircich, 1980, for a comparison of approaches to social science.) Some would even deny constructivism the status of science because of these differences. Despite these challenges, it is clear that there is growing use of ethnographic methods in organizational analysis. The resolution of the philosophic questions are beyond the scope of this chapter.

4. Perhaps it helps to consider a loose physical analogy—the building of sand castles on a beach. Efforts must be made to build the shared reality (castle) and there is a continual erosion (from wind and water) that must be overcome for the shared reality to survive or expand.

5. One might question whether these were just stories or whether they truly reflect the work environment. Observations indicated there were many occasions when it was that intense.

6. The author was able to locate and read all the issues from the initial year through Year 10.

7. Camelot had dozens of products and teams that were specialized for particular design tasks.

8. Camelot employees never used the term *locus of control*. The work is reviewed by Leftcourt (1982), who classified people into "internals," who see the world largely as "I make it happen," versus "externals," whose perceptions are more often "it happens to me."

9. This testing had a considerable cost because the hardware supplier was on the east coast and all computers had to be shipped first to Camelot's headquarters on the west coast, tested, and then reshipped to customers around the country. Shipping the computers directly to the customer and then installing Camelot's software would have been less expensive.

10. At the time, this was a newly written language and the engineers had little experience with this different genre—object-oriented languages.

11. Their two major competitors did build their own hardware—a strategy that offered higher margins than Camelot's software-only business model.

12. Including the "parking lot lights" and "fish tank" stories among others.

References

Bem, D. J. (1970). *Beliefs, attitudes and human affairs.* Belmont, CA: Wadsworth.

Bennett, M. (1977). *The forming/feeling model.* Unpublished doctoral dissertation, University of Minnesota, Minneapolis/St. Paul.

Bennett, M. (1986). Towards ethnorelativism: A developmental model of intercultural sensitivity. In M. Paige (Ed.), *Cross cultural orientation: New conceptualizations and applications* (pp. 27-69). Lanham, MD: University Press of America.

Berger, P., & Luckman, T. (1966). *The social construction of reality.* Garden City, NJ: Doubleday.

Deal, T. E., & Kennedy, A. (1982). *Corporate cultures.* Reading, MA: Addison-Wesley.

Kelly, G. (1955). *A theory of personality: The psychology of personal constructs.* New York: Norton.

Kenny, V. (Ed.). (1988). Radical constructivism, autopoiesis & psychotherapy [Special issue]. *Irish Journal of Psychology, 9*(1).

Leftcourt, H. M. (1982). *Locus of control: Current trends in theory and research.* Hillsdale, NJ: Lawrence Erlbaum.

Maturana, H. R. (1988). Reality: The search for objectivity or the quest for a compelling argument. *Irish Journal of Psychology, 9,* 25-82.

Migliore & Martin, J. (1994, March-April). Use of a corporate culture index for strategic planning. *Journal of Strategic Choice, 3*(2). Despres' reply is in Vol. 4, No. 2, March-April, 1995.

Morey, N., & Luthans, F. (1984). An emic perspective and ethnoscience methods for organizational research. *Academy of Management Review, 9,* 27-36.

Morey, N., & Luthans, F. (1985). Refining the displacement of culture and the use of scenes and themes in organizational studies. *Academy of Management Review, 10,* 219-229.

Morgan, G., & Smircich, L. (1980). The case for qualitative research. *Academy of Management Review, 5,* 491-500.

Peters, T. (1987). *Thriving on chaos.* New York: Harper & Row.

Peters, T., & Waterman, R. (1982). *In search of excellence.* New York: Harper & Row.

Reger, R. K., Mullane, J. V., Gustafson, L. T., & DeMarie, S. M. (1994). Creating earthquakes to change organizational mindsets. *Academy of Management Executive, 8*(4), 31-46.

Reichers, A. E., & Schneider, B. (1990). Climate and culture: An evolution of constructs. In B. Schneider (Ed.), *Organizational climate and culture.* San Francisco: Jossey-Bass.

Schein, E. (1985). *Organizational culture and leadership.* San Francisco: Jossey-Bass.

Schumacher, T. R. (1992a). *Simulation design, role identification and attitude change in a high technology culture.* Unpublished doctoral dissertation, Portland State University, Portland, OR.

Schumacher, T. R. (1992b). *Changing organizational culture with simulation experience.* Paper presented at the 1992 Academy of Management Conference, Organizational Development Division, Las Vegas, NV.

Schumacher, T. R. (1996). *Guidelines for creating effective microworld simulation-games.* Paper presented at the 5th International Conference on Management of Technology, Miami, FL.

Spradley, J. P. (1979). *The ethnographic interview.* New York: Holt, Rinehart & Winston.

Spradley, J. P. (1980). *Participant observation.* New York: Holt, Rinehart & Winston.

Swartz, H., & Davis, S. (1981, Summer). Matching corporate culture and business strategy. *Organizational Dynamics,* 32-48.

Taylor, S. E., & Crocker, J. (1978). Schematic bases of social information processing. In E. T. Higgins, C. P. Herman, & M. P. Zanna (Eds.), *Social cognition: The Ontario symposium* (Vol. 1).

Watzlawick, P. (Ed.). (1984). *The invented reality (contributions to constructivism).* New York: Norton.

Chapter 7

Cultural Contrasts in a Democratic Nonprofit Organization

The Case of a Swiss Reading Society

Thomas S. Eberle

A long-term case study of a Swiss reading society is presented based on historical documents that cover 187 years. Reading societies were social inventions of the 18th century. They often lasted into the 20th century and played an important role in the cultural process of modernization. Like other societies founded in the spirit of the Enlightenment, they were nonprofit organizations with a democratic structure. With regard to their programmatic goals, their legal structure, and their formal procedures, reading societies were conspicuously similar and uniform. On closer look, however, each had its specific cultural complexity. In the following case study, three cultural contrasts inherent in the organization are reconstructed, each of which shaped the organizational life for several decades.

Reading Societies: Carriers of
the Modernization Process

Reading and writing have penetrated nearly all the realms of modern society. These practices have become so common that nowadays it is difficult to grasp how fundamental the cultural change was that took place during the past few centuries. Up to the high Middle Ages, reading and writing were a privilege of the clergy. Ordinary people communicated orally. Consequently, much of the lived culture was passed on to the next generation by way of an oral tradition. Only gradually did a culture of reading emerge throughout the society. The invention of printing paved the way for new forms of literature, and the expansion of education advanced literacy. More and more social areas required paperwork: public administration, administration of justice, book-keeping, science, and literature. Finally, during the age of Enlightenment, reading also became an activity of leisure (Dann, 1981a, p. 9).

During the 18th century, a significant change in the style of reading occurred—a change from an intensive, repetitive reading of the same few publications (particularly the Bible, religious publications, and calendars) to an extensive reading of new information (Engelsing, 1970). The soaring middle class, the economic and educational elite, was oriented toward the sciences and arts and demanded more and more information about all areas of knowledge and social life. This thirst for knowledge exceeded the potential of oral communication; written communication became a new social ideal (Dann, 1981a, p. 13; Engelsing, 1974, p. 216ff).

The change in reading styles was paralleled by a change in the structure of literary production. The book market adapted to the demands of the new reading classes. During the 18th century, Latin, the language of the scholars, was thrust aside by the national languages (English, German, French, Italian, Spanish, etc.), and theological literature was replaced by books that provided entertainment and general knowledge. An even more fundamental change was introduced by two new printing products—journals and newspapers. Both set new standards for written information and had an explosive quantitative growth in the second half of the 18th century—journals for a specialized audience and newspapers for a general audience (Dann, 1981a, p. 15).

The reading societies were one important element in the social organization of this cultural change. Their primary goal was to motivate people to read and to provide them with literature. Reading societies were a cultural invention of the

18th century and emerged throughout Europe in increasing numbers. In Germany alone, historical research found more than 600 reading societies in the 18th century (Prüsener, 1973; Reckmann & Dann, 1978). The term *reading society* first appeared in 1770 (Prüsener, 1973, p. 384) and is already a key word in an encyclopedia printed in 1790: "**Reading Society** is a number of persons who have associated to read certain books and publications" (Krünitz, 1790, p. 278). Presumably, the financial advantage was an important motive for forming such associations because the prices of books and journals at the time were too high for most readers to afford (Stützel-Prüsener, 1981, p. 72). Such readers' associations had many forms and different labels. All of them, however, had the same fundamental purpose: to make people read. All of them also pursued an educational goal: to spark people's interest in "good" literature, in scientific knowledge, and in general information about what was going on in the world (Dann, 1981a, p. 13; Engelsing, 1974, p. 216ff). In this sense, reading societies were—to use a term of Max Weber's—"carriers" of the modernization process; carriers of a cultural change that is often overlooked by focusing on only the technical and economic side of modernization.

Societies: New Social Forms Originating in the 18th Century

Historical research in Switzerland and Germany (which began investigating reading societies only since the 1970s)[1] views reading societies as part of the vast society movement that unfolded above all in the second half of the 18th century (Im Hof, 1982). At the end of the century, the whole of Europe—in particular, France, Switzerland, Germany, and Northern Italy—as well as European America were covered by hundreds of "societies." Academies, scholarly and literary societies, reading cabinets, and charitable, economic, agricultural, and patriotic and political societies as well as freemason's lodges were founded everywhere. These societies represented new social forms in the spirit of the Enlightenment: They were oriented toward the future, and their objectives were to improve and reform given states of affairs; they were based on voluntariness, codetermination, and joint responsibility; and they had a republican organization and formed a new social stratum between the old classes. All these societies can be characterized by two criteria. First, they had a formal structure; thus, they are to be differentiated from informal, unorganized associations such as the French "salons," the English "clubs," or the German *"Zirkel"* (circles) of all kinds. Second, they have to be distinguished from all religious communities, orders, or brotherhoods; these lacked voluntariness and served a worldview other than that of Enlightenment (Im Hof, 1982).

Accordingly, historical research draws two distinctions: between reading societies and informal readers' associations (Dann, 1981a) and between the reading societies of the Enlightenment and those of the past (Weisz, 1934a, 1934b). The informal readers' associations or readers' circles, although serving the same goal of buying and circulating books, journals, and newspapers, had no documented organizational structure. Over the years, thousands have been founded and dissolved within short periods of time, leaving no written testimony. In contrast, the reading societies were institutions with a clear, formal structure that in principle allowed them to exist longer than one person's lifespan. In addition, historical research also draws a distinction between the reading societies of the Enlightenment and the literary societies of the past. These were institutions with formal structures as well, but they were esoteric societies of the upper class, of aristocracy and clergy, lacking a democratic orientation and organization (Milstein, 1972).

Comparative studies show that the objectives and formal structure of the new, democratic reading societies were very much alike (Prüsener, 1973). The goals typically were to provide literature and organize social and cultural events for their members. To this purpose, they usually maintained a library with books, a reading room with newspapers and journals, and often additional rooms for gatherings, lectures, and social events. How these services, the general management tasks, and the democratic control were best organized was intensively discussed and written down in formal rules. In the founding era—the second half of the 18th century— these organizing processes were very lively and an interesting topic for research.[2] At every general assembly, established rules were confirmed, modified, replaced, or complemented by new ones. The reading societies of the 19th century built on the collected experiences and usually copied many of the rules of former societies. In the course of time, the typical formal structures had been developed that nowadays are still constitutive of societies and other formal associations; a managing committee with a president or chair and other members who had specialized functions (such as a vice president, a treasurer, a secretary, a librarian, etc.), financial revisers, and a general assembly of the members that elected the persons into these functions, determined the bylaws, and controlled the proper course of affairs.

Reading societies were thus carriers of the modernization process in two ways; they not only spread the ideals of reading and of acquiring knowledge but also represented—together with other organizations[3]—new social formations in which democratic behaviors were trained and practiced on a local, organizational level. In states with a feudal structure, such democratic practices were rather revolutionary; not surprisingly, aristocratic authorities often censored or even prohibited reading societies (see Prüsener, 1973).

The Museum Society: The Case of a Swiss Reading Society

What was life inside these organizations like? Despite their resemblance with regard to their programmatic goals, their legal structure, and their formal procedures, each reading society developed a specific, complex organizational structure. The following case study deals with the Museum Society in St. Gallen, a small Swiss town of about 70,000 inhabitants (since 1900). There were several reading societies in town but only two of them were of major importance: the Büsch Society (1836-1980) and the Museum Society (1856-1974; its main predecessor, the Literary Society, was founded in 1789). The Büsch Society was a reading society for the lower classes, and the Museum Society a reading society for the upper classes. The latter was selected for a case study because most historical documents of the Museum Society have been preserved (in contrast to the Büsch Society), which makes it easier to reconstruct the inherent contrasts in its organizational life.

Research Methodology

How does one study the organizational culture of a reading society? From an anthropological standpoint, all the experiences, views, and activities of the members in their local, temporal, and spatial arrangements and in their material surroundings have to be examined. The definition of organizational culture should not be restricted to "a pattern of basic assumptions" of a given group "taught to new members as the correct way to perceive, think, and feel" (Schein, 1985, p. 9) or to the informal aspects of an organization such as myths, stories, or special jargon (Jelinek, Smircich, & Hirsch, 1983). Reading societies represent an instructive example that the notion of organizational culture must also include the formal aspects of an organization:[4] All these societies had a conspicuous inclination to formalize and institutionalize nearly every aspect of the society's life. The bylaws regulated the conditions of becoming a member; the members' rights and duties;

the conditions for resigning or being expelled; the tasks of the managing committee and the revisers as well as the mode of their election; the procedures of making suggestions and referendums; the rules of borrowing books and circulating journals; and even norms for all kinds of members' behavior (where and when to speak or not to speak, to smoke or not to smoke, in which rooms women were allowed and in which ones only men were allowed, how to be disciplined when coming late to a meeting, how to handle the different kinds of publications, how misbehavior was punished and by whom, etc.). Thus, the statute book also informs us, beyond the generally uniform structures, about many cultural specifics of a society.

An organization does not have a culture but rather it is a culture. Ethnography is the most promising method for investigating it in all its complexity. Ethnographic fieldwork, however, is bound to the present;[5] past cultures are the object of historical research. Most reading societies, including the one in this case study, do not exist anymore. They are past cultural realities that cannot be entered anymore and that can no longer be experienced in any direct way. They have to be reconstructed on the basis of all kinds of objectivations[6] that have been preserved. Fortunately, the reading societies not only fostered reading but also practiced writing. Many aspects of a society's life were documented in writing—there were not only the statute book, the library decree, or the bookkeeping but also the minutes of the managing committee, the proceedings of the general assembly, the annual reports of the presidents, a members' and a visitors' book, correspondence, and other documents. In addition, some members wrote a review of the society's history on the occasion of a society's "big" anniversary (like the 10th, 25th, 50th, 100th, 150th, etc.). Each reading society, in other words, created its own little "symbolic universe" that documents the society's specific history. If preserved (much was lost![7]), these documents may be a rich resource for historical analysis—much richer than the personal memory of people who try to remember what happened many years ago.[8]

In the case of the Museum Society in St. Gallen, nearly all the documents ever written seem to have been preserved. When it was dissolved in 1974, the documents were handed over to the state library. An early president wrote the history of the first 15 years including that of its forerunners (Linden, 1871), and another one wrote the history of the first 58 years (Seiler, 1914). Ample information can be found in the annual reports by the presidents, the bylaws, and the library decree. There are also guest books, legal documents, correspondence, and so on, and even some furniture of the former reading room is left. Interestingly, there are no minutes of the committee's meetings or proceedings of the general assembly (except for the final years—1965-1974). It seems that, in contrast to other reading societies, they were simply not produced. To grasp some key aspects of the society's life, we have to concentrate on the annual reports[9] by the presidents and the early historical review by Linden (1871). These materials are detailed enough to reconstruct some essentials of the cultural life as it is reflected in the president's perspective.

Contrast Between Literary Objectives and the Goal of Social Entertainment

Merger of Three Forerunner Societies

The Museum Society in St. Gallen was founded in 1856. There is no hint whatsoever why the founding fathers chose this name. Read nowadays, the name may be misleading because the society had nothing to do with a "museum" in the common sense of the word. Rather, the name was oriented to its ancient origin from which in Latin *museum* (stemming from Greek "mouseîon") meant "a site for scholarly work; library; academy" (Herkunftswörterbuch, 1989, p. 475). Several other reading societies were previously named Museum Society in Switzerland as well as in Germany.[10] The goals of the Museum Society (1856) are described in the first two articles of the statute book:

Art. 1. The Museum Society in St. Gallen has as its purpose the literary and social entertainment of its members.

Art. 2. To this purpose it maintains reading rooms with journals with a political, entertaining and generally educating contents, a library and adequate rooms and facilities for social entertainment. (p. 3)[11]

These goals are typical of reading societies and can be found in nearly the same wording elsewhere. Although these goals were not changed for more than 100 years,[12] life in the Museum Society changed quite a bit over time. The first decades were shaped by the heritage of the merger. The Museum Society was not a new foundation but rather the result of a merger of three locally prominent societies. To understand the cultural contrasts and tensions that developed within the new organization, the three forerunner societies must be examined.[13]

The Cercle, often called the Casino, was founded in 1788 as a society "for pleasant entertainment, as a meeting point of the educated classes, and for the furtherance of good form" (Cercle, 1788-1792). The idea came from young businessmen who, on their business trips, were introduced into noble circles of other cities. Like the reading societies, the Cercle was organized as a formal association with all major rules put down in bylaws. The primary goal was not reading, however, but rather social entertainment. There were some newspapers offered but no journals or books. Most popular were card games and billiards. Gambling, however, was explicitly prohibited. Membership was restricted to men of high professional and social positions, such as businessmen, medical doctors, senior civil servants, and so on. In 1814, the Cercle acquired the old Weavers' House in the heart of the old town that was soon called the Casino. From that point on, the Cercle held soirées and balls on a regular basis and lent out its hall and other rooms to other societies of the town.

The Literary Society was founded in 1789, one year after the Cercle. Its statute book is introduced with detailed reflections about the reasons why the individual activity of reading shall be combined with a membership in a society. Among the most important reasons mentioned were the opportunity to share the feelings and thoughts one had while reading literature, to learn about pieces of literature one did not know about, to get inspired and more knowledgeable by such discussions, and to increase one's appreciation of literature, of ideas, and of "the good and the beautiful." In addition, this society had the explicit goal "to bring together citizens of different classes, to raise mutual esteem and love and envigorate trust and solidarity" (Literary Society, 1816, p. 3). The Literary Society maintained a library and had approximately two dozens newspapers and journals in a reading room. It also organized scholarly lectures by members and sometimes by guest speakers. For a long time, games of all kinds were prohibited; later, some of them were allowed on Sunday afternoons. In 1814, it began renting rooms in the house of the Cercle.

The Reading Society to the Sun (in brief, the Sun Society), named after the public house where its rooms were located, was founded in 1835 by members of the Literary Society. These members had attempted to rejuvenate the Literary Society and to modernize the facilities after the model of the reading societies in Zurich and Geneva (Linden, 1871, p. 35). When they failed, a number of prominent civil servants, lawyers, and college professors decided to form a new reading society. Many of them sustained their membership to the Literary Society, others left, and new people joined. Only a few years later, the new society offered to merge with the old one, this time attempting to introduce the reforms from the outside. Because they could not find a suitable locality in town, they also asked the Cercle to join the merger. The Cercle refused, and there was no rapprochement between the two reading societies. The members of the new society called the leading members of the Literary Society "pigtails" (conservatives), whereas the members of the Literary Society considered the others disdainfully as "furious radicals."

Subsequently, the new Sun Society developed into a modern reading society on its own with a well-organized library, several dozen journals and newspapers, and, since 1848, even a billiard facility.

In 1856, the three societies finally merged. This time, the initiative came from the Cercle. It is quite informative to look at the motives for the merger (see Linden, 1871, pp. 42-50). All three societies had a weak financial base and hoped to create a solid ground by joining forces. There were diverse interests, however; the two reading societies were still primarily interested in the house owned by the Cercle (in which the Literary Society had already been a tenant) because of its big hall. The Cercle, however, strived for higher membership fees after having suffered a sudden and significant loss of members. Indeed, there was a total of 259 members: 61 from the Cercle, 43 from the Literary Society, and 155 from the Reading Society to the Sun. The members of the Cercle, however, were hardly inclined to exchange or complement their goal of cultivated social entertainment with an interest in literature. Therefore, this merger left cultural contrasts and tensions within the Museum Society for decades to come.

Cultural Schism:
A Heritage of the Merger

The formal goals, "the literary and social entertainment of its members," seemed to encompass the objectives of all three former societies. Each organizational culture, however, persisted as a subculture in the new society. In 1871, the president stated that the particularities of the three former societies could still be recognized and that the new members of the Museum Society usually joined one of the subcultures instead of compensating the contrasts (Linden, 1871, p. 53). Presumably, the contrasts between the members of the two former reading societies was an ongoing difference between generations and between conservative versus progressive convictions. There is no further information available on this issue. This fact in itself suggests that the two subcultures were not as diverse as to evoke major problems. Much more fundamental—and reported in more detail—was the cultural contrast between these two subcultures and the subculture of the former Cercle. This group of members was not interested in any literary activity but rather exclusively in social entertainment, as was the goal of their former society. Although in the first 7 years of the Museum Society many lectures were held, by members as well as by guest speakers (an occasion that combined literary and social entertainment), the members of the former Cercle interpreted the goal of social entertainment differently: playing card games and billiards and having banquets and balls. This was a clear divergence of objectives that caused a cultural schism in the society and posed a persistent problem for the management.

The schism in the early Museum Society illustrates how informal views prevailed even when contradicting the formal rules. The former members of the Cercle were still called the "Casino-Gentlemen" and regarded as nobler and treated with considerable respect. Although the bylaws determined that every member had equal rights, those who did not belong to this illustrious circle did not venture to enter the drawing rooms in which the games were played (Linden, 1871, p. 53). After 1862, when reading rooms and drawing rooms were separated and located on two different floors of the building, the cultural schism was even more discernible by the spatial separation of the subcultures. The Casino-Gentlemen managed, in other words, to continue their social life among themselves although they had merged with two other societies.

This schism produced a major problem for the managing committee. To ensure a vivid social life, the Museum Society maintained a pub in its house. Because many members shied away from using the drawing rooms or did not feel comfortable among the "Casino-people," consumption in the pub was little. As a result, profitability was low, the leaseholders often changed, and the managing committee of the Museum Society faced again and again the problems of finding a new pubkeeper and coming to terms with another financial loss. Time and again, longtime president Alfred Linden called on the members to visit the pub more frequently. He also explicitly encouraged the members to be more self-conscious toward the Casino-Gentlemen (Linden, 1871, p. 53) but had little success. Finally in 1884, he came up with the more radical suggestion to close the Casino pub and thereby reduce the functions of the society to a "pure Reading Society." Because the society had a democratic structure, such decisions had to be made by the general assembly of the members, and here Linden's suggestion met a strong opposition (Museum Society, 1884).

Let us consider this situation in more detail. Alfred Linden was the last secretary of the Sun Society before the merger. In the first year of the Museum Society, he had the mandate to organize the society's archive, which meant to take an inventory and sort out all the files of the three former societies. In the following year, he became a member of the managing committee, in 1863 he became vice president, and from 1869 to 1889 he was president of the Museum Society. It is owing to him that much of the new society's activities were described. When president, he wrote a book on the history of the three former societies and the first 15 years of the Museum Society. Then, sanctioned by the general assembly, he introduced the tradition that the annual reports by the president be printed and distributed among the members—a tradition that lasted until 1938. (All these reports have been preserved.) Linden was obviously interested in history but also in literature. From 1860 onward, he headed the "literary committee," a subcommittee of the managing committee like the "economic committee." When elected president, he became responsible for the general management issues but requested to remain head of the literary commission too.

Interestingly, in his annual reports Linden hardly ever mentions literary issues but describes, above all, managerial problems. His reports are an illustrative account of the typical issues the managing committee of a society was confronted with at the time: renovating parts of the house, acquiring a new heating system, getting better gas lights and later introducing electricity and telephone, buying decoration material for anniversaries or town festivals, finding a new pubkeeper, laying down rent and lease, dealing with authorities, making contracts with neighbors, and so on. His annual reports give the impression that the president, who was so interested in literary issues, mostly dealt with economic, financial, and other managerial matters. Many of the problems resulted from the ownership of the house and, not surprisingly, Linden repeatedly suggested selling the house to get rid of that burden.

The Casino pub was just one of the many management problems, but it was a rather persistent one. Maintaining the pub was directly connected to the society's goal of "social entertainment." At the general assembly in 1875, after presenting the annual report the president was also asked, in the form of an interpellation, to say something about the social life of the society. In a detailed account, he disclosed his view in the printed version of the report (Museum Society, 1875, pp. 8-11): There was no getting around that the Museum Society, like her sister societies in other Swiss towns, was primarily (approximately 80%) a reading society and only secondarily a Casino or a Cercle. The original idea to make the Museum Society into a center of the higher social life in town had to be buried. How low the members' demand for social entertainment actually was is demonstrated by the fact that in that year the annual banquet had to be canceled for lack of interest. "Social life cannot be commanded," Linden stated (Museum Society, 1875, p. 9) and added the following as an explanation:

> Social life in this town has become completely different. It is so manifold and split up that it is impossible to compete in more than one respect. Much of what was believed that the "Museum" should or wished to offer, has become the purpose of particular Societies. (p. 10)

Which societies he referred to remains unclear. The rather defensive account of more than four pages, however, makes it quite obvious that this president was not a great advocate or even lover of social events.

It was no surprise that in 1884 president Linden, after another pubkeeper had left, suggested abolishing the Casino pub. The managing committee had called a special general meeting on this issue and urged the members to make a fundamental decision—either to give up the pub or to return to a pure society pub (without admittance of nonmembers). For the latter option, a sound financial solution was demanded. The president and the secretary who diagnosed a financial impasse voted for abolishment, and the rest of the managing committee and the majority of the present members voted for a return to a pure society pub—a "real Casino." "It was called a testimonium paupertatis, a certificate of poverty, if the city of St. Gallen cannot even afford a Casino" (Museum Society, 1884, p. 7), and it was suggested that donations be collected (which was done for years to come). In the president's judgment, it was above all the supporters of the Casino pub who attended this special general meeting, and he was particularly upset that the rupture also went right through the managing committee (p. 3f). In 1989, he made a final remark on this cultural schism: "If last year the centenary of the Casino pub was celebrated with a solemn banquet, the centenary of the Reading Society [of the Literary Society] has passed by quietly, as yet being silent is a main virtue in Reading Societies" (Museum Society, 1888, p. 5).

When Linden resigned at the end of 1889 (he died shortly thereafter), the new managing committee immediately began a wave of social events. Soirées and balls were given, lectures were held, and musical and theatrical performances were staged, all with considerable success, which seemed to prove Linden's assessments wrong. In 1894, an "entertainment committee" was formed, and a few years later the budget for social events was increased and the new president soon stated that "our social evenings play a major role in the social life of our town" (Museum Society, 1893, p. 7). The Museum Society was financially restructured, right after Linden's resignation, by renting out the rooms on the first floor of the building, which yielded additional income. In this way, the Casino pub was saved, although with less rooms. In 1898, the Casino pub was questioned once again and finally given up in 1912 when the house was expropriated by the city council (for their own purposes) and a new house was built. This did not, however, reduce the functions of the Museum Society to a "pure Reading Society" as was Linden's intention; social life in the society had been flourishing for more than two decades. Among the initiatives from the 1890s, three types of social events became firmly institutionalized: public lectures, readings by authors, and balls. After 1912, rooms outside were rented for these occasions at a prominent local inn, at the university, or at the concert hall of the city.

Hence, after Linden's resignation the Museum Society seemed to succeed in integrating the twofold objective—the business of reading and the organization of social events. Whether the cultural schism between the different groups of members had finally been overcome is difficult to judge. Both goals, however, were actually strived for in parallel and no annual report ever mentioned this schism again. The fresh approach by the new management seemed fruitful and was, after the turn of the century, supported by favorable socioeconomic conditions—that is, by a booming economy in town.

Cultural Gender Contrast as a Nonissue

Another cultural contrast was based on gender. It became visible when for the first time women were admitted as members in 1891. Previously, the Museum Society—like most reading and other societies of the 18th and 19th centuries—was a male society excluding women from membership. This exclusion, however, concerned the social life but not the reading. The wife of a member as well as his children were entitled to use the library. What if a member died, however, and left his wife a widow? Did this entitlement then become invalid? Was she not allowed to use the library anymore only because her husband had died? Such questions made many reading societies issue library cards to certain people who could not become members. The Museum Society also had such library cards. Thus, to abolish these library cards and allow women to become full members was quite a revolutionary act. This step was initiated, once again, by the new managing committee right after Linden's resignation. It contradicted the rules of the bylaws but this did not bother the new president, Dr. Vetsch (Museum Society, 1891):

> Among the new members there are—for the first time—three ladies. These have applied for membership in order to participate in the circulation of reading folders, and we have complied with this wish most readily although the by-laws did not provide that. (p. 3)

The "reading folder," a social institution that had been invented in the 18th century, had just been introduced in the Museum Society when the ladies applied. Reading folders contained several magazines and journals and were circulated once or twice a week from household to household—one was passed on and another arrived. This institution was obviously quite popular at the time, in particular among women. This was not the first time that a strong interest of women in such reading folders was reported. The other major reading society in town, the Büsch Society, which was founded in 1836 as a society of the lower classes, had introduced reading folders half a century earlier in 1842. Chroniclers of that reading society report that by this act the Büsch Society became "an institution of the family" (Koch, 1911, p. 5), and that it was above all women and daughters who enjoyed the reading folders (Amrein, 1886),

> Even if here and there the potatoes get burned and the milk boils over because of the reading folder, it is yet the most widespread, most welcome and most discreet friend of the house in all our town, comforting those women whose husbands are sitting over a glass of wine or beer. (p. 16)

That is, in the pub. The reading folders were so popular that the Büsch Society, which concentrated exclusively on circulating reading folders and maintaining a library, in the 1870s became a mass society with many more members than the Museum Society ever had. It is interesting to note that the reading society for the lower classes, the Büsch Society, allowed women to become full members almost 20 years before the Museum Society, the reading society of the upper classes, did.

In the Museum Society of 1891, the only mentioned motive of the ladies to apply for membership was to become a recipient of the reading folders (Museum Society, 1891, p. 3). Were they interested only in the reading folders or in the other rights and privileges of a member as well? If so, were they allowed to exercise these rights or were their formally equal rights overridden and restricted by informal rules? Presumably, they did not venture to enter the Casino pub on their own and did not participate in the general meetings or the political life of the society. Unfortunately, there is no data available on this issue because no proceedings are left of those meetings. Concerning the other social events, there was hardly any gender barrier and balls especially presupposed couples anyway. What can be reconstructed is that 30 years later the quota of women was 10% (54 of 537 members; Museum Society, 1920) and another 30 years later 17.6% (45 of 255 members; Museum Society, 1950). When the Museum Society was dissolved in 1974, 20% of members attending the general meeting were women (4 of 19 members). Since 1921, there were also several female librarians mentioned who became members but were not part of the managing committee. It appears[14] that up to the dissolution of the Museum Society there has never been a woman elected into the managing committee, although there were several who held PhDs.[15]

Research on gender issues suggests that it makes sense to distinguish a male and a female culture, that each has different characteristics, and that there are different forms of how they can be combined (Harding, 1991). If this holds true, it makes sense to assume that in the Museum Society a cultural contrast existed between the minority of female and the majority of male members who dominated the general assembly as well as the managing committee. The women's perceptions, interests, values, motives, and so on have not been recorded in any written document of the Museum Society and have therefore perished. In a document of the Büsch Society, however, gender issues are mentioned. In 1911, the (male) author of a commemorative publication for the 75th anniversary of the Büsch Society complained that the male majority had always treated women as "quantité négligeable" and as "superfluous accessories" and had always made them feel inferior (Koch, 1911, p. 16ff). Several instances are mentioned to provide some evidence that gender issues were repeatedly discussed; this reading society postponed granting women full membership until 1872. In the following year, there was a big debate on the question of whether dancing was dignified enough to include in an evening program (which implied inviting women to dance with men). When some women requested by way of a poetic petition to include a fashion magazine in the reading folder (family magazines did not yet include fashion themes at the time), the managing committee proudly refused with all kinds of excuses including a sniffy remark that the fashion would be out of date anyway by the time the women got the reading folder (Koch, 1911, p. 16ff). Presumably, comparable instances of paternalistic behavior toward women have also happened in the Museum Society.

Contrast Between Elitist Expert Quality Standards and the Tastes of Laypersons

From the outset, reading societies had the explicit goal to make people read, to spark their interest in all areas of knowledge, and to provide them with good literature. What good literature was, however, had to be defined. What experts considered to be good was often not what people liked to read. When women in the 18th century (men were hardly mentioned) began to read novels, a new cultural product, reading societies were founded with the specific objective to fight the diagnosed "reading addiction" or "reading mania." The goal was not to prevent them from reading but rather to replace the "cheap novels" by "good literature" (Weisz, 1934a, 1934b). How were such educational intentions handled in a reading society with a democratic structure, in which the general assembly was the highest power and the members were the clients as well as the owners of the organization? Here, too, we can observe an ongoing cultural contrast between what experts defined as good literature and what members actually demanded.

The Museum Society had collected books from all areas: geography, ethnology, history, history of arts, history of literature, biography, belles lettres, Helvetica, books in foreign languages, and others (see Museum Society, 1883, p. 9). A statistical analysis, however, showed that members' actual demand was preferably belles lettres and, above all, novels and novellettes.[16] President Linden concluded that the Museum Society should reduce its aspiration to build up a scientific library and concentrate on belles lettres (Museum Society, 1878, p. 9). There was still a difference, however, between good and "cheap" belles lettres. In the 1920s, a strange ritual emerged; in the annual reports, the presidents time and again reproached the members for their bad literary taste. This judgment was regularly based on a survey by the librarian that showed which 8 or 10 books were most requested. The validity of this procedure—to infer from the most requested 8 or 10 books the general literary taste of all the members—was, of course, more than questionable. Nevertheless, it was repeated by many presidents. In 1946, the president noted (Museum Society, 1946, p. 4), "The most often read books are, as the experience of many decades teaches, time and again best-sellers, while the rich and precious stocks of older books are used only rarely or never at all." In 1949, the following phrase was created that stereotypically was repeated year after year: "that the quantity of the lent out books was generally larger than the quality" as was shown by the list of the most demanded books (Museum Society, 1949, p. 6). This reproaching ritual, which persisted for nearly four decades, indicated once again a rather paternalistic attitude of the presidents toward the members. The members were not treated as clients or even owners of the reading society but rather as people who needed guidance. Such an educational pose was hardly apt to stop the decrease of membership or even acquire new members.

This tension between the quality standards of literary experts and the taste and demand of laypersons persisted in the modern debate on quality assessments versus audience rating of radio and TV broadcastings. The librarians or heads of literary committees in reading societies were usually professionals—often college professors of German literature—who aspired after high-quality standards of their library. They had to conceive of the members as clients, however, and therefore had to balance their diverse tastes and interests. After all, the society was democratically organized—each member had the right to make suggestions and the general assembly could take votes on every issue. How a librarian attempted to meet the different claims of quality standards and client demands is shown by the following quote in which a librarian draws, based on the usual list of best-sellers, the following conclusion (Museum Society, 1953):

> The literary taste of our readers is, as is shown once more by this list, of a remarkable stability. This shall not prevent the librarian . . . from smuggling in some demanding books of high poetic quality, which no doubt are rarely requested but which later will be desired again and again, while the best-seller after a span of 10 years mostly perishes unheralded and unsung. (p. 3)

Literary ratings, however, changed over time. A brief analysis shows that many a best-seller of former times is considered a "classic" nowadays, whereas it may well be that those books that the quoted librarian smuggled in have never found a reader.

Similar cultural contrasts can be identified concerning the social events. As noted previously, three types of social events had become firmly institutionalized in the 1890s: public lectures, readings by authors, and balls. The so-called Museum Balls were organized nearly every year, except for the years of war and crisis. They symbolized that the Museum Society was a distinguished, noble society that struck people in town with awe.[17] Only some of the members enjoyed these balls, however; others designated them "as a boring and stiff institution" (Museum Society, 1925, p. 7). The managing committee was determined to keep this tradition, even when members made alternative suggestions: "Proposals to organize a ball more in the sense of an entertainment evening should not be attached too much importance to as we want to keep up the tradition of a ball in proper style" (Museum Society, 1949, p. 6f). The question was how to keep up a tradition the members did not want anymore. Only 3 years later, in 1952, a "certain ball tiredness among the members" was reported (Museum Society, 1952, p. 7) and after 1953, "after the distressing experiences of the past years" (Museum Society, 1954, p. 5), no balls took place.

The same happened with readings by authors and public lectures. The contrast between expert criteria used to select the speakers' and members' tastes and interests was clearly measurable by the size of the audience. After World War I, the success of these events was rather modest, and time and again the managing committee questioned whether such readings and lectures actually met a demand or if the Museum Society should retreat to a pure reading society. As the president stated in 1935 (Museum Society, 1935), however,

> We could not decide so far to abandon the good old tradition of our Society and to change to let our selection be guided only by the thought of the attraction of a big name and the box-office success. It is one of the noblest tasks of a literary Society to help poets who are less known and successful to find their way to the reader. The poet is not always the best but always the most interesting conveyor of his work. (p. 3)

The tradition was kept, but the society suffered a financial loss every year. In 1952, the revisers uttered the explicit wish "to make some concessions to the general taste when selecting authors" (Museum Society, 1952, p. 5). In 1954, the same managing committee whose president used to reproach the members with their bad literary taste invited an author of a best-seller. This event attracted a much bigger audience than the hall could accommodate and was a tremendous success. The president concluded, "Perhaps we must . . . concentrate more on best-seller-poets who can, as this example has shown, be of a high caliber, too" (Museum Society, 1954, p. 3f). This statement, however, rather expressed how deep the president's conviction actually was that a best-seller cannot be good literature and that a best-seller author is usually not of a high caliber. It is only logical that this remained the last best-seller poet invited. When in 1958 a renowned German expert of contemporary stage and play was announced for a lecture, only 3 persons instead of the expected 700 showed up. Furious, the same president resigned because of "this failure of the audience of St. Gallen" and stated, "Only when we come up with big names, people show up to see the famous woman or the important man. A true love for literature is missing in St. Gallen" (Museum Society, 1958, p. 4).

Decline and Death of the Museum Society

No doubt, the Museum Society had its heyday in the period between 1890 and World War I. Membership peaked in 1919 with 573 members, then it decreased continually to less than 100 in 1974 when the society was dissolved. Already in 1952, the president stated that there were too many old people and hardly any young ones among the members. Many publicity campaigns were made but with no success. Of the remaining 100 members in 1974, 70% of the members were retired and there had been no new entries for many years (Museum Society, 1974). Since 1930, the society had suffered a steady financial loss, and by 1965 the assets had vanished by half. During the last 20 years of the society, the managing committee attempted all kinds of little innovations but without much success. In 1966, radical measures were taken; the reading folders were canceled, the library integrated into the city library, and the Museum Society's activities were restricted to the organization of lectures (Museum Society, 1966). Death was inevitable, however. The small library next to the large library and the small reading room next to the large reading room were hardly attractive enough, and the lectures did not draw much of an audience either.

Was the decline of the Museum Society the result of the demonstrated cultural contrasts within the organization or was it rather caused by external factors? Undoubtedly, the change in the environment had been a tremendous one. Modern society is characterized by detraditionalization, individualization, multiple options, pluralized life worlds, different lifestyles, high spatial mobility, and new media such as radio, TV, telecommunications, and computers.[18] Radio and TV have changed the sense of topicality dramatically and made reading folders anachronistic. No one in modern societies is interested in reading magazines that have been outdated for weeks. In addition, the increasing economic wealth allows virtually everybody to subscribe to a newspaper and a magazine or buy a book, especially in the era of paperbacks and pocket books. These factors, each in its own intricate way, made the conventional goals of the reading society somewhat obsolete. People buy much of their reading material themselves, lectures are competing with information from radio, TV, and the Internet, and there is much diversity concerning social events. It was no coincidence that many reading societies were founded in the 18th and 19th century; we must conclude that it is also no coincidence that nearly all of them have died in the 20th century. Of the 36 reading societies that were counted in the canton (state) of St. Gallen in 1871 (Erne, 1988), none has survived,[19] and of the 123 in the canton of Zurich only a few still exist (Bachmann, 1993).

The reasons why some reading societies have managed to survive despite such unfavorable conditions remain a topic for further research. They have obviously found a cultural niche in which they are still attractive for many people. The Museum Society in St. Gallen, however, seemed to have become rigid and frozen during the past 50 years and failed to rejuvenate. It lacked a fresh management approach and a wave of innovations as it had experienced in the 1890s after Linden's resignation. Instead, the managing committees clung persistently to the traditions that were created in the last century, although the worsening crisis was well perceived and acknowledged. The cultural contrast and sometimes contradiction between an elitist, traditional interpretation of the society's goal and the tastes and interests of the members and clients was certainly aggravating the crisis. The educational style and the paternalistic attitude of the managing committee toward the members was hardly apt to attract new members, in particular young ones. In the declining years, however, the Museum Society found itself in a vicious circle: The vast majority of the members were old people who were eager to keep up the society's traditions, but this was exactly what did not inspire the young.

Conclusions

Modern society consists to a vast degree of organizations. Reading societies were typical organizations as they emerged in the 18th century and persisted until today: associations with voluntary membership and self-determined objectives, structures, and processes. In contrast to many other organizations of modernity, they were nonprofit organizations and had a democratic structure. Born in the age of the Enlightenment, they were pragmatic, future-oriented, and educational. They organized civic sense around specific goals— namely, to provide good literature for their members and to ensure a cultivated form of social entertainment. Reading societies represented a vast social movement throughout western Europe, advanced cultural change, and thus were carriers of the modernization process. Despite the similarities among them, each developed a specific, complex organizational culture. The case study of the Museum Society in St. Gallen, Switzerland, allowed to elicit some cultural contrasts within the organization that determined the organizational life for several decades. The following paragraphs present a summary of some major insights of this case study.

The first decades of the Museum Society and the history of its forerunners represent an interesting case of organizational politics. When a minority of people in the Literary Society did not succeed in reforming the society democratically, they founded a new society with the same goals (the Sun Society). Soon, they suggested a merger with the old society, thereby attempting to introduce the reforms from the outside. The same people also invited the Cercle to join the merger, although they were not interested in those people and their goals at all—they had the sole motive of acquiring the house of the Cercle that provided a suitable locality with a big hall. Later, sometime after the merger, they suggested giving up the Casino and withdrawing to a pure reading society; because they had the house, they wanted to abolish the goals and activities of the former Cercle. This process happened over a time span of 50 years; thus, it was hardly a conscious, goal-oriented, and politically calculated strategy. It was, however, presumably a cultural mind-set that was passed on within the Sun Society and from there, in the person of the secretary and later longtime president and in many other members, to the Museum Society.

This case study shows how diverse the motives for a merger can be and what kind of a cultural schism they may produce. The Cercle wanted the additional income of membership fees to pursue their hitherto goals and activities, and the two reading societies were interested only in the house of the Cercle. The diverse orientations could be subsumed under the goals of the Museum Society, but there was a persistent cultural schism inherited by the merger between those interested in the business of reading and those interested in social entertainment. The subcultures persisted for decades and even new members did not bridge and integrate the cultural diversity but rather joined one of the preexisting subcultures. The managing committee and the president had quite an influence on advancing one kind of activity (reading) over the others (social events), and the longtime president disclosed clearly his view that the Museum Society should give up the goal of social entertainment. It is difficult, however, to judge if he was just lacking in initiative for social events or if he systematically demotivated or even suppressed other people's potential initiatives. In any case, it is amazing to observe what kind of innovations took place and how social life suddenly soared after his resignation.

Introducing innovations that met the formal goals of the society was obviously easier than changing the goals themselves. The democratic organization of the society did not allow for radical change. When the longtime president suggested radical measures, such as giving up the Casino pub, the opposing members showed up at the general meeting to smash the suggestion, and because there were only a few people attending the general meetings[20] it was easy even for a minority of members to become a voting majority. This mechanism may have prevented later managing committees from suggesting a radical change even when the society suffered a continuous financial loss. It took 30 years, up to the 1960s, until radical measures were suggested and implemented. Before that, the presidents only posed rhetorical questions as to whether one possibly should consider doing this or that, and they added immediately that the managing committee had decided to go on with business as usual. When radical measures were finally suggested in 1966 and 1974, the managing committee developed a careful operational plan to build up a coalition strong enough to win the vote: There was a written plan determining who had to convince whom of the committee's proposal and motivate him or her to attend the general meeting and to vote for it. Thus, it may well be that the democratic structure of the organization accounts for a certain inertia of the managing committee to take adequate measures in a perceived crisis and to delay radical change as long as possible.

In connection with the democratic structure, the nonprofit orientation proved to be fatal in one way. Although during the first half of the society's lifetime the managing committees tried hard and, on average, succeeded in achieving a balanced budget, the managing committees after 1930 got used to reporting a financial loss. Although they undertook all kinds of measures to reduce costs and increase membership fees, the annual statement of accounts continued to show a deficit. With a nonprofit orientation, the financial loss could be legitimized by the honorable goals and activities of the society, and nobody wanted to value the virtue of a balanced budget over those. Thus, each managing committee diagnosed the problem but went on with business as usual hoping for a better next year. The alarm clock calling for radical measures was set off only in 1965, when an extrapolated scenario of business as usual showed that the society would go bankrupt within 10 years. The managing committee of 1966 took action, sanctioned by the vote of the general meeting, and thereby preserved some of the society's assets.

The decline of the Museum Society, like that of other reading societies, may be attributed above all to the change in the social environment. Reading societies emerged as carriers of the modernization process and later became victims of the very same process. The cultural contrast within the Museum Society between an elitist, traditional interpretation of the society's goal and the tastes and interests of the members and clients, as described in this case study, was not a main cause of the decline but certainly aggravated the crisis. Presumably, the actual problem was not so much the committee's striving for elitist standards and cultural values as the way it communicated them and the way it dealt with other people's tastes. The annual presidential ritual to reproach the members for their tastes may well be an indicator of a generally repulsive climate within the society, with people applying many kinds of impression management techniques to appear to be scholarly and savant while showing disrespect for ordinary people with ordinary tastes. This type of behavior and communication—this educational, paternalistic style—was hardly apt to attract new and young members, especially during and after the 1950s when the offered advantages (reading folder, library, and lectures) became less attractive. When a democratic organization with voluntary membership fails to rejuvenate its membership, however, it runs the risk of rotating in a vicious circle, with increasingly older members who foster traditions that do not appeal to the young generation. Failure to rejuvenate means aging of members and organizations, and death becomes inevitable.

Notes

1. For Germany, see Prüsener (1973), Göpfert (1976), and Prüsener and Göpfert (1977). In autumn of 1977, there was a conference in the "Herzog August" Library in Wolfenbüttel, Germany, where researchers from seven European countries presented their work on reading societies (see Dann, 1981b; see also Dann, 1977, 1984; Galitz, 1986; van Dülmen, 1996). For Switzerland, see Im Hof (1982), Bernard and Reichen (1982), and Erne (1988) regarding societies; regarding reading societies, see Braun (1965), Milstein (1972), Eberle (1989, 1997), and Bachmann (1993).

2. Most historical research on reading societies focused on this period, except Braun (1965), Eberle (1989, 1997), and Bachmann (1993).

3. The term *organization* emerged in France during the 18th century (Herkunftswörterbuch, 1989, p. 581f) as a designation of these new, modern social formations with voluntary membership, voluntary objectives, and voluntary structures and processes (see Türk, 1989).

4. For a review of different anthropological concepts of organizational culture concerning formal and informal aspects, see Schwartzman (1993) and Gregory (1983).

5. Regarding the subject of anthropology through temporal concepts and devices as a political act, see Fabian (1983).

6. Regarding the term *objectivation,* see Berger and Luckmann (1966).

7. As previous research by the author has shown (Eberle, 1989), the materials were passed on from secretary to secretary, sometimes got lost, sometimes were forgotten in a closet or thrown away, or they burnt down in a house fire.

8. In previous research, many interviews were conducted with persons who had been members of a reading society. Compared to the richness of the historical documents, the memory of people proved to be scanty. For a theoretical discussion on the relationship of memory and history, see Halbwachs (1980) and Assmann (1988).

9. The annual reports are cited by the year the report is concerned with; the printed report, however, was usually published in the first months of the next year.

10. In the Swiss cities of Zurich since 1834 and of Berne since 1847; in the German cities of Hannover since 1789 and of Karlsruhe since 1808.

11. All quotes from the bylaws, the annual reports, and other historical documents were translated from German into English by the author. The sometimes heavy, complicated style reflects the German original.

12. The goals changed in their wording—especially because the civil code defined some legal rules for associations—but not in their substance.

13. See Linden (1871, pp. 1-50) and the preserved documents of each society.

14. This cannot be reconstructed with ultimate certainty on the basis of the preserved materials.

15. Being an academic and having a title was obviously important for getting elected into the managing committee.

16. The same was the case in other reading societies: See Amrein (1886, 1897), Koch (1911), and Eberle (1997).

17. Personal interview by the author with someone who moved to town and later became a member. The interviewee reported that everyone talked with great respect about the Museum Society and that he felt greatly honored when being admitted as a member.

18. For a further sociological analysis of these phenomena, see Berger, Berger, and Kellner (1974), Giddens (1991), Bauman (1991, 1993), Beck, Giddens, and Lash (1994), and Gross (1994).

19. Survey by the author in 1994 (see Eberle, 1997).

20. Linden stated in 1875 (Museum Society, 1875, p. 11) that the seven members of the managing committee and the three revisers usually represent the majority at the general meetings.

References

Amrein, K. C. (1886). *Jubiläums-Bericht über den fünfzigjährigen Bestand der Lesegesellschaft Büsch* [Anniversary report on the fifty year long existence of the Reading Society Büsch]. St. Gallen, Switzerland: Zollikofer.

Amrein, K. C. (1897, January 14). *Festbericht für die Sechste Dezenniumsfeier der Lesegesellschaft Büsch* [Anniversary report for the sixth decade celebration of the Reading Society Büsch]. Unpublished manuscript.

Assmann, J. (1988). Kollektives Gedächtnis und kulturelle Identität [Collective memory and cultural identity]. In J. Assmann & T. Hölscher (Eds.), *Kultur und Gedächtnis* (pp. 9-19). Frankfurt, Germany: Suhrkamp.

Bachmann, M. (1993). *Lektüre, Politik und Bildung. Die schweizerischen Lesegesellschaften des 19. Jahrhunderts unter besonderer Berücksichtigung des Kantons Zürich* [Reading, politics and education. The Swiss reading societies of the 19th century, with special consideration of the canton of Zurich]. Bern, Switzerland: P. Lang.

Bauman, Z. (1991). *Modernity and ambivalence*. Cambridge, MA: Polity.

Bauman, Z. (1993). *Postmodern ethics*. Cambridge, MA: Blackwell.

Beck, U., Giddens, A., & Lash, S. (1994). *Reflexive modernization: Politics, tradition and aesthetics in the modern social order.* Cambridge, MA: Polity.

Berger, P., Berger, B., & Kellner, H. (1974). *The homeless mind. Modernization and consciousness.* New York: Vintage.

Berger, P., & Luckmann, T. (1966). *The social construction of reality.* London: Penguin.

Bernard, N., & Reichen, Q. (Eds.). (1982). *Gesellschaft und Gesellschaften. Festschrift zum 65. Geburtstag von Prof. Dr. Ulrich Im Hof* [Society and societies. Festschrift for the 65th anniversary of Prof. Dr. Ulrich Im Hof]. Bern, Switzerland: Wyss (University of Berne, Institute of History).

Braun, R. (1965). *Sozialer und kultureller Wandel in einem ländlichen Industriegebiet (Zürcher Oberland) unter Einwirkung des Maschinen—und Fabrikwesens im 19. und 20. Jahrhundert* [Social and cultural change in a rural industrial area ("Oberland" of Zurich) as a result of the industrialization in the 19th and 20th century]. Stuttgart, Germany: Eugen Rentsch.

Cercle. (1788-1792). *Protokollbuch* [Proceedings]. Unpublished manuscripts.

Dann, O. (1977). Die Lesegesellschaften des 18. Jahrhunderts und der gesellschaftliche Aufbruch des deutschen Bürgertums [The reading societies of the 18th century and the social awakening of the German bourgeoisie]. In H. G. Göpfert (Hrsg.), *Buch und Leser. Schriften des Wolfenbütteler Arbeitskreises für Geschichte des Buchwesens* (Vol. 1, p. 162ff). Hamburg, Germany: Hauswedell.

Dann, O. (1981a). Die Lesegesellschaften und die Herausbildung einer modernen bürgerlichen Gesellschaft in Europa [The reading societies and the formation of a modern bourgeois society in Europe]. In O. Dann (Ed.), *Lesegesellschaften und bürgerliche Emanzipation. Ein europäischer Vergleich* (pp. 9-28). München, Germany: Beck.

Dann, O. (Ed.). (1981b). *Lesegesellschaften und bürgerliche Emanzipation. Ein europäischer Vergleich* [Reading societies and bourgeois emancipation. A European comparison]. München, Germany: Beck.

Dann, O. (Ed.). (1984). Vereinswesen und bürgerliche Gesellschaft in Deutschland [Associations and the bourgeois society in Germany]. *Historische Zeitschrift 1, Beiheft 9.*

Eberle, T. S. (1989). Die Appenzeller Lesegesellschaften im Fernsehzeitalter [The reading societies of Appenzell in the age of television]. In R. Dubs, Y. Hangartner, & A. Nydegger (Eds.), *Der*

Kanton St. Gallen und seine Hochschule. Beiträge zur Eröffnung des Bibliothekbaus (pp. 169-185). St. Gallen, Switzerland: University of St. Gallen.

Eberle, T. S. (1997). Aufstieg und Niedergang der st. gallischen Lesegesellschaften [The rise and fall of the reading societies in St. Gallen]. In W. Wunderlich (Ed.), *St. Gallen—Kloster, Stadt, Kanton, Region. Eine Geschichte der literarischen Kultur* (Vol. 1). St. Gallen, Switzerland: University Press Constance.

Engelsing, R. (1970). Die Perioden der Lesergeschichte in der Neuzeit [Periods of reader history in modern age]. In *Archiv für Geschichte des Buchwesens 10* (pp. 945-1002). Frankfurt, Germany: Buchhändler-Vereinigung.

Engelsing, R. (1974). *Der Bürger als Leser. Lesergeschichte in Deutschland 1500-1800* [The citizen as reader. Reader history in Germany 1500-1800]. Stuttgart, Germany: Metzler.

Erne, E. (1988). *Die schweizerischen Sozietäten. Lexikalische Darstellung der Reformgesellschaften des 18. Jahrhunderts* [The Swiss societies. Lexical account of the reform societies in the 18th century]. Zurich, Germany: Chronos.

Fabian, J. (1983). *Time and the other. How anthropology makes its object.* New York: Columbia University Press.

Galitz, R. (1986). *Literarische Basisöffentlichkeit als politische Kraft. Lesegesellschaften des 17ten bis 19ten Jahrhunderts unter besonderer Berücksichtigung des 18ten. Jahrhunderts* [Literary grassroots public as a political force. Reading societies in the 17th till 19th century, with special consideration of the 18th century]. Bern, Switzerland: P. Lang.

Giddens, A. (1991). *Modernity and self-identity.* Cambridge, MA: Polity.

Göpfert, H. G. (1976). Lesegesellschaften im 18. Jahrhundert [Reading societies in the 18th century]. In F. Kopitzsch (Ed.), *Aufklärung, Absolutismus und Bürgertum in Deutschland.* München, Germany: Nymphenburger Verlagshaus.

Gregory, K. (1983). Native-view paradigms: Multiple cultures and culture conflicts in organizations. *Administrative Science Quarterly, 28,* 359-376.

Gross, P. (1994). *Die Multioptionsgesellschaft* [The multiple options society]. Frankfurt, Germany: Suhrkamp.

Halbwachs, M. (1980). *The collective memory.* New York: Harper & Row.

Harding, S. (1991). *Whose science? Whose knowledge? Thinking from women's lives.* Milton Keynes: Open University Press.

Das Herkunftswörterbuch: Etymologie der deutschen Sprache [Etymological dictionary](Vol. 7). (1989). Mannheim, Vienna, Zürich: Duden, Bibliographisches Institut.

Im Hof, U. (1982). *Das gesellige Jahrhundert. Gesellschaft und Gesellschaften im Zeitalter der Aufklärung* [The sociable century. Society and societies in the age of Enlightenment]. München, Germany: C. H. Beck.

Jelinek, M., Smircich, L., & Hirsch, P. (1983). Introduction: A code of many colors. *Administrative Science Quarterly, 28,* 331-333.

Koch, H. (1911). *Lebens-Erinnerungen der "Frau Büsch," ihrer Familie gewidmet an ihrem 75. Geburtstage* [Reminiscences of the life of "Mrs. Büsch," dedicated to her family on her 75th anniversary]. St. Gallen, Switzerland: A. Loehrer.

Krünitz, J. G. (1790). *Oekonomisches Wörterbuch* [Economic encyclopedia] (Vol. 175). Berlin.

Linden, A. (1871). *Die Museumsgesellschaft in St. Gallen. Geschichtliche Rückblicke und gegenwärtige Zustände, zugleich erster bis fünfzehnter Jahresbericht (1856-1870) über die Museumsgesellschaft* [The Museum Society in St. Gallen. Historical survey and present states, at the same time first till fifteenth annual report (1856-1870) of the Museum Society]. St. Gallen, Switzerland: Zollikofer & Züblin.

Literarische Gesellschaft [Literary Society]. (1816). *Statuten* [Statute book]. St. Gallen, Switzerland: Zollikofer & Züblin.

Milstein, B. M. (1972). *Eight eighteenth century reading societies. A sociological contribution to the history of German literature.* Frankfurt, Germany: H. Lang.

Museumsgesellschaft St. Gallen [Museum Society of St. Gallen]. (1856). *Statuten* [Statute book]. St. Gallen, Switzerland: Author.

Museumsgesellschaft St. Gallen [Museum Society of St. Gallen]. (1875). *Jahresberichte* [Annual report]. St. Gallen, Switzerland: Author.

Museumsgesellschaft St. Gallen [Museum Society of St. Gallen]. (1878). *Jahresberichte* [Annual report]. St. Gallen, Switzerland: Author.

Museumsgesellschaft St. Gallen [Museum Society of St. Gallen]. (1883). *Jahresberichte* [Annual report]. St. Gallen, Switzerland: Author.

Museumsgesellschaft St. Gallen [Museum Society of St. Gallen]. (1884). *Jahresberichte* [Annual report]. St. Gallen, Switzerland: Author.

Museumsgesellschaft St. Gallen [Museum Society of St. Gallen]. (1888). *Jahresberichte* [Annual report]. St. Gallen, Switzerland: Author.

Museumsgesellschaft St. Gallen [Museum Society of St. Gallen]. (1891). *Jahresberichte* [Annual report]. St. Gallen, Switzerland: Author.

Museumsgesellschaft St. Gallen [Museum Society of St. Gallen]. (1893). *Jahresberichte* [Annual report]. St. Gallen, Switzerland: Author.

Museumsgesellschaft St. Gallen [Museum Society of St. Gallen]. (1920). *Jahresberichte* [Annual report]. St. Gallen, Switzerland: Author.

Museumsgesellschaft St. Gallen [Museum Society of St. Gallen]. (1925). *Jahresberichte* [Annual report]. St. Gallen, Switzerland: Author.

Museumsgesellschaft St. Gallen [Museum Society of St. Gallen]. (1935). *Jahresberichte* [Annual report]. St. Gallen, Switzerland: Author.

Museumsgesellschaft St. Gallen [Museum Society of St. Gallen]. (1946). *Jahresberichte* [Annual report]. St. Gallen, Switzerland: Author.

Museumsgesellschaft St. Gallen [Museum Society of St. Gallen]. (1949). *Jahresberichte* [Annual report]. St. Gallen, Switzerland: Author.

Museumsgesellschaft St. Gallen [Museum Society of St. Gallen]. (1950). *Jahresberichte* [Annual report]. St. Gallen, Switzerland: Author.

Museumsgesellschaft St. Gallen [Museum Society of St. Gallen]. (1952). *Jahresberichte* [Annual report]. St. Gallen, Switzerland: Author.

Museumsgesellschaft St. Gallen [Museum Society of St. Gallen]. (1953). *Jahresberichte* [Annual report]. St. Gallen, Switzerland: Author.

Museumsgesellschaft St. Gallen [Museum Society of St. Gallen]. (1954). *Jahresberichte* [Annual report]. St. Gallen, Switzerland: Author.

Museumsgesellschaft St. Gallen [Museum Society of St. Gallen]. (1958). *Jahresberichte* [Annual report]. St. Gallen, Switzerland: Author.

Museumsgesellschaft St. Gallen [Museum Society of St. Gallen]. (1966, March 3). *Protokoll der Generalversammlung* [Proceedings of the General Meetings]. St. Gallen, Switzerland: Author.

Museumsgesellschaft St. Gallen [Museum Society of St. Gallen]. (1974, December 12). *Protokoll der Generalversammlung* [Proceedings of the General Meetings]. St. Gallen, Switzerland: Author.

Prüsener, M. (1973). Lesegesellschaften im 18. Jahrhundert. Ein Beitrag zur Lesergeschichte [Reading societies in the 18th century. A treatise in reader history]. *Archiv für Geschichte des Buchwesens, 13,* 369-594.

Prüsener, M., & Göpfert, H. G. (1977). Lesegesellschaften [Reading societies]. In E. L. Hauswedell & Chr. Voigt (Eds.), *Buchkunst und Literatur in Deutschland 1750 bis 1850* (pp. 287ff). Hamburg, Germany: Hauswedell.

Reckmann, J., & Dann, O. (1978, April 21). Lesegesellschaften und bürgerliche Gesellschaft im 18ten Jahrhundert. Probleme der Forschung im europäischen Vergleich [Reading societies and bourgeois societies in the 18th century. Problems of research in a European comparison]. *AHF Informationen, 16,* 1-4.

Schein, E. H. (1985). *Organizational culture and leadership. A dynamic view.* San Francicso: Jossey-Bass.

Schwartzman, H. B. (1993). Ethnography in organizations. *Qualitative Research Methods, 27,* 1-83.

Seiler, O. (1914). *Weberhaus und Rösslitor. Festschrift der Museumsgesellschaft St. Gallen* [The Weber house and the Rössli gate. Festschrift of the Museum Society St. Gallen]. St. Gallen, Switzerland: Zollikofer.

Stützel-Prüsener, M. (1981). Die deutschen Lesegesellschaften im Zeitalter der Aufklärung [The German reading societies in the age of Enlightenment]. In O. Dann (Ed.), *Lesegesellschaften und bürgerliche Emanzipation. Ein europäischer Vergleich* (pp. 71-86). München, Germany: Beck.

Türk, K. (1989). Organisationssoziologie [Sociology of organization]. In G. Endruweit & G. Trommsdorff (Eds.), *Wörterbuch der Soziologie* (Vol. 2). Stuttgart, Germany: Enke (dtv).

van Dülmen, R. (1996). *Die Gesellschaft der Aufklärer. Zur bürgerlichen Emanzipation und Aufklärerischen Kultur in Deutschland* [The society of the Enlightenment. Bourgeois emancipation and the culture of Enlightenment in Germany]. Frankfurt, Germany: Fischer.

Weisz, L. (1934a, December 18). Alt-Zürcher Lesezirkel I. *Neue Zürcher Zeitung, 2299.*

Weisz, L. (1934b, December 22). Alt-Zürcher Lesezirkel II. *Neue Zürcher Zeitung, 2333.*

Chapter 8

Telling Tales

Contrasts and Commonalities Within the Organization of an Amusement Park— Confronting and Combining Different Perspectives

Sierk B. Ybema

The question of unity or division is a central theme in discussions about culture in organizations (e.g., Frost, Moore, Louis, Lundberg, & Martin, 1991). Some studies portray organizations as cultural breeding grounds for shared sentiments. Other studies regard and describe an organization as a battle area dominated by ideological and political struggles. Martin (1992) thoroughly described these two views (labeled integration and differentiation perspective) and added a third one (the fragmentation perspective) that underlines the chaotic and unstable nature of organizational reality (see Meyerson & Martin, 1987). These authors do not address, however, how these different readings of reality relate to each other. In this chapter, quantitative and qualitative data from a study of a Dutch amusement park are used to explore if and how findings from different perspectives are interrelated. I first address the different ways in which culture researchers deal with the issue of order and disorder in organizations, discuss a multiperspective view, and sketch the theoretical outlines of an alternative approach. I argue that, contrary to Martin's multiperspective approach, our reasoning and research should aim at confronting and combining the insights of different views. Particularly, the paradox of unity and disunity existing jointly—people being "opposed" and "together" at the same time—seems to point in a promising direction.

From Integration to Fragmentation

The consensus and dissent views on organizational culture partly correspond with a difference between a pragmatic or theoretical interest of culture researchers (Barley, Meyer, & Gash, 1988). Practitioners' accounts depict culture as a tool of management (e.g., Deal & Kennedy, 1982; Ouchi, 1981; Peters & Waterman, 1982). They reason that culture brings about social cohesion, which in turn will increase production. Excellent companies are said to be distinguished by a "corporate culture"—shared values, a family feeling, and mutual concord. Culture in this sense is the harmony model embodied: Culture means consensus.

This idea has been criticized by academics. Organizations usually contain a great many different cultures rather than one single, pervasive culture (Gregory, 1983; Louis, 1985; Lucas, 1987; Morey & Luthans, 1985; Riley, 1983; Van Maanen & Barley, 1985; see Chapter 2, this volume). Van Maanen and Barley point out that classical studies by Whyte (1948), Selznick (1949), Homans (1950), Gouldner (1954), Blau (1955), and Dalton (1959) also portray organizations as penetrated by conflicts of interest fought out between groups with divergent ideologies and interpretations. "Culture, as invented by various groups of an organization, was found to be a differentiating, rather than an integrating, mechanism" (Van Maanen & Barley, 1985, p. 39). Culture is not so much a force that will keep things together as it is a force that makes a mess of things. Culture is being placed within the political paradigm—the conflict model.

The two views are diametrically opposed. "Organizational culture, it seems, is about either pervasive unity or pervasive division" (Young, 1989, p. 187). Recently, various authors drew attention to the complexity (sometimes called ambiguity) of boundaries between people and the dynamic and diverse nature of social and cultural networks (e.g., Alvesson, 1993; Hannerz, 1992; Martin, 1992). Organizations are seen from a fragmentation perspective (Martin, 1992), a local, management-centric and a "great culture" perspective (Alvesson, 1993), and considered crossroads of cultures—a "nexus" (Meyerson & Martin, 1987) where broader, societal "feeder cultures" (Louis, 1985) come together. This perspective is a sharpened version of the second one because it sheds light on the variety and variability of patterns of consensus and dissent.[1] Boundaries between (sub)cultures appear blurred and susceptible to change from this viewpoint.

Confronting and Combining Unity, Diversity, and Ambiguity

Once different perspectives have been detected and described, we are inspired to go beyond a single perspective approach. Martin (1992) makes a challenging attempt to take into account all three perspectives (integration, differentiation, and fragmentation) and adopt a multiperspective view (pp. 168-188). She argues that if we are looking from one single perspective we may see certain aspects sharply but be blind to other at the same time. By taking a multiperspective view, we might overcome shortcomings of a single perspective approach and avoid drawing a one-sided picture of cultural reality.

This seems to be a promising and plausible thought. We are easily locked up in one single perspective, which does not do justice to the complexity of culture in everyday organizational life. For the greater part, however, the promise remains unfulfilled. Martin (1992) eloquently describes different approaches in organizational theory and research and is dedicated to preserving the "integrity" of each approach: "As in a conversation, each perspective is given its turn to speak fully, in its own words" (p. 17). Theoretical thoughts and empirical data are thus classed in closed categories, presented each in turn, and held apart scrupulously. Martin further states, "It is essential to keep each perspective separate. . . . Pressures toward assimilation would undermine a perspective's inherently oppositional stance toward the other viewpoints" (p. 187). This way, differences between these viewpoints are described but not discussed. So, in fact, the conversation never really starts. I doubt whether a multiperspective approach that does not point out if and how divergent theoretical and empirical findings are interrelated really "broadens and deepens understanding" as Martin (1992, p. 15) asserts. Simply adding up different views does not make us automatically better off.

Rigid categorization keeps us from going in two different directions: confrontations or combinations. First, perspectives may very well offer contradictory rather than complementary readings of cultural reality. This does not so much ask for quiet conversation, as for discussion and debate between perspectives that then will stand face to face rather than shoulder to shoulder.

Second, a real conversation between oppositional perspectives may also lead to their combination. If different viewpoints are not mutually exclusive, why keep them strictly separated? The three perspectives have been put away in a rather rigid framework as clear-cut categories, designed, as it were, from a differentiation perspective. It could be more challenging to view them from an integration and fragmentation perspective, thereby moving across boundaries and mingling insights from different categories.

A fine example of cultural unity and diversity occurring simultaneously is provided by Young (1989). Some organizational events in a production factory expressed a sense of collectivity and common interest of all personnel but also contained the seeds of discord between different departments: "Unity and division existed in tandem" (Young, 1989, p. 188; see also Chapter 3, this volume). This idea has been elaborated by anthropologists stating that group members attach a personal meaning to group symbols and rituals. Cultural forms are inherently ambiguous. They allow for divergent interpretations, giving the individual room to move and placing him within a community at the same time (see Cohen, 1985, pp. 15-21; Kertzer, 1988, p. 11). In this chapter, illustrations of both confrontations and combinations of the consensus and dissent view will be given.

Social and Cultural Boundaries

How can we picture cultural borderlines if unity and division go together? If organizations house several (sub)cultures, what is their location? Van Maanen and Barley's (1985) theory of (sub)cultural creation gives us some clues. One of their basic assumptions is that culture is closely linked to interactions between people, which leads to shared interpretations: "As a subgroup's members interact over time and address problems cooperatively, collective understandings form to support concerted action" (p. 37). The division of work and workers into different groups and levels is a breeding ground for cultural division within organizations. People with a common place or position, the same office or canteen, interact frequently, start to form a group, and may develop a distinctive group culture. Consequently, culture in organizations is tied to a workplace, a department, or a hierarchic level (see Louis, 1985, pp. 75-79; Trice & Beyer, 1993). Structural differentiation has cultural consequences, but this process may also go the other way around. Different cultural backgrounds and opposing ideologies of employees may shape interaction patterns profoundly. Contradictory views can divide a group into different camps, which eventually may lead to a structural cleavage such as the schism of a church or controversies between scientific schools of thought (Van Maanen & Barley, 1985). The outcome of both formation processes is that structural and cultural dividing lines start to overlap within organizations.

Clearly, given the complexity of these differentiation processes, patterns of interaction and interpretation can cross-cut formal lines of division within the organization and often transcend organizational boundaries. Social networks may grow out of shared interests or ideologies and common professional, ethnic, or social backgrounds, subsequently leading to friendship groups, cliques, cabals and coalitions, occupational and managerial subcultures (Trice & Beyer, 1993), and oppositional groups or movements (Martin & Siehl, 1983; Van Maanen & Barley, 1985). These groupings are often poorly or not at all reflected in the formal structure of the organization (e.g., see Sackmann, 1992, pp. 154-155).

Furthermore, people are more likely than not members of different groups at the same time (see Allen, Wilder, & Atkinson, 1983; Chapter 2, this volume). For example, doctors and nurses are members of both a profession and the organizational unit in which they work (Chapter 16, this volume). This means that relations between organization members are socially defined in more than one way. A new manager can be "boss," "colleague," and "less experienced organization member" to his direct subordinates at the same time. Consequently, people may be culturally and socially far apart and simultaneously have certain ideas, interests, and identities in common. Certain issues and specific situations may trigger certain cultural and social commonalities or differences and determine whether people stand together or are divided (e.g., Chapter 17, this volume). This leads to paradoxical patterns of unity and disunity in organizations. Boundaries between people appear and disappear, and they are marked or ignored depending on the ideas, interests, and identities that are at stake and the setting in which the interactions take place.

Under "Conclusions and Discussion," I address the theme of cultural order and disorder, exploring different ways of dealing with contrasting views. The question will be answered if and how divergent empirical findings are interrelated, building on the descriptive data presented in the following sections.

Method

The empirical material that will be presented in this chapter is drawn from a case study of a medium-sized service company in the south of the Netherlands—

the amusement park "de Efteling." The park draws more than 2 million visitors a year. As will become clear from the description, the 1,300 people who work for the company tell quite some tales about one another, maybe inspired by the well-known fairy tales on which the attractions in the park are based. The research was conducted in 1991 and was originally set up as a reaction against the corporate culture cult that depicts culture as a unifying force in organizations. Therefore, the organization was studied primarily from a differentiation perspective to describe cultural differences between groups within the organization. The richness of the qualitative data allows for a secondary analysis that does justice to the integration perspective as well. The findings can illustrate both confrontations and combinations of different perspectives.

Data Gathering

Different research methods have been used to gather data: document analysis, (participant) observation, interviews, questionnaires, and feedback sessions. A first orientation consisted of an analysis of various documents and informal interviews with key figures within the company. To get an in-depth understanding of the organization's structure and culture, I worked as a "vacation worker" at different places in the park (on the pleasure grounds) and attended receptions, celebrations, training sessions for new employees, and two-week sessions for top management and some high staff members with a management consultant regarding the current company policy, daily routines, and mutual cooperation. Interviews of one or two hours' duration were conducted with 18 employees at different places and positions in the organization, chosen in consultation with the personnel manager. They included, among others, the top manager and his secretary, all members of the management team, staff personnel, some old-timers and newcomers, and an employee representative. The interview checklist contained open questions about the history and future of the company, the current power and friendship relations, and current changes in the company ("changes" proved to be relevant in other research settings as well—e.g., Sackmann, 1992, pp. 144, 156), thereby probing for ideas and interests of people in their work situation. Furthermore, a standardized survey questionnaire has been administered to a sample of organization members, from which 70 usable questionnaires have been collected. Finally, the results of the interviews, observations, and the questionnaire were discussed with members of the management team and some staff personnel. Their comments and interpretations have been used in the data analysis.

Dimensions and Questionnaire

The questionnaire was adopted from the research conducted by Hofstede, Neuijen, Ohayiv, and Sanders (1990). Sixty-one questions assessed "perceived practices in one's work situation" (p. 295). The respondent is asked about values and practices concerning his or her work situation. The questions are in a bipolar format under the general heading "Where I work . . ." using 5-point scales on which, for example, 1 = "meeting times are kept punctually" and 5 = "meeting times are only kept approximately." Five questions about divergent matters, such as stress at work and commitment to the company, were also adopted. The items assessing personal values were not adopted because they were not related to organizational life.

Hofstede et al. (1990) looked for cultural differences between 20 organizational units from 10 divergent organizations—5 in Denmark and 5 in the Netherlands (a total of 1,295 respondents). Differences between organizational units could be measured on six dimensions: process oriented versus results oriented, employee oriented versus job oriented, parochial versus professional, open system versus closed system, loose versus tight control, and normative versus pragmatic. Although the authors are careful not to claim generalizability too explicitly, they certainly seem to suggest that the six dimensions could be used outside the sample of organizational units in their research to describe both organizational cultures and group cultures (p. 313). There are good reasons to doubt the validity of this assumption. As a model to describe subcultural differences, it is contaminated by organizational variance, whereas some subcultural differentiation has clearly been ignored such as possible differences between executive levels, departments, or occupational groups. For this reason, we cannot a priori assume these dimensions to be valid to describe subcultural differences within an organization. Therefore, the research data have been (factor) analyzed to find out on what dimensions cultural differences within the company can be described in this particular case.

Sample and Statistical Issues

At the time of the research, 1,150 people worked for the organization— approximately 140 with a permanent appointment, more than 400 seasonal workers, and more than half vacation workers (700-800 in the summertime, and a total of approximately 1,300 organizational members). In informal conversations and interviews, it appeared that distinctions between organizational members were primarily drawn on the basis of differences in department, executive level, and contract. These differences divided organization members into seven groups: two executive levels (top and middle management), staff personnel (members of the commercial, financial, and personnel department all working in the office), technical engineers (designers, decorators, bricklayers, gardeners, and technicians), two departments working in the park (catering service and attraction or park personnel), and vacation personnel (working at different work locations). Vacation personnel usually worked a couple of weeks and weekends and park personnel seven or eight months (the park is closed during the winter season). A stratified, random sample of 105 employees was drawn from the organization. Within each of the seven groups, a certain number of members were selected following the systematic sampling method with a random start. Seventy usable questionnaires were collected that were more or less equally divided across the groups (top and middle management, staff, technical, catering, attraction, and vacation personnel), consisting of approximately 10 respondents each (respectively, 8, 10, 9, 11, 11, 10, and 11).

A multivariate analysis on the aggregated data of the seven groups provides insights into the cultural factors or dimensions that may distinguish groups. Culture is a characteristic of a collectivity. Statements about cultural differences can therefore be based only on an analysis of aggregated data. Hence, a factor analysis should be performed on group mean scores rather than on individual scores to prevent "methodical fallacies" (Hofstede, Bond, & Luk, 1993; Hofstede et al., 1990) or, in this case, the so-called atomistic (Swanborn, 1981/1984, p. 184) or reverse ecological fallacy (Hofstede, 1980, p. 29)—interpreting individual data as if they could be applied to groups. A mean score of a group, however, is a vague, if not false, indication of "the" group culture when contrasts within the group have been leveled out. Therefore, an analysis of variance should precede an analysis of mean group scores. When between-group variance is significantly larger than within-group variance, differences between groups can be said to be meaningful.

Inevitably, an "ecological" factor analysis has only a few cases in comparison to the number of variables. The number of cases should be much larger, otherwise factors become unstable and unduly dependent on the whims of individual respondents. This constraint does not apply, however, to factor analyses of aggregate data in which each mean is based on a large number of individual scores. These scores are relatively stable (Hofstede et al., 1990, p. 299). Because correlations between mean scores tend to be stronger than individual correlations, we can expect to find a high percentage of variance explained. To avoid paying attention to trivialities, it is advisable to keep the number of factors much smaller than the number of cases and smaller than what is technically possible based on the eigenvalues larger than 1.0. In addition, one should consider only variables with high loadings on a factor (p. 299).

Multimethod Approach

The research consisted of both quantitative and qualitative elements. Culture researchers mostly show a distinct preference for either qualitative or quantitative methods. A choice for quantifiable data has long been (and for many still is) self-evident in organization research. For a substantive group of mainly academic researchers, however, organizational culture offered an empirical alternative to mainstream organization research aimed at objectivistic quantification (Barley et al., 1988), as becomes apparent from various accounts advocating ethnographic research (e.g., Frost et al., 1991, pp. 165-240; Gregory, 1983; Jones, 1988; Rosen, 1986; Van Maanen, 1979, 1983, 1988). This polarizing antagonism led to what Martin (1990) calls "mono-method monopolies." Martin makes a case for adopting a multimethod approach because "one method's strengths are another method's weaknesses" (p. 39; see also Rousseau, 1990).

This also holds for the Efteling study in which I intended to combine different data sources. The "hard," quantitative data drawn from the questionnaire showed whether and on what points groups could be distinguished from a cultural viewpoint mapping out some cultural differences within the organization. Such a description offers a useful characterization and typification because it highlights only certain cultural characteristics. We then know how personnel typified their workplace in a certain way, but we do not know why. To uncover the meaning behind the typification, observations and interviews were conducted.

In the quantitative part of this study, culture is understood as perceptions of values and practices more or less shared by members of a group that distinguish one group from the other. These values and practices are related to the work situation; they are (re)produced within and refer to organizational life. Values are approved and disapproved ways of thinking and acting; practices are common ways of behaving within an organization. These are not personal values and practices but rather perceptions "in the third person" of values and practices that are ascribed to the organization or the group. This concept of culture is very similar to definitions of the concept of organizational climate (e.g., Reiches & Schneider, 1990). In observations and interviews, attention is focused on actual behavior patterns (as opposed to perceived practices) and personal ideas and values of organizational members that are manifested in discourses (traditional lore, corporate creed, gossip, etc.) and practices (the ways in which people act and interact).

Results

Quantitative Data: Two Dimensions of Subcultures

Analyses of variance (*F* tests) for all variables across the seven groups showed that group means differed significantly on 25 questions (*p* value smaller than .05). The between-group variance on these variables was considerably larger than the within-group variance. A significant share of the total variance in answers of organizational members on these items could be ascribed to membership of groups within the organization. For these 25 variables, an ecological principal component factor analysis was performed with orthogonal varimax rotation. The optimal number of factors was two, which explained 75% of the variance. The eigenvalues of higher factors were substantially smaller than the eigenvalues of the first two factors (15.8 and 4.5 as opposed to 2.6, 1.8, 1.4, and 0.8), and according to independent judgment their meaning was vague. These higher factors served as a repository for isolated items with relatively low loadings on the first two factors. Hence, the main differences between the groups could be described on two dimensions (see Appendix).

Open Versus Closed (Tight Versus Loose)

The first factor refers to a distinction between open and closed groups. Some regard their workplace as a private club in which only special people are admitted (Items 30 and 49). New employees need quite some time to feel at home (Item 36). People are closed with one another. Conflicts are covered up (Item 56) and fought out indirectly (Item 59). In other groups, members are more open and direct with one another. Everyone fits in the organization, and new employees are easily accepted and quickly feel at home. Conflicts are openly talked about. People are straightforward and direct. Furthermore, mutual trust exists between departments, and people work together rather than work against each other (Items 9, 47, and 55). In addition, the way of working by open groups seems to be more precise and punctual. Promises are kept (Item 47) and time and money expenses are carefully watched (Items 15 and 31). Closed groups, however, typify their work environment as somewhat loose. Meeting times are not as strict. They do not keep such a tight grip on time and money expenses and seem to have an easier attitude toward their work and fellow workers.

Factor I makes a distinction between groups working in the park (catering, attraction, and vacation personnel) and groups with the office building as their common workplace (top management and staff). The culture in the park is open, and the office culture is closed. The position of the other two groups on this dimension is somewhere in the middle. Middle management works both in the park and in the office building and technical engineers have their own workplaces (see Figure 8.1). The culture difference between office and park personnel is probably connected to different work, different terms of employment, and a different workplace. Park personnel work on the pleasure grounds and in the restaurants, whereas office employees retire to tidy rooms connected by straight corridors and solid stairs. Park workers have seasonal, vacation, and standby contracts, whereas office employees usually have permanent appointments. Furthermore, these groups have a different kind of work. Shop floor workers are smiling, selling drinks and helping children, and wearing uniforms, whereas white-collar administrators are writing memos, keeping up the paperwork, holding meetings, and wearing suits. As Factor I shows, administrative work is more challenging, whereas executive work is a little monotonous (Items 42, 8, and 28). Office work is more formalized; more meetings are held (Item 44) and communication is more often on paper (Item 11). Unlike the services of park personnel, activities of office employees are not visible to customers—a difference in so-called front-office and back-office activities (Langeard, 1980). Because of temporary appointments of employees and regular contact with visitors, park personnel see new faces every day. New employees are easily accepted and quickly feel at home. Everyone fits into the organization. Office employees see the same faces every day. They are thrown together. Interaction is more formalized and conflicts are covered up. Relations between people are politically loaded. People do not always know where they stand. New employees are left to find their own way. The organization is hard to fathom and is experienced as impenetrable, closed, and secretive.

Autonomous Versus Conformist

Factor II distinguishes groups in which members worry about losing their job (Item 20), are aware of competition (Item 34), and are afraid of making a mistake because then they are on their own (Item 61). These items seem to denote a degree of uncertainty that is experienced by group members in their work situation. The danger stems from competitors, colleagues who might ditch you, and bosses who may fire you. They want to remain working for this company (Item 64), experience a lot of rules and procedures (Item 45), and maintain a formal way of dealing with

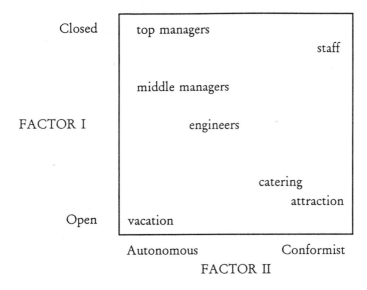

Figure 8.1. Position of the Seven Groups on the Dimensions Open Versus Closed and Autonomous Versus Conformist

each other (Item 33). By holding on to their jobs and maintaining formal ways of dealing with their work and with each other, it seems that these groups of workers want to build in security.[2] They are guided by their organization, its rules and regulations, and its competitors.

As the antidote to this dimension, we find groups in which members are apparently less worried about losing their job, competitors, colleagues, mistakes, rules, or procedures. They have an informal way of dealing with each other. Less troubled by uncertainty and less bound to their job, they will also be less inclined to conform to the organization. They follow their own judgment, starting from their own strengths. In short, Factor II makes a distinction between groups from which members work with caution, keep the rules, and accommodate the organization and groups in which people confidently go their own way: independent and autonomous versus cautious and conformist.

Factor II distinguishes between vacation workers and superiors (top and middle management), on the one hand, and subordinates (staff, catering, and attraction workers) on the other hand. Again, the technical department scores somewhere in the middle. In comparison to their subordinates, superiors have a self-assured, autonomous way of working, with one exception: Vacation workers are less insecure than staff or seasonal workers, probably because their job is just a sideline. These employees are relatively independent because of a position above (superiors) or somewhat outside the organization (vacation workers), whereas subordinates who are tied to the organization feel their boss breathing down their neck and find themselves confronted with rules and regulations, colleagues, and competitors. Therefore, they carefully stay in line.

To conclude, the dimensions of subcultures point at possible differences between the work climate among shop floor service workers and among white-collar office workers (open vs. closed and tight vs. loose) and between superiors and subordinates (independent and autonomous vs. cautious and conformist). The implications of these results for Hofstede et al.'s (1990) model will be discussed under Conclusions and Discussion. The critique will illustrate one part of the theoretical argument set out in the first two paragraphs: confronting and choosing between different perspectives. We cannot hold on to different views when they offer contradictory readings of reality.

The Established and the Outsiders: Qualitative Data

The dimensions found in the quantitative part of this study can serve as a preliminary sketch of some cultural characteristics of different groups in de Efteling. Despite the appealing simplicity of a description in terms of dimensions, the reality behind a dimension score comes alive only if we detect its meaning. Respondents are restricted to answer predefined questions that catch only a little of what actually moves people in everyday organizational life. The quantitative analysis provides a useful grip on a complex phenomenon such as organizational culture, but to get a broader and deeper understanding we need to turn to data from interviews and observations of daily routines, anniversaries, and meetings. To limit the scope of the research, I focused on the work situation among office employees who typified their workplace as both closed and loose.

Double Character of the Office Culture

The informal and often friendly manner of the office personnel gave the impression to some newcomers (including myself) of a very open organization.

People exchanged greetings rather jovially and had cozy chats in the corridors. They often left their door open; people could drop in any time they wanted. Once the door was closed, however, the "loose" conversation immediately turned confidential: "This must remain between us." It appeared there were busy under-cover communications that were considered to be somewhat illegal. People called it "gossiping," and participants adopted a conspirational tone in these conversations. This squabbling and babbling about one another fit a picture of a rather parochial culture in which work and private life are hard to keep separate. As one respondent stated, "Even if you remain distant, you're still subject of conversation. Your private life is an open secret."[3] The gossiping had considerable entertainment value; it was a break in the everyday routine. However, business matters as well as people were discussed. In these private conversations, ideas were considered, coalitions were formed, policies were set out, and actions were prepared. Clearly, this vital, informal communication circuit obscured decision processes. People often felt there were things going on that they had no grip on or knowledge of. They had to go by what their informants confided to them. This is why office employees found their workplace to be both loose and closed. The office culture was a curious combination of direct conversation and secrecy—a jovial attitude and repressed tensions.

Professionalization

In these confidential conversations, a new, hidden reality unfolded, revealing an ideological and political conflict among office personnel. The organization was involved in a transformation process that frequently gave rise to arguments. Roughly two antagonistic discourses could be detected—one more parochial and the other more professional. Parochial ideas could be heard in complaints about current changes, often accompanied by references to the past of the company that revealed a distinct pride of the organization's history and its founder, a highly respected Dutch popular artist. De Efteling started in the 1950s as a nonprofit organization strongly tied to the local community. A small group of dedicated laborers from the region, most of them semi- or unskilled, built a fairyland in the woods inspired by well-known fairy tales. An old-timer typified these workers as "flopped fish and chips sellers who wanted to try something new in life." He sketched their work as "making a quality product out of simple means, sitting between the trees." According to these stories, a hard-working attitude and a warm-hearted atmosphere among employees were typical for this period.

De Efteling became widely known in the country and attracted large crowds. In the late 1970s, it was decided to build new attractions because the number of visitors had stagnated. Some of these were characteristic of de Efteling, offering a fantasy world that appeals to the imagination. Other attractions, such as roller coasters, offered thrill and excitement to attract not only young children and their (grand)parents but also teenagers for whom fairy tales were boring. This was a successful policy; toward the end of the 1980s, the park started to draw more visitors than any other European amusement park (more than 2 million).

The rather rapid growth started a process of professionalization. The organization gradually grew into a commercial company and financial policy and personnel management (e.g., in relation to selection and dismissal procedures) became more businesslike. This process undermined traditional ideas and practices. The original ideology of offering fairy-tale amusement to visitors was turned into a commercial formula to sell fun to as many people as possible. Quality had to be weighed carefully against costs and benefits. The easy manner and pleasant work atmosphere were also put under strain and partly made way for a more stressful and businesslike way of working. The increased number of workers and visitors reinforced this process and made relations between people more impersonal.

Clash of Cultures

Parochial ideas and practices were personified by employees who won their spurs as staff and middle managers and during a lengthy period of service became one with de Efteling. They cherished romantic memories of the past: the shared passion for producing a quality product and the personal attention of the founder to his employees. They considered the commercialization a destruction of the corporation's cultural heritage. For them, it was like a closely knit Gemeinschaft turning into a loose Gesellschaft. Novelties such as a hotel and roller coasters were most positively seen as a necessary evil. The cool managerial pragmatism was at odds with the fairy tale of de Efteling. One of the members of the old guard portrayed his view of the demystification and prosaization in a sketch (see Figure 8.2). He added a quotation by the Austrian writer Karl Kraus: "When the sun of culture is low in the sky, even dwarfs cast long shadows."

The professional counterpart of these parochial craftsmen was a group of young and middle-aged financial, commercial, and personnel administrators. These highly educated professionals were seen as the representatives of the commercialization. They were selected mostly from outside the organization (and

Figure 8.2. Impression of the Office Culture Drawn by an Old-Timer

outside the region) to introduce a more pragmatic way of thinking within the company. Tales were told about these professional outsiders in which they were caricatured as rather dubious money-makers—for example, gossip about a manager's alleged fraud in his past as a businessman. In particular, the new board of directors (named "management team"), appointed a few years before and during my research, were identified with this new reality, especially after the symbolic act of doing away with the traditional (and expensive) personnel trip. They advocated well-known and widely accepted managerial values, such as cost consciousness, financial health, and further growth of the company, to be able to compete with Euro Disney. In line with these concerns, they were not as proud of the glorious past of de Efteling as of the record-breaking number of visitors of that year. For them, de Efteling was not a fairy tale. It was leisure industry.

The differences between the old guard and the new management team have so far been presented as a clear dichotomy, depicting the groups as each other's opposites. In fact, this black-and-white picture of parochials versus professionals was much more blurred. Managers adopted some of the parochial ideas and practices and were aware of the impact of traditional values, and seniors did see the necessity of professional management. One senior manager stated,

> For a long time I identified myself completely with Pieck's [the founder] view that there was no place for such modern things like a roller coaster. Until I started to see the import of the words of the then chairman of the board, who said, "I don't feel a damn for dying a beautiful death in this fine tradition." What he meant was that we would miss the boat, if we would hold on stringently to the values we so much cherished up till then.

Starting from their own parochial or professional perspective, both parties had some understanding for the other's position and arguments. Mutual understanding existed alongside mutual discontent and disagreements.

Conflicting Power Structures

The friction between the old guard and the new management team was not only a cultural question; it was both a conflict between contradictory ideologies and a clash of interests. Some seniors used to have a central position in top-level consultations within the company. The general manager at that time directly supervised 11 different departments. Every head of department had a personal connection with him. This simple structure worked well when the organization was small. It began to get inefficient when the organization grew in size and the 11 departments started to function like 11 separate islands. Toward the end of the 1980s, a new general manager was appointed who reorganized the company, structuring the organization in four staff departments (e.g., personnel, design, and development) and three (later four) line departments (technical, commercial, financial, and operational matters). New professional managers were brought in and put in charge of these four departments. Consequently, the old guard's position in the formal hierarchy changed profoundly. A new executive level was pushed between the general manager and these former heads of department, who were now called staff or middle managers. As a result, they lost considerable influence.

In the informal communication network, however, seniors kept a central position. They were frequently consulted because of their experience and expertise. New managers were generally left out of this informal circuit and they, in particular, experienced the organization as closed and secretive. The board of directors was dependent on the old guard's cooperation and had to take their opinions seriously into account (Willemier Westra, 1996). This was one of the reasons for setting up an advisory body for policy consultations—a monthly gathering of the board, staff managers, and a selection of senior staff members and middle managers. One old-timer, a skilled craftsman stashed away in the margin of the diagram of the new formal organization, was allowed to participate in top-level meetings in which company policy and cooperation problems were discussed. Apparently, formal leaders were not able to get around the old guard. Because of their technical skill and know-how, senior employees still enjoyed a high position in the informal hierarchy, comparable to the status of honorary members of a club (see Figure 8.3). The high position of the board of directors in the official hierarchy gave them formal authority. In the informal "club structure," however, they were not always entitled to speak, because here one was weighed by seniority and experience. Reactions were often rather reserved when these newfangled managers came up with new ideas and plans. Managers themselves indicated that they often felt misunderstood. In a way, it seemed they were considered candidates for membership in the club. Their ideas did not need to be taken too seriously yet.

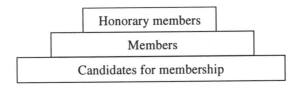

Figure 8.3. The Informal Club Structure

Not all office personnel fit into the black-and-white picture of professionals and parochials, honorary members, and candidates. Different office workers felt that they stood between the contending parties or completely out of the controversy and did not take a particular standpoint in the dispute. A rather young staff member serves as an example here. He was familiar with both professional and parochial ideas because his father was a retired honorary member of the Efteling club and he himself was a highly educated commercial professional. Therefore, he could switch easily between the two cultural programs—sometimes choosing sides and sometimes reluctant to choose—looking at things from both sides and putting them in perspective. Most of the office workers who had no pronounced professional or parochial opinion were young or middle-aged professionals just like this staff member. They contributed to a further professionalization, but at the same time they often sympathized with the parochial past. Most of them had no special position (high or low) in either the formal or the informal structure. Therefore, they were not forced to take sides nor were they held responsible for the ideas or actions of either of the two parties. They were the members of the club who could be partners with both parties because they could understand both sides. Their role was to interface with the two cultures. As far as their less pronounced opinions mattered to management or to the old guard, they created both a buffer between the two parties and a political playground. They could be the "floating votes" or the "cultural brokers" that either worsened or weakened the conflict.

To conclude, it appears that the cultural conflict between parochials and professionals was also a political clash between formal and informal authority. Two contradictory power structures ran parallel to the opposing ideologies of the old guard and the new professionals: the official hierarchy laid down in the organization chart and the informal club structure of honorary members, members, and candidates. Thus, ideological discussions had a clear political undertone and people's ideas were mixed with their personal interests. One party justified its opinions by pointing to experiences from the past, whereas the other bragged about current numbers (financial results and visitors). The professional subculture asserted widely accepted managerial values, such as profitability, further growth, and cost consciousness, that clearly transcended organizational boundaries (Alvesson, 1993). These ideas are largely taken for granted and carry a self-evident character that makes them hard to challenge. In this way, cultural ideas were used to support political interests. In this case, power and culture go hand in hand.

Certainly, no one case can be a model for all variations in professional-parochial relations in organizations. This situation, however, is probably not atypical of organizations entering into a midlife stage (see Schein, 1992, p. 254), involved in processes of ideological differentiation, or confronted with imported profes-sional subcultures or countercultural movements (Van Maanen & Barley, 1985). The case study of a mine factory administration by Gouldner (1954), for example, shows the same shift toward a more businesslike orientation with the entrance of a new manager and the same subsequent opposition of employees (see Chapter 6, this volume). A club structure model of the informal organization might well be recognized in other organizations such as in international firms and joint ventures. Wels's (1996) study of a Sino-Western joint venture in China describes a situation in which Western "outsiders" with high formal authority are confronted with an established informal order of Chinese managers. The Westerners noticed that some of their plans were never carried out because—as they found out—the Chinese managers held secret meetings in which Western decisions first had to be approved before they were executed. Smith and Eisenberg (1987) describe a conflict between management and employees of Disneyland in which shared symbols from the past were used strategically by both parties. Employees cherished the friendly, tight-knit family image of the organization. They remembered the founder of the company, Walt Disney, as a caring employer. The family image was supposed to be typical of his vision. Disneyland managers had a different interpretation of Disney's "philosophy." Confronted with financial problems due to the economic recession in the 1980s, they stressed the "business of show business." " 'Walt' knew how to make a buck"—he was a shrewd businessman who was selling a highly calculated fantasy world. Therefore, the visions of the organizational hero, the very symbol of the values and beliefs that were supposed to be widely shared in this "excellent" organization (Peters & Waterman, 1982), were interpreted differently by the two parties. This eventually led to a strike by the employees (Smith & Eisenberg, 1987, pp. 367-380).

Conclusions and Discussion

To obtain a good understanding of patterns and processes of integration, differentiation, and fragmentation in organizations, we need to look from all three perspectives simultaneously (Martin, 1992). The crucial question then is, Are the findings from different perspectives contradictory or complemen-tary? It was argued in the first section of this chapter that we should adopt a multiperspective approach that, in contrast with Martin's approach, confronts and combines unity, diversity, and ambiguity. The results presented here illustrate a multiperspective approach and provide some first answers to the question of how findings from different perspectives are related.

Confrontation

The factor analyses produced two dimensions, with one of them being a combination of two dimensions also found by Hofstede and colleagues (1990)— open versus closed and tight versus loose. The organization as a whole does not have an extreme mean score on these dimensions, suggesting the culture is neither open nor closed. In fact, this dimension draws a clear distinction between two groups within the organization: The culture appears to be open and closed. Consequently, these dimensions cannot describe the culture of the organization as a whole. It appears that we cannot a priori assume the six dimensions found by Hofstede and colleagues to be valid to describe the culture of an organization or any group of people because huge differences within the group (and thus a much more salient cultural reality) could be ignored.

The results in this example clearly contradict the assumption that the organization can be described as one cultural unit. The findings are incompatible with a view from an integration perspective. For a critical evaluation of a single perspective study, such as Hofstede et al.'s (1990), the results need to be put in another perspective. This may lead to confrontations typical of scientific debate between different views that have contradictory readings of reality. Of course, the quantitative results that have been presented here may be criticized in the same way. For example, an integration view may in turn be critical of its one-sidedness, drawing attention away from possible similarities within the organization. The study describes cultural differences while ignoring shared values and practices. The critique from the perspective of a fragmentist could relate to the stable, clear-cut character of the subcultures. Subcultures are presented almost as pieces of a mosaic, homogeneously colored, with hard, well-defined edges (Hannerz, 1992, p. 73). This does not add up to the often fragmented, fluctuating nature of cultural patterns. Apparently, the method that has been followed inevitably leads to a focus on diversity while ignoring unity and ambiguity.

Combination

The multiperspective approach that confronts and chooses between different views is familiar scientific practice. More complicated and less common in culture theory and research are combinations of different views. If ideas and findings from different perspectives are not mutually exclusive, a combination is the logical next step. In this way, we redirect our thinking from an "either-or" perspective to a "both-and" orientation.

The qualitative data support and offer some interesting clues for such an approach. The combination of unity and division was most obvious in the widespread habit of professing faith in the company. Both the parochial old-timers and the professional managers took a distinct pride in de Efteling's success. In different situations, members of both groups stated how wonderful it was to work for the company and praised the "club spirit." This could be understood as a sign of hidden tensions, denial of dissent, and "false consciousness" (Kunda as cited in Martin, 1992, p. 100). The club demanded full dedication of all members, whereas in fact its structure marked those who were insiders from those who were outsiders. I believe, however, that these statements were both false and true, both showing only one side of the picture. This is illustrated by the fact that all members felt they belonged to a unique organization—one group pointed to current results of the company to express their pride and the other group to its glorious past (see Smith & Eisenberg, 1987; Young, 1989).

Their being "together" and "opposed" at the same time is also reflected in the paradoxical combination of friendly chats in the corridors and secretive conversations: front-stage harmony and backstage conflict (Koot, 1996). The common (and possibly counterproductive) practice of banishing distrust and discord from the scene, pushing it behind closed doors, shows the same paradox in a more subtle manner. The friendly conversations in the corridors and the secretive way of dealing with conflicts clearly cut across cultural borderlines. Mutual communications and agreements between the groups existed next to miscommunications and disagreements. Members of both groups were opposed as old guard versus new professionals, top versus staff and middle management, and members versus nonmembers, but they were also colleagues who worked together in the same building for the same company, often with the same concerns, the same practices, and some common ideas and interests. Consequently, the group boundary was rather ambiguous. It existed in one way or at a certain time and was nonexistent in another way or at other times.[4]

These examples show that consensus and dissent and harmony and conflict do not exist separately but rather occur simultaneously or successively. If there is a close connection between convergent and divergent forces, processes of inclusion and exclusion, a question for future research could be how and in what circumstances are they interrelated. Clearly, this way of confronting and combining knowledge from different viewpoints and "exchanging partners" between perspectives enables us to draw a more comprehensive and coherent or maybe a complex and paradoxical picture of cultural reality. A multiperspective approach understood in this way can cut across old lines of thought and explore new ways of thinking about culture in organizations.

Notes

1. Consensus is one of the three defining features of these three perspectives. The other two features, consistency and clarity, are not considered here.

2. Formal relations, procedures, and rules are often connected with uncertainty and anxiety (e.g., Blau, 1955, p. 188). Bureaucracy provides something to hold on to. It releases people from their responsibility. They can do their job almost without thinking and can always appeal to "standard procedures." Hirschhorn (1988) argues that bureaucratic interventions function as a defense against feelings of anxiety aroused in the work situation. Rules and procedures are the materialization of people's fear of entering into confrontations and taking responsibility. The starting point of Kets de Vries and Miller's (1986) theory is also anxiety. They discuss different types of organizational cultures in the emotionally charged terminology of psychopathology. In the paranoid organization, extreme bureaucratization of work processes is justified by "dangers" in the environment of the organization.

3. In comparison to 20 organizational units in Hofstede et al.'s (1990) research, de Efteling had a low score on the parochial versus professional dimension—31 on a scale from 0 to 100, where the poles are the lowest and highest score in the sample of 20 organizational units. De Efteling employees paid less attention to competitors and did not think about the long term as much. They were more concerned with their work situation, their boss, and colleagues—with what happens inside de Efteling.

4. These combinations of consensus and dissent, which are rather unusual in organization theory and analysis, are elaborated theoretically and empirically in my contribution to a book on organizational paradoxes (Ybema, 1996).

Appendix

Results of Factor Analysis of Unit Group Scores on 25 Items

Factor/Item	Factor[a] I	II
I. Closed versus open		
44. We hardly ever attend meetings	.97	.10
12. One easily leaves the organization for a better job elsewhere	.96	−.17
42. Every day is more or less the same	.96	−.17
55. Departments are helpful to the company	.95	−.18
32. We don't talk much of the company's past	.94	.10
31. Meeting times are kept punctually	.92	.21
36. New employees quickly feel at home	.91	.01
35. Decisions are made by experts	.91	−.24
8. Always the same approved products/services are delivered	.91	−.15
15. Everybody is conscious of costs of time/material	.90	.29
9. Cooperation and trust between departments are normal	.88	.05
56. Conflicts are openly talked about	.87	−.15
47. People usually keep their promises	.85	.06
11. Contacts are mostly vocal	.82	−.07
49. New employees are easily accepted in the informal network	.77	−.04
59. Communication is very direct	.72	.10
30. Everyone fits in the organization	.66	.26
28. We are traditional in technology and working methods	.46	−.41
II. Autonomous versus conformist		
20. People worry about losing their job	−.16	.96
34. People are strongly aware of competition	.05	.91
33. Formal style of dealing with each other	.33	.80
45. There are many rules and procedures	.56	.66
61. You are on your own, if you make a mistake	−.39	.61
40. Pragmatic, not dogmatic in matters of ethics	.11	.60
64. I want to remain working for this company	−.47	.59

a. Items with negative loadings have been reworded negatively. The two factors together explain 75% of the variance.

References

Allen, V. L., Wilder, D. A., & Atkinson, M. L. (1983). Multiple group membership and social identity. In T. R. Sarbin & K. E. Scheibe (Eds.), *Studies in social identity.* New York: Praeger.

Alvesson, M. (1993). *Cultural perspectives on organizations.* Cambridge, UK: Cambridge University Press.

Barley, S. R., Meyer, G. W., & Gash, D. C. (1988). Cultures of culture: Academics, practitioners and the pragmatics of normative control. *Administrative Science Quarterly, 33,* 24-60.

Blau, P. M. (1955). *The dynamics of bureaucracy: A study of interpersonal relationships in two government agencies.* Chicago: University of Chicago Press.

Cohen, A. P. (1985). *The symbolic construction of community.* Chichester/London: Horwood/Tavistock.

Dalton, M. (1959). *Men who manage.* New York: John Wiley.

Deal, T. E., & Kennedy, A. A. (1982). *Corporate cultures: The rites and rituals of corporate life.* Reading, MA: Addison-Wesley.

Frost, P., Moore, L., Louis, M., Lundberg, C., & Martin, J. (Eds.). (1991). *Reframing organizational culture.* Newbury Park, CA: Sage.

Gouldner, A. W. (1954). *Patterns of industrial bureaucracy.* New York: Free Press.

Gregory, K. L. (1983). Native-view paradigms. Multiple cultures and culture conflicts in organizations. *Administrative Science Quarterly, 28,* 359-376.

Hannerz, U. (1992). *Cultural complexity: Studies in the social organization of meaning.* New York: Columbia University Press.

Hirschhorn, L. (1988). *The workplace within: Psychodynamics of organizational life.* Cambridge, MA: MIT Press.

Hofstede, G. H. (1980). *Culture's consequences: International differences in work-related values.* Beverly Hills, CA: Sage.

Hofstede, G. H., Bond, M. H., & Luk, C. (1993). Individual perceptions of organizational cultures: A methodological treatise on levels of analysis. *Organization Studies, 14*(4), 483-503.

Hofstede, G. H., Neuijen, B., Ohayiv, D. D., & Sanders, G. (1990). Measuring organizational cultures. *Administrative Science Quarterly, 35,* 286-316.

Homans, G. C. (1950). *The human group.* New York: Harcourt, Brace & World.

Jones, M. O. (1988). In search of meaning: Using qualitative methods in research and application. In M. O. Jones, M. D. Moore, & R. C. Snyder (Eds.), *Inside organizations: Understanding the human dimension* (pp. 31-48). Newbury Park, CA: Sage.

Kertzer, D. I. (1988). *Ritual, politics and power.* New Haven, CT: Yale University Press.

Kets de Vries, M. F. R., & Miller, D. (1986). *The neurotic organization.* San Francisco: Jossey-Bass.

Koot, W. (1996). The rhetoric of synergy and the practice of increasing ethnic rivalry in organizations. In W. Koot, I. Sabelis, & S. Ybema (Eds.), *Contradictions in context: Puzzling over paradoxes in contemporary organizations* (pp. 63-86). Amsterdam: VU University Press.

Langeard, E. (1980). Service marketing: State of the art. *Marketing, 10,* 16-29.

Louis, M. R. (1985). Organizations as culture-bearing milieus. In P. J. Frost, L. F. Moore, M. R. Louis, C. C. Lundberg, & J. Martin (Eds.), *Organizational culture* (pp. 73-93). Beverly Hills, CA: Sage.

Lucas, R. (1987). Political-cultural analysis of organizations. *Academy of Management Review, 12,* 144-156.

Martin, J. (1990). Breaking up the mono-method monopolies in organizational analysis. In J. Hassard & D. Pym (Eds.), *The theory and philosophy of organizations: Critical issues and new perspectives* (pp. 30-43). London: Routledge.

Martin, J. (1992). *Cultures in organizations: Three perspectives.* New York: Oxford University Press.

Martin, J., & Siehl, C. (1983). Organizational culture and counterculture: An uneasy symbiosis. *Organizational Dynamics, 12,* 52-64.

Meyerson, D., & Martin, J. (1987). Cultural change: An integration of three different views. *Journal of Management Studies, 24,* 623-647.

Morey, N., & Luthans, F. (1985). Refining the concept of culture and the use of scenes and themes in organizational studies. *Academy of Management Review, 10,* 219-229.

Ouchi, W. G. (1981). *Theory Z: How American business can meet the Japanese challenge.* Reading, MA: Addison-Wesley.

Peters, T. J., & Waterman, R. H. (1982). *In search of excellence.* New York: Harper & Row.

Reiches, A. E., & Schneider, B. (1990). Climate and culture: An evolution of constructs. In B. Schneider (Ed.), *Organizational climate and culture.* San Francisco: Jossey-Bass.

Riley, P. (1983). A structurationist account of political cultures. *Administrative Science Quarterly, 28,* 414-437.

Rosen, M. (1986). Some notes from the field: On ethnography and organizational science. *Dragon, 6,* 57-67.

Rousseau, D. M. (1990). Assessing organizational culture: The case for multiple methods. In B. Schneider (Ed.), *Organizational climate and culture.* San Francisco: Jossey-Bass.

Sackmann, S. A. (1992). Culture and subcultures: An analysis of organizational knowledge. *Administrative Science Quarterly, 37,* 140-161.

Schein, E. H. (1992). *Organizational culture and leadership* (2nd ed.). San Francisco: Jossey-Bass.

Selznick, P. (1949). *TVA and the grass roots: A study in the sociology of formal organizations.* Berkeley: University of California Press.

Smith, R. C., & Eisenberg, E. M. (1987). Conflict at Disneyland: A root-metaphor analysis. *Communication Monographs, 54,* 367-380.

Swanborn, P. G. (1984). *Methoden van sociaal-wetenschappelijk onderzoek: Inleiding in ontwerp strategieèn* [Methods of social-scientific research: Introduction in design strategies]. Meppel: Boom. (Original work published 1981)

Trice, H., & Beyer, J. (1993). *The cultures of work organizations.* Englewood Cliffs, NJ: Prentice Hall.

Van Maanen, J. (1979). The fact of fiction in organizational ethnography. *Administrative Science Quarterly, 24,* 539-550.

Van Maanen, J. (1983). *Qualitative methodology.* Beverly Hills, CA: Sage.

Van Maanen, J. (1988). *Tales of the field: On writing ethnography.* Chicago: University of Chicago Press.

Van Maanen, J., & Barley, S. R. (1985). Cultural organization: Fragments of a theory. In P. J. Frost, L. F. Moore, M. R. Louis, C. C. Lundberg, & J. Martin (Eds.), *Organizational culture* (pp. 31-53). Beverly Hills, CA: Sage.

Wels, H. (1996). Strategy as paradox and paradox as strategy: Images of and paradoxes in Chinese culture: Expatriate managers in Sino-Western joint ventures. In W. Koot, I. Sabelis, & S. Ybema (Eds.), *Contradictions in context: Puzzling over paradoxes in contemporary organizations* (pp. 133-150). Amsterdam: VU University Press.

Whyte, W. F. (1948). *Human relations in the restaurant industry.* New York: McGraw-Hill.

Willemier Westra, A. W. (1996). Between contrariness and complaisance: The paradox of power: About tools of upward influence in the Netherlands. In W. Koot, I. Sabelis, & S. Ybema (Eds.), *Contradictions in context: Puzzling over paradoxes in contemporary organizations* (pp. 151-170). Amsterdam: VU University Press.

Ybema, S. B. (1996). A duck-billed platypus in the theory and analysis of organizations: Combinations of consensus and dissensus. In W. Koot, I. Sabelis, & S. Ybema (Eds.), *Contradictions in context: Puzzling over paradoxes in contemporary organizations* (pp. 39-62). Amsterdam: VU University Press.

Young, E. (1989). On the naming of the rose: Interests and multiple meanings as elements of organizational culture. *Organization Studies, 10*(2), 187-206.

Chapter 9

Inside Hewlett-Packard

Corporate Culture and Bureaucratic Control

Patrick McGovern
Veronica Hope-Hailey

Corporate culture was one of the most fashionable of management topics in the 1980s. Much of the interest in the subject was inspired by the central role that it occupied in best-selling books by Peters and Waterman (1982), Deal and Kennedy (1982), and William Ouchi (1981), among others. This management-oriented literature, which described and promoted the role of organizational culture in corporate success, was based on a mixture of personal impressions and experiences, company documentation, and occasional interviews drawn from a sample of highly successful companies. Although the quality of the research behind these

We thank the managers and staff of Hewlett-Packard (especially the human resources department) for their participation in this research; The Leading Edge Forum—including Arthur D. Little—for funding the research; our colleagues on the project—Lynda Gratton, Philip Stiles, and Katie Truss; and finally the participants of the EGOS 1995 conference on "Cultural Complexity in Organizations" for their comments on an earlier version of this chapter. Quotations from *The HP Way: How Bill Hewlett and I Built Our Company,* by David Packard, are used with permission.

books has been challenged (e.g., Guest, 1992; Hitt & Ireland, 1987), the companies named in these texts have assumed something approaching the status of icons in management discourse because they are so frequently cited as exemplars of corporate culture and of "excellence" in action.

This chapter is based on research into one of these organizations—Hewlett-Packard (HP). Hewlett-Packard is one of the world's leading manufacturers of computer systems and peripheral equipment, electronic test and measurement equipment, electronic components, medical electronic equipment, instruments for chemical analysis, and hand-held calculators. One of the remarkable features about HP is that although much has been written about it, little has been based on actual research inside the company or, if it was, it did not use the name Hewlett-Packard when published. The primary goal of this chapter is to show that some of the popular representations of this company have oversimplified the nature and significance of its culture.[1]

We draw on empirical research into HP that covers two areas. The first concerns the introduction of a recent "downsizing" program by the company and employee responses to what was apparently the destruction of one of the central tenets of the corporate philosophy: jobs for life. The second area covers HP's planning, work organization, and performance management policies. The focus on HP's culture in the popular management discourse has meant that these areas of management practice have traditionally been underplayed in accounts of the success of this leading U.S. multinational corporation. We argue, contrary to this view, that HP's ability to formulate and implement a battery of planning, work control, and performance measures should be given greater significance. This does not mean that workplace rules and procedures—what Edwards (1979) has termed bureaucratic control—are more important than corporate culture. Rather, we draw attention to the continuing role played by bureaucratic control in the context of a corporate culture by showing how the two exist as a combination within a corporation such as HP.

The chapter is structured as follows. We begin by examining the prescriptive literature on corporate culture before moving on to a consideration of the sociological literature that seeks to analyze corporate culture as a form of labor control. Next, we provide an account of HP that draws on the popular management literature before describing the research methodology employed in this study. The rest of the chapter contains findings from our in-depth research into a division of HP based in the United Kingdom.

Corporate Culture: Traits and Strength

The general message of the corporate culture literature is that the culture of an organization—its values, beliefs, ethos, and way of doing things—influences its performance and, furthermore, that this culture can be actively manipulated by management. The message also has a prescriptive element, if not always a practical one (Guest, 1992). The organization's culture can be manipulated (e.g., through a change in management style and the use of mission statements) so that management come to believe in profitability through people, employees came to believe in the value of being close to the customer, and the search for excellence becomes both a shared challenge and the means of boosting corporate profitability.

One of the more common assumptions in this literature is that if culture is to contribute to performance then it must possess distinctive "traits" and be "strong" in nature. This line of argument can be found in at least three of the most widely known best-sellers on this subject. For the authors of *In Search of Excellence* (Peters & Waterman, 1982), the traits include a deeply ingrained people-oriented philosophy that is summarized as "respect the individual." This, combined with an apparent lack of rigid chains of command, helps to produce a sense of family feeling within the organization. All these traits are, according to Peters and Waterman, part of a highly successful business philosophy of generating "productivity through people."

The distinguishing traits of Ouchi's (1981) *Theory Z* firm are that the organization and its culture are homogenous in nature and the organization provides secure employment (no layoffs) and encourages collective decision making. Overall, Ouchi claims that they behave more like a clan than a market, or bureaucracy, in that they do not resort to price mechanisms or close monitoring to govern behavior. Clans are superior to markets or bureaucracies in that they are able to control behavior in situations of high uncertainty and complexity because employees have been socialized to do what is in the firm's best interests.

Finally, the traits listed by Deal and Kennedy (1982) include organizational heroes (usually the company founders), a widely shared set of values that emphasize the importance of people, and a variety of stories, rituals, and ceremonies that are specific to the organization. They also claim that companies with strong cultures, where "everyone knows the goals of the corporation, and they are working for them" (p. 4), perform better than companies with weak cultures in which employee goals are either fragmented or divergent from those of management.

Finally, one of the most notable features of the prescriptive literature is the focus on corporate culture to the point where other forms of labor control have been ignored or judged to be of little value within "strong cultures." This tendency is possibly a consequence of the need to simplify and package the culture message (e.g., lists of traits, etc.) to sell it to a managerial audience.

Corporate Culture as a Form of Labor Control

Much of the sociological literature on the subject of corporate culture is concerned with its use as a management tool for maintaining control over employees while simultaneously increasing their commitment. Some of the major contributions in this area have argued that corporate culture is being used as a means of generating normative control over employees as their hearts and minds become sites for corporate influence (e.g., Casey, 1995; Kunda, 1992; Ray, 1986; Willmott, 1993). It should be noted that the focus on culture as a means of control over employees is not just of academic concern because this usage has also been made explicit in the "pop" management literature. Peters and Waterman (1982), for example, claim that a strong corporate culture acts as a control over individual behavior, thus allowing for considerable individual discretion without any concomitant cost to the company.

We make two points in relation to the arguments about corporate culture as a form of labor control. These relate to its origins and limitations. First, there is a tendency to interpret corporate culture as the solution to what is perceived to be a crisis in existing forms of labor management (Ray, 1986) or as a response to the dissolution of traditional and modern bonds of social solidarity brought about by the postindustrial age (Casey, 1995).

Ray's (1986) argument is that the manipulation of a corporation's culture has emerged as the latest and most powerful form of control following crises in bureaucratic and humanistic forms of control. According to Edwards (1979), the workplaces of the United States have been transformed since the start of the 20th century. Corporations in the United States adopted bureaucratic forms of control following earlier experiences with control through direct supervision (simple control) and through assembly line systems that established the pace of work (technical control). The bureaucratic form of labor management consisted of elaborate formal procedures for recruitment, remuneration, promotion, and discipline, with the result that corporate employees are now managed through policies rather than through the whims of supervisors. Ray argues that this form of employee management, in turn, was superseded by humanistic forms of control derived from the human relations school (see Mayo, 1949). These typically included job enrichment, job enlargement, and job rotation plans. Ray claims, however, that this approach was also limited because it could not elicit the moral commitment of employees to the organization and its goals. Corporate culture, in her view, is potentially a much more powerful form of employee management precisely because it seeks to foster and capture their moral commitment.

Casey (1995, p. 5), in her analysis of the impact of changes in work on self-formation, contends that the advent of deliberately designed corporate cultures is a phenomenon of the postindustrial age. These "designer" cultures have emerged, in her view, in response to a broad crisis in the industrial production, work organization, and culture of modern society. She stresses that employees have not been "duped" by such cultures. Rather, "they have been *reasonably* convinced of the merits of organizational reforms and affectively attracted to the ethos of familial caring and belonging not offered by typical industrial companies" (p. 135).

The second point we make is that the actual effectiveness of corporate culture as a management tool has not been as impressive as might be expected from popular management texts. A number of writers have, for instance, pointed out inherent contradictions in the nature of organizational change and the limited potential for the achievement of uniform corporate cultures (e.g., Willmott, 1993).

These indicate that attempts to impose desirable cultures in a top-down fashion by senior managers often fail. The paradox is that a cultural change process often works in the opposite direction to the values it is trying to inculcate. This is particularly apparent when cultural values statements contain terms such as *innovation* or *empowerment,* but are inculcated using top-down communication systems, bureaucratic controls, or organizationwide planned interventions (Hope & Hendry, 1995). Beer, Eisenstat, and Spector (1990) have reported on research that shows that those very companies that tried to impose cultural change of this kind often fail. Instead, they suggest that this form of change should be allowed to emerge in an organic fashion on the periphery of organizations.

There is also evidence that points to important cultural differences within organizations—between divisions, departments, staff groupings, and national operations—and also demonstrates that attempts to impose uniformity on these subcultures are often counterproductive (Hofstede, 1991; Kunda, 1992; Lawrence & Lorsch, 1967). Research from the United States by Kotter and Heskett (1992) found that even when a strong culture does exist, it does not always lead to a competitive advantage and may even hinder, or hold back, those who perform poorly. The pressures for conformity can stifle individual initiative, even if this is also espoused as a value underpinning the culture (Hope, 1990). Furthermore, research conducted by one of the authors of this chapter on three "heuristic" models of culture (paternalism, bureaucracy, and human resource management [HRM]) and their forms of people management showed that intuitively held forms of paternalistic culture were far stronger in gaining staff commitment than purposefully managed corporate cultures under HRM models (Hope, 1993).

The limitations of corporate culture are even more convincingly demonstrated by evidence that shows that employees who are subjected to designer cultures do not become cultural dupes or clones. Whittington (1992) and Kunda (1992), for instance, have pointed to the importance of human agency in reinterpreting and reenacting corporate cultures. Kunda, in his study of culture as a form of normative control at "Tech," suggests that the interplay between culture and human agency, or self, may be somewhat more complex than that suggested by prescriptive management texts. He found that staff at the company were engaged in a complex negotiation between themselves as "selves" and the organization. Their loyalty, allegiance, and commitment to the organization were strongly influenced by their sense of self. This meant that, in some cases, their responses were actually the direct opposite to what management had intended.

Finally, it can be argued, contrary to Casey (1995), that recent changes in the world of work have undermined rather than contributed to the role of corporate cultures. For example, many of the major multinational corporations have, through delayering and restructuring, moved toward project working and multifunctional groups that rely heavily on "professional knowledge workers" (Drucker, 1992). There are now numerous examples in which vertical lines of control and career paths are giving way to horizontal peer networks and authority to expertise (Kanter, 1989). The so-called knowledge workers who will flourish in these new organizations may perhaps be those least open to cultural manipulation because they seek to build their careers along "cosmopolitan" rather than "local" lines (Gouldner, 1957). Moreover, those organizations that have implemented redundancy programs may well be left with a cynical and demoralized staff (McGovern, Hope-Hailey, & Stiles, 1995) who respond sarcastically to calls for extra commitment (Hendry & Hope, 1994; Hope, 1993).

Despite these limitations, the theoretical and empirical case for treating corporate culture as a form of labor control is well established. We believe that it can and should be examined alongside other forms of employee management, especially when its value as a management tool has been challenged and when one of the conditions conducive to its existence—job security—has been dramatically weakened. There is, we argue, a need to do this because many of the studies which have examined its controlling aspects (e.g., Kunda, 1992; Casey, 1995) tended to focus almost exclusively on cultural control without reference to other forms of workforce management. Others, such as Ray (1986) and Casey (1995), have done so because they believe that corporate culture has supplanted what are deemed to be less effective forms of labor control.[2] Moreover, if we assume that corporate culture in a multinational firm may vary across different national contexts, then the need to investigate other forms of labor control alongside that of corporate culture is of even greater importance if we are to understand how the workforce is managed. Given these reasons, a case study of one of the original strong-culture companies should prove to be a useful starting point.

Hewlett-Packard

Best-Selling Image

The management style and culture of Hewlett-Packard became famous after they were featured in the two major management best-sellers of the early 1980s by Ouchi (1981) and Peters and Waterman (1982). The popular image of this organization was further shaped by Deal and Kennedy's (1988) book on corporate cultures, by case studies written for master's degree teaching purposes (Mintzberg & Quinn, 1991; von Werssowetz & Beer, 1982), and by David Packard's (1995) account of his years with the company he helped to create. In addition, there are numerous newspaper and magazine stories (e.g., "Britain's Non-Union Leaders," 1980) that add to the image. The overall picture is one of a corporation that was created by two remarkable cofounders who have now come to hold the status of corporate heroes (Deal & Kennedy, 1982, p. 38). The founding heroes, Bill Hewlett and David Packard, established a reputation for hands-on management and created a set of practices that grew up around the company. These included ad hoc informal meetings, along with ritual "beer busts" and "coffee klatches." There are many widely known stories about the founders—such as how "Bill and Dave" founded the company in a garage, and how on one Saturday afternoon Bill Hewlett visited a plant and, on finding the lab stock area locked, cut the padlock and left a note saying "Don't ever lock this door again. Thanks Bill." The company that they created also became famous for its strong sense of team commitment allied to a philosophy of innovation through people. Peters and Waterman (1982, pp. 243-246) reinforced this picture when they judged it to be an excellent company with a people-oriented philosophy (see Peters, 1985).

The most famous aspect of the company's approach to management is the "HP Way" (especially the "People Related" section; Figure 9.1), which stated the company's basic values and philosophy. These objectives, which were first put in writing in 1957, are credited within the company as the basis for its success and strong sense of employee loyalty.

The HP Way, along with the company's products, has come to represent what Hewlett-Packard stands for across the globe. Many writers and academics have used the HP Way as a crude explanation of the culture, and even of the success, of this organization (Levering, Moskowitz, & Katz, 1984; Mintzberg & Quinn, 1986; Ouchi, 1981; Peters & Waterman, 1982; Reynolds, 1989; von Werssowetz & Beer, 1982). Given this level of exposure—and indeed glorification—HP has come to represent one of the classic archetypes of corporate culture even though none of these accounts is actually based on any kind of detailed research inside the company.

Recent History

Hewlett-Packard had grown at least ten-fold by the late 1980s before it encountered its first major slump in performance. Like its competitors, HP faced the same difficulties brought on by increased competition, sluggish markets, decreasing profitability, and a declining stock market valuation. Despite these circumstances, the group still managed to record a 41% rise in first-quarter net profits by February 1994. Furthermore, in 1993 the U.K. subsidiary increased their turnover by 43%, generating profits of $85 million compared with a break-even position in 1992.

A number of factors appear to have contributed to this turnaround, including market changes, new product launches, and cost-cutting measures. The most dramatic change, however, was to the organization structure. Advisers urged that the company, which had originally been started by entrepreneurial engineers, had become too centralized. In addition, new ideas were being squashed if they appeared too unorthodox. Hewlett-Packard's response was to return to a decentral-

---

The HP Way

People Related

1. *Beliefs* in our people
   - Confidence in, and respect for, our people as opposed to depending upon extensive rules, procedures, etc.
   - Depend upon people to do their job right (individual freedom) without constant directives.
   - Opportunity for meaningful participation (job dignity).

2. Emphasis on working *together* and *sharing* rewards (teamwork and partnership)
   - Share responsibilities; help each other, learn from each other; chance to make mistakes.
   - Recognition based on contribution results—sense of achievement and self-esteem.
   - Profit sharing stock purchase plan, retirement program, etc.; aimed at employees and company sharing in each other's successes.

3. A *superior* work environment which other companies seek but few achieve
   - Informality—open, honest, communications; no artificial distinction between employees (first-name basis); management by walking around; and open door communication policy.
   - Develop and promote from within—lifetime training, education, career counseling to help employees get maximum opportunity to grow and develop with the company.
   - Decentralization—emphasis on keeping work groups as small as possible for maximum employee identification with our business and customers.

Figure 9.1. The "People Related" Excerpt From the HP Way (From The Hewlett-Packard Company)

ized structure that gave freedom back to the individual business units (Packard, 1995, pp. 148-151). The result was impressive. In the United Kingdom, for example, one HP division was able to expand rapidly and capture a significant proportion of a new product market.

In addition to decentralizing, the company also implemented a number of other changes, one of the most controversial being the voluntary severance program with several thousand people being "released" from the company. This was the first such program HP had ever introduced. It was targeted at the middle-management level with the aim, as in all delayering exercises, of reducing the number of managerial levels between the bottom and top of the organization. It was not, however, the number of those released that proved controversial. Many HP employees had come to assume that the company offered "jobs for life." The basis for this assumption probably started with HP's previous efforts to avoid layoffs on occasions, a practice that was generally interpreted to be part of a no layoff policy and reported as such ("The Corporate," 1985; Levering et al., 1984; "The No Lay-Off," 1985). The shattering of this assumption led some employees, as we shall see, to question the weight that the corporation now placed on its values.

Research Methods

The research conducted at HP is part of a 5-year research project that was commissioned by a consortium of 14 major British-based firms that are collectively known as the Leading Edge Forum Ltd. This project examines human resource strategies, policies, and procedures and their implementation by senior, line, and general managers (Truss & Gratton, 1994). A particular focus of the research is the relationship between the informal organization and human resource management in practice. Interest in HP's culture in the aftermath of job losses, and the way it contrasted with the best-selling perceptions of it, emerged in the course of our fieldwork within this organization.

This research was based within the U.K. head office of HP, which is located in the south of England. The head office consists of 1,600 white-collar employees, none of whom are trade union members. The U.K. operations comprise a field operations management team and three other divisions based within other offices in Britain. There is a board of directors for the U.K. division, although the main managing body is an executive council. The corporation as a whole employs a staff of 96,200 worldwide, of which 20,200 are employed within Europe as a whole and

5,000 within the United Kingdom. The U.K. operations account for 11% of international orders.

The empirical material, which was collected between January and March 1994, was gathered through qualitative and quantitative methods. These included a focus group, semistructured interviews with employees at all levels, 12 "unwritten rules," interviews, and a questionnaire survey. Out of the total of 36 interviews held with members of the Customer Support Centre and the Computer Systems Organization, 12 were conducted with middle managers from the Computer Systems Organization using a methodology called "The Unwritten Rules of the Game." This was developed by Peter Scott-Morgan (1994) at the A. D. Little consultancy, another sponsor of the research. The design of this methodology is such that, with some modification, it was possible to use it as another qualitative research method (McGovern, 1995).

A total of 400 questionnaires were distributed to randomly selected employees in the entire head office staff. Two hundred fifteen questionnaires were completed and returned, giving a response rate of 56%. The widely used organizational commitment questionnaire (OCQ), developed and validated by Mowday, Steers, and Porter (1979), was among the items included in the questionnaire schedule. This consists of 15 items that seek information on the employee's loyalty to, identification with, and willingness to exert effort on behalf of the company's goals.

The material reported here is drawn primarily from the "unwritten rules" interviews with managers (whose names and titles have been changed) and from the section of the survey instrument that examined organizational commitment among all employees in addition to some other items.

Downsizing: A Cultural Crisis?

Although many employees had assumed that HP had formally made a commitment to lifetime employment, this had never actually been explicitly stated by HP. Nor does it appear in the original HP Way. Therefore, when faced with difficult decisions about downsizing in 1992 in the wake of the economic downturn, it was possible for senior management to successfully remind staff of the historical emphasis on business performance and management by objectives. Senior managers who we interviewed described the arguments they used as follows:

> The HP Way is respect for the individual, but they have to deliver results. This is not a holiday camp. We do a lot of things to create a positive environment for our people to succeed. People forget the "having to succeed" part and can confuse some of the downside of not succeeding with an abandonment of the Hewlett-Packard Way. . . . You can't grow and make a profit by just being nice to people. (senior executive)

Another stated, "The Hewlett-Packard Way is not jobs for life. It's jobs for performers. . . . We're a business, not a philanthropic enterprise" (Fred, Technical Applications Manager).

One of the personnel officers did admit that the company was changing its policy but without rupturing any previous commitments. It was, in her words, "moving from guaranteed employment to guaranteed employability." This meant that HP would continue to help employees to develop their skills and expertise but it could not guarantee that such skills would always be required within HP. They could, however, be sold elsewhere.

Although senior management insisted that it was not reneging on any commitments, many of the staff were shaken up by the layoffs. Interviews revealed that changes had occurred in the implicit psychological contract with the company. One manager, George, stated that the "long-timers," in particular, who had devoted many years to the company "took it badly." He has now come to the view that the HP Way works only when the company is successful. Others held a similar view. Hewlett-Packard would never be quite the same people-oriented company again because it had become more "realistic" and "hardened up": "HP has hardened up a lot. It's difficult to have core values when you are getting rid of people. There is an underlying nervousness. We're OK now but who knows tomorrow" (Linda, Sales Manager); "HP is like any other company when the chips are down. We needed the dose of realism. You can't have that [the HP Way] unless you bring in revenue" (Ernie, Marketing Manager).

Some employees had a crisis of faith in relation to HP's supposed values and noted that the "huge uncertainty" that had appeared with the delayering "lingers on," having "left scars." It still remained after the redundancies even though the company had begun to perform quite well. Among the "scars" left in the organization was a reduction in the number of promotion possibilities on the managerial ladder. Promotion would now be more infrequent and involve greater increases in responsibility than before. Managers also had to deal with wider spans of control in the new structure, which meant that larger numbers of staff now reported directly to them. Meanwhile, the company was expanding its market share. To illustrate the impact of downsizing within HP United Kingdom, one manager described the effects on his department as follows: "Three or four years ago there were 34 managers in this group. Now there are only eight managers with a business three times the size" (Linda, Sales Manager).

The increased workload had consequences for the division between work and family life. Many had to work longer and longer hours. Some managers admitted in the course of the interviews that they were having difficulty in coping with the loss of time with their families. A few others also stated that they were having stress problems.

Despite the negative impact of the delayering exercise, HP staff still retain a relatively high level of commitment toward the organization. This was most clearly expressed in the survey evidence on organizational commitment. In comparison to the other organizations that participated in this research, the summary indicator for organizational commitment in HP (4.6) was significantly higher than that for any of the other organizations (ranging from 3.4 down to 2.4).[3] Furthermore, HP's managers did not have a lower level of organizational commitment than nonman-agerial staff even though it was primarily management jobs that were made redundant. When the evidence is disaggregated to the level of individual question-naire items, we found that 85% of the respondents strongly agreed or agreed with the statement that they "talk up this organization to my friends as a great place to work," 87% strongly agreed or agreed that they really "care about the fate of this organization," 73% strongly disagreed or disagreed with the statement that "it would take very little change in my present circumstances to cause me to leave," whereas 92% strongly agreed or agreed that still they "are willing to put in a great deal of effort beyond that normally expected in order to help this organization be successful."

Employees also expressed positive views on the people-oriented culture of the organization in the course of the interviews. Although many of these acknowl-edged that they had doubts, or that it would never be quite the same after the recent upheaval, they still judged HP to be a "damn good place to work." This was summed up by the following comment from a sales executive: "It's very good from a people point of view. It still is though I doubted it for a while" (John, Sales Executive).

Interestingly, more than a few also spoke of the way HP's values aligned or fitted with their own. This sense of moral commitment, of employees who give of their "hearts and minds," corresponds with the images of HP found in the popular management texts: "It's my choice to be here. The core values are outstanding and there is a re-emergence of the belief in people" (Linda, Sales Manager); "There is an alignment between the core values and mine. You're not here to be rich but to be satisfied" (Fred, Technical Applications Manager); "The difference is the culture. It's very professional and very straight. I love it. I fit the culture and it fits me" (Julie, Marketing Executive).

With growth occurring again in the early 1990s, senior management is leading a revival of the "Hewlett-Packard Way" and has publicly declared that there has been too much deviation from the original creed. It is, however, unclear to what extent it is a complete return to the ideals of 1957 and how much of these have had to be sacrificed *de facto* because of the demands of the marketplace. Still, it would appear that HP has weathered the crisis with most of its culture and traditions intact, at least for those who remain with the company. Its ability to survive, despite the removal of what some believed to be a core corporate value, is indicative of the attraction of employees to the culture of this organization and the control that it is consequently able to exert over them.

Performance Management: The Hewlett-Packard Way

Given the traditional focus on the HP culture, the most surprising finding was the prominence of elaborate policies and procedures for business planning, work organization, and human resource management. The prevalence and sophistication of such policies has never been discussed in the existing literature on HP. We were informed that these reflect the engineering and systems culture of the company, which in turn is molded by top management who virtually all have a technical background.

The formality of these processes meant that the planning process, for instance, could be described precisely from the corporate headquarter level down to U.K. business units and through to the personal objectives of individual members of staff. The company states that the reason for this close attention to detail is paradoxically the promotion of individual freedom, innovation, and entrepreneurial spirit. As one of the original founders, Dave Packard (as quoted in von Werssowetz & Beer, 1982), has frequently explained:

Early in the history of the company, whilst thinking about how a company like this should be managed, I kept getting back to one concept: if we could simply get everybody to agree on what our objectives were and to understand what we were trying to do, then we could turn everybody loose and they would move along in a common direction. (p. 3)

Thus, individuals have their personal objectives defined for them but the actual process by which they achieve those objectives, in terms of innovative activity or specific behavior, is formally left undefined. So how are these objectives defined?

There are three main planning processes conducted at a corporate level: the "Ten Step Approach," which consists of a long-range plan and an annual plan. The annual plan is made up of two components. One of these identifies areas that need immediate and substantial attention because they are critical for immediate business success. These are called "breakthrough" areas. The other area in the annual plan focuses on the daily management of the business and the key process measures. In all these planning exercises, human resource issues are included alongside commercial factors. Therefore, for instance, one of the Business Fundamentals for 1995 is that all performance evaluations should be received on time. This is not seen as a Human Resources initiative but rather as a business initiative.

At an individual level, HP also uses a variety of mechanisms to plan, monitor, and assess individual performance: performance evaluation, ranking, and self-development plans. As one sales manager explained,

There are three key measures: quota, costs and how you lead your people. Without that your unit can't perform. . . . All are equally important. You can succeed on quota and not people but in the long term you have got to get the balance between all three. (Steve, Sales Manager)

The documentation for all these processes stresses measures for success. In recent years, one of the many planning and monitoring devices to be developed is "Framework," a tool that means that an employee's principal duties are clearly defined. Business Fundamentals drive the roles that are carried out:

They are linked to the Business Fundamentals of the Business Unit, thus ensuring that an individual understands the goals of the unit in which they work and how their performance is measured against the success of their contribution to achieving those Business Fundamentals. (extract from the "How to Use Framework" guide)

Arising from this, each employee has Key Result Areas that prioritize those objectives that are considered to be of most importance to the business at any given point in time.

The emphasis placed on people and people management is also formally institutionalized into the work of managers as one of their Business Fundamentals. Those managers who have employees reporting to them must conduct regular performance evaluations for their staff. These formal discussions include not only the employees' actual performance on the job but also their training and career needs. This activity is not viewed as simply another piece of bureaucratic red tape that can be ignored. It is included in managers' performance evaluations and is subsequently reflected in their performance-related pay. In other words, "HP takes PEs seriously. We are measured on it. It goes on your file and follows you around. The CSO director does read them all. We have to do them" (Alan, Marketing Accounts Manager), and "Those who don't [take them seriously] do eventually get found out and it affects their own ranking. . . . The management commitment is absolute at the highest level" (David, Marketing Executive).

These procedures are clearly the result of strong rationalizing tendencies within the company culture. One training manager commented, "If something goes wrong, we tend to blame the system rather than the individual—we're engineers after all." The institutional emphasis that is placed on work outputs and on making the links between individual performance and corporate performance transparent highlighted, what was for us, one of the most prominent although unsung features of the culture of this organization: the preoccupation with measurement. One employee claimed that this was actually one of the defining features of HP's corporate culture: "We're a measurement culture. If it moves we measure it. It's not only a performance driven company, it's a measurement culture" (Dennis, Technical Services).

How are these various planning processes viewed by staff? Those who were interviewed responded very favorably. For example, "The whole structure of the way we are measured gets to the heart of the business" (Alan, Marketing Accounts Manager).

Another manager, who had worked in other companies, considered the pay for performance policy to be the best he had witnessed anywhere. He stated, "They have a better process of doing it [paying for performance] well than I've seen anywhere else" (Alan, Marketing Executive).

More generally, the questionnaire results indicate that HP employees believe that the company has a strong sense of direction and that it will achieve its objectives: 73% agree with the statement "I know what management are trying to achieve," 81% agree with the statement "My organization has a clear corporate strategy," and 88% agree that the "organization will achieve its aims."

Conclusion

The research reported here arose from a unique opportunity to examine HP's designer culture not only from the inside but also in the aftermath of a downsizing program that might be assumed to have had a traumatic effect on its culture. Rather than finding traumatized employees, however, we found that they had a high degree of organizational commitment and remained, for the most part, quite positive about the company and its culture. There was also, however, a view that the cultural magic could never be quite the same again, although it would continue to differentiate HP from other organizations.

The generally positive nature of the response may, perhaps, stem from the way HP's culture grew up around the company rather than being imposed in a classic top-down fashion. One explanation might be that the senior management at HP is less ambitious in its values statement than other organizations. In other words, although they recognize that the HP Way does buy a certain element of goodwill, they do not overemphasize it because of the costs associated with "turning employees off" by enforcing the culture in a uniform manner. If so, then companies that have tried to impose certain values and beliefs on their employees, following on the wave of interest generated in corporate culture by popular accounts of HP and others, may not have been allowed to get away as lightly as the originals of the species.

This research in HP also contradicts some of the notions of culture as a management tool. In particular, we found that a highly developed form of bureaucratic control existed as an essential part of the culture. This is significant because it demonstrates that corporate culture had not supplanted other forms of labor control as suggested by Ray (1986) and Casey (1995). In Ouchi's (1981) terms, the bureaucratic form coexisted profitably with the clan form. The policies and procedures, particularly those connected with performance management systems, actually had a very large part to play in the management of the organization. This was, perhaps, most obviously illustrated by the effort that management put into the measurement of various work outputs. What this means is that management relied quite heavily on bureaucratic controls to help extract, monitor, and reward employee performance rather than simply depending on HP's culture for this purpose. What is also significant is that the existence of these measures came into being precisely because of the need to design a culture that promoted innovation and freedom for the individual employee. Although other forms of labor control, such as supervision, may exist elsewhere in the corporation, the two that we have identified here (cultural and bureaucratic control) were of most significance in the business we studied.

The establishment of clear targets and objectives (the what) did not necessitate the means of achieving those objectives (the how) also being prescribed. This can be contrasted with many classic bureaucracies of the kind described by Max Weber in which the functions and actions (the how) are prescribed to reduce individual discretion as a means of increasing efficiency. Weber's "iron cage of rationality" can be witnessed in the planning systems and in the quasi-Taylorist, engineering approach applied to measuring work output. The cultural emphasis on measurement is, arguably, further evidence of what Ritzer (1993) describes as "McDonaldization" tendencies. The aim in this case is to produce efficiency, calculability, and predictability in work performance. The question that remains to be asked is whether the combination of bureaucratic control and corporate culture is unique to HP or whether it is part of a wider tendency within certain corporations that we might term "Hewlett-Packardization."

Notes

1. This myth-destroying exercise is of importance because simplification of HP's culture does a disservice to both it and those who seek to learn from it.

2. It should, however, be acknowledged that Kunda (1992, p. 220) and Ray (1986, p. n3) have at least noted that progressive U.S. firms use a number of approaches simultaneously. Van Maanen and Kunda (1989) have suggested that there may even be up to four different forms of control operating simultaneously.

3. The scale ranges from 1 to 5. A summary indicator that is greater than 2.5 represents positive organizational commitment, whereas less than 2.5 indicates the opposite. A 5-point Likert response format was used for each of the 15 items in the OCQ. The summary indicator was calculated by summing the results from each of the 15 items and then dividing them by 15. Several of the items, which are negatively phrased to reduce bias, are reverse scored (see Mowday et al., 1979, p. 227).

References

Beer, M., Eisenstat, A., & Spector, B. (1990, November/December). Why change programmes don't produce change. *Harvard Business Review,* 158-166.

Britain's non-union leaders. (1980, July). *Management Today,* 58-65.

Casey, C. (1995). *Work, self and society: After industrialism.* London: Routledge.

The corporate responsibility champs . . . and chumps. (1985, Winter). *Business and Society,* 4-10.

Deal, T., & Kennedy, A. (1982). *Corporate cultures: The rites and rituals of corporate life.* London: Penguin.

Drucker, P. (1992, September/October). The new society of organizations. *Harvard Business Review,* 95-104.

Edwards, R. (1979). *Contested terrain: The transformation of the workplace in the twentieth century.* New York: Basic Books.

Gouldner, A. (1957). Cosmopolitans and locals. *Administrative Science Quarterly, 2*(3), 281-306.

Guest, D. (1992). Right enough to be dangerously wrong: An analysis of the In Search of Excellence phenomenon. In G. Salaman (Ed.), *Human resource strategies* (pp. 5-19). London: Sage.

Hendry, J., & Hope, V. (1994, December). Cultural change and competitive performance. *European Management Journal, 12*(4), 401-406.

Hitt, M., & Ireland, D. (1987, Fall). Peters and Waterman revisited: The unending quest for excellence. *Journal of Business Strategy,* 52-62.

Hofstede, G. (1991). *Culture and organizations: Software of the mind.* London: McGraw-Hill.

Hope, V. (1990). People are our greatest asset. *Personnel Review, 10*(5), 14-23.

Hope, V. (1993). *The wrong kind of attitude: A study in control and consent in human resource management.* Unpublished PhD thesis, University of Manchester, Manchester, UK.

Hope, V., & Hendry, J. (1995). Corporate cultural change—Is it relevant for the organizations of the 1990s? *Human Resource Management Journal, 5*(4), 61-73.

Kanter, R. M. (1989, November/December). The new managerial work. *Harvard Business Review,* 85-92.

Kotter, J. P., & Heskett, J. L. (1992). *Corporate culture and performance.* New York: Free Press.

Kunda, G. (1992). *Engineering culture: Control and commitment in a hi-tech corporation.* Philadelphia: Temple University Press.

Lawrence, P. R., & Lorsch, J. W. (1967). *Organization and environment.* Cambridge, MA: Harvard University.

Levering, R., Moskowitz, M., & Katz, M. (1984). *The 100 best companies to work for in America.* New York: Addison-Wesley.

Mayo, E. (1949). *The social problems of an industrial civilization.* London: Routledge.

McGovern, P. (1995). Learning from the gurus: Managers' responses to the unwritten rules of the game. *Business Strategy Review, 6*(3), 13-26.

McGovern. P., Hope-Hailey, V., & Stiles, P. (1995, September). *Career management in an era of insecurity.* Paper presented at the annual conference of the Employment Research Unit, Cardiff Business School, Cardiff, CA.

Mintzberg, H., & Quinn, B. P. (1991). The Hewlett Packard Company. In H. Mintzberg & B. P. Quinn (Eds.), *The strategy process: Concepts, contexts, cases* (2nd ed., pp. 456-480). London: Prentice Hall.

Mowday, R. T., Steers, R. M., & Porter, L. W. (1979). The measurement of organizational commitment. *Journal of Vocational Behavior, 14,* 224-247.

The no lay-off payoff. (1985, July). *Dun's Business Month, 126,* 64-66.

Ouchi, W. G. (1981). *Theory Z: How American business can meet the Japanese challenge.* New York: Avon.

Packard, D. (1995). *The HP way: How Bill Hewlett and I built our company.* New York: HarperCollins.

Peters, T. (with Austin, N.). (1985). *A passion for excellence: The leadership difference.* London: Collins.

Peters, T., & Waterman, R. (1982). *In search of excellence: Lessons from America's best-run companies.* New York: Harper & Row.

Ray, C. A. (1986). Corporate culture: The last frontier of control? *Journal of Management Studies, 23*(3), 287-297.

Reynolds, B. (1989). *The 100 best companies to work for in the UK*. London: Fontana/Collins.

Ritzer, G. (1993). *The McDonaldization of society*. Newbury Park, CA: Pine Forge Press.

Scott-Morgan, P. (1994). *The unwritten rules of the game*. New York: McGraw-Hill.

Truss, C., & Gratton, L. (1994). Strategic human resource management: A conceptual approach. *International Journal of Human Resource Management, 5*(3), 664-686.

Van Maanen, J., & Kunda, G. (1989). "Real feelings": Emotional expression and organizational culture. In L. L. Cummings & B. M. Staw (Eds.), *Research in organizational behavior* (Vol. 1). Greenwich, CT: JAI.

von Werssowetz, R. O., & Beer, M. (1982). Human resources at Hewlett Packard. In *Harvard Business School case services*. Cambridge, MA: Harvard University, Harvard Business School.

Whittington, R. (1992). Putting Giddens into action: Social systems and managerial agency. *Journal of Management Studies, 29*(6), 693-713.

Willmott, H. (1993). Strength is ignorance, slavery is freedom: Managing culture in modern organizations. *Journal of Management Studies, 30*(4), 515-552.

Part III

Culture With a Focus on the Suborganizational Level

This part contains four studies that focus predominantly on issues at the suborganizational level of culture. Again, all studies were conducted in different cultural contexts regarding nation, industry, and region.

Chapter 10, by Katrina Burrus, explores the dynamics of perceptual and behavioral culture clashes on the basis of differences in gender and nationality in a decision-making situation within a large Swiss bank located in the Swiss region of Geneva. The reader experiences most of the unfolding events from a North American professional woman's perspective, although the reader is also invited to take the role of one of the male decision makers at one instance. For a traditional organizational scholar, this narrative as such may appear quite unusual. Despite its idiosyncratic nature, the narrative characterizes that particular cultural context extraordinarily well and may help people (especially North American women) prepare if they need to conduct business in that part of the world.

Chapter 11, by Diana Rosemary Sharpe, also explores cultural complexity and its inherent dynamics but in the cultural context of the automobile industry, a specific region in the United Kingdom, and a Japanese transplant company. In the role of an assembly line worker, she investigates the complex dynamic interplay of different subcultures that come to bear at the shop floor level, including the Japanese overlay, local managers, authority, and age subcultures. Most of the time, these different subcultures oppose each other, but there are a few examples of the subcultures being indifferent toward each other. Her study also shows how the members of different subcultures handle the same control strategies quite differently.

Chapter 12, by Juha Laurila, is a case study that focuses on profession by investigating managerial subcultures within the cultural context of Finland and the paper industry. Similar to McGovern and Hope-Hailey in Part II, Juha Laurila uses a situation of change—in this case, a discontinuous technological change—to investigate the cultural dynamics involved at the suborganizational level. In contrast to McGovern and Hope-Hailey, however, Laurila focuses on the suborganizational level and starts from the situation of existing subcultures. Because the technological introduction is attractive for members of all different managerial subcultures, although for different reasons, these different subcultures join forces and all support the change—but only as long as it promises to be successful.

The last chapter in Part III explores cultural agreement versus diversity at the suborganizational level within the cultural context of the retail industry in The Netherlands. Bas A. Koene, Christophe A. J. J. Boone, and Joseph L. Soeters draw on quantitative data collected from 50 supermarket stores to explain cultural dynamics at the store level—for example, how apparent contrasts (a higher degree of cultural homogeneity associated with greater demographic diversity and number of departments) may make sense. Methodologically, the study represents an enriching contrast to the other three studies included in this section.

Chapter 10

National Culture and Gender Diversity Within One of the Universal Swiss Banks

An Experiential Description of a Professional Woman Officer and President of the Women Managers' Association

Katrina Burrus

A Phenomenological Exercise according to Max Van Maanen's (1990) four existentials: lived space (spatiality), lived body (corporeality), lived time (temporality), and lived human relation (relationality or communality).

This chapter is an attempt to lace anecdotal narrative into more formal textual discourse to create a tension between the prereflective and reflective pulls of

AUTHOR'S NOTE: This narrative is based on a lived experience, and names of all individuals and institutions are pseudonyms.

languages (Van Maanen, 1990, p. 121). This approach is also selected to bring out experientially the inherent contrasts and contradictions of cultural and gender diversity in a Swiss Universal Bank as seen by a bicultural professional woman. This narrative is the story of a North American woman whose U.S. parents moved to Italy when she was 2 years old and then divorced and remarried Europeans when she was 5 years old. Switzerland became her home until she returned to the United States for graduate and postgraduate school. With diplomas in hand, she returned to work for a large Swiss bank at the tip of Lake Geneva. Five years after her return, the following is her story.

Narrative

> *I was nervously perched on a little sofa outside the conference room. The general director of Mont Blanc Bank, Geneva, was holding his meeting with his men. I must remember! Before the reengineering process, they were termed directors of departments. Now, they were chiefs of division, or were they? It made no difference to me what they were termed. They were, nevertheless, the most powerful men of Mont Blanc Bank, Geneva. Furthermore, the vocabulary describing the hierarchy of the bank was still a carbon copy of the military system. Was this not an indication of the spirit of the bank? Previously, the men who climbed the military ladder were lured into enticing jobs at one of the three largest banks in Switzerland: Union Bank of Switzerland, Swiss Bank Corporation, and Credit Suisse. It was believed that they made better managers because they had plenty of practice at leading, ordering, planning for, and controlling their soldiers. To be a high ranking military official was almost a must to pursue a career in one of the big banks. It always surprised me, as a foreign woman, that this paradox could exist in a country that prided itself in its neutrality. Many Swiss still assumed that neutrality required a strong military force to protect it. The Swiss Universal bankers, in particular, have some strange nostalgia for the military system. They participated aggressively strategically and tactically in world events, which has made them astute international bankers but will their "military" banking systems be the most appropriate structure when change seems to be accelerating in the global financial environment?*

As soon as the voices I was hearing through the conference room door ceased, the impressive wooden door would open. Apart from a former Jesuit, I would walk into a room of men that vouched for the military system. Rumor had it that this was changing. Was it just a coincidence that they used military jargon profusely?

I wondered whether the animated talk I was hearing through the walls was ever going to come to an end. I was impatient to deliver my speech. I believed in my mission "to strengthen professional women's identities and working conditions in the bank." Granted, we were asking for a better quality of work and an enforcement of equal opportunities for women. In counterpart, we would create events that would attract professional women outside the bank to invest in a more "progressive" bank. Was this not also appealing to a capitalistic stance?

In preparation for this meeting, every night after work I had reviewed what other companies were doing to ameliorate the conditions and opportunities of the women working in their institutions. I thought I had gained a "sense" of what Swiss companies were ready to change. I had been president of several professional women's organizations and had created programs to promote women.

The sense that was felt by this professional woman corresponded to the emergence of entrepreneurial project-based groups—a microclimate in which patch dynamics can work. These are operations at the peripheral boundaries of the organizations where experiments can thrive and perpetuate the variety necessary to preserve the system as a whole. The sense expressed here, however, was not representative of the whole organization. Inevitably, this activity entails the potential creation of crisis for existing mature operations (Hurst & Zimmerman, 1994, p. 350) such as the Swiss banks. In other words, maybe nothing less than a crisis could have instigated large-scale change.

Legally, women had equal rights, or at least that is what I believed. But did the heads of companies want to enforce the women's newly acknowledged rights? How could one explain why French or German international banks had many more women managers?

Big Brother, the head officer of Mont Blanc Bank, seemed a little embarrassed by the large discrepancy between the image the bank portrayed of a global bank and its local management with regard to women. Dr. Tug himself, the god of the gods, gave his

> *men directives! Listen to the women in the bank! Was this not our opportunity to have women's voices heard? As president of the Women Managers' Association, I was the representative of our project.*

What were the chances of this woman succeeding in her project? Where was this organization on the ecocycle? According to Hurst and Zimmerman (1994), an organization goes through four phases of the ecocycle. An organization evolves from the exploitation phase to the conservation phase to the creative destruction phase and, finally, to the renewal phase. These authors draw parallels between organizational change and the formation of a forest. The exploitation phase of the ecosystem is characterized by the rapid colonization of an available space, such as a gap in a forest due to the fall of a large tree. A "microclimate" is created. The newly opened space now offers equal access to resources to more organisms. There are many different ways for resources to flow through the system. Slowly, this newly opened field becomes dominated by a few large systems and differentiates into a hierarchy of smaller niches. At this point, a more mature phase of the ecocycle is reached. Successful organisms produce fewer successors, investing their energy in protecting them for longer periods of time and in defending their territories. In organizations, large hierarchical structures will control a set of niches beneath them. Seen from afar, the forest or the organization will look impressive and stable. Many organisms in the system will be specialized, however, and therefore the total diversity of the system will be less than that in the exploitation phase. "It is precisely the homogeneity of such systems in age, species type and their specialized adaptation to protected niches that renders them susceptible to catastrophe" (Hurst & Zimmerman, 1994, p. 343).

The Swiss banking industry is in its mature phase of development. According to Hurst and Zimmerman (1994), it is the conservation phase of the ecocycle that entails that the next ecocycle is the "creative destruction" phase. A significant decrease in the number of banks has taken place in the Swiss financial market in the 1990s. There is a process of concentration in the industry (Andersen, 1992). Is the forest being dominated by a few large trees? Is the organizational system highly articulated with specialists?

> *I was anxiously fidgeting with the papers I was going to distribute when suddenly the general director appeared in front of me. He very kindly told me that they were looking forward to my intervention. They were resolving important issues and would appreciate*

the relaxation during my 10-minute speech. He would call me in a few minutes. He then disappeared behind those large, heavy doors.

Was the "more pressing matter" alluded to by the general director an indication of his preoccupation with the banking industry entering a more competitive environment? The young lady could speculate that if the organization was in its phase of "large hierarchical structure that controls available resources" (Hurst & Zimmerman, 1994), it would be less likely that the bank would be susceptible to any form of change altering the status quo. The bank would be in a tightly connected system in which few alternative pathways existed to use the resources.

Lived Time (Temporality)

Was my speech going to be their 10-minute cigar break? Were these issues that I was going to fight for classified as being of minor importance?

Seven thousand dollars, the amount requested from the Mont Blanc Bank, Geneva, for the women's association that year was indeed minor for this prestigious bank and its over $100 billion in assets. The reality and impact of this matter did not really enter my consciousness.

Like many women, my impression was colored by my relationship with my father. Insidiously, I heard my father's vociferation coming to me from my past. He was speaking with a loud and overbearing voice to his four sons seated on the staircase leading to the second floor. He was standing up, waving his hands as an orator would to stress his main points. "YOU my son, John, will be the director of the company. You, my son, Kelly, will market our products in the rest of Europe. You, my son . . ."

My father's voice was slowly dimming in my mind as if he was receding once again into my past. I only barely remembered him noticing my presence where I was perched on the last step of the staircase. Did I even hear him say "Oh Micky Ticky, learn how to type"?

Present experience in any given now has a "historical" dimension, issuing from a past life and leading into a future life. This is related to what Schutz (as cited in Wagner, 1983) called our "biographical situation."

Today, I was fighting for my rights and my women colleagues'
rights to be respected as three-dimensional persons. I had worked
endless hours for this recognition and produced effectively above
and beyond my yearly quotas. The revenues of my mutual fund
department had soared to unprecedented heights.

My colleagues and I labored to create a project that would
narrow the discrimination between the percentage of female and
male managers within the next five years. Furthermore, we envi-
sioned a possibility of more flexible working schedules at reduced
rates for both men and women. Would that not be a win-win
situation for the bank?

The Old Boy Network

While the woman officer was ruminating in her thoughts, muffled sounds
filtered through the walls. She was too preoccupied to notice the agitated
sounds emanating from the conference room. The general director was facing
his men and one in particular—the director of credits, Mr. Patrick Shultz. He
was a man of 53 years, sharp and shrewd, and after 25 years of a successful
career in the bank he could easily recognize when his favors were losing their
allure. He had been the model of entrepreneurship when the bank was making
loans at an ever-increasing rate. As interest rates were persistently creeping
up, more credit defaults were being witnessed. Today, the credit market called
for extreme prudence. What was once seen as a dynamic business approach
was now perceived as dangerously overextending the bank's risk.

Patrick Shultz was shuffling his papers until he realized that his internal
agitation might be noticed. He laid his hands gently on his papers and looked up
to meet the general director's gaze. He uttered his figures calmly even though he
knew better than anyone that troubled waters lay ahead. Patrick Shultz gauged
incisively his auditors' reactions, but they were demonstrating the usual collegial
responses. Confronted with negative financial figures, he knew his colleagues'
loyalties and political allegiances to him were going to be put to the test in the next
year. His mind wandered but his voice did not. His usual discourse was peppered
with witty irony at crucial moments to reduce the increasing tension in the room.

Increasing interest rates were reducing real estate values by up to 30% and
40%, which reduced the bank's guaranty on their loans. Consequently, the bank
was going to be reluctant to loan more money to his clients in difficulty, which

might set another cascade of defaults. With each credit failure, his accounts would be further scrutinized, and each mistake would be brought to light. If, temporarily, realtors could increase the rent to their renters and banks could see their interest rates increase substantially, the commercial department might see itself through this credit difficulty. He knew, however, that this was not easily done in a society composed of more than 70% renters without provoking a social upheaval. Politically, this option would be difficult to take. His speech came to an end, and the director general asked him to describe the client profile most affected by the economic slowdown. He mumbled a clever response that set his auditors chuckling, but Schultz knew that in the enthusiasm of making new loans much of the data on the client's profile were missing in the dossier. Faced with adversity, Schultz and his men were going to go busily to work to consolidate their portfolios. The pendulum had swung the other way. The more meticulous, conservative bankers would have their time of favor. Patrick Schultz knew he had only bought time.

When the director general got up with a smile to announce that the president of the women managers' association was next on the agenda, Schultz was relieved and told a dirty joke about women that set the boy network laughing in unison. It was the most cohesive moment of the afternoon. Because the director general was known to have a healthy appreciation for women, the joke was welcomed by this chief in command. When the laughter subsided, the head of Mont Blanc Bank, Geneva, Mr. Ladefond, a gentle man in his sixties, mentioned in a serious tone that headquarters wanted the directors to be more proactive in integrating women in management. "Active intaking!" echoed a young ambitious director while glancing at his colleagues playfully and rocking his chair backward. "Gentlemen, gentlemen," said Mr. Ladefond while raising his hand, "The Head Office has asked us to sponsor the Women Managers' Association."

Reputedly, the German Swiss and French Swiss regions had more than just a language and cultural barrier between them. The German Swiss area accounted for 70% of the country and harbored most of the industry. The French Swiss area (Romandie) accounted for 27% of the country and jealously guarded the tertiary activities. They were known for banks and insurances. Mont Blanc Bank, Geneva, was the most successful branch office in Mont Blanc, Switzerland, and this was with the conscious effort of its directors to hold as many resources in the Geneva branch office as possible. This time, the German Swiss director general, who was part of the Director Generals Mont Blanc worldwide and whose headquarters were located in the German Swiss area, was also politically interested in maintaining as much power in the French Swiss area. It was under his area of responsibility. For the local directors, headquarters was the big brother to comply with but not in any way to concede to. Most directives from the German Swiss headquarters were perceived as undermining their authority and were, at times, resented. The German Swiss, however, generally thought of the French Swiss as the southerners—the Latin minority: not serious workers nor rigorous in their methods but who lived in a great place to spend the holidays. The French Swiss shared this attribute with the Italian Swiss who held 3% of the sunniest part of the country—on the border of Italy.

Mr. Ladefond could not pursue his comments because the director general was already personally walking over to open the door to the next item on the agenda.

> *I heard through the walls a few more voices and then silence. The door opened and out peered the general director to invite me in. I bounced up. I must have had as much adrenaline in my system as a sprinter before a race. I was going to face the gods of finance of my company—The Mont Blanc Bank. This company had been my life, maybe even my soul, for five years. Of course, five years for a Swiss banker was a short time—stability being of essence. Consistency and durability were cherished values. Brilliance or outright ambition were suspicious qualities in this society in which decisions were made in a civilized consensus form. Open confrontation was something the Descartian French might relish, but the Swiss—"God forbid!" mused the U.S. voice in me.*
>
> *Typically, the Swiss were nonconfrontational. How could the Swiss ever come to any decision if their style was confrontational? Every canton, each of which could not be much bigger than Santa Barbara, California, has its own rules and regulations. Each canton has its own school system. If you drive a half hour in one direction, you will most likely be out of one canton and well into the next. There are four official languages in Switzerland, and this country is only 41,000 square kilometers with a population of 7,000,000 people, which is half the population of New York. With the Swiss borders touching Germany, France, Austria, Liechtenstein, and Italy, consensus ensured the country's diversity and survival.*

Lived Space (Spaciality)

> *Before I knew it, I was standing before nine gods of finance with snow white temples who were sitting around a large U-shaped*

conference table. The light was a dim glow. We were floors beneath the surface of the earth—near those gold safes. No exterior sound reached us. The ceiling appeared endlessly high, and yet the room seemed confining after accommodating these nine gnomes of finance. The general director was on his throne at the far end of the table. Each director's power could be measured precisely by the distance of his seat from that of the general director's. His court consisted of the young or ambitious opportunists or both who were at the tip of the U table. The more submissive consensus buffers were seated at the middle of the table. Were the buffers the general director's men at the end of their careers in this bank, waiting for their retirement, or were they here at interim waiting for their next promotion? The buffers, nevertheless, adopted the same policy—no risks, no mistakes. Finally, the core decision makers were concentrated at the head of the table. The general director's bodyguards were competing for his favors. There was no doubt who ruled this roost. Unprotected by any of this hierarchy, I felt very insecure in front of these colossal decision makers, who in a snapshot would decide my career in the bank.

Lived Body (Corporeality)

Patrick Shultz stretched out his upper body, determined to make these next 10 minutes last. Now that he was out of the center of focus, the gnawing pain in his back came to his consciousness. He shuffled his papers again like a pack of cards and mechanically placed them in his familiar folder, worn and faint in the corners where he had searched for comfort by rubbing them numerous times with his fingers.

He was jolted into the present time when he witnessed a young woman racing into the quaint and familiar room where decisions with his colleagues were made with conscious deliberation. Like a young mare, isolated from the troupe, she rushed into the conference room with a mixture of brute force characteristic of youthful conviction and an awkwardness from being in uncharted territory. Her gaze settled for an instant on Patrick Shultz, who matched her glance while judging the strength of her body dressed in a tight black suit. Her hands and body moved expansively while she was stressing a point on the graph projected on the screen. What was it about North American women, he thought, that left you with the impression that they were trespassing on your private space? Their innate democratic attitude did not leave you with a comfortable hierarchical distance. He had noticed that many North American women's faces expressed an apparent "naïveté" as if American women were unhampered by the same historical and traditional references or constraints as the Europeans. She was unabashedly ambitious and wanted to play with the big boys, and she even seemed to demand it as a right. It was unusual, appealing, and maybe even exciting but to be controlled. Patrick Shultz was reflecting on a previous presentation given by a Japanese woman officer. In contrast, she was so reserved, shy, and controlled in her movements that he felt he had been invited to peek in a china store full of hidden treasures too fine and small for him not to feel clumsy and awkward. Her unassuming behavior and her soft-spoken voice made him lean forward to hear because there seemed to be more distance between them than necessary. Suddenly, Schultz was distracted from his thoughts by someone nudging him in the arm. A second later, a note was slipped into his hand. He discreetly opened it under the table. Scribbled in pencil was the message, "Some pair of legs! By the way, could you facilitate that loan to Mr. X of Company Y?" Patrick Shultz's eyes blinked a second longer than usual, which assured his colleague's dossier would be examined with a positive bias.

I wonder what the Spartans felt when they were thrown into the ring to fight the wild lion. Seconds before the beast was released, the Spartan stole a quick look at the public. Did the public appear serene, amused, or untouchable? Would the Spartan draw the public's attention first to his body, then to his look of defiance?

The spectators would probably gauge his success in combat and then continue talking or laughing. A moment of silence would follow when the lion ran into the ring. Curious spectators would evaluate the force of the beast. If he was forceful or different in any way, the lion would hold their glances, their minds, their breaths, the time between two drops of water, before spectators resumed their conversations.

I walked briskly into my ring, ready to fight in earnest for women's recognition. I challenged the glances of these nine men looking at my attire, my suit, and my hair. I suddenly was aware not only of their power and my lack of it but also of my body and my gender. I was the only woman in the room. Did I expect anything different? Of course not! No professional women reached this level of power in the bank. Although I cognitively knew that I would be faced only by men, physically I was finding my bearings. I was young, maybe attractive, but I felt foreign among this boy network. My body, for a fleeting second, was no longer part of me.

It stood out awkwardly. It lost its naturalness and behaved clumsily. There was no room to move. The room barely contained the large conference table. Mostly venerable older men sat around it. They were chatting while occasionally glancing my way. Was I the buffoon called in to amuse them for the equivalent of the 10-minute cigar break?

It was not until three minutes into my speech, as most of these important men continued their conversations, albeit more hushed, that I was beginning to feel ill at ease. I was losing my bearings. I began to go into the details of my outline instead of giving them the global view. It would be similar to a Spartan worrying about the strength of his spear instead of gauging the reactions of the lion facing him. After all, the lion, with one strategic leap, could snuff out his last sigh. I felt vulnerable. Two directors were laughing at their own jokes while slipping notes to each other. Now, what lions were these? Here I was called in to provide them with a program to improve women's conditions, and I felt I was in front of a kindergarten class watching small boys being disruptive and oblivious to the school teacher. Two good students, at the tip of the U table, were looking straight at me, which drew my attention to them in search of spectators or any sign of positive recognition of my presence.

I should have tapped my ruler on the desk, stopped dead in my tracks, and called on them: "Why do you call on us?" "What do you expect from the women of the bank?" "What are you ready to change?" "Do you have the power or will to enforce equal opportunities in your division?" "Are you going to establish a dialogue with us and answer these questions directly to us?"

Instead, I did not call on them to take positions or to act as adults. I continued with my statistics. "One woman out of every four men is in middle management. Only two women out of 1,700 employees are vice presidents, and approximately fifty percent of all the employees are women.

"May a group of women make a survey investigating what the professional women of the bank would like to change to ensure equal opportunities?"

A survey seemed the most adequate procedure. After all, were these directors not constantly asking us to know what our clients want inside and outside of the bank? Total quality management, TQM, was all I had heard in the last six months. No response came from the directors. "Are you content with this situation?" I

wanted to scream! But I did not. I gave in to the unspoken collusion,
"One does not question authority."

The typification, "gods of finance," served to predetermine the intersubjective agenda, assuring that "they'll have their way" without thoughtfulness or much effort (Rehorick, 1994). In other words, the author's biographical situation predisposed her to submit to the authority structure and not attempt to alter the status quo.

At the end of the speech, I felt I was making a plea. I felt like the Spartan waiting for the verdict for a performance that barely held the spectators' attention. I felt condemned as a bad fighter. My lion had the better of me. I instilled more power in him than he actually possessed.

The speech had finished, and the conference room was finally silent. It was time for questions. A few polite inquiries followed from one of the bodyguards. The Swiss are so very composed. It was such a contrast to my internal agitation. I heard myself answer one of the questions in what I thought might have appeared as my last breath. "There is a trend that started in the USA. It will sooner or later come to Switzerland." I saw a few heads nod among the directors. I continued, "How do you want to position the bank within this trend: before? amongst? or after the trend?" This was another direct question, albeit timid. It received no answer. I was dismissed cordially, and with due form, from the conference room.

The 10 minutes were already up, thought Patrick Shultz. The meeting was coming to a close with a few polite questions and answers. The thud of the conference door announced that the men's club was in its familiar room again. Of course, the $7,000 would be approved. The sum demanded was insignificant. Furthermore, it was both politically correct to approve what headquarters asked for and wise not to overtly counter a women's association when more than 50% of the bank's workforce were women. He thought,

But she wanted to play with the big boys, did she . . . in a market that was ever more highly competitive and where overcapacity of human resources was becoming a serious problem. There were enough players among the men of the bank for every chosen spot, and if she wanted to play the game, she would have to start learning the rules of the big boys.

Patrick Shultz scanned his colleagues to evaluate their potential resistance to his next remark. First, he judged the ambitious director at the end of the table. As a fine sailer, the younger and ambitious director knew how to take advantage of favorable winds. Next, he glanced at the director in chief of the president of the women's association. He was seated in the buffer zone and was not going to take any undue risk for anyone under his responsibility. Furthermore, the women's association president in question was not now representing a department under his authority, and she was too low in the hierarchical structure for her successes or failures to be associated with his. Patrick Schultz was already internally chuckling when assessing the remaining directors. With one controlled ironic statement, he set his audience laughing spiritedly at the woman officer's expense. Finally, the general director tapped his hand and ordered his men to pay attention to the next item on the agenda, "downsizing."

> *As soon as I heard the closing thud of the large conference door, I felt a lonely, desolate, and uncomfortable feeling of having not been recognized as a person. I had received no feedback. How were these gnomes of finance going to make their decision? But of course, it was going to be behind closed doors.*
>
> *Now what did I expect? Gods of finance do not negotiate directly with the commoners. Gods make the rules of the cosmos; commoners live by them.*
>
> *As I walked out of the bank, which stretched out for an entire block, I saw that the building was almost empty, and it was dark outside. Was it already nighttime, or was I feeling somber and gloomy, which tainted my vision? What had happened during the meeting? There had been no real communication or sharing of ideas. I left the conference room not knowing what the directors were thinking nor what they would decide, which left me with a heavy load to carry—a sense of failure.*

When system members back away from change "because of resignation, inertia, passivity, or despair" (Levinson, 1978, p. 52), the closing of the transitional opportunity often brings a sense of failure or stagnation (Gersick, 1991, p. 31). Was this the case with this woman? Was she feeling a sense of despair? In mature and successful organizations, managers will naturally tend to restrict activities to those that have proven to work, leading to tightly coupled practices (Hedberg, Nystrom, & Starbuck, 1976; Hurst & Zimmerman, 1994; Tushman & Romanelli,

1985). Cost reductions and efficiency are priorities during the mature phase of the ecocycle. "It seems that just as the trees in the forest go up in smoke when faced with fire, rigid inertial structures and systems within organizations can be destroyed only by crisis" (Hurst & Zimmerman, p. 347). The women's association was not a priority to the Mont Blanc Bank, Geneva branch. It was not going to help the directors out of their current difficulties. The boy network was a cohesive force between members, and no advantage was to accrue to the directors if they integrated women actively in management. Furthermore, the program was initiated by headquarters, which made any outcome a political decision.

The other possibility for a systemwide change on every scale to occur is a major crisis as described by Hurst's (Hurst & Zimmerman, 1994) creative destruction phase. The creative destruction phase may allow a new system to emerge with different values. Punctuated equilibrium, however, suggests that for most systems' histories, there are limits beyond which "change is actively prevented rather than always potential but merely suppressed because no adaptive advantage would accrue" (Gould, 1989, p. 124).

> *I must have walked a mile before realizing where I was. I was still in the conference room arguing for more equal opportunities. I saw those 10 minutes repeated endlessly in my mind . . . as if somehow, the "gods" would finally hear me. What I said during the conference echoed in my head:*

> Have you not been talking to us profusely about Total Quality Management: Find out what the clients want . . . to serve them better! . . . OK! Let us do a survey among the women in the bank to find out what would enable them to be happier and more productive in this bank.

> *Another echo came to me: "Here is a minute detail of how the funds would be allocated if given to the association of women managers of the bank. A woman guest would be invited to talk to the women inside and outside the bank about . . ."*

Inner experiences occur within a continuous flow of "duration"; no isolated things appear in it but only ongoing happenings (Wagner, 1983, p. 26). The woman's inner and exterior world are being experienced as the same during her walk from the bank. She is experiencing duration; her sense of time is totally subjective and does not correspond to the objective time of a clock. Consciousness is then experienced as a flow of happenings (Wagner, 1983).

I heard tires screech and a horn blow, which jolted me out of my thoughts in time to pull out of the way of a car racing at me. The endless film of the conference room resumed like a bad movie, but this time it was reviewed in slower motion. Was the adrenaline wearing off?

Two days later, when I was back in the hustle and bustle of a trading room, my phone rang yet again. It must have been for the thirtieth time that day at only 10:30 in the morning. Whether the phone rang or someone talked to me, my eyes never left for long one of the numerous screens encircling my desk. I had the pulse of the world's markets half a meter from my body. I grabbed the phone and answered a curt "yes" only to be answered by an unusually serene and poised voice. I heard him say, "The $7,000 has been attributed to the Swiss Bank's women managers' project for the year 6/92 to 6/93. Thank you and congratulations for your project, Mrs. Odier."

The dollar against the yen was weakening on the screen in front of me. The information did not register consciously. I was asking myself if I had killed the lion. Had the emperor judged the fight valiant enough to show his thumb upward to the public? Did he grace the Spartan with his life? Did I misjudge the impact of my fight? Had I killed the lion? I was so relieved that as the representative of the women in the bank I had succeeded in my mission. I felt a surge of love for my women colleagues, my friends. I felt thankful to the directors. I know this was no major achievement in itself. It was only a step, but like a baby's first steps, it implied that it might walk someday to its independence.

Indeed, two years later the Women Managers' Association, my baby, was beginning to walk alone. Each year new projects were gathering vital force. Women were working together—proposing ideas, creating events. However, the idea of a survey asking professional women what they believed would make them more productive professionals was never allowed to blossom. The project was nipped in the bud. The director said, "The survey would create expectations."

Of any change, I thought.

I keep regular accounts of what I felt was my biological child. Yes, I left the Mont Blanc Bank a few months after the women's project had first been approved. I never believed I would ever see this child grow to adulthood. Was I going to be co-opted by this token gesture from management or did I abandon this newborn?

Should I have stayed with this baby even if it did not grow beyond childhood? I see my friend, the child's adoptive mother, leading the group. She is providing for its growth with her patience and care. She has faith that change occurs by incremental, cumulative, and gradual steps. On the other hand, I believed that incremental adaptation was far inferior to the economic, social dislocation taking place in the environment. With regards to women, Swiss banking organizations were not in alignment with the rest of the banking institutions in Europe, or was my North American culture affecting my perception?

Maybe my father's ghost still hurts me, and the pain has distorted my vision of reality. Change has occurred. Was it more than cosmetic? Did I make a mistake by leaving the bank?

My mind wanders off into a daydream. I remember sitting next to the general director at a wedding. We talked and laughed until he geared the conversation to professional women. The general director leaned over to me and said, "Women should be in the kitchen sweeping the floors"—but of course, this was a joke of his! Did I not have a sense of humor?

It reminds me of one of the negotiation meetings that I held with the second in command of several hundred people in the Geneva branch of the Mont Blanc Bank. After an endless discussion of the purpose of our projects, I embarked on a light social conversation to end the meeting by asking our number two general director, "Do you have children?," to which he answered, "Yes, three girls, all of whom are in secretarial school." I took a second look at this tough but kind man and thought he resembled my father too much.

While at a luncheon with 20 of the women managers of the bank, I was seated next to another one of my directors, the host of the luncheon. He gave us an impressive speech on how he had given equal opportunities to the women in the bank. Once he had finished his speech, he and I continued a more private conversation about women working in the bank.

"Yes," he said, "my wife keeps pestering me about wanting to work. I do not think she should take the place of a woman who really needs to work." He took another look at me and paused. He assumed that with the well-known last name I carry, I did not need to work, and he corrected his remark to, "I prefer that my wife does not work since she does not need to. I provide for her." Strangely

enough, I felt relieved by his candor. Finally, my god of finance was looking me in the eye and telling me his true thoughts.

Did I make the right decision to leave the Mont Blanc Bank? I felt gratitude for the opportunity to initiate a women's program with one of the most prestigious banks in Switzerland. But I equally knew that my child would take several generations to grow to adulthood in the Mont Blanc Bank. While it was an immediate and tangible gesture, was it not only a token?

And yet, I could not keep myself from wishing that some external crisis or the internal psychological makeup of the professional women might reach such cognitive dissonance that the process of change would be accelerated.

Kuhn (1970) states that crises are necessary precursors to scientific revolutions. Tushman and Romanelli (1985) identify "performance pressures . . . whether anticipated or actual" as being fundamental agents of organizational reorientation. Here again, there were no crises. The banking industry as a whole was doing fairly well. One questions whether management would have even been concerned with equal rights if its bottom line was in jeopardy. Under stress, management would probably have reverted to its conservative behavior. In summary, change was demanded from the chief executive officer of the bank during a period of relative stability, but the sense of urgency to address the change desired was not transmitted to these directors. Tushman, Newman, and Romanelli (1986) found that change can occur during equilibrium periods but through broad participation. They also found that top teams are the only instigators strong enough to mount successful reorientations. In the narrative, headquarters expressed the desire to reorient gender issues, but no will was expressed by the branch's directors. Through the hierarchy, the order to "listen to the women of the bank" was acquitted by accepting the professional women managers' association's budget, but no communication was allowed that might have addressed some of the more fundamental issues of gender discrimination. Gersick (1991) would have suggested that the banking system was in an equilibrium state that allowed only incremental adjustments to compensate for internal or external perturbations without changing their deep structures (p. 16).

How could change be dispersed through this banking institution? Prigogine and Stengers (1984) propose that organizations begin with a "nucleus" where the change must first become established firmly before it can take over the rest of the system (p. 187). The more articulated the system—that is, the more mature the organization—the stronger and larger the nucleus must be if it is to result in a systemwide change. In summary, this entails that if patch dynamics takes place and women's groups gather in informal networks throughout the organization, these groups may gather momentum to have systemwide influence. Gould (1972) states that the nucleus must be formed rapidly and in groups that are small and isolated enough for the change to take hold so as not to be diluted by the parent company. In other words, these groups must have enough autonomy to have a self-referential system. Groups create their own agendas and start questioning the status quo. Self-referential systems, if they are not co-opted into the larger system, have lives of their own. Finally, Gersick (1991) states that for a new direction to emerge, random environmental events or circumstances are required. Does that mean that the outcome of the narrative would be a question of chance or is the "unexpected" an integral part of change?

On the individual level, Levinson (1986) argues that transitions in adult development are stimulated by deficiencies in the current life structure (p. 5). In other words, the narrator's life structure no longer adapted to this environment and, therefore, permitted the narrator to shift developmentally. This may explain why the narrator took the presidency of the Professional Women Managers' Association and why she left the bank. Maybe the directors' attitudes toward the lady were too similar to her father's stifling behavior, and her vision of reality was tainted by her biographical history.

Kuhn (1970) notes that perception is a subjective phenomenon; there is always more than one plausible way to interpret reality.

References

Andersen, A. (1992). *Les banques en Suisse l'aube des annees 2000* (Survey No. 2). Zurich, Switzerland: Andersen Consulting.

Gersick, C. J. G. (1991, January). Revolutionary change theories: A multilevel exploration of the punctuated equilibrium paradigm. *Academy of Management, 16*(1), 10-36.

Gould, S. J. (1989). Punctuated equilibrium in fact and theory. *Journal of Social Biological Structure, 12,* 117-136.

Hedberg, B. L. T., Nystrom, P. C., & Starbuck, W. H. (1976). Camping on seesaws: Prescription for a self-designing organization. *Administrative Science Quarterly, 21,* 41-65.

Hurst, D. K., & Zimmerman, B. J. (1994). From life cycle to ecocycle: A new perspective on the growth, maturity, destruction, and renewal of complex systems. *Journal of Management Inquiry, 3*(4), 339-354.

Kuhn, T. S. (1970). *The structure of scientific revolution* (2nd ed.). Chicago: University of Chicago Press.

Levinson, D. J. (1978). *The seasons of a man's life.* New York: Knopf.

Levinson, D. J. (1986). A conception of adult development. *American Psychologist, 41,* 3-13.

Prigogine, I., & Stengers, I. (1984). *Order out of chaos: Man's new dialogue with nature.* New York: Bantam.

Rehorick, D. (1994, October). *"Schutzian critiques of corporate lifeworlds." Searching for meaning: Three reflective commentaries.* Commentary presented at the Society for Phenomenology and the Human Sciences, Seattle, WA.

Tushman, M., & Romanelli, E. (1985). *Organizational evolution: A metamorphosis model of convergence and reorientation.* Greenwich: CT: JAI.

Tushman, M. L., Newman, W. H., & Romanelli, E. (1986). Convergence and upheaval: Managing the unsteady pace of organizational evolution. *California Management Review, 29*(1), 29-44.

Van Maanen, M. (1990). *Researching lived experience: Human science for an action sensitive pedagogy.* New York: State University of New York.

Wagner, R. H. (1983). *Phenomenology of consciousness and sociology of the life-world.* Alberta, Canada: University of Alberta Press.

Chapter 11

Managerial Control Strategies and Subcultural Processes

On the Shop Floor in a Japanese Manufacturing Organization in the United Kingdom

Diana Rosemary Sharpe

Overview of Some Related Research

The shop floor work organization associated with a Japanese style of management has been identified and discussed in previous research (e.g., Kenney & Florida, 1993; Lincoln & Kalleberg, 1985) as having variations in organizational design, structuring of internal labor markets, and the organization of

AUTHOR'S NOTE: I thank all the people at Machine Co. who have helped me to learn about shop floor life. I am particularly grateful for the opportunity to work on the shop floor provided by the directors and I am indebted to the associates on the line who I worked with. A first draft of this work was presented at the 12th EGOS Colloquium, "Contrasts and Contradictions in Organizations," Istanbul, July 6 through 8, 1995. I acknowledge the encouragement and suggestions provided by participants in the Cultural Diversity tract including Sonja Sackmann, Nakige Boyacigiller, and industrial relations compared to Western (particularly U.S.) models of work organization. It tends to be characterized as incorporating a just-in-time production system, total quality management, and lean production.

Increased attention has been given to researching various aspects of this management system in attempts to explain the success of Japanese organizations in world markets (e.g., Womack, Jones, & Roos, 1990), analyzing the social construction of the Japanese business system (Whitley, 1992), comparing the Japanese form of work organization to Western models of work organization (e.g., Jurgens, 1993; Lincoln & Kalleberg, 1990), and assessing if and how aspects of this system can be adopted by Western organizations (Florida & Kenney, 1991; Tayeb, 1994; Westney, 1993).

There has been much less attention given to exploring social relations on the shop floor under this form of management system, however, especially in a Western context. A notable exception is the work of Delbridge (1995). Interesting issues that remain relatively unexplored include the nature of unfolding and evolving social relations and social processes on the shop floor within this form of management system.

Theoretical debates have developed, recognizing the need to incorporate analysis of objective and subjective factors, the structure and agency in any analysis, and an explanation of managerial control and countercontrol in work organizations (e.g., Burawoy, 1979, 1985; Knights, 1995; Knights & Willmott, 1985, 1989; Storey, 1985; Willmott, 1995).

These debates, however, have been accompanied by a relative paucity of empirical work, of an ethnographic nature, suited to the exploration of such social processes and relations as they unfold, evolve, and adapt over time. Notable exceptions include the work of Collinson (1992) and Kunda (1992). Research addressing these issues in the context of a Japanese form of work organization is limited; one exception is Kleinberg (1994), who performed a study of work group culture formation in a Japanese subsidiary in North America. This chapter is based on a research project focusing on changing forms of work organization and managerial control systems.

Margaret Phillips. I thank Jos Benders, Hugh Willmott, and David Knights for their feedback on my work. I express my gratitude to my supervisor, Richard Whitley, for first inspiring me with the "philosophy of the social sciences" course at the school and then continuing to inspire me through his informed guidance, encouragement, constant intellectual challenges, and unrelenting expectation of Kaizen from me during my doctoral studies, which were made possible by a scholarship from Manchester Business School, England.

Research Methodology
and Setting

Research Method

Research methods such as questionnaire surveys or structured interviews were considered superficial, remote, and a mechanistic means of attempting to access such issues as the actual process of work, the informal work groups, and the less obvious forms of resistance and conflict on the shop floor (Braverman, 1974; Thompson, 1986). These issues need to be addressed in exploring the dynamics of shop floor cultural processes. It was equally important to attempt a longitudinal study in which actual processes could be captured as they emerged and evolved over time in interplay with emerging and evolving managerial control strategies. By definition, ethnography is a longitudinal method geared toward a process-based understanding of organizational life. As Rosen (1991) argues, "At its best ethnography is a method of 'seeing' the components of social structure and the processes through which they interact" (p. 13).

Such requirements justified the adoption of an approach that allowed an extended period of stay in the field. Participant observation was preferred over nonparticipant observation because I wanted to understand and experience shop floor work and shop floor culture for myself and, as a member of the shop floor, reflect on my own and others' behavior in developing cultural interpretations of events. I joined the organization as an associate (shop floor worker) on a six-month student job-placement contract after having been given permission by the company to do so as part of my doctoral studies. Participant observation enabled me to enter into routines, rituals, and practices as a member of the shop floor. By immersing myself in the shop floor life, I believed I would be able to offer a richer, reflexive understanding of social processes and dynamics than if I took a more conventional approach of research as an outsider or distant observer.

The work of Lupton (1963), Burawoy (1979), Cavendish (1982), Purcell (1986), Collinson (1992), and Lee (1993) provides examples of the contribution that a participant observation approach can make in the study of shop floor cultures. Participant observation studies within Japanese forms of work organizations have been few. A notable contribution is the work of Kamata (1982) on working for Toyota in Japan. In a Western context, the work of Gottfried and Graham (1993) and Graham (1993) provided important accounts and analysis of working on the shop floor within a Japanese automobile company in the United States. In the

United Kingdom, Delbridge (1995) has contributed by detailing workers' experiences of a just-in-time/total quality management system and outlining a significant impact on social relations by the adoption of these systems.

In adopting an ethnographic approach to the research project, I was aware of the recent challenges made—not from outside the field but from within the field—concerning the status of ethnography—for example, see Hammersley (1992) and Porter (1993), who stresses the need to bring structural factors back into any analysis and explanation of social phenomenon.

Research Organization

"Machine Co.," an international joint venture between a European and a Japanese organization, was established as a new company in the early 1990s, and a manufacturing plant was built on previously undeveloped land in the United Kingdom (a greenfield site), with the major shareholder being the Japanese parent. Within four years, it had expanded to employ more than 300 direct shop floor workers and was operating in light engineering manufacture and assembly.

Because I had permission from management to work on the shop floor as part of my research to understand shop floor practices and social processes within Japanese forms of work organization, people on the shop floor knew that I was working as part of my studies and that I wished to gain experience on shop floor practices. The Japanese expatriate managers were somewhat surprised at my strong will to work on the shop floor considering that a spell in the offices was probably a more conventional way to learn about Japanese management techniques. The managing director mentioned to me that in the parent company in Japan graduates had to be persuaded and pushed to work on the shop floor to gain experience. It was not considered as useful by the Japanese graduate recruits. People on the shop floor did treat me as "different" at first. This was partly because I was there for only six months rather than as a permanent worker. The organization, however, had only recently been established. Recruitment was ongoing and I soon dropped the title of "new associate." Being recruited during this period was advantageous because it allowed me to settle into the company and gain a degree of tenure and to be accepted into shop floor formal and informal groups. The fact that I was a student did not seem to create a great deal of curiosity. People in general saw it as a reflection of the company's wider plans to develop training opportunities for employees. Shop floor employees seemed to be more concerned that I was not a local but rather someone from another part of the country, as outlined in the following section.

The Town

Starting work at Machine Co. involved relocating to the town where the factory was located. The town was designated as a "new town" in the late 1960s by the central government and received an investment of more than £1 billion to provide an infrastructure to attract new business and 20,000 new jobs. Today, it boasts the largest number of Japanese organizations in a single town in the country and has attracted a considerable amount of foreign direct investment in manufacturing facilities, including more than 20 Japanese companies, more than 60 European companies, and more than 30 American companies. The Japanese organizations in the town have taken on the largest share of employees of all the overseas investors.

Interesting features of the town that are promoted to foreign investors include the exceptionally low level of industrial disputes in recent years compared to the region or the country as a whole and the absence of trade union representation in the majority of new companies moving into the area. Wage levels in the area are also significantly below the national average and government financial incentives have encouraged foreign investment in the area.

The majority of workers on the shop floor lived in the town, with only a small proportion traveling to work from neighboring towns. Because it is a small town, many workers know each other from outside of the factory. Many people on the shop floor were related to others who were working there, exaggerating the feeling for me of being in a small, closed community. Some workers did look surprised when I told them I was not from the area. I did feel like a stranger in this respect. During my stay, I came to understand that the nature of the local community, less cosmopolitan in outlook and ethnocentric, was an interesting factor mediating the relations of the shop floor workers with each other.

Induction and Socialization

All new associates, as new employees are called, had to complete a four-day induction program. On my first day, I was to meet with other new recruits in the public relations (PR) hall. As I entered the room, I was told to find the seat that had a file with my name on it and sit in that particular seat. The files had been arranged so that men and women sat in alternating chairs.

The induction course, or orientation course as some people preferred to call it, also served as a means of socializing new recruits into the organization's culture, norms, rules, spirit, and philosophy. The Japanese managing director gave a speech in which an analogy of the work organization to a football team was made. Each player was described as having a position but also interfacing and overlapping with others. The general manager continued this analogy: "As in a football team, ensure all parts of the playing field are covered, support your team members and harness that force." He continued,

> In the Western culture there is individualism. It is more difficult to have a consensus. Teams should aim for a consensus. You have the responsibility to speak up and listen to others, to discuss and debate and try to reach a general agreement.

We were told the company operated on a single status system. This manifested itself along a number of dimensions including the company uniform that everyone had to wear, the shared dining room, car parking without reserved spaces, time cards for everyone in the organization, and the open general office in which the managing director would share a desk alongside everyone else in the office.

The company philosophy and motto were presented—that people were the company's most important asset and that safety and quality must come first. We were introduced to the concept of Kaizen, which the general manager explained to us meant continuous improvement, involving everyone in the company and being based on the philosophy that our way of life—working life, social life, and home life—deserves to be constantly improved. An outline of how we should try to apply this concept to the workplace was presented. A member of quality control told us that TQI stood for total quality improvement and involved achieving total quality by harnessing everyone's commitment.

As the induction sessions ended, my first impression of the response of new associates was that the spirit and commitment being communicated by the managers did not seem to be making a resounding impact on them. During breaks, paper airplanes were flung around the room by the younger group of men and women aged approximately 18 to 22. People who recognized each other from outside the factory got together and talked. When we were left to watch a video of the parent company in Japan, few people actually watched the video. The airplanes returned and jokes were told. Some people just sat, looking very bored, not talking to anyone but also not interested in watching the video. Those I spoke to talked about wanting to "get on and start doing something."

The contrast between the commitment, dedication, and discipline being espoused by the Japanese managing director and the blank, resigned faces of the new recruits remained in my mind. Some recruits sounded as though they had an understanding of what taking up employment anywhere meant, and they just wanted to get on with it. This was my first impression of the response of the local workforce to the management's initial efforts to foster a sense of company spirit in new associates. I wondered what it was going to be like on the shop floor. I also realized the enormous challenge faced by the Japanese expatriates in working with the local workforce. I would learn what enormous pressure they were in fact under during their overseas assignments, with their future careers in the parent company resting very much on their performance in this overseas assignment.

Almost half of the 30 managerial positions in the organization were filled by Japanese expatriates. They filled senior management positions in the areas of manufacturing, production engineering, engineering, distribution, and accounting. The only senior management position not held by an expatriate was in personnel, following a strategic decision in line with other Japanese subsidiaries in the town to employ local nationals to deal with personnel and administration issues. The managing director was a Japanese expatriate of considerable experience and tenure in the parent organization, with previous experience in setting up overseas operations. The general management position was filled by the European partner's representative in the joint venture. He was the sole representative in the organization of the European partner, again having considerable experience in working in a multicultural environment. For many of the expatriates, however, this was their first posting overseas.

The following account presents findings from my time spent working on the Hano assembly line. The line provided the most direct attempt by the organization to implement the majority of the technical elements and many of the social elements of the work organization found in the parent organization in Japan. Therefore, it provided an interesting example of an experiment in the transfer of Japanese work practices. Because the organization was set up on a greenfield site, there were opportunities to design and experiment with forms of work organization. During interviews with senior managers, I was told that what was evolving was a hybrid system that retained many of what were considered the advantages of the Japanese form of technical and social work organization, with some adaptation of practices, especially in the area of human resource practices to the local environment, particularly the local labor market—for example, regarding remuneration and employment conditions.

A Study of Subcultural Processes
on the Hano Assembly Line

"Managing" the Culture to
Become the "Model" Line

I spent three months working on the Hano assembly line. The Hano assembly line was dedicated to producing systems for a Japanese customer. Other lines were set up to build systems for European customers. During this three-month period, I was part of the Hano team striving for continuous improvement and zero defects on the line. New recruits on the line were introduced to the culture of Kaizen and zero defects at an early stage through the job responsibilities they were immediately given to complete their work without any faults. There was little time allowed for new recruits to get up to the pace of the line; the expectation for zero defects in work was almost immediate.

As time passed, I realized that the Hano line had its own distinct culture on the shop floor that seemed to be related to some extent to managerial control strategies, which included human resource practices in recruitment, selection, and appraisal and Kaizen activities that were most advanced on the Hano line. The Hano line had a sign hanging over it that read "Achieving high productivity through Kaizen." It was the first of the assembly lines to be set up in the factory. I was told that the layout of the line had been copied almost exactly from the line in the parent company in Japan. When we had visitors on the shop floor, which was a regular event, senior management would show them the Hano line as the exemplar of the drive toward zero defects and increased productivity through Kaizen activities.

The Role of Hot Corners

Associates assembled before the start of work in specific areas on the shop floor assigned to their section. These were called hot corners. They had tables and chairs and lockers as well as sections for the use of the team leader and supervisor. The hot corners served to facilitate control of the workforce by providing a designated area for them to congregate during their breaks. It thus restricted communication by workers across different sections and served to facilitate a sense of belonging with the immediate work team. In my case, it was the other people on the Hano line. This physical separation of the workers during breaks also facilitated the development of a sense of identity to a particular section as opposed to another section through the hot corner meetings that were held in most sections at the beginning of every day. In these meetings, the team leaders or supervisors would run a meeting with the workers in which performance, output targets, and quality issues would usually be addressed.

One day, our supervisor commented on the new hot corners, implying that because of safety requirements the dividing walls between sections would be removed: "The new hot corners won't be ready for a week or so, so I want you to be very careful and tidy. We don't want to slump to their level" (indicating the team in the adjoining hot corner). "In the new hot corners there will be no dividing sections so keep our part of the corner tidy."

We did keep our corner tidy. With a cleaning rotation that was kept to, our line cleaned the hot corner twice a day. This was an example of the commitment that our supervisor was seeking to develop in us to being the best line in the factory with the best performance on quality and "5 S," the overall organizing and tidying of work in the workplace that the Japanese managers practiced so well and sought to instill in the local workers. The hot corners thus facilitated the development of a distinct and separate identity by the Hano assembly line workers in relation to assembly line workers on the other lines. The hot corner meetings furthered this sense of identity through the efforts of supervisors and team leaders to foster a sense of team loyalty and commitment to the team, and by seeking to instill other work-related values and attitudes in the associates as illustrated in the following paragraphs.

The supervisor and team leader of the Hano line were key actors in managing the culture on the line. The supervisor appeared to come to the line whenever he believed quality or productivity was not up to the level that management had set in their targets for the line. On a day-to-day basis, however it was the team leader who would manage the line.

During the time that I worked on the line, approximately 27 people were involved directly in the activities of the Hano line. This included the supervisor, team leader, and usually two setters who would work off the line. There were also sub-assembly activities involving one or two associates. The remaining associates worked on the line—the majority at assembly workstations along the line. Toward the end of the line, there was an "in-process inspector" followed down the line by a "QA" (quality assurance) associate who would do the final inspection of the assembled systems at the end of the line. This person was not directly accountable to the supervisor or team leader on the line but rather to his own supervisor of the QA department. The QA associate's role was to record any defects in products coming off the line. This formed part of the statistical process control system for monitoring performance on the line, a feature of the total quality management program implemented in the organization. This information was communicated back to the Hano team in the form of visual charts and graphs, displayed in our hot corner and discussed with us by the team leader in the team briefings that took place at the beginning of every day. There was also a record kept of "in-process" faults, which were faults identified and corrected by the in-process associate before they reached QA. The in-process associate was part of the Hano team, having been recruited to work on the Hano line rather than in QA.

Although all these people interacted in the running of the line, there were clearly identifiable emergent subcultures formed among these associates that, it is argued, were related to the underlying managerial control strategies.

Task and Subcultural Processes

One such subgrouping was associated with the nature of the task that the associate was performing as part of the work process. The QA associate at the end of the line was usually treated as an outsider rather than as a member of the Hano team. He would take his breaks with the rest of the QA team in their own QA hot corner. There was sometimes friction between the QA associate and the Hano line members. The QA associate was under pressure to prevent any defects passing through because the next inspector, to use the language of the culture we worked in, was the customer. The in-process inspector was also under pressure because the more faults that passed through that stage the more risk there was of QA missing one. It also reflected badly on the person in the in-process inspection role if faults were allowed through.

The daily team briefings in the hot corner focused on how many in-process faults there had been on the previous day, how many QA faults, and the output we had achieved against planned output. During my three months on the line, I observed and experienced the range of managerial control strategies utilized on the line in attempts to improve output and quality performance. In addition to the technical forms of monitoring faults and securing output along the assembly line, including such activities as statistical process control, time and motion studies, and the use of the Andon system, there were social pressures applied to capture the commitment of associates to the Kaizen philosophy. In a discussion with an associate off another line, I was told,

Really you have to be able to do the job of the person before you and the person after you. This is because you are supposed to check the quality of the person before you and your own. It's a quality network. If you see a defect you have to press your red light and the line will stop. If you let a defect pass you, then quality inspectors at the end of the line will put the defect down to all the people on the line past the workstation where the defect was made. This will then look bad on all the team.

The concept of "letting the team down" was used frequently by the supervisor, team leader, and setter to push people to improve their performance on the line. Through the hot corner team meetings, it was easy to understand which people had not been achieving the quality targets expected of them, and although reference to individuals was rarely made, the team leader's attention would focus on presenting which workstations were having the most defects. This proved to be a powerful means of putting pressure on individuals through presenting their performance to the rest of the team.

Authority and Subcultural Processes

In addition to task subcultures on the Hano line, a second subculture identified was associated with the authority hierarchy on the shop floor. The team leader and supervisor were directly accountable to management for performance on the line, and in trying to meet expectations placed on them for productivity and quality standards they would exercise a range of disciplinary and motivational forces on associates seeking to harness the efforts and commitment of everyone. Social interaction on the line thus revolved around the need to secure production and quality targets and the efforts of those in positions of authority to achieve this.

Both the team leader and the supervisor became exemplars of the spirit of commitment and positive attitude that was being encouraged in everyone on the line. In difficult times, associates on the line sometimes broke away from this culture and displayed, overtly or covertly, a counterculture of dissatisfaction, lack of commitment, apathy, and resistance to authority. In this way, two emergent subcultures sometimes became manifest and coexisted and interacted on the line—that of the positive, committed culture displayed through the team leader and the supervisor and that of the counterculture of antagonism and dissatisfaction among the rest of the line workers. As outlined previously, these two subcultures appeared to emerge in relation to efforts by those in positions of formal authority on the line to meet the demands of the TQM, just-in-time, lean production system.

The desire to nurture a culture that was not a "blame culture" came across several times in the induction program with emphasis on the need to pull together and help each other—all of us being responsible for the work of the team. In that program, we had been told by the production manager, "If you make a mistake tell the team leader. We do not operate a blame culture. If defects get back to the line it will be to say, for example, that the Sato team has failed." This philosophy, however, was sometimes difficult to implement in practice. Given the demanding production and quality targets, those responsible for managing the Sato line, who were local workers, would sometimes, under pressure, abandon these notions in favor of strategies they thought would have a stronger impact on the local workforce. In this way, there was the enactment of the beliefs, norms, and attitudes of the locals' wider cultural context in juxtaposition with the philosophy and culture being espoused by the Japanese expatriates. For example, the supervisor intervened whenever he considered things were going badly on the line.

During my first few weeks on the line, there was one very bad day when, from the beginning of work in the morning, the line was frequently being stopped because of faults. While we were working on that day, the line was stopped by the supervisor and he told us to gather around him. He told us angrily, "We have had eleven faults in the first hour. I am wasting my breath speaking. Come on. Wake up. Stop talking to each other and concentrate on what you are doing. This is disgraceful." Our supervisor was quick to point out following our increase in faults that "If senior management decide the situation cannot be tolerated anymore, then they may take drastic action and everyone will be out of the door."

The supervisor was himself under much pressure to reach the output and quality targets he had been given by senior management. The strive for continuous improvement meant that targets were never stable but rather would be set to improve on previous performance. The long-term objective was to aim for the kind of productivity and quality levels that were sustained in the Japanese parent company—an ambitious target for the local and the expatriate workforce to deal with.

The previous analysis indicates how the process of developing a strong organization-wide value system that is assimilated by the locals is still in its early stages. First-level managers have the challenging task of mediating relations and managing the interplay, contrasts, and contradictions in the cultural baggage of the local and expatriate workforce.

Age and Subcultural Processes

It was in this context of management efforts directed at the Hano line that the line culture evolved. As Pamela, a lady that I trained on the line who had moved from another line, said,

> I am nervous moving over here. I am more nervous than when I first started in the company. It is this line, they say it's really strict over here with mistakes and that the people don't talk to you very much, that it's not friendly.

Brenda, who worked up the line from us, commented,

> Well, there are the young ones and the old ones, like two groups on this line. That's it. I don't know where I fit in. I think they've put me with the old ones, but I'm not that old.

She was 28 years old.

At first, Brenda's comment may appear to be strange, one that does not follow from the concerns that Pamela had voiced. To me, it did make sense in the context of social relations and processes that were evolving on the line in association with management's attempts at securing control and commitment. As outlined in the sections that follow, this involved managerial control strategies being mediated by two distinct subcultures associated with age, with each subculture having its own response to managerial demands.

Age Subcultures and the Mediation of
Managerial Control Strategies

The main issues that the supervisor was concerned about were output levels and quality. Concern for continuous improvement by senior management was passed down to the supervisors on the shop floor in the form of continuous improvement targets in such areas as productivity, quality, and absenteeism levels. Hot corner meetings revolved around attempts to win the commitment of the workers to these targets through a combination of carrot and stick approaches. It is in this context that the social relations and processes on the line can best be understood and the comment by Brenda appreciated more fully.

There were clear groups of people who seemed, over time, to be identified by their different responses to the demands of the managerial control system. One group included the young men and women on the line. As in the induction course, they were approximately 18 to 22 years old. A second group was made up of older middle-aged women. A team leader from another section made the following comment about workers in general on the shop floor:

> There are three types of people. The young ones who are only passing through, and will go off and do something else. The older ones who work because they need the money and have a family and the older ones who want to make a go of it and are thinking of pensions.

She went on to say that the company should encourage the older ones because they were the most interested in doing a good job.

As Brenda had commented, there were indeed two groups of people on the line identified by their age: the young men and women approximately 18 to 22 years of age and the older women approximately 40 to 50 years old. I believe that recruitment and selection practices had encouraged these two groups to be over-represented on the line. Because they worked days, assembly line workers were the lowest paid workers on the shop floor. People who had experience in a manufacturing environment, especially engineering, seemed to be placed in the manufacturing section, leaving two distinct groups of people: the young and relatively inexperienced who did not have dependents and the middle-aged female group who did not have dependents or were taking home a second wage with children no longer dependent on them.

The two subcultures on the line could be differentiated by the nature of their reaction to managerial control strategies on a day to day basis. The younger group could be characterized as having a more overt display of resistance to control strategies. For example, they often broke the norms and rules set by the team leader and supervisor for conduct on the line—for example, by talking to each other or leaving the workstation to "stretch their legs" whenever the line had stopped. An unwillingness to exert peer pressure on their fellow workers on the line was a further example of resistance to managerial control attempts. The majority of young workers I spoke to on the line would often respond when things were not running well by saying that this job was only temporary because they had intentions of doing something else such as go to college at a later date. In this way, the younger workers appeared to console themselves and accommodate the pressures they faced in their work by considering that they had the "option" to leave.

In contrast, the older group of workers expressed a more resigned approach that things were not any better elsewhere and often appeared to accommodate to the demands of the managerial control system more readily, although not always enthusiastically and often with skepticism among themselves. In general, they were willing to use peer pressure to reduce defects on the line and were more actively involved in quality circle activities. When pressure built up on the line, they would often tend to deflect any criticism or blame onto the younger workers.

The responses of the two groups to overtime tended to be different and this was often commented on by the supervisor, who would criticize the younger group for not doing enough overtime: "Look at them. They are leaving [referring to the younger workers on the line who chose not to hang around in search of overtime when the buzzer went]. . . . They are just not bothered."

Within the Kaizen culture and the overall spirit of the company, doing overtime was interpreted as a sign of commitment to the company and of a positive attitude by people not on the shop floor. The just-in-time production system made it imperative to have a workforce that could respond to fluctuations in output requirements and production progress on a day-to-day basis. Overtime was therefore an important means for management to secure output levels in times of unexpected changes. For the younger workers on the line, however, the opportunity to "work over" was not often welcomed. From discussions I had with the younger workers on the line, I realized that it was often seen as an infringement on their spare time and social life outside the factory. Working alongside the younger workers, I was privileged to be given the opportunity by them to enter their "world" for a short period of time. I learned of their lives outside the factory and their spare-time activities that they always talked about. Again, I sensed the local community influence, with many of the young people on the line going to the same places and knowing the same people. There was a disco in the center of the town that attracted most of the youth in the town. Working overtime on a Saturday would mean Friday night social events would have to be restricted.

Such dilemmas seemed to lead to the younger workers displaying a less positive attitude to overtime, and the older workers, who were much more consistent in doing overtime, would comment on this. When the line needed to be kept running, then all the team had to be there. It was difficult to replace people who were absent because there was not a great deal of flexibility of workers. People in general had been trained and gained experience in just a few positions. This was probably partly explained by the fact that this was still a relatively new operation, with the majority of employees on the line having worked there for less than two years. In this situation, the supervisor would tell us in the hot corner meetings that we all must come in and if someone did not, then we would be letting the whole team down. This is demonstrated by the following episode:

> In the break, our supervisor told us that there would have to be some overtime done because we were behind in achieving our next delivery (a just-in-time

delivery system operated). He suggested Saturday, but some shouted that it was the social club's trip out. He told us that we should get together then and decide as a team when we would like to do the overtime and to get back to him later that day. Later, he asked us what our decision had been. We had not discussed the issue so he asked us to raise our hands if we preferred Saturday to coming in early during the week. The majority raised their hand and so it was decided. (extract from field notes)

The supervisor continued,

You made that decision as a team, so you have to stick to it as a team. So I want all of you to be here on Saturday. It is no good if some of you don't come. We need all of you, you are a team.

There was a tendency for the young workers to join together in their resistance to managerial pressure. A communication network was maintained along the line in which several of the young workers were able to interpret sign language and read lips. Sometimes there were ongoing conversations about what had happened the night before or whether they were going out that night. From my contact with the young workers, I came to appreciate this network because it served to ease boredom and frustration from the routine, repetitive nature of the job. I worked alongside two of the younger workers during my period on the line and I joined with them in the pastimes they played as a way of alleviating boredom on the line. As Sheila, who worked next to me, told me, she would "crack up" if she was not allowed to talk on the job.

The supervisor, however, tried to cut down on talking by arguing that people were not concentrating on their work and defects would be made if people talked. Pressure was again placed on the young ones to stop talking. The young ones, however, maintained their informal communication system along the line out of the immediate eye of the supervisor. Sometimes, one or two of the more rebellious boys would blatantly talk in front of the team leader, saying that as long as they did their job they should be able to talk. Sally and Brian, both in their early 20s, were dating. They amazed me with their ability to walk up and down the line and talk with each other, find out what was happening, and joke whenever there were a few seconds to spare. The supervisor tried to crack down on this as well and the young workers became more frustrated. Workers were moved around to try and break up any signs of informal cliques that may be damaging to performance on the line.

Antagonism Across Age Subcultures: A Response
to Managerial Control Strategies to Reduce
Defects on the Line

The just-in-time system had an impact on social relations on the line through the demands it placed on the line performance. The just-in-time system required flexibility of workers to respond to an unexpected shortfall in output through overtime and through keeping the line going (i.e., not stopping the line). It placed demands on the line workers to get things right the first time, avoiding delays in having goods ready for shipment to customers. This was reinforced by the total quality management system that the company was in the process of implementing. It was in the context of this system and efforts to develop a commitment to quality by everyone on the line as part of their job that the antagonism between the old and the young workers was clearly displayed in the PR room incident outlined previously.

Operating a relatively lean production system put additional pressures on the line workers. Without buffer stock, the line was vulnerable to defective parts or shortages of parts. Pressure on the line would mount when defective parts were found and line workers were held responsible for inspecting the parts they were assembling as well as checking their own work. Thus, these pressures led to reactions by subcultures on the line. The age, task, and authority subcultures were identifiable by their reactions to these pressures on the line.

The older women on the line had agreed to form a quality control circle to look at some of the technical problems on the line. With the older women being together in the QC circle, this further reinforced the gulf between the young and the older workers on the line. As shown in the following episode, a confrontation developed following pressure from the supervisor to reduce the number of reworks coming off the line:

> The supervisor told us in the hot corner that we needed to consider ways to reduce the reworks coming off the line. The team leader took us into the PR room and asked for our ideas. She prompted that she thought peer pressure might help. (extract from field notes)

She continued, "What do you think of a yellow card and a red card for too many faults?"

At the time, all faults found by in-process inspection at the bottom of the line (carried out by a middle-aged woman) were written down and finally displayed on a chart showing the faults of each person on the line. Final inspection by quality control at the end of the line also identified the nature of the faults found and these were also placed on the faults chart displayed in the hot corner. One middle-aged lady retorted that it would be like school. The team leader continued, "What if we all tell them in the hot corner 'Come on, we don't want to be correcting your faults, you are making the faults on the line and we don't want you to make them.' " The in-process inspector at the end of the line replied,

> That's not going to work, is it, because people are not going to say anything about their friends. The thing is here, as you know, there are the young ones and the old ones. The young ones are not bothered. They couldn't care less if the faults don't come down. Don't tell me they are going to change, they are not going to put pressure on each other.

The next day, the young girl working next to me complained, "It's always us [implying the young ones] that are at fault. People will leave if it gets worse."

I had the opportunity to work alongside two of the young workers. What I noticed was that they worked very hard—as hard as anyone else on the line (technically, there was little choice)—and most of the time were very committed to their task at hand in that they were concerned about not making a mistake and would be quick to correct mistakes they spotted from others up the line. I had no reason to interpret their conscientiousness as a product of my presence on the line. They would talk openly to me when they were feeling bored or did not feel like working. They would mention when their mind was not on the job. On a typical day, there were approximately 400 units that had to be assembled. Each of these units may require approximately five or six assembly processes to be completed within the time allowed (approximately 40 seconds). This amounted to a total of approximately 2,400 processes by each worker every day. The target that we were told to aim for was to have zero defects off final inspection.

The standards of performance and concentration expected of everyone on the line were so high that a small lapse in concentration was not acceptable. One or two defects for the whole line were accepted by the team leader, but if we went higher than this, then we would be told to do better. If a person had one fault during a day, this was considered very serious. Two faults and the person would be spoken to by the team leader as a usual practice. Brian, working next to me, made two faults one day and he was given a severe telling off by the team leader who told him that he was not concentrating and that this did not look good with his appraisal coming up soon.

When reacting against increased pressure from management, however, the particular form of resistance practiced by the young ones was more overt than that of the older women. In both cases, however, resistance never led to direct confrontation with management in which work on the line actually had to be halted. In this sense, it may be argued that there were underlying latent subcultures on the line that became manifest when the expectations on the workers by the formal management system were seen as too demanding. This process was associated with the nature of the work organization, which involved a just-in-time, lean production, total quality management system.

Contradictions in Managerial Control Strategies

During the period of time I spent on the Hano line, it was possible to identify contradictions in the managerial control strategies being used, as shown in the following example: "The team leader came down the line saying that she was keeping a file on where the reworks were coming from. This really got everybody's attention on to the faults files" (extract from field notes). A few days later, she announced that there was to be a new chart that recorded defects taken off the line and defects spotted on the line.

Management attempted to increase surveillance on the line by having the team leader encourage workers to report defects they found on the line. In some cases, however, the informal resistance to the control came through the wish of workers not to be reported by their workmates working alongside them. One young girl said to me,

> If we do what Laura [the team leader] wants us to do, there will be things done behind other people's backs. There will be a lot of trouble because people will be getting their own back if someone says something about faults to Laura and it will just make the whole line go bad.

I felt the pressure on the line increase at that time. I understood that the informal help that people had been giving each other to correct faults on the line had been a strength of the team to ensure that no defects reached the end of the line. This cooperation between people on the line was now being challenged by management who, in seeking to make us suppliers and customers of each other, wished to formalize the TQM system further through more extensive monitoring of individual performance (defects) on the line. In seeking to increase their control by the reporting of defects on the line, management was in fact inadvertently breaking down the cooperative effort of the team pulling together. This provides another example of first-line managers' attempts to meet the demands placed on them and the complex way in which cultural baggage influences interpretation of these actions by the local workforce. I came to understand that the younger workers on the line had as much interest in making a go of it in their job as did the older ones. It was their response to situations that they felt were unfair or unjust, such as the incident described previously, that led many of them to take a negative attitude to their work and people in authority over them.

Some Reflections

The previous analysis of social processes along one assembly line operating with a just-in-time, TQM, lean production system has sought to explore the emergence and interaction of subcultures on the line and relate them to the managerial control system. It has been argued that the just-in-time, TQM, lean production system that operated was associated with the social relations and social processes that evolved on the line through the performance and quality demands that the combined effects of these systems placed on the line. The emergence of subcultures was analyzed in association with managerial control strategies used to secure output and quality requirements demanded by the just-in-time, total quality management, lean production system. This interaction of managerial control strategies with subcultural processes is conceptualized in Figure 11.1. The figure also seeks to incorporate an awareness of the further cultural complexity on the shop floor created by the interplay of broader local workforce and Japanese expatriate subcultures.

Local Workforce and Japanese Expatriate Subcultures

In working in a multicultural environment in which Japanese expatriates and local nationals seek to comprehend each other, cope with cultural diversity, and assimilate some of the cultural traits of the other, the Hano assembly line has provided an example of the day-to-day struggles at the heart of the production process in dealing with the challenges that this creates. The interpretation of management practices by the setter and team leader, the local figures of authority

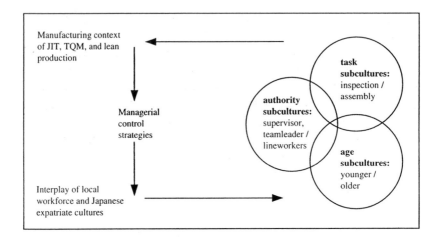

Figure 11.1. Managerial Control Strategies and Subcultural Processes on the Hano Line

on the line, indicates the difficulties they face in seeking to mold the culture of a local workforce on the assembly line.

Interesting questions raised by this analysis relate to the extent to which the subcultural processes along the line are influenced by the wider national culture of the local workforce in their efforts to adopt and respond to management practices transferred from the parent organization. The organization is still in its early stages of developing a strong formal organization culture that, as senior management have outlined, will involve adapting Japanese best practice to the local situation and in this sense creating a hybrid system (Abo, 1994). The technical and social means of securing control on the assembly line involved the application and adaptation of management practices and principles related to attitudes and values of the parent organization's managers brought with them from their own national culture and context that, in turn, were interpreted, refined, sometimes adjusted, and sometimes ignored by the local managers in seeking to achieve their production objectives. This formed the framework in which further subcultural processes among the local workforce were explored in this chapter. Thus, the shop floor activities explored in this chapter involving the local workforce were contingent on the evolving style of management being utilized—a style transferred and adapted to the local conditions from the parent company in Japan.

Concluding Points

This chapter has focused on outlining the emergence and interaction of subcultures in a shop floor manufacturing environment characterized by just-in-time, total quality management, and lean production systems. In exploring the interaction of managerial control strategies and subcultural processes, these manufacturing systems were believed to place demands on the output and quality standards of the assembly line. The following points summarize the results of the research findings described in this chapter:

1. The systems required a fast response time to changes in production orders, flexibility of workers to work overtime, and the critical importance of getting things right the first time due to the low level of slack in the system. Managerial control strategies were aimed at securing these targets through being continually adapted and revised.

2. The evolving control strategies utilized were influenced by the complex interplay between parent organization expectations as translated by the Japanese expatriates into the local cultural context and the local manager's interaction with the workforce in which control strategies were adapted, refined, and adjusted to cope with the responses and actions of the local workers.

3. The Hano assembly line was analyzed as having its own distinct culture on the shop floor that evolved during the interplay of managerial control strategies and worker responses to these strategies.

4. This chapter has explored the emergence of authority, task, and age subcultures on the Hano line. Subcultures could be differentiated by the contrasting reactions of their members to managerial control initiatives on a day-to-day basis. The emergence of subcultural identities and their enactment appeared to be related to the pressures of the managerial control system, with the subcultures becoming more divisive and active when pressure on the line increased. On such occasions subcultures were often in conflict on the line. This conflict seemed to strengthen the cultural identity of members of both groups.

5. Management practices along the line would sometimes draw on the cultural identities of these groups. This was clear in the instance of age subcultures, in which there were challenges and provocation addressed at the younger workers to do better. Such practices, however, in strengthening subculture identities, divided

the line and contradicted the objective of securing a sense of team spirit along the whole of the line.

6. The inherent complexity in transferring management practices across cultural boundaries is recognized. It is argued that those in positions of authority on the line interpreted, refined, sometimes adjusted, and sometimes ignored the management practices and principles that were being transferred in their attempts to meet the production targets they were given.

In this sense, a hybrid management system was evolving at the point of production through the ongoing social processes and social relations on the line. The task of those in positions of authority on the line was seen as complex in negotiating the demands of the production system and working with the web of cultural expectations, norms, values, and attitudes that emerged in the multicultural work context.

References

Abo, T. (1994). The analysis of Japanese factories located overseas. In T. Abo (Ed.), *Hybrid factory: The Japanese production system in the United States* (pp. 3-25). Oxford, UK: Oxford University Press.

Braverman, H. (1974). *Labor and monopoly capital: The degradation of work in the twentieth century.* London: Monthly Review Press.

Burawoy, M. (1979). *Manufacturing consent: Changes in the labour process under monopoly capitalism.* London: University of Chicago Press.

Burawoy, M. (1985). *The politics of production.* London: Bookcraft.

Cavendish, R. (1982). *Women on the line.* London: Routledge Kegan Paul.

Collinson, D. L. (1992). *Managing the shop floor: Subjectivity, masculinity and workplace culture.* New York: de Gruyter.

Delbridge, R. (1995). Surviving JIT: Control and resistance in a Japanese transplant. *Journal of Management Studies, 32*(6), 803-817.

Florida, R., & Kenney, M. (1991). Organisation v culture: Japanese automotive transplants in the U.S. *Industrial Relations Journal, 22,* 181-196.

Gottfried, H., & Graham, L. (1993, November). Constructing difference: The making of gendered subcultures in a Japanese assembly plant. *Sociology, 27*(4), 611-628.

Graham, L. (1993, May). Inside a Japanese transplant: A critical perspective. *Work and Occupations, 20*(2), 147-173.

Hammersley, M. (1992). *What's wrong with ethnography? Methodological explorations.* London: Routledge.

Jurgens, U. (1993). National and company differences in organizing production work in the car industry. In B. Kogut (Ed.), *Country competitiveness: Technology and organizing of work* (pp. 106-123). Oxford, UK: Oxford University Press.

Kamata, S. (1982). *Japan in the passing lane.* New York: Pantheon.

Kenney, M., & Florida, R. (1993). *Beyond mass production. The Japanese system and its transfer to the US.* Oxford, UK: Oxford University Press.

Kleinberg, M., & Florida, R. (1994). The crazy group: Emergent culture in a Japanese-American binational workgroup. *Research in International Business and International Relations, 6,* 1-45.

Knights, D. (1995, April). *Labour process theory in the age of deconstruction.* Paper presented at the 13th Annual Labour Process Conference, Blackpool, UK.

Knights, D., & Willmott, H. (1985, February). Power and identity in theory and practice. *Sociology Review, 33*(1), 22-46.

Knights, D., & Willmott, H. (1989, November). Power and subjectivity at work: From degradation to subjugation in social relations. *Sociology, 23*(4), 535-558.

Kunda, G. (1992). *Engineering culture: Control and commitment in a high-tech corporation.* Philadelphia: Temple University Press.

Lee, C. K. (1993, December). Familial hegemony: Gender and production politics on Hong Kong's electronics shopfloor. *Gender and Society, 7*(4), 529-547.

Lincoln, J. R., & Kalleberg, A. L. (1985, December). Work organisation and workforce commitment: A study of plants and employees in the U.S. and Japan. *American Sociological Review, 50,* 738-760.

Lincoln, J. R., & Kalleberg, A. L. (1990). *Culture, control and commitment: A study of work organisation and work attitudes in the United States and Japan.* Cambridge, UK: Cambridge University Press.

Lupton, T. (1963). *On the shop floor: Two studies of workshop organisation and output.* London: Pergamon.

Porter, S. (1993, November). Critical realist ethnography: The case of racism and professionalism in a medical setting. *Sociology, 27*(4), 591-609.

Purcell, K. (1986). *Gender and experience at work: An ethnographic study of work and social interaction in a manufacturing workshop.* Unpublished doctoral dissertation, Manchester University, Manchester, UK.

Rosen, M. (1991). Coming to terms with the field: Understanding and doing organisational ethnography. *Journal of Management Studies, 28,* 1-24.

Storey, J. (1985, May). The means of management control. *Sociology, 19*(2), 193-211.

Tayeb, M. (1994, February). Japanese managers and British culture: A comparative case study. *International Journal of Human Resource Management, 5*(1), 145-166.

Thompson, P. (1986). *The nature of work. An introduction to debates on the labour process.* London: Macmillan.

Westney, E. (1993). Country patterns in R & D management: The United States and Japan. In B. Kogut (Ed.), *Country competitiveness: Technology and organizing of work* (pp. 36-53). Oxford, UK: Oxford University Press.

Whitley, R. (1992). *Business systems in East Asia: Firms, markets and societies.* London: Sage.

Willmott, H. (1995, April). *Action, structure and the labour process debate.* Paper presented at the 13th Annual Labour Process Conference, Blackpool, UK.

Womack, J. P., Jones, D. T., & Roos, D. (1990). *The machine that changed the world.* New York: Harper Perennial.

Chapter 12

Discontinuous Technological Change as a Trigger for Temporary Reconciliation of Managerial Subcultures

A Case Study of a Finnish Paper Industry Company

Juha Laurila

After a short period of dominance by the integrative approaches within the organization culture literature (e.g., Pettigrew, 1979; Schein, 1985), work emphasizing cultural differentiation and fragmentation has taken over the field (e.g., Gregory, 1983; Meyerson & Martin, 1987; Saffold, 1988). The conceptualizations of organizational subcultures have so far identified various types of subcultures and

AUTHOR'S NOTE: Financial support from the Academy of Finland, Marcus Wallenberg Foundation, and the Helsinki School of Economics and its research project Finnish Managerial Competence and National Competitiveness in Transition is gratefully acknowledged. I thank Peter Dahler-Larsen, Margaret Grieco, Kari Lilja, Maggie Phillips, Sonja Sackmann, and Risto Tainio for encouragement and comments on an earlier draft.

sources of these cultural divisions (Martin & Siehl, 1983; Wilkins & Dyer, 1988). It has thus been understood that even organizations that appear to be culturally united contain several sectional groups with their specific ways of thinking and acting (Brown & Duguid, 1991; Jermier, Slocum, Fry, & Gaines, 1991).

It seems, however, that despite recognition of the forms and sources of subcultures very little is known about the situational mechanisms that might be able to produce consensus across these subcultural boundaries. For example, it should be further elaborated how and why subdivided management may be united in situations in which managerial actors must signal commitment to a specific innovation to provide the necessary external resources for its realization (Burgelman & Sayles, 1986). This line of study has been lacking, although some seminal works have already noted how, for example, social indulgence (Gouldner, 1954) or temporary resource munificence (Cyert & March, 1963) enforce feelings of community and commitment by permitting various actors to promote their objectives through common means. More empirical research is needed to conceptualize the situational mechanisms and "unsettled periods" (Bloor & Dawson, 1994) during which the relationships between different subcultures become rearranged.

This chapter aims to make a contribution to previous literature on organizational subcultures through empirical investigation of subcultural factions within management. This is a novel starting point merely in the sense that even in organizational culture studies, management is mostly treated as a culturally unified actor (e.g., Lewis, 1994; Rouse & Fleising, 1995). Instead, this chapter assumes that management, like any other constellation of individuals, is divided into various subcultural factions that are continuously in flux (Parker, 1995) and can be identified most easily in relation to a concrete managerial problem (Harris, 1994). One example of this kind of problem is discontinuous technological change, which is used here as a research experiment and as a tool for analytical generalizations on managerial and organizational subcultures (Dyer & Wilkins, 1991; Tsoukas, 1989). This problem is prominent in the paper industry because the uncertainties and risks related to the major capital expenditures required in the acquisition of necessary new technologies compel various subcultural actors to reveal their ideological stance in relation to the alternative technological designs. Situations of discontinuous change are also especially interesting for theorizing on subcultural reconciliation in the sense that they pose a major challenge for creating consensus within management. A single key executive or even a dominant coalition in management cannot authorize this kind of change, which depends on the cooperative action of managers representing different levels and functions in the managerial hierarchy. Examination of this situation in an in-depth case analysis will demonstrate how the expansion of operations through technological change temporarily unites actors representing conflicting managerial subcultures.

The fieldwork was conducted in the Finnish forest industry corporation, Tampella, during a period of several years.[1] During that period of time, several reports were published on different issues. In general, the research project focused on managers and their actions, especially in relation to technological change. Although the research was not ethnographic in the sense that the researcher had systematically used participant observation and stayed for long periods in the field, it was based on a variety of data shedding light on subcultural patterns in management. In addition to formal individual interviews and collective discussions with 20 key managers related to the specific change situation examined here, the researcher and author of this chapter visited the mill shop floor several times, spoke with managers in their offices during lunch and in a company limousine, and spent days content-analyzing files at company headquarters. These data were combined into an aggregated view of management as a constellation of subcultures. In addition, the researcher belonged to a research group that worked on the same case and also on five other cases within the same industry, which provided additional information and opportunity for information cross-checking and case contextualization (see Eisenhardt, 1989, pp. 540-541).

As a result, the researcher was provided with a mixed collection of documentary and oral history material, including data from a corporate culture survey conducted throughout Tampella. In addition, several years' research access has permitted longitudinal analysis partly in real time, allowing the researcher to follow-up the changing "native-views" (Gregory, 1983) on specific events during a longer period of time. For example, it was possible to compare the arguments related to new technology at the time of their introduction with those a few years later.

In the following section, some previous conceptualizations of organizational and managerial subcultures are reviewed with a focus on factors that seem to function as bases of subculture formation. The second section elaborates on the mechanisms that seem to blur these subcultural boundaries. The third section describes and analyzes the case before concluding and making suggestions for further study.

Sources of Subcultural Division
Within Management

If organizational culture is defined as a patterned system of values and meanings, making individuals susceptible to specific ways of action in organizations (see Golden, 1992, p. 5), then organizational subcultures can be interpreted as deviating in some way from this general pattern. In other words, organizations often carry a consistent cultural image that, however, covers a variety of practices (Jermier et al., 1991) and meanings attached to those practices (Meek, 1988). Cultural diversity can thus be found both at the level of social practices and at the level of the values and meanings that the former manifest (Trice & Beyer, 1993).

At the level of social practices, the identification of subcultures has emphasized the view of organizations as conflict-intensive constructions (Young, 1989). For example, it has been demonstrated how organizations that appear to be homogeneous may contain significant contradictions because individuals have opportunities to oppose the dominant cultural patterns, and this leads to the emergence of subcultures (Carnall, 1986; Golden, 1992). In this sense, the subcultural perspective conforms to the organizational politics perspective (e.g., Mintzberg, 1985). The current literature on subcultures, however, exceeds these limits because it does not assume that all actors necessarily pursue similar objectives or that they interpret the organizational acts in the same manner (Young, 1989). This implies, in the managerial context, that subcultural factions may find deviating ways to promote the general managerial objectives that they all accept (Golden, 1992). Hence, subcultures may exist if a concrete managerial problem is treated differently by identifiable groups of managerial actors (Harris, 1994).

What then produces subcultural division within management? Numerous factors may contribute. Among them are demographic factors such as gender, age, race, religion, and language. Taking a more formal point of view, management may be divided horizontally into functions (Lawrence & Lorsch, 1967) and into geographical or product lines and staff (Dalton, 1950). In addition, management is divided vertically into hierarchical levels with specific responsibilities (Teulings, 1986). In the case of multidivisional companies, the specific features of industry such as technology produce subcultural diversity (Gordon, 1991; Pennings & Gresov, 1986; Reynolds, 1986; Sackmann, 1992). Thus, managerial subcultures emerge because these differences between the formal responsibilities of managerial actors are coupled with differences in their career paths, methods of operation, and sources of power. From a socioemotional perspective on management subdivisions, it is necessary to refer to the shared experiences and background within management as a social (Dalton, 1959) or an occupational community (Van Maanen & Barley, 1984). This does not necessarily mean that the managerial factions sharing an occupational background agree. Instead, intraprofessional groupings may be based, for example, on the differences between cosmopolitan and local bases of loyalty (Gouldner, 1957) and on background (Gouldner, 1954). Moreover, the same managerial community may include several subcultures based, for example, on differences in operational traditions (Bierly & Spender, 1995).

The existing literature thus suggests that although management has some shared functions, it can and should be conceptualized as a social constellation of subcultural factions connected and divided by several factors acting in concert. This is not to say that managerial actors are unable to cooperate and to sustain a coherent public image (see Parker, 1995, pp. 542-543). A coherent facade, however, is not enough in situations of discontinuous change that necessitate adoption of new managerial skills and actions and also determined cooperation throughout management because successful implementation depends on the skills and capabilities of each actor (Pettigrew & Whipp, 1991). Subcultural reconciliation is also important because precluding some actors from this cooperation may lead to "foot-dragging" and negative criticism that endangers efforts to overcome the discontinuity (Kanter, 1982). It can therefore be expected that the necessary cooperation and revolutionary momentum will not be created without at least temporary cultural homogeneity and consensus within management.

Approaches to Subcultural Reconciliation Within Management

It is argued that the problem of subcultural reconciliation within management can be tackled in at least three different ways. The first is to deny the whole problem by assuming that although subcultural factions exist, specific mechanisms for overcoming subcultural conflicts are not needed because the operational pressures of managerial work compel actors to cooperate (Young, 1989, p. 203) and, thus, smooth functioning does not require collectively shared objectives and meanings (Grieco, 1988). Another assumption that can be made is that little consensus is needed for organizational actions (Cohen, March, & Olsen, 1972) partly because of the shared means and conventions of communication (Donnellon, Gray, & Bougon, 1986). On a more general level, it has been argued that because managerial actors also work for their living, they are motivated to find ways that combine even contrasting objectives into joint action (Weick, 1979).

The problem with this kind of approach, however, is that it cannot explain why managerial actors take part in actions that require personal sacrifices and cooperation with actors representing dissimilar values and ideologies. It cannot illuminate how, for example, conflicting managers in a paper industry company come to an agreement over the timing and design of a large-scale technological change project.

Another way to treat the problem is to link needed cooperation to the persuasion executed by individual managers either at top- or middle-level management. It is assumed that key individuals may act as liaisons between conflicting subcultural factions through ongoing negotiation and by providing adequate rewards and messages for each faction (Trice & Beyer, 1991, pp. 163-164).

The success of individual managers in their efforts to bring about cultural reconciliation depends on their abilities to create a positive interpretation of future events (e.g., Westley & Mintzberg, 1989). Thus, each subcultural grouping is addressed with messages "framed" in a way that secures its commitment to or at least participation in the intended cooperation (Snow, Rochford, Worden, & Benford, 1986). In addition, an inspiring vision may in itself promote its own realization (Field, 1989; Gagliardi, 1986). From this perspective, the managers' actual skills, capabilities, and personal charisma (Trice & Beyer, 1986) affect their power to create and enforce cooperation within the managerial hierarchy. In successful cases, this may lead to the emergence of an "integrative" management culture (Kanter, 1983).

Such an entrepreneurial approach (e.g., Fulop, 1991) can be criticized for its implicit assumption that the capabilities and charisma of individual managers are sufficient to reconcile subcultural conflicts. This assumption is problematic because processes of managerial persuasion are time-consuming, individual managers have varying amounts of skill (Hosking, 1991), and it is questionable whether charismatic individuals who can sustain their charisma will be found (Trice & Beyer, 1986). In addition, some actors may implicitly or explicitly oppose and act against such a process of reconciliation (e.g., Carnall, 1986; Golden, 1992; Hirschman, 1970).

Efforts to advocate unified corporate cultures may even produce new conceptual tools that organizational actors can use to legitimate oppositional acts (Chapter 17, this volume). For these reasons, acts of individual managers represent only a limited mechanism of subcultural reconciliation.

Because neither the operational pressures nor the specific capabilities of individual managers can provide the necessary subcultural reconciliation, for example, in situations of discontinuous change, one needs to be sensitive to the situation-specific mechanisms of subcultural reconciliation and locate the basis of intramanagerial consensus in the specific content of managerial work. Such a situational approach to subcultural reconciliation assumes that managerial subcultures emerge in critical phases such as new technology introduction and result in changes in subcultural power relations (Bloor & Dawson, 1994; Pettigrew, 1973). The existing literature on managerial subcultures does not systematically address situational aspects that might produce subcultural reconciliation.

This chapter proposes that discontinuous technological change is an example of a situational mechanism that may trigger temporarily subcultural reconciliation within management because it may in itself entail various positive outcomes for those who participate in its design and implementation. For example, besides the usual official objectives for new technology, such as increasing profitability or gaining competitiveness, an emerging business exploiting new technology permits "scientists" to increase their knowledge and "business people" to expand their businesses although these groups are at the same time competing within the same managerial hierarchy (Burgelman & Sayles, 1986). The creation of subcultural reconciliation is not obvious even in companies dominated by a specific profession because the actors holding similar professional objectives may not be able to agree on the ways of how to implement them (Strauss, Schatzman, Erlich, Bucher, & Sabshin, 1963). The following case analysis is aimed at supporting the argument that discontinuous technological change should be understood as a mechanism that may temporarily unite managerial actors.

Subcultural Reconciliation in the Case of Tampella

Some Facts on Tampella and the Structure of the Analysis

Tampella is an industrial company founded in the middle of the 19th century. Its turnover at the time of study was about $1.5 billion. The company's operations consisted of several business units, most of which were related to the forest industry sector. This chapter focuses on the period of discontinuous technological change made at the beginning of the 1990s in one of these business units—a paper mill.[2] In 1987, after approximately 20 years of low profitability and lack of capital investment, Tampella changed ownership to a new dominant owner who wanted to modernize the company. The changes in this specific facility included replacing a significant part of the old machinery (i.e., a paper machine) with a new one through a major investment project. This discontinuous technological change deviated from previous ones undertaken at Tampella in that this time machinery more than five decades old was replaced with "state-of-the-art" machinery based on the most sophisticated technological design available at that time,[3] which permitted the production of "leading edge" products.[4] The novelty of both products and their manufacturing process necessitated significant recruitment of personnel at all management levels. The ways in which this specific situation of discontinuous technological change affected Tampella's management as a subcultural constellation are examined in detail in the following subsections.

The following case description should be considered one ideal type of construction of managerial subcultures that by their very nature are indefinite and ambiguous. The major features of each subcultural fraction and their mutual contradictions are described before exploring how actors who represented clearly deviating managerial subcultures found themselves supporting the same ambitious change design.

Management as a Constellation of Four Subcultures

The managerial subcultures involved are described and characterized according to features, the specific ideological patterns that characterize each subculture, and the ways in which these ideologies are materialized in managerial action (see Jermier et al., 1991). In the case of Tampella, at the time of the study management was composed of four subcultures that were produced by two parallel divisions. One subcultural division was between company- and mill-level management. It implied that managers at these levels faced different work responsibilities, had systematically varying lengths of previous working careers, and, in addition, the former were usually the supervisors of the latter. Another division also proved to be vital: the division between the "old-timers" and the "newcomers" in management (Gouldner, 1954). The old-timers consisted of individuals who had been managers at Tampella either at the mill or company level for several years. The newcomers had entered management positions in Tampella at either of these levels

Table 12.1 Comparison of the Characteristics of the Subcultures at the Management of Tampella

| | Subculture | | | |
| | Company-Level | | Mill-Level | |
Feature	Old-timers	Newcomers	Old-timers	Newcomers
Typical age and education	55 Years; MSc (engineering)	45 Years; MSc (engineering)	45 Years; MSc or BSc	32 Years; MSc or PhD
Typical work history	Four previous positions at Tampella	Two or three previous employers	Two previous positions at Tampella	One previous employer
Ideology	Local	Cosmopolitan	Local	Cosmopolitan
Management style	Centralization	Empowerment	Compliance	Opportunism
Implications for strategy	Maintenance of traditions	Aim for the "state of the art"	Minor improvements	Supporting modernization

only a short while ago and had acquired management experience outside the company. These four subcultures are characterized in Table 12.1.

In terms of background features, these four subcultures in the management of Tampella can be characterized by identifying their typical representatives. The typical old-timer at the company level was a rather aged (55 years old) paper industry civil engineer who had for his whole working career served Tampella first in concrete technical planning and later in various management positions. He had experienced the company expansion in the 1960s and threats of bankruptcy in the 1970s. In addition, the typical old-timer was born in one of the Tampella localities and most likely still lived in one.

In contrast, the typical old-timer at the mill level was slightly younger (about 45 years old) and, instead of a master of science (MSc) degree in paper industry engineering, he held an MSc or bachelor of science degree in some other technical subject. He resembled the typical old-timer at the company level, however, in that he also had worked during his whole career at Tampella in different positions but had not left the vicinity of the facility in which he was well-known. In contrast, the newcomers had quite a different background. A typical representative of the newcomers at the company level was approximately the same age as a typical old-timer at the mill level (45 years old), and he held an MSc degree in paper industry engineering.[5] Most of these newcomers had been employed by several companies and facilities and participated in various development projects within the industry.

Participation in these visible endeavors had made them well-known within the sector, whereas the old-timers had mainly gained their reputation within Tampella.

Newcomers who were recruited at the company management level were naturally more experienced (and aged) than those who were recruited at the mill level, although some of the younger newcomers might even hold a doctoral degree in engineering. In this sense, newcomers were not a uniform group that was still enforced by different positions in the managerial hierarchy. The typical newcomer at the mill level resembled newcomers at the company level in the sense that both of them were mobile and had moved around according to their employer. Hence, they lacked the strong connections to the local community that were typical of all the old-timers.

It can be argued that the participation in numerous industry projects and their mobility had acculturated the newcomers to a cosmopolitan (Gouldner, 1957) appreciation of competence instead of hierarchy. That is, the subculture of new-comers produced both leading-edge development projects and was a production of earlier participation in such projects. One of the more experienced newcomers stated,

> An organization is thriving when it takes on big challenges, preferably too difficult rather than too easy. Then the entire personnel has to develop new solutions, new ways of acting and more efficient ways of planning for the future. ... We all are the same kind of fellows, no matter at what level we are, everybody is important.

In contrast, among the old-timers, the most central ideological cornerstones were related to locality. Many of them had a long career at Tampella and, therefore, only a few had the chance to go elsewhere. This provided a strong motive to emphasize a company perspective and the continuity of the local operations. For example, company units experiencing problems with profitability were taken care of even at the cost of the other facilities. A company executive stated, "It's up to us, the company management, whether we can employ people in a way which secures profitable production. And of course, all lines of business will eventually show a profit."

At the mill level, this ideology suppressed enthusiasm for presenting ideas of new products and, instead, efforts were made to prolong the life cycles of existing products with minor changes in the production process.

From the perspective of managerial action, mobility of old-timers in and out of Tampella was rare. Thus, it was the custom that academically educated managers gradually became qualified for company management, and seniority was an important determinant of managerial authority. For example, extracts from a company memo summarizing Tampella's managers' opinions on the management of their company reveals the centralized management mode (see Goold & Campbell, 1987) at Tampella: "Company headquarters is bureaucratized . . . governmental . . . and it gets too involved in operational details of the business . . . and it demands too much reporting on every activity . . . with tight schedules . . . and too much detail."

Low mobility in the management of Tampella was supported by the fact that development projects had been few; therefore, no new specialists were needed. This tendency not to increase the number of educated personnel was also fostered by the old-timers' earlier experiences of company crisis when "good people had to be let go," and this was to be avoided in the future. As a consequence, the number of managerial positions was low, and they were defined largely according to the individual managers' preferences.

Whereas the old-timers maintained the company traditions, the newcomers' ideologies materialized in a tendency to change them. These activities required people to formulate ideas and implement them. For example, a challenging vision was formulated in the following way by a newcomer in company management:

> Every division of Tampella will end up being the market leader in their business area. To reach that objective we must create growth together and no other thoughts can be allowed. We must be extremely upset by every unprofitable business unit. This cannot go on. Something must be done and it must be radical.

The ambitious business objectives were (especially as far as the more experienced newcomers were concerned) related to the general aim of a more democratic atmosphere within management. This was manifested by transferring some managers to less critical positions and replacing them with younger ones who were considered more competent. Moreover, the newcomers emphasized that the "boss is not always right." One of them expressed it as follows:

> I believe in teamwork. Nobody is good enough alone, but when the whole group aims in the same direction we get results. As a supervisor, I insist especially that my subordinates work hard. In our meetings, I value individuals who have their own opinions. I don't want them to echo mine. This would kill all progress . . . it is wrong to imagine that I am always right.

In addition to the dimensions used, managerial subcultures can also be characterized on the basis of what their representatives say about each other. It can be expected that a change situation stimulates expressions in which actors emphasize their own positive sides and the negative ones of the others (see Parker, 1995, p. 541). For example, the old-timers argued that the high aspirations of the newcomers exposed their incompetence. In addition, they felt that the newcomers spent too much money on general expenses and hired too many new people with a good salary who were lacking experience in relation to their responsibilities. One of the old-timers in the company management stated, "A huge number of these new managers entered both company headquarters and lower management levels. 'Brains' were hired for Tampella and for example division staff got some freshmen, but those positions were too demanding for rehearsing."

The newcomers, however, also expressed strong criticism of the old-timers. They argued, for example, that the previous management at Tampella in general and at the company level in particular was too small in number, too authoritarian and discouraging, and too burdened by operational pressures. As a consequence, the old-timers were always too dependent on external advice such as that from consultants in the case of development projects. Moreover, they considered the old-timers' company management as a hotbed of cliques and intrigues in which some of the company businesses and their heads were systematically favored, and the major decisions were made virtually outside the formal management system. Representatives of the newcomers stated, "The company management suffered 'a disease of the neck.' In other words, every time the key figure said something, all the others just nodded. Moreover, they partied together and made the critical decisions then." They also declared, "The company management was full of skilled intriguers, but successfully managing a company the size of Tampella was beyond their abilities."

In addition, controversies were also to be found within the newcomers' and the old-timers' factions. For example, mill-level managers might complain that their supervisors wanted to put their finger into every detail in the activities of the mill although their knowledge had long been outdated. According to one of the mill managers,

> The company managers might encourage adding a new paper grade in production without taking into account that at the same time they demanded a high level of production efficiency which was more easily reached with only a few paper grades in production.

In relation to the presented conceptualization of managerial subcultures in the case of Tampella, at least two reservations need to be made. First, although it has been demonstrated how the mentioned subcultural fractions differed from each other, this does not mean that the actors representing these different subcultures were dissimilar to each other in all respects. For example, most of the individuals in question had a technical education that they had received at the same universities, and they also belonged to the same professional associations. They also had a variety of shared experiences in the context of managing paper industry facilities. Moreover, almost all managers at Tampella were men, who (at least as far as the researcher was able to observe) shared middle-class values and lifestyles.

Second, the fact that the managerial subcultures were conceptualized this way does not mean that no other divisions existed. A complete depiction of all managerial subcultures is, however, not the focus of this chapter, which aims to analyze how the identified subcultural boundaries were crossed in a situation of discontinuous technological change. This requires relating the specificities of the change to each of the subcultures and especially to the ways the characteristics of the latter were in and out of line with the former. This is the subject of the following section.

Subcultural Reconciliation in a Situation of Discontinuous Technological Change

Why were the conflicting subcultures described previously able to cooperate in a situation of discontinuous technological change? Actors with significantly different backgrounds supported the same quickly launched and executed project in a spirit that can be illustrated by the statements of individual managers involved. Two of them described the spirit at Tampella as follows:

> In the initial stage of project implementation the spirit of action within manage-ment was high. However, the expectations of what the change would bring and what each one should have been doing were not quite clear. . . . It seems that expectations of the actual changes in relation to both timetable and operational performance were overly optimistic. But at the time all felt realistic and we went a bit crazy. The situation was so unusual that although we should have been able to restrain ourselves, we just all believed in it.

More important than the assessments by individual managers, however, are the reasons concerning the basis of each subcultural faction's enthusiasm and will to participate in and support the change. Before answering the question why the change was positive from the perspective of specific subcultures, why this specific change project was also problematic for them must be discussed. From the old-timers' point of view, the novelty of the adopted design invalidated a large part of their previous capabilities. They could interpret this as a threat to the company's competitiveness. The change implied that the old-timers had to learn many new things that had not been relevant for the current production process and the previous "learning curve." From the newcomers' viewpoint, most of the problems were related to the fact that although many of them had encountered many similar projects, there was also something quite new and, in addition, the context in which these new things were being implemented was unfamiliar to them. It was therefore not clear whether the project would succeed, and it also meant a risk for the newcomers' careers, which in most cases had so far been successful.

The anticipated change, however, also had several positive features. Because the old-timers were strongly committed to the continuity of Tampella's traditions, this change project was welcomed because it would enhance the company's competitiveness and support the local community. Although the simultaneous renewal of products and production technology was risky, the leading-edge design offered prospects for long-term competitiveness. Also, although the change partly broke with the previous technological trajectory, it continued the company's tradition of implementation in that Tampella manufactured the new paper machinery at its own engineering works, which facilitated later deliveries for other facilities. In addition, because the old-timers readily complied with formal authority, they wanted to fulfill the owners' aspirations for ambitious development projects despite the latter's limited knowledge of the paper industry.

Despite all these positive aspects, some grumbling occurred among the old-timers at the mill level because they perceived that their opportunity to move upward in the managerial hierarchy had diminished. In contrast, the old-timers at the company level felt that they had secured their position, at least for a short time. That is, the risks related to the change were particularly perceived by the individuals lower down on the ladders of management because of their personal investment in a different kind of technological development. One manager stated,

> It seems that I was not sufficiently aware of what was involved when I took a managerial position and responsibility for the production process. As a consequence, I focused too narrowly on the day-to-day responsibilities of the position and neglected to think about development of the mill in general and my personal professional development in particular.

The doubts of the newcomers were partly dispelled by strong support from the owners and by the fact that the material resources provided permitted the employment of the best external specialists. Moreover, from a general strategic perspective, the discontinuous technological change was a chance for the newcomers to upgrade the product portfolio and adopt a more "market-driven" orientation at Tampella. Thus, they were fascinated by the prospects offered by the applications of new technology and new products in bringing the previous "laggard" up to date. This justified contact-building with numerous customers, but it also offered a chance for career advancement to those individuals who had already concentrated on these issues through either their education or working experience. Tampella's management at the mill level especially had traditionally been dominated by actors specializing in technical issues, but now, as the mill entered a new market area, the marketing function became more critical. Even more driving was the newcomers' combination of high ambition with the will to be in places where state-of-the-art processes were developed. This was especially the case with the more experienced newcomers. One of them stated,

> The main reason why I came here was the novelty and maybe partly the challenge: how to make an established mill produce a new product range and to solve the many problems this naturally causes. But I felt that the mill needed to be able to face the demands of manufacturing coated paper grades.

In contrast, the younger newcomers were interested in the development projects because they had little previous experience of this kind. Thus, the ambitious change offered them an opportunity to expand their skills and capabilities and to advance in their careers by having responsibilities in real change projects.

In summary, temporary reconciliation in the management of Tampella implied that each subculture had some ideological features in line with the ambitious change design. Thus, the potential conflicts between the subcultures temporarily lost their importance as the actors' attentions were focused on the positive potential of the change. For example, the old-timers did not pay much attention to the significant market risks related to product upgrading despite their preference to "stick to their knitting." The long-term upward potential seemed to be stronger. The newcomers, however, accepted the potential flaws in the adopted design because it basically seemed to be the right thing to do and the project offered a chance for a successful episode in their careers. Thus, the discontinuous technological change let "a thousand flowers bloom" (Kanter, 1988), and the company, which had long been characterized by lack of innovation, was now abruptly characterized by a high level of ambition and a desire to establish state-of-the-art technology within the industry.

The duration of such a temporary subcultural reconciliation, however, is most likely short because the actors' enthusiasm for the project was based partly on contradictory and also unrealistic expectations. In this case, the problems with the implementation of the discontinuous technological change gradually dampened the enthusiasm that characterized the management of Tampella in the earlier stages of the project. In particular, after about 18 months of planning and before the construction and installation of the new machinery, it was clear that many of the project's objectives, such as the budget and the start-up, would not be reached. The fact that a promising project began to look like a failure started to reproduce and enforce the underlying boundaries within the management of Tampella and resulted in a situation in which blame on the emerging problems was placed on "the others." One manager describes the phenomenon as follows:

> More problematic than the actual technical difficulties was the quarreling they caused within management. It became more important to argue about who was responsible for the failures than how they would be overcome. In that situation the actors loudly questioned each other's competence.

Further Discussion and Some Conclusions

This study was intended to contribute to the current understanding of managerial subcultures by empirically investigating the process of their temporary reconciliation in the context of technological change. Such a temporary reconciliation is especially needed in situations of discontinuous change that create opportunities for the various subcultural factions involved to promote their objectives toward an apparently common goal that overlays potentially existing conflicts. Hence, new technology provides a mechanism that can be used as a tool to reduce tension and to enhance cooperation between conflicting actors who have to operate in the same arena (Grieco & Lilja, 1996).

Further research is needed with regard to at least four areas. First, the findings support the use of a context- and sector-specific approach (e.g., Child, 1988) in the study of organizational subcultures. Studies have demonstrated, for example, that in addition to strategic recipes, industries and sectors also have an effect on the cultural orientations of the organizational actors (Phillips, 1994; Sackmann, 1992). These findings are in contrast to earlier work that claims that cultural patterns are more consistent across industry boundaries than within them (Buono, Bowditch, & Lewis, 1985). Only contextually sensitive research, however, can yield more knowledge about which mechanisms may function, for example, as triggers for temporary reconciliation of managerial subcultures.

Second, further studies on the cultural effects of technology promise to be fruitful because technology has usually been treated as an independent factor influencing organizational culture (e.g., Chatman & Jehn, 1994; Zammuto & O'Connor, 1992). The more subtle issues of how varying processes of technological change affect culture, however, have not been adequately investigated despite the fact that specific requirements set by discontinuous technological change for voluntary action have been highlighted at both the firm (Tushman & Romanelli, 1985) and the industry level (Dosi, 1982).

Third, by focusing on the issues of subcultural reconciliation, this study shares a recently developed view that argues that cultural fragmentation (Martin, 1992) does not necessarily lead to increasing individualism (Golden, 1992; Harris, 1994). Beliefs and norms can produce conflicts as well as consensus, especially in management, which necessarily is a "melting pot" (Alvesson & Sandkull, 1988) for numerous occupational subcultures (Meek, 1988, p. 461; Chapter 17, this volume). Despite the subcultural fragmentation, managers as individuals and groups of individuals may (at least in specific situations) perform similar acts but still interpret those acts differently (Young, 1989). This means that monolithic or strong cultural patterns (e.g., Peters & Waterman, 1982) should be considered as emerging cultural forms in organizations in which attempts are made to achieve unity through "corporate culturism" (Willmott, 1993).

Finally, it is expected that the phenomenon of subcultural reconciliation developed here may benefit from the social movement approach that has been emerging within the field of organization and management studies. The conceptualization of subcultural reconciliation in terms of social movements offers a variety of concepts and ideas concerning the rapid rise and decay of cooperation between actors holding dissimilar ideologies and values (Soeters, 1986; Zald & Berger, 1978). In addition, managerial control may then be considered inherently limited by the social dynamics inside and outside corporations (Davis & Thompson, 1994). From this point of view, the pluralism of actors and the operational pressures of organizational actions produce cultural dynamics that have been examined here in the managerial context of the paper industry.

Notes

1. A more detailed description of the nature of the evidence and the research process has been presented by Laurila (1995).

2. This specific change project was only one part of a companywide investment. It was chosen for this investigation because of its potential to identify managerial subcultures.

3. More specifically, the production could be doubled on that production line and the new product (coated magazine paper) was clearly more refined (e.g., soft calendered and coated) than the previous one (uncoated book paper).

4. A continuous process of this kind (on-line calendering and coating instead of off-line processes) is more demanding than a discontinuous one because in the latter the dysfunctions in the coating part stop the entire machine.

5. Paper industry engineering education and paper manufacturing education have been regarded as identical, although they are at many times separate lines of study.

References

Alvesson, M., & Sandkull, B. (1988). The organizational melting-pot: An arena for different cultures. *Scandinavian Journal of Management, 4,* 135-145.

Bierly, P., & Spender, J. C. (1995). Culture and high reliability organizations: The case of the nuclear submarine. *Journal of Management, 21,* 639-656.

Bloor, G., & Dawson, P. (1994). Understanding professional culture in organizational context. *Organization Studies, 15,* 275-295.

Brown, J., & Duguid, P. (1991). Organizational learning and communities-of-practice: Toward a unified view of working, learning and innovation. *Organization Science, 2,* 40-57.

Buono, A., Bowditch, J., & Lewis, J. (1985). When cultures collide: The anatomy of a merger. *Human Relations, 38,* 477-500.

Burgelman, R., & Sayles, L. (1986). *Inside corporate innovation: Strategy, structure and managerial skills.* New York: Free Press.

Carnall, C. (1986). Toward a theory for the evaluation of organizational change. *Human Relations, 39,* 745-766.

Chatman, J., & Jehn, K. (1994). Assessing the relationship between industry characteristics and organizational culture: How different can you be? *Academy of Management Journal, 37,* 522-553.

Child, J. (1988). On organizations in their sectors. *Organization Studies, 9,* 13-19.

Cohen, M., March, J., & Olsen, J. (1972). A garbage can model of organizational choice. *Administrative Science Quarterly, 17,* 1-25.

Cyert, R., & March, J. (1963). *A behavioral theory of the firm.* Englewood Cliffs, NJ: Prentice Hall.

Dalton, M. (1950). Conflicts between staff and line managerial officers. *American Sociological Review, 15,* 342-351.

Dalton, M. (1959). *Men who manage.* New York: John Wiley.

Davis, G., & Thompson, T. (1994). A social movement perspective on corporate control. *Administrative Science Quarterly, 39,* 141-173.

Donnellon, A., Gray, B., & Bougon, M. (1986). Communication, meaning, and organized action. *Administrative Science Quarterly, 31,* 43-55.

Dosi, G. (1982). Technological paradigms and technological trajectories: A suggested interpretation of the determinants and directions of technical change. *Research Policy, 6,* 147-162.

Dyer, W., & Wilkins, A. (1991). Better stories, not better constructs, to generate a better theory: A rejoinder to Eisenhardt. *Academy of Management Review, 16,* 613-619.

Eisenhardt, K. (1989). Building theories from case study research. *Academy of Management Review, 14,* 532-550.

Field, R. (1989). The self-fulfilling prophecy leader: Achieving the metharme effect. *Journal of Management Studies, 26,* 151-175.

Fulop, L. (1991). Middle managers: Victims or vanguards of the entrepreneurial movement? *Journal of Management Studies, 28,* 25-44.

Gagliardi, P. (1986). The creation and change of organizational cultures: A conceptual framework. *Organization Studies, 7,* 117-134.

Golden, K. (1992). The individual and organizational culture: Strategies for action in highly-ordered contexts. *Journal of Management Studies, 29,* 1-21.

Goold, M., & Campbell, A. (1987). *Strategies and styles: The role of the centre in managing diversified corporations.* Oxford, UK: Basil Blackwell.

Gordon, G. (1991). Industry determinants of organizational culture. *Academy of Management Review, 16,* 396-415.

Gouldner, A. (1954). *Patterns of industrial bureaucracy.* New York: Free Press.

Gouldner, A. (1957). Cosmopolitans and locals: Toward an analysis of latent social roles—1. *Administrative Science Quarterly, 2,* 281-306.

Gregory, K. (1983). Native-view paradigms: Multiple cultures and culture conflicts in organizations. *Administrative Science Quarterly, 28,* 359-376.

Grieco, M. (1988). Birth-marked? A critical view on analyzing organizational culture. *Human Organization, 47,* 84-86.

Grieco, M., & Lilja, K. (1996). Contradictory couplings: Culture and the synchronisation of opponents. *Organization Studies, 17,* 131-137.

Harris, S. (1994). Organizational culture and individual sensemaking: A schema based perspective. *Organization Science, 5,* 309-321.

Hirschman, A. (1970). *Exit, voice and loyalty: Responses to decline in firms, organizations and states.* Cambridge, MA: Harvard University Press.

Hosking, D. (1991). Chief executives, organising processes and skill. *European Review of Applied Psychology, 41,* 95-103.

Jermier, J., Slocum, J., Fry, L., & Gaines, J. (1991). Organizational subcultures in a soft bureaucracy: Resistance behind the myth and facade of an official culture. *Organization Science, 2,* 170-194.

Kanter, R. M. (1982). The middle manager as innovator. *Harvard Business Review, 60,* 95-105.

Kanter, R. M. (1983). *The change masters: Corporate entrepreneurs at work.* New York: Simon & Schuster.

Kanter, R. M. (1988). When a thousand flowers bloom: Structural, collective and social conditions for innovation in organization. *Research in Organizational Behavior, 10,* 169-211.

Laurila, J. (1995). *Social movements in management: Making a technological leap in the case of the Anjala paper mill* (Series A-100). Helsinki: Helsinki School of Economics.

Lawrence, P., & Lorsch, J. (1967). *Organization and environment.* Cambridge, MA: Harvard University Press.

Lewis, D. (1994). Organizational change: Relationship between reactions, behaviour and organizational performance. *Journal of Organizational Change Management, 7,* 41-55.

Martin, J. (1992). *Cultures in organizations: Three perspectives.* New York: Oxford University Press.

Martin, J., & Siehl, C. (1983). Organizational culture and counterculture: An uneasy symbiosis. *Organizational Dynamics, 12,* 52-65.

Meek, V. L. (1988). Organizational culture: Origins and weaknesses. *Organization Studies, 9,* 453-473.

Meyerson, D., & Martin, J. (1987). Cultural change: An integration of three different views. *Journal of Management Studies, 24,* 623-647.

Mintzberg, H. (1985). The organization as a political arena. *Journal of Management Studies, 22,* 133-154.

Parker, M. (1995). Working together, working apart: Management culture in a manufacturing firm. *Sociological Review, 43,* 518-547.

Pennings, J., & Gresov, C. (1986). Technoeconomic and structural correlates of organizational culture: An integrative framework. *Organization Studies, 7,* 317-344.

Peters, T., & Waterman, R. (1982). *In search of excellence.* New York: Harper & Row.

Pettigrew, A. (1973). *The politics of organizational decision-making.* London: Tavistock.

Pettigrew, A. (1979). On studying organizational cultures. *Administrative Science Quarterly, 24,* 570-581.

Pettigrew, A., & Whipp, R. (1991). *Managing change for competitive success.* Oxford, UK: Basil Blackwell.

Phillips, M. (1994). Industry mindsets: Exploring the cultures of two macro-organizational settings. *Organization Science, 5,* 384-401.

Reynolds, P. (1986). Organizational culture as related to industry, position and performance: A preliminary report. *Journal of Management Studies, 23,* 333-345.

Rouse, M., & Fleising, U. (1995). Miners and managers: Workplace cultures in a British Columbia coal mine. *Human Organization, 54,* 238-248.

Sackmann, S. (1992). Culture and subculture: An analysis of organizational knowledge. *Administrative Science Quarterly, 37,* 140-161.

Saffold, G. (1988). Culture traits, strength and organizational performance: Moving beyond strong culture. *Academy of Management Review, 13,* 546-558.

Schein, E. (1985). *Organizational culture and leadership.* San Francisco: Jossey-Bass.

Snow, D., Rochford, B., Worden, S., & Benford, R. (1986). Frame alignment processes, micromobilization and and movement participation. *American Sociological Review, 51,* 464-481.

Soeters, J. (1986). Excellent companies as social movements. *Journal of Management Studies, 23,* 299-312.

Strauss, A., Schatzman, L., Erlich, D., Bucher, R., & Sabshin, M. (1963). The hospital and its negotiated order. In E. Friedson (Ed.), *The hospital in modern society* (pp. 147-169). New York: Macmillan.

Teulings, A. (1986). Managerial labour processes in organized capitalism: The power of corporate management and the powerlessness of the manager. In D. Knights & H. Willmott (Eds.), *Managing the labour process* (pp. 142-165). Aldershot, UK: Gower.

Trice, H., & Beyer, J. (1986). Charisma and its routinization in two social movement organizations. *Research in Organizational Behavior, 8,* 113-164.

Trice, H., & Beyer, J. (1991). Cultural leadership in organizations. *Organization Science, 2,* 149-169.

Trice, H., & Beyer, J. (1993). *The cultures of work organizations.* Englewood Cliffs, NJ: Prentice Hall.

Tsoukas, H. (1989). The validity of idiographic research explanations. *Academy of Management Review, 14,* 551-561.

Tushman, M., & Romanelli, E. (1985). Organizational evolution: A metamorphosis model of convergence and reorientation. *Research in Organizational Behavior, 7,* 171-222.

Van Maanen, J., & Barley, S. (1984). Occupational communities: Culture and control in organizations. *Research in Organizational Behavior, 6,* 287-365.

Weick, K. (1979). *The social psychology of organizing.* Reading, MA: Addison-Wesley.

Westley, F., & Mintzberg, H. (1989). Visionary leadership and strategic management. *Strategic Management Journal, 10,* 17-32.

Wilkins, A., & Dyer, W. (1988). Towards culturally sensitive theories of culture change. *Academy of Management Review, 13,* 522-533.

Willmott, H. (1993). Strength is ignorance; Slavery is freedom: Managing culture in modern organizations. *Journal of Management Studies, 30,* 515-552.

Young, E. (1989). On the naming of the rose: Interests and multiple meanings as elements of organisational culture. *Organization Studies, 10,* 87-206.

Zald, M., & Berger, M. (1978). Social movements in organizations: Coup d'etat, bureaucratic insurgency and mass movement. *American Journal of Sociology, 83,* 823-861.

Zammuto, R., & O'Connor, E. (1992). Gaining advanced manufacturing technologies' benefits: The roles of organization design and culture. *Academy of Management Review, 17,* 701-728.

Chapter 13

Organizational Factors Influencing Homogeneity and Heterogeneity of Organizational Cultures

Bas A. Koene
Christophe A. J. J. Boone
Joseph L. Soeters

During the past several years, organizational culture has been established as an important aspect of organizations. Handbooks on organizational culture have been published (e.g., Schein, 1992; Trice & Beyer, 1993), thus taking their place next to books about organizational strategy and organizational structure. In empirical research, the topic has been studied in various ways. Organizational culture has been the focus of both qualitative (e.g., "Special issue," 1983) and quantitative studies (e.g., Hofstede, Neuyen, Ohayv, & Sanders, 1990; O'Reilly, Chatman, & Caldwell, 1991). The quantitative empirical research on the topic has focused mainly on the content of organizational culture. These studies either aim to develop measurement instruments identifying dimensions of organizational culture (e.g., Hofstede et al., 1990; O'Reilly et al., 1991) or they focus on the impact of the content of organizational culture on topics such as job satisfaction (O'Reilly et al., 1991), job turnover (Tett & Meyer, 1993), and financial performance of organizations (Denison, 1990; Hansen & Wernerfelt, 1989; Koene, 1996). This interest in the content of organizational culture is important to advance our understanding of what is organizational culture. Nevertheless, understanding the causes of agreement or disagreement on perceptions of organizational culture can be considered of both practical and methodological importance.

The fact that the level of agreement varies between organizations is a widely accepted assumption. The early popular writers on organizational culture argued that a "strong culture" distinguishes successful organizations from other organizations (e.g., Peters & Waterman, 1982). In their view, a strong culture facilitates coordination and communication and thus gives strong-culture companies a competitive advantage over their competitors (Ouchi, 1980; Weick, 1985). In empirical evaluations of the impact of "cultural strength," the argument has become more subtle but not less compelling. A strong culture seems to show a positive correlation with short-term performance and a weak or even negative correlation with long-term performance (Denison, 1990; Gordon & DiTomaso, 1992). Theoretically, the argument was similarly refined. Cultural strength is just one aspect of organizational culture (Saffold, 1988). It is an important phenomenon, supporting organizational coordination and employee motivation in the short run but causing strategic myopia and lack of flexibility in the long run (Denison, 1990; Earl, 1984; Soeters, 1986). The issue of within-organization agreement is also important methodologically. Agreement on perceptions of organizational culture between individuals in an organization validates the use of aggregated individual level data as proxies for the organizational-level construct (Dansereau, Alutto, & Yammarino, 1984; George & James, 1993; James, 1982; Klein, Dansereau, & Hall, 1994).

Quantitative researchers have paid only scant attention to the variation in cultural diversity itself and to the organizational aspects influencing this diversity. Studies that primarily investigated cultural diversity in organizations and its antecedents did not focus on a comparative evaluation of the differences in the level of cultural diversity between organizations. These studies mostly used a richer definition of organizational culture, often relying on qualitative research methods to develop "thick" descriptions of differences in culture within one organization. Examples include Sackmann's (1992) study investigating cultural diversity in three units of a U.S.-based conglomerate, identifying nine cultural groupings, and Dougherty's (1990) study that used in-depth interviewing to analyze the diversity in understandings of new markets between planners, field personnel, technical personnel, and manufacturing personnel in five American firms.

In this study, we try to bridge the gap between the one-sided comparative quantitative focus on cultural diversity as an independent variable (influencing organizational performance and determining the level of analysis at which the variable has to be understood) and the qualitative in-depth focus on the issue of diversity and its antecedents. This chapter reports the outcomes of a study investigating the variation in cultural agreement in an empirical data set of 50 supermarket stores and the impact of social and organizational factors on cultural agreement within the stores. In the analysis, two issues are addressed. First, the meaning of cultural agreement and its variation are discussed focusing on how the cultural agreement information can support the interpretation of culture and leadership variables. Second, the influence of organizational structure, demographic, and social variables on the level of agreement on organizational culture and leadership is evaluated.

The chapter begins with a theoretical analysis of the impact of social and organizational factors on cultural agreement in organizations. Then, the methodological implications of within-group agreement and the possibility of variations in it are addressed. The subsequent section describes the research methodology, variables, and empirical setting. In this section, special attention is paid to the procedure for measuring within-organization agreement. Finally, in the last two sections, we present our findings and discuss them. We shall first determine the level of agreement on six dimensions of leadership and organizational climate for each organization in our sample. On the basis of these scores, we can evaluate the validity of aggregation to the organizational level for each of the leadership and climate variables and show how the separate evaluation of within-group agreement and between-group variation can aid our interpretation of the variables. Then, we focus on the differences in agreement between the organizations and correlate the agreement scores with the social and organizational factors of the organizations in our sample.

Factors Influencing Cultural Agreement in Organizations

What factors influence the agreement on organizational climate and culture in organizations? Schneider and Reichers (1983) organize the answers to this question into three categories: the structural approach, the selection-attraction-attrition (SAA) approach, and the social interactionist approach. Studies taking the structural approach focus on the impact of organizational structure and objective work conditions on the (perceived) organizational climate. The SAA argument explains how an organizational climate arises from the process of hiring and firing employees, thus influencing the kind of people employed by the organization. The outcomes of this process are reflected in the organization's demography. The social interactionist approach explains the emergence of a coherent organizational climate through the social interaction between organization members. Poole (1985) argues that social interaction is a cornerstone of culture formation and is influenced by the favorableness of the organization's communication climate. Therefore, we discuss the hypothesized impact of the organizational structure, organizational demography, and organization's communication climate on cultural agreement in the organization (Figure 13.1).

Organization Structure

Researchers using the structural approach argue that the organizational setting influences people's attitudes, values, and perceptions of organizational events. In this view, climates arise from the objective aspects of the work context. The structural approach argues that the type of work and the experience of individuals in their work directly influence people's perception of their work situation. Common work experience increases with the similarity of people's work. Presumably, specialization in the organization will decrease the level of agreement on perceived organizational culture in the organization because of an increasing diversity of experiences and a lack of interaction between organization members. Previous research has shown a relationship between organizational structure and organizational climate (Payne & Pugh, 1976), but it focused on the content of climate rather than on the agreement about it.

SAA and Organizational Demography

The SAA model explains the growth of within-organization agreement through three processes at the individual level: selection, attraction, and attrition (Schneider, 1987; Schneider & Reichers, 1983). Two assumptions underlie this approach. First, organizations select people that fit the organization and resemble the members of the organization (and fire people that do not fit the group). Second, individuals are attracted to jobs that fit their personalities, in which they can implement their self-concept, and from which they can obtain desirable outcomes (and will quit jobs that are not congruent with their personalities).

These processes at the individual level of selection, attraction to, and attrition from the organization can thus create a relatively homogenous group of organization members with a high level of agreement on organizational culture. In this line

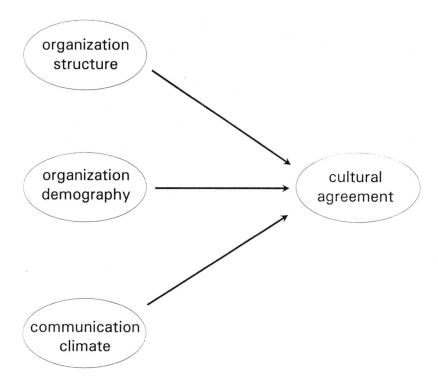

Figure 13.1. Factors Contributing to Cultural Agreement (SAA Model)

of reasoning, it is assumed that an organization's culture is strengthened by weeding out individuals with different opinions and hiring employees with personal views congruent with those of the other organization members. According to Staw, Bell, and Clausen (1986), the influence of personality on individuals' understandings of their work situation is far more important than we think. Large personality differences may thus point to disagreement in the evaluation of the social organizational context. The selection-attraction-attrition process has a trial-and-error quality to it, making it more effective over time.

The three processes can vary in intensity, thus influencing the expected level of cultural agreement in the organization. In a computer simulation of the process of enculturation, Harrison and Carroll (1991, 1995) showed that both the content (the mean level of culture) and the level of agreement (the standard deviation of the mean level of culture) differed when selection, socialization, and turnover parameters were varied in the simulation. These processes can differ in practice in various ways. Selection processes can be more or less uniform, the image of the organization will influence who is attracted to it, and, finally, criteria for and levels of employee turnover can also vary between organizations.

The SAA process can be expected to influence organizational demography. Studies of organizational demography show that similarity in experience and attitudes is reflected by demographic features such as time of entry in the organization, age, race, and sex. This similarity is important because it is one of the most important bases of interpersonal attraction (Pfeffer, 1985, p. 69). Using the SAA approach, we can expect agreement on perceptions of organizational climate and leadership in organizations in which the demographic variables indicate similarity.

Social Interactionism and Communication Climate

Finally, the symbolic interactionist approach argues that an agreed-on organizational culture emerges from the interaction between people (Schneider & Reichers, 1983, p. 32). Social interactionists emphasize the impact of interaction between individuals in organizations as the source of adaptation of an individual's understandings of the work setting toward greater congruence with the organizational culture. According to Salancik and Pfeffer (1978), the social context has the following two general effects on individuals:

(1) it provides a direct construction of meaning through guides to socially acceptable beliefs, attitudes and needs, and acceptable reasons for action; (2) it focuses an individual's attention on certain information, making that information more salient, and provides expectations concerning individual behavior and the logical consequences of such behavior. (p. 69)

These effects of the social context have an affect on culture in two ways. First, socialization processes of training and indoctrination mold the newcomers' understanding of the work situation. These processes can be more or less extensively used and vary in their formalization and reach. Second, the impact of the social context can also arise from the interaction between organization members, who are all part of the social context. Organizational culture then "emerges out of the interactions that members of a work group have with each other" (Schneider & Reichers, 1983).

An important facilitator of this second kind of interaction is the communication climate in the organization (Poole, 1985). When a positive communication climate stimulates interaction between organization members, we expect more agreement on perceptions of organizational culture. We also expect that a longer exposure to each other (operationalized in terms of tenure) will increase mutual experiences and will result in stronger agreement on perceptions of organizational culture by organization members.

Methodological Implications of Within-Group Agreement

Given that systematic differences may exist in the way people perceive the organizational context, it is important to assess whether and, if so, to what extent culture and climate can be considered unitary characteristics at the organizational level. The issue of a level of analysis is at the core of a recent methodological discussion about the validity of empirical studies relying on aggregated individual-level perceptual data for measuring organizational culture (e.g., George, 1990; George & James, 1993; Hofstede, Bond, & Luk, 1993; Klein et al., 1994; Yammarino & Markham, 1992). Here, two issues need to be discussed. First, the discussion about the measurement of within-group homogeneity because it explains our choice of James's (1982) measure of agreement. Second, the question of whether we can use a measure of agreement for evaluating the validity of an aggregated organization level variable when the level of agreement differs between organizations.

Homogeneity Discussion

The existence of cultural diversity in itself poses important methodological issues for empirical organizational culture research. To derive measures of organizational culture, perceptions of individuals are aggregated to composite organizational variables. When is this aggregation valid? Klein et al. (1994) argue that the choice of a level of analysis is dependent on three assumptions about the data. Aggregation of data to the organization or group level, for example, assumes homogeneity at the "individual" level, meaning that group members have to agree to a certain extent on the organization-level variable. Second, it assumes independence of the units (organizations and groups) from higher-level units (e.g., industry-level variables). This means that the variation in the variables studied should not be determined at a higher level of analysis. In that case, we would not measure organizational attributes but rather higher-level (e.g., industry level) variables. Finally, it assumes heterogeneity of responses at the organizational or group level: To be of significance, the organizational-level variables should show some significant variation at the organizational level of analysis. Following this line of reasoning, one needs to determine both the level of within-group agreement (as evidence for the within-group homogeneity) and the existence of between-group variation (to determine heterogeneity or significant variation of responses at the group level) to validate the appropriate level of analysis for organizational culture. The problem here, however, is to determine what level of agreement is "good enough." Some argue that the within-group variation should be smaller than the between-group variation to be able to speak of an organization-level phenomenon (e.g., Dansereau et al., 1984; Yammarino & Markham, 1992).

This position, however, is not shared by everyone. George and James (1993) summarize the arguments against this approach:

> This [conclusion] is problematic because it essentially implies that unless a group stamps out all individual differences, it is essentially not having any meaningful effects. Individuals do not lose their individuality by being members of a group. Group effects can be powerful, and yet one might still observe variation and co-variation within groups. (p. 800)

Therefore, analyses that compare the within-group variation to the between-group variation miss the point of the separate assumptions asking for within-group homogeneity and between-group variation. Ideally, both within-group agreement and between-group variation should be determined by comparing them against independent objective bases. In this chapter, we use the agreement measure developed by James (1982) to evaluate the level of within-group agreement. A traditional analysis of variance (ANOVA) F test is used to determine the significance of between-group variation.

Interpreting Variations in Agreement

When using the level of agreement as a measure for evaluating the validity of the level of analysis of organizational culture variables, we must decide how to interpret the variation in levels of agreement between organizations. What should we decide in a situation in which the agreement indicator points to the valid aggregation of a variable to the organizational level in one organization and shows much less agreement in another organization? To answer this question, it is useful to think of organizations in terms of cultures and subcultures (see Harrison & Carroll, 1995).

Organizations can be seen as composed of a multiplicity of discrete subcultures that are held together, more or less strongly, by an overall culture. The overall culture consists of a number of elements that are embraced by practically everybody in the organization (Trice & Beyer, 1993, p. 174). This view shows that when studying organizational culture empirically, studying some aspects of culture will give the impression of cultural diversity, whereas other aspects are agreed on by most members of the organization. An analytical description of this view is proposed by Poole (1985). In his view, cultures (Poole uses the term *climates*) are "collective schemes of meaning established through interactions focused on organizational practices" (p. 101).

Describing culture, Poole (1985) distinguishes different layers of culture in the organization including a common-concept pool, a kernel climate, and particularized climates to the behavioral and affective reactions of individual organization members. The common-concept pool is the most basic level of shared understandings in the organization; it describes the words and concepts used by the organization members to understand their organizational world. The second level is labeled the "kernel climate." It contains the aspects of the general organizational culture that pervade the behaviors of all organization members. Third, there are the specific particularized climates (subcultures) of the different working groups in the organizations and, finally, an even wider variety of behavioral and affective reactions of individuals in the organization. Poole argued that researchers measuring organizational culture would find high agreement between organization members' evaluation of the organization's culture if the measures happened to tap the kernel and if the sample is limited to a group with no particular climates (p. 100). Recognition of these levels of culture adds another dimension to the evaluation of agreement scores. Measures of culture that consistently show a high agreement can be considered aspects of the kernel climate. Measures of culture that show consistently low agreement can either be considered aspects of a particularized climate (a subculture) or individual "behavioral and affective reactions" (thus, not indicators of climate). Measures of culture that show varying levels of agreement point to aspects of culture reflecting particularized climates that arise depending on the organizational context.

Method

The current study is part of a quantitative empirical study of the impact of organizational culture and leadership on organizational performance in supermarket stores. Data are reported from 1,229 lower-level employees in 50 stores of a large retail chain in The Netherlands. We sent questionnaires to all employees working more than 12 hours per week in the stores—2,156 in total. This procedure resulted in a response percentage of 57%. This report is based on the quantitative measures of leadership and organizational climate from the data set. The data were collected using a questionnaire that included, among other items, translated items from Bass's (1989) charismatic leadership scale, an updated version of a Dutch translation of a questionnaire in the Ohio State tradition (Syroit, 1979), and items measuring three aspects of organizational climate. Organizational climate was measured with items from the *organisatie-klimaat-index voor profit-organisaties* (OKIPO) (de Cock, Bouwen, de Witte, & de Visch, 1984), a Dutch translation of the Business Organization Climate Index (Payne & Mansfield, 1973) and one dimension from a 1989 study.

Using separate factor analyses for leadership and climate (both at the individual level of analysis; $N = 1,229$), three leadership and three climate factors were established. The leadership factor analysis confirmed the three ex ante dimensions of charisma, consideration, and initiating structure. The charisma dimension points to a personal influence of the leader (the store manager) on his subordinates' motivation. It was measured with statements such as ". . . is a model for me to follow" and ". . . has a sense of mission which he/she transmits to me." The consideration dimension points to the amount of attention the leader pays to the social aspects of his workgroup. It was measured with statements such as "he is friendly and approachable" and "he looks out for the personal welfare of group members." The initiating structure dimension points to the amount of attention the leader pays to structuring the work task of his workgroup. It was measured with statements such as "he maintains definite standards of performance" and "he schedules the work to be done."

In the factor analysis for organizational climate, three scales were confirmed: task communication and innovation (based on the OKIPO items) and general communication (based on the Pennings items). The task communication dimension points to the clarity and quality of task descriptions. Statements used to measure task communication were "everybody here always knows what to do" and "the work is well organized here." The innovation dimension points to the readiness to innovate in the organization. Statements used to measure innovation were "many new ideas are tried out here" and "finding a new approach is encouraged here." Finally, the general communication dimension points to the amount of information about the general situation of the business that reaches the employees of the supermarket stores. Statements used to measure general communication were "my boss makes an effort to inform me about changes that could be important for me" and "my boss informs me about what is happening in our store." The psychometric properties of the six scales were evaluated at the level of individual respondents ($N = 1,229$). The internal consistency of the scales was further checked using Cronbach's alpha coefficient. The alpha coefficient scores for the leadership scales and the organizational climate scales are shown in Table 13.1.

For the assessment of within-group agreement, we used James, Demaree, and Wolf's (1984, 1993) measure of within-group interrater agreement (Rwg). This measure is independent of between-group variation and is able to capture different levels of agreement in groups. Basically, the Rwg compares the actual distribution of responses (showing the actual agreement in the response group) to an expected distribution of responses in the case of a complete lack of within-group agreement. Rwg compares the actual within-group variance, S_x^2, with the expected variance in the case of completely random response, $(\sigma)_E^2$ (the theoretical benchmark). Within-group agreement is then assessed as "the degree to which the observed ratings reflect a reduction in error variance relative to the theoretical benchmark" (James et al., 1993, p. 307). The formula for calculating the Rwg is

$$Rwg = (\sigma_E^2 - S_x^2)/\sigma_E^2 = 1 - (S_x^2/\sigma_E^2)$$

In this study, the agreement scores were calculated using the Rwg(j), the multiple-item version of James et al.'s (1984) agreement index. It is important to notice that the Rwg is not without flaws. Its interpretation, although "logical, legitimate and meaningful," is a matter of judgment (James et al., 1993). There is still a lack of empirical evidence on the behavior of the Rwg index. Furthermore, it "suffers from the same problems inherent in all such agreement indexes: the ambiguity of establishing the distribution of expected variance" (Kozlowski & Hattrup, 1992, p. 166). For the interpretation of Rwg index scores, we follow James et al. (1993). Rwg = 1.0 is the outcome in the case of perfect agreement of all raters; Rwg = 0.0 is the outcome in the case of a perfectly random response of all raters; Rwg = .86 suggests a "high, but not perfect level" of interrater agreement; and Rwg = .47 suggests a "reasonably low level" of interrater agreement (James et al., 1993, p. 308). To suggest acceptable levels of agreement, Rwg scores should be higher than "the Rwg = 0.70 ballpark figure for a 'good' amount of agreement" for most of the units under study (George, 1990, p. 110). Building on this logic, we can extend the interpretation of the Rwg scores to the point at which Rwg scores can be seen as indicative of subcultures. This is shown in Figure 13.2.

Table 13.1 Cronbach's Alpha for Leadership and Climate Scales
($N = 1,229$)

Scale[a]	Alpha	No. Items
Leadership		
Charismatic leadership (CHLDS)	.93	6
Consideration leadership (COLDS)	.89	7
Initiating structure leadership (ISLDS)	.69	4
Organizational climate		
Task communication (TCOM)	.73	4
Readiness to innovate (INNO)	.82	3
General communication (GCOM)	.80	3

a. Scales based on factor analysis.

Central in this reasoning is the use of the theoretical benchmark of completely random response. Because in essence the Rwg measure compares the found sample variance to a theoretical benchmark of perfectly random response, it is clear that a variation in responses that is larger than the variance in a situation of random responses can point to the existence of distinct subcultures. Hence, a negative score on the agreement scale should not be discarded as uninformative and consequently be set to zero as James et al. (1993, p. 308) propose. Rather, it can be interpreted as reflecting a nonrandom, large variance in the sample, pointing to the existence of notably different subcultures.

To evaluate the empirical support for our expectations of the impact of social and organizational factors on within-store cultural agreement, the level of agreement on the six climate and leadership variables was related to a number of store-specific factors indicative of organizational structure, organizational demography, and the organization's communication climate. The organization's communication climate was measured using the mean values of the climate and leadership variables, assuming that these variables showed sufficient within-store agreement to be considered valid store-level indicators of climate and leadership. The variables used as indicators are presented in Table 13.2.

Results

The results are analyzed in two steps. First, the agreement scores and the ANOVA F test scores for the six organizational climate and leadership

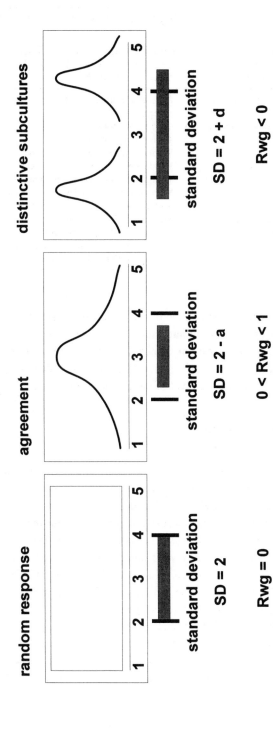

Figure 13.2. Within-Group Agreement Rwg Measure

Table 13.2 Social and Organizational Factors and Their Measurement

Store Attribute	Measurement Variable
Organizational structure	Number of full-time employees (= store size), number of departments
Organizational demography	Time in this store
	Time with the company
	Within-store mean age, standard deviation age
	Within-store standard deviation level of school training
	Within-store standard deviation function
	Within-store standard deviation tenure in this store
	Within-store standard deviation tenure in company
Communication climate variables	Mean level of climate variables for each store (TCOM, INNO, and GCOM)
	Mean level of leadership variables for each store (CHLDS, COLDS, and ISLDS)

variables are presented. On the basis of this information, we can evaluate the validity of our level of analysis assumptions of within-group agreement and between-group variation. Second, we show the empirical evidence for the hypothesized impact of organizational structure, demography, and communication climate on the level of cultural agreement in the organization.

Within-Group Agreement and Between-Group Variation

Table 13.3 shows the mean, minimum, maximum, and standard deviation for the agreement scores. Furthermore, Table 13.3 also shows the number of stores for which $Rwg(j)$ exceeded .70, .80, and .90.

Table 13.3 indicates that in the 50 stores the employees most consistently agree on their evaluations of leader consideration (COLDS) and the climate variable innovation (INNO). The level of agreement differs most in their assessment of the store manager's charisma (CHLDS) and the climate variable general communication (GCOM)—that is, the perceived quality of top-down communication in the store. The mean level of agreement is also weakest for charisma and general communication. Thus, overall employee agreement is lowest for charismatic leadership and the climate variable general communication. At the same time, these variables show the highest variation in agreement scores between the stores. The mean level of agreement is highest for consideration leadership and the climate variable innovation.

Table 13.3 Within-Store Agreement for 50 Stores

| | | Agreement score [Rwg(j)] | | | | No. of Stores for Which | | |
Scale	No. of Items	Mean	Minimum	Maximum	SD	Rwg(j) > .70	Rwg(j) > .80	Rwg(j) > .90
CHLDS	6	.79	.26	.94	.12	40	31	6
COLDS	7	.88	.42	.97	.08	49	46	24
ISLDS	4	.80	.50	.91	.08	45	30	1
TCOM	4	.81	.60	.92	.07	46	35	4
INNO	3	.88	.46	.96	.09	47	47	26
GCOM	3	.62	−.19	.802	.19	24	1	0

The statistical significance of the leadership and climate differences between stores is determined with an ANOVA F test. Table 13.4 shows the results of the F test for the six organizational climate and leadership variables.

The scores in Table 13.4 show that for all leadership and organizational climate variables except task communication (TCOM), the mean scores differ significantly ($p < 0.001$) between stores. These results show that in general the organizational climate and leadership scales show relatively high levels of agreement, indicating the validity of an organizational-level analysis of the climate and leadership variables. For the TCOM variable, the findings are interesting. This variable combines high within-store agreement with insignificant between-store variation. It can be argued that TCOM, measuring the perceived clarity of individual tasks in the organization, is strongly related to corporate job design and task definitions. This might strongly limit the amount of variance of this variable between stores.

Determinants of Within-Store Agreement

To estimate the empirical support of the impact of situational factors on within-store agreement, the level of agreement on the six climate and leadership variables was related to the three store attributes described previously: organizational structure, organizational demography, and communication climate. This has been done by means of a multivariate regression analysis. Table 13.5 shows the results of a backward regression analysis. This analysis provided the highest level of predicted variance of the various (forward and backward and stepwise and direct) multivariate analyses we have performed on the data. In this procedure, variables are removed one by one from the model until all variables left in the

Table 13.4 ANOVA Scores With F Test for Between-Store Analysis of Variance

Scale	No. of Stores	F Value	Pr > F
CHLDS	50	6.97	.0001
COLDS	50	4.13	.0001
ISLDS	50	4.06	.0001
TCOM	50	1.17	.1985
INNO	50	2.30	.0001
GCOM	50	2.18	.0001

model add significantly (parameters significant at $p < .10$) to the explanation of the dependent variable. The standardized parameter estimates are reported.

As can be seen in Table 13.5, the store structure variables show the strongest relationships with the level of agreement. Store size (measured in full-time equivalents) has a negative influence on the level of agreement on virtually all climate and leadership variables. The bigger the store, the lesser the level of agreement and, hence, the more extended the degree of cultural diversity within the stores. This result conforms to everyday logic. There are also, however, organizational explanations for this result based on the structure of organizations. The larger the organization, the more elaborate is its structure—that is, the more specialized tasks are, the more differentiated are its units and the more developed is its administrative component (Mintzberg, 1979, p. 230). Cultural differentiation apparently reflects the degree of structural differentiation in larger organizations.

The second result seems to be somewhat complicated and paradoxical. The more the stores are subdivided into separate departments, the greater is the degree of cultural homogeneity. To understand this result, it is essential to realize that larger organizations normally tend to have larger and thus relatively fewer separate units (Mintzberg, 1979, p. 232). Organizations, however, may counterbalance this tendency by intentionally dividing the organization in more separate and hence relatively smaller departments. This way of organizing may lead to a coordinating effect in that extra efforts are spent to communicate the organizational mission and messages in a rather controlled way. Then, the larger the number of departments, the smaller the span of control. The role of the department supervisors has a significant impact in this regard. This result suggests that an organizational policy specifically directed toward dividing the organization into more relatively smaller departments may provide the mechanism to create more cultural homogeneity in the organization.

Table 13.5 Backward Multiple Regression

Store Attribute	Parameter Estimate (p Value) for Dependent Variables: Rwg(j) (Level of Agreement) for					
	CHLDS	COLDS	ISLDS	TCOM	INNO	GCOM
Store size	−.64 (.06)		−1.13 (.0006)	−.90 (.0022)	−.59 (.06)	−.71 (.03)
No. of departments	.62 (.06)		.98 (.0023)	1.04 (.0008)	.81 (.01)	.88 (.008)
Mean age				.24 (.05)		
Time with store						
Time with company						
SD^a age						
SD time with store	.25 (.09)		.49 (.01)		.31 (.03)	.25 (.09)
SD time with company			−.41 (.02)			
CHLDS	—			.24 (.09)		
COLDS		—				
ISLDS			—			
TCOM	—	—	—	—	—	—
INNO				.61 (.0001)	—	
GCOMR	.26 (.07)	.49 (.0004)				—
R^2	.25	.24	.32	.45	.28	.23
adj. R^2	.18	.23	.25	.39	.23	.18

a. *SD*, standard deviation.

The demographic variables show relations with the level of agreement in the organization as well. Striking is the positive correlation between demographic diversity (measured as a standard deviation of time with the store) and the level of agreement on most of the climate aspects measured in this study. An explanation for this could be the need for a more personal approach of the leader toward each employee in the case of greater demographic diversity. When employees have joined the store at different times, the supervisor may communicate more meanings regarding "the way we work here" and thus leave less room for interpretations. If demographic variation refers to "time with company" and not to "time with store," however, this specific effect is absent and, in one case (agreement on initiating structure), turns into the opposite. Presumably, the supervisor is not aware that tenure at a store leads to different interpretations. It may be that employees having worked in other stores of the companies perceive their supervisor's leadership style differently when compared to colleagues who have worked at only one store.

Third, the social interactionist approach seems to be supported by demographic data. First, the higher the average age of the personnel in the stores, the greater the agreement on the aspect of task communication. This result may point to the impact of more task experience of relatively older employees. For younger, less experienced employees, task communication may be more diffuse, implying a generally smaller degree of agreement on the dimension of task communication ("the work is well organized here" and "everybody knows always what to do"). In addition, the social organizational context (especially the communication climate and charismatic leadership) shows significant correlations with the level of agreement on leadership and cultural issues. These results confirm our expectations.

Finally, there is a striking result indicating that a climate of innovation produces a relatively low level of agreement with regard to task communication. A climate of innovation ("many new ideas are tried out here") probably implies a kind of insecurity in the organization with regard to the way things have to be done.

Summary

The analysis in this chapter shows the importance of a careful analysis of the level of within-group agreement and its variation between organizations. This type of analysis is important for understanding the meaning of the various indicators of culture and for determining the level of aggregation at which organizational variables have to be understood. Separating the evaluation of within-group agreement from the evaluation of significant between-group variation enriches our interpretation of the sources of variation and the appropriate level of analysis for the cultural variables under scrutiny. Furthermore, not all climate and leadership variables showed equally wide variations in the levels of agreement between stores. Extreme variation in level of agreement of a variable between organizations might be interpreted as an indicator of the vulnerability of that variable for the development of particularized climates in the organizations.

The careful analysis of the level of within-group agreement, its variation between organizations, and its causes is also crucial for understanding the factors that support the development of particularized climates or subcultures in organizations. The lesser the degree of agreement, the more likely is the chance that subcultures (have) emerge(d). The comparison of the impact of structural, demographic, and social variables on the level of cultural agreement indicated the importance of mostly structural and social interactionist explanations of the causes of cultural agreement. The structural variables show a differentiated affect on the level of agreement in organizations. The negative impact of organizational size points to the negative impact of task specialization on cultural agreement in organizations. The positive impact of the number of departments points to a possible positive impact of a more elaborate organizational structure on the ability to communicate organizational expectations throughout the organization. The demographic and social variables also showed clear relationships with the level of cultural agreement in the organization. These relationships mostly pointed to social interactionist mechanisms influencing the level of cultural agreement in organizations, emphasizing the role of the leader and the stimulating impact of the communication climate on cultural agreement in the organization.

References

Bass, B. M. (1989). Evolving perspectives on charismatic leadership. In J. A. Conger & R. N. Kanungo (Eds.), *Charismatic leadership, the elusive factor in organizational effectiveness.* San Francisco: Jossey-Bass.

Dansereau, F., Alutto, J. A., & Yammarino, F. J. (1984). *Theory testing in organizational behavior: The variant approach.* Englewood Cliffs, NJ: Prentice Hall.

de Cock, G., Bouwen, R., de Witte, K., & de Visch, J. (1984). *Organisatieklimaat en cultuur: Theorie en praktische toepassing van de organisatie-klimaat-index voor profit-organisaties (OKIPO) en de verkkorte vorm (VOKIPO)* [Organizational climate and culture: Theory and practical application of the organizational climate index for profit organizations (OKIPO) and the short version (VOKIPO)]. Leuven, Belgium: Acco.

Denison, D. R. (1990). *Corporate culture and organizational effectiveness.* New York: John Wiley.

Dougherty, D. (1990). Understanding new markets for new products. *Strategic Management Journal, 11,* 59-78.

Earl, P. (1984). *The corporate imagination: How big companies make mistakes.* New York: Sharpe.

George, J. M. (1990). Personality, affect, and behavior in groups. *Journal of Applied Psychology, 75,* 107-116.

George, J. M., & James, L. R. (1993). Personality, affect, and behavior in groups revisited: Comment on aggregation, levels of analysis, and a recent application of within and between analysis. *Journal of Applied Psychology, 78*(5), 798-804.

Gordon, G. G., & DiTomaso, N. (1992, November). Predicting corporate performance from organizational culture. *Journal of Management Studies, 29*(6), 783-798.

Hansen, G. S., & Wernerfelt, B. (1989). Determinants of firm performance: The relative importance of economic and organizational factors. *Strategic Management Journal, 10,* 399-411.

Harrison, J. R., & Carroll, G. R. (1991). Keeping the faith: A model of cultural transmission in formal organizations. *Administrative Science Quarterly, 36,* 552-582.

Harrison, J. R., & Carroll, G. R. (1995, July). *Manufacturing dissent: The emergence of organizational subcultures.* Paper presented at the EGOS conference, Istanbul, Turkey.

Hofstede, G., Bond, M. H., & Luk, C. (1993). Individual perceptions of organizational cultures: A methodological treatise on levels of analysis. *Organization Studies, 14*(4), 483-503.

Hofstede, G., Neuyen, B., Ohayv, D. D., & Sanders, G. (1990). Measuring organizational cultures: A qualitative and quantitative study across twenty cases. *Administrative Science Quarterly, 35,* 286-316.

James, L. R. (1982). Aggregation bias in estimates of perceptual agreement. *Journal of Applied Psychology, 67,* 219-229.

James, L. R., Demaree, R. G., & Wolf, G. (1984). Estimating within-group interrater reliability with and without response bias. *Journal of Applied Psychology, 69,* 85-98.

James, L. R., Demaree, R. G., & Wolf, G. (1993). rwg: An assessment of within-group interrater agreement. *Journal of Applied Psychology, 78*(2), 306-309.

Klein, K. J., Dansereau, F., & Hall, R. J. (1994). Levels issues in theory development, data collection, and analysis. *Academy of Management Review, 19,* 195-229.

Koene, B. A. S. (1996). *Organizational culture, leadership and performance in context: Trust and rationality in organizations.* Doctoral dissertation, University Maastricht, The Netherlands.

Kozlowski, S. W. J., & Hattrup, K. (1992). A disagreement about within-group agreement: Disentangling issues of consistency versus consensus. *Journal of Applied Psychology, 77,* 161-167.

Mintzberg, H. (1979). *The structuring of organizations.* Englewood Cliffs, NJ: Prentice Hall.

O'Reilly, C. A., Chatman, J., & Caldwell, D. F. (1991). People and organizational culture: A profile comparison approach to assessing person-organization fit. *Academy of Management Journal, 34*(3), 487-516.

Ouchi, W. G. (1980). Markets, bureaucracies, and clans. *Administrative Science Quarterly, 25,* 129-141.

Payne, R. L., & Mansfield, R. M. (1973). Relationships of perceptions of organizational climate to organizational structure, context, and hierarchical position. *Administrative Science Quarterly, 18,* 515-526.

Payne, R. L., & Pugh, S. S. (1976). Organization structure and organization climate. In M. D. Dunette (Ed.), *Handbook of industrial and organizational psychology* (pp. 1125-1173). Chicago: Rand McNally.

Peters, T. J., & Waterman, R. H. (1982). *In search of excellence: Lessons from America's best-run companies.* New York: Harper & Row.

Pfeffer, J. (1985). Organizational demography: Implications for management. *California Management Review, 28*(1), 67-81.

Poole, M. S. (1985). Communication and organizational climates: Review, critique, and a new perspective. In R. D. McPhee & P. K. Tompkins (Eds.), *Organizational communication* (pp. 79-108). Beverly Hills, CA: Sage.

Sackmann, S. A. (1992). Culture and subcultures: An analysis of organizational knowledge. *Administrative Science Quarterly, 37,* 140-161.

Saffold, G. S. (1988). Culture traits, strength, and organizational performance: Moving beyond "strong" culture. *Academy of Management Review, 13,* 546-558.

Salancik, G. R., & Pfeffer, J. (1978). A social information processing approach to job attitudes and task design. *Administrative Science Quarterly, 23,* 224-252.

Schein, E. H. (1992). *Organizational culture and leadership* (2nd ed.). San Francisco: Jossey-Bass.

Schneider, B. (1987). The people make the place. *Personnel Psychology, 40,* 437-453.

Schneider, B., & Reichers, A. E. (1983). On the etiology of climates. *Personnel Psychology, 36,* 19-39.

Soeters, J. L. (1986). Excellent companies as social movements. *Journal of Management Studies, 23,* 299-312.

Special issue on organizational culture research. (1983). *Administrative Science Quarterly, 28.*

Staw, B. M., Bell, N. E., & Clausen, J. A. (1986). The dispositional approach to job attitudes: A lifetime longitudinal test. *Administrative Science Quarterly, 31,* 56-77.

Syroit, J. (1979). *Mens-en taakgerichtheid: Constructie en validering van een verkorte leiderschapsschaal [People and task orientation: Construction and validation of a short leadership scale].* Gedrag, tijdschrift voor psychologie, 3, 176-192.

Tett, R. P., & Meyer, J. P. (1993). Job satisfaction, organizational commitment, turnover intention, and turnover: Path analyses based on meta-analytic findings. *Personnel Psychology, 46,* 259-290.

Trice, H. M., & Beyer, J. (1993). *The cultures of work organizations.* Englewood Cliffs, NJ: Prentice Hall.

Weick, K. (1985). The significance of corporate culture. In P. Frost, L. Moore, C. Lundberg, & J. Martin, (Eds.), *Organizational culture* (pp. 381-389). Beverly Hills, CA: Sage.

Yammarino, F. J., & Markham, S. E. (1992). On the application of within and between analysis: Are absence and affect really group-based phenomena? *Journal of Applied Psychology, 77,* 168-176.

Part **IV**

Ethnicity Cross-Cutting Organizational Boundaries

The two chapters in Part IV focus on ethnicity, which cross-cuts cultures at the suborganizational, organizational, regional, industry, national, and greater regional levels. Again, both chapters explore the issue of ethnicity but within quite different cultural contexts.

The study conducted by Sjiera de Vries investigates the problem of ethnic diversity within the cultural context of multiethnic teams in the Dutch police force. Her specific focus and sampling strategy, including the triad composed of minority and majority officers and their supervisor, gives insights into issues of ethnic diversity from different perspectives. In addition, the data and discussion shed light on how diversity may be managed and, if managed successfully, may contribute to better understanding and less prejudices.

Willem C. J. Koot explores ethnicity in the cultural contexts of the consumer electronics industry located in two different regions of Austria as well as the oil refinery industry in the Caribbean. Koot's focus on ethnicity differs from de Vries's. Koot argues that, in contrast to the view that cultural differences should be used synergistically, ethnic diversity, or rather ethnic rivalry, is much more powerful because of the amounts of energy and power it may generate and he uses the two cases as illustrations. Koot argues rather forcefully from a political point of view and also raises power issues. This line of argumentation, as well as the specific style of the discussion (openly taking a value-based stand), is more typical for European academicians than for their North American colleagues.

Chapter 14

Ethnic Diversity in Organizations

A Dutch Experience

Sjiera de Vries

The Netherlands has a wide variety of ethnic groups in its population. Gradually, more members of ethnic minority groups enter work organizations, and these organizations become more diverse. From American research, we learn that minority workers in organizations have to deal with "triple jeopardy," a set of problems their majority colleagues do not have to face (discrimination, solo role, and the special position of being hired under a program of affirmative action). In this research project, we tried to find out whether this is also true for ethnic minority workers in The Netherlands. We also wanted to learn about how both majority and minority workers evaluate working in multiethnic teams. The research was done within the Dutch police force. Before discussing this research, some background information on the position of ethnic minorities in The Netherlands is presented.

AUTHOR'S NOTE: I thank Professor T. F. Pettigrew and Professor T. M. Willemsen for their help and suggestions on the research.

Ethnic Minorities in The Netherlands

The population in The Netherlands is becoming more and more diverse. Currently, approximately 16% of the population was born outside of The Netherlands or has at least one parent born outside this country. Part of this group is defined as an "ethnic minority." Ethnic groups are groups that share a common ancestry and culture (real or reputed). An ethnic group is seen as an ethnic minority group when the members of that group are generally in a low socioeconomic position (de Vries, 1992).

The largest ethnic minority groups in The Netherlands are the Surinamese, Turks, Moroccans, and people from the Dutch Antilles and Aruba (Table 14.1). In its policy relating to ethnic minority groups, the Dutch government also considers some specific groups of refugees as ethnic minorities. This includes refugees from Ethiopia, Iran, Iraq, the former Yugoslavia, Somalia, and Vietnam. Together, the different ethnic minority groups make up approximately 7% of the Dutch population. In the larger cities, however, the numbers are much higher. In Amsterdam, the capital, approximately 20% of the population is considered to be an ethnic minority. The numbers are currently increasing; of children younger than age 15, approximately 11% belong to an ethnic minority group (Martens, Roijen, & Veenman, 1994).

Unemployment

As stated in the definition of ethnic minority groups, these groups are in a low socioeconomic position. For members of ethnic minority groups in The Netherlands, this means jobs at lower wage scales and a high unemployment rate. Although the unemployment rate of the native Dutch population is 5%, for Turks and Moroccans this number is approximately six times higher (Martens et al., 1994).

There are several explanations for this uneven distribution of unemployment. Part of the difference can be explained by differences in demographic variables such as age, sex, and level of education. These, however, explain only a small part of the difference (see Veenman & Roelandt, 1990). A variable that accounts for a larger part of the difference is discrimination. Considerable research shows that Dutch employers, when asked explicitly, prefer majority group job applicants over applicants from minority groups (e.g., Van Beek, 1993).

Table 14.1 Largest Ethnic Minority Groups in The Netherlands
(January 1, 1992)

Total population	15,129,150
Surinamese	262,839
Turks	240,810
Moroccans	195,536
Antilleans and Arubans	90,650

From Martens et al. (1994).

Apart from these direct forms of discrimination, institutional or systemic discrimination hinders the chances of minority applicants. *Institutional discrimination* is the term used to describe rules, practices, and procedures that have a negative effect on certain groups, often without any intention to do so. An example of this is selection tests, many of which work well for native Dutch applicants but not for minority applicants because of the cultural bias present in these tests (Hofstede et al., 1990).

In the past few years, a great number of activities have been undertaken to overcome the high unemployment of minority members. Most activities are focused on finding better ways of recruitment and selection to give minorities a fair chance. In 1994, a new law was introduced that was modeled after the equal employment laws of Canada. This law (Wet Bevordering Evenredige Arbeidsdeelname Allochtonen) states that employers must register the ethnic background of their employees and provide a yearly overview of the ethnic makeup of their employees and the changes in this makeup. When ethnic minorities are underrepresented, the employer has to name activities that will be undertaken to come to a more equal representation.

Problems Within the Work Organization

In this section, we describe the disadvantaged position of people from an ethnic minority background when applying for a job. They are confronted with direct and indirect discrimination. Many members of minority groups, however, do have jobs. What is their position when they become members of an organization? In an extensive overview of the research on the position of black Americans in organizations, Pettigrew and Martin (1987) concluded that minority workers in predominantly white organizations are confronted with several problems that make their position more challenging than that of their white colleagues. The authors summarize these problems as so-called triple jeopardy:

1. the "normal" prejudice and discrimination that most minority employees face;
2. the strain of the solo role among those minority employees who are the only minority worker in their group; and
3. the token role—the special role that arises when one is an affirmative action candidate.

Prejudice and discrimination toward minority people are part of daily life for many minority members (e.g., Essed, 1991), and the workplace is no exception (Morrison & Von Glinow, 1990). Indeed, several Dutch researchers have reported on discrimination and prejudice at the workplace (Bouw & Nelissen, 1988; Sikking & Brassé, 1987). Prejudice and discrimination may have a negative effect on the position of minorities at work. They can result in less well-being and less motivation and thus lead to a decrease in performance. Also, negative prejudices about the capacities of minority workers may work as self-fulfilling prophecies; the minority workers may start believing what is said about them and so may the persons who evaluate their performances (Jussim, 1990).

A "solo" is a person who is the only one in a group who differs significantly from the other group members. Sometimes the term is used more loosely to describe a person or subgroup that is a minority (less than 20%) in the group (e.g., Kanter, 1977). According to Kanter, solo workers are highly visible, and this places a strain on their ability to function. They are also judged more extremely (Taylor, Fiske, Etcoff, & Ruderman, 1978); therefore, feedback does not accurately inform them of their performance. This deprives them of a tool for improving their performance. In addition, other group members often force the solo to behave according to the general image of the social group to which the solo belongs. Ott (1985, 1989) and Yoder and Sinnett (1985) have shown that the mechanism is not the same for all solos. For example, the position of a solo man in a group of women is much more favorable than the position of a solo woman in a group of men.

Being a token—an affirmative action candidate—is also difficult because majority persons have negative expectations about the performance of minority workers who are hired under affirmative action (e.g., Heilman & Herlihy, 1984). The negative expectations come from the belief that if minorities were really good, they would not need affirmative action. Again, these negative expectations can work as self-fulfilling prophecies.

Research Questions

The problems summarized in the triple jeopardy concept suggest that the position of minority workers in organizations will be more difficult than that of their majority colleagues and even more so when the minority worker is a solo or a token or both. Because the Dutch situation is quite different from the situation in the United States (see de Vries, 1992), it is not clear whether problems of the triple jeopardy occur in the Dutch situation. This research project tried to investigate this question. In addition, we were interested in the general evaluation of ethnically diverse teams. Do people like working in them, and what are the effects on the quality of the work?

Research Setting

The research was carried out within the Dutch police force. The police force is one of the few Dutch organizations with a reasonable number of minority and majority workers on the same jobs. In the mid-1980s, the police force introduced ethnic diversity in the organization to work well in an ethnically diverse population. They were one of the first Dutch organizations to implement an affirmative action program—a policy aimed at attracting and employing more minority officers. The program has been revised and improved over the years and consists of efforts in the field of recruitment, selection, extra schooling, and training of minority applicants. After some years, this was completed with training in working with ethnic diversity in the organization for the staff of the police training institutes and for the police forces.

Respondents

Interviews were conducted at police stations in several Dutch cities with three groups of respondents: minority officers, a majority colleague of each of them, and their supervisor. This procedure enabled us to compare three views on one situation. For the selection of respondents, random sampling was not possible. The police department does not register the ethnic background of its employees; therefore, a listing of minority officers was not available. Because of the small percentage of minority officers (with a maximum of 3.2% in Amsterdam), a random sample of the total force would not provide enough minority officers for the purpose of this study. We had to find a different way of recruiting respondents.

First, we selected seven cities with minority officers in their police forces: two big cities (Rotterdam and Den Haag), two medium-sized cities (Enschede and Amersfoort), two smaller cities (Assen and Tegelen), and Amsterdam, which has the highest number of minority officers. In each city, there was a contact person, usually a personnel consultant. These contact persons knew the police forces and knew the minority officers. We discussed whom to contact with them. In some cases, they presented a list of names so that we could make a random choice. In other cases, the contact person decided who to contact. Although we resisted this "steering" by the contact persons, it was the only way to get in touch with the respondents.

The initial contact was made by the contact persons. They handed the potential respondents a letter from us and asked them to cooperate in the research. If they agreed or were willing to discuss this question with the researcher, they were called for an appointment.

In all cases, the minority officer was contacted first. If he or she agreed to cooperate, the contact person contacted the supervisor and a majority officer. To compare the minority and majority officers, we had asked our contact persons to match as well as possible the officers according to sex and years of service in the police.

As far as we know, all the approached majority officers cooperated. A few minority officers refused. Among the reasons they gave were that they did not want to be approached as an ethnic minority person or that they did not think of themselves as belonging to an ethnic minority group. They were also reluctant to focus extra attention on themselves. Other reasons were that they were tired of interviews or that researchers always focus on problems and difficulties and they did not want to be seen as a problem. Apart from refusals, there were minority officers who were not asked to participate because the contact person thought they would be offended or that their position in the group was so feeble that taking them out of their normal work would cause difficulties. Some of those who initially refused were persuaded to give us the benefit of the doubt and tried the interview. Their view of the study turned out to be positive afterward.

It must be noted that the selection procedure and the refusal of some of the potential respondents may have an influence on the results of this study. Because of the selection procedure, we do not have a precise figure of how many persons refused to cooperate.

In total, there were 31 groups of three persons (minority officer, majority officer, and supervisor). Three supervisors were interviewed about four officers instead of two officers so that we conducted a total of 90 interviews.

Most of the respondents were male. Of the minority officers, six were female; of the majority officers, two were female. There was one female supervisor. Eleven minority officers had a Surinamese background and seven had a Turkish background. There were five Antilleans, three Moroccans, three Moluccans, and two officers who described themselves as "blacks of mixed background." None of the supervisors had a minority background.

Interviews

Each person was interviewed individually.[1] Interviews lasted approximately two hours each. For the interviews, a structured list of questions was used with some of the questions closed and others open. In most instances, respondents were first asked to give their opinion on a scale (closed question) and were then asked to tell more about the subject (open question). In this way, both quantitative and qualitative data were systematically gathered. This chapter discusses the qualitative data. The quantitative data are discussed in de Vries (1992) and de Vries and Pettigrew (1994).

The interview questions focused on well-being and the perceived effects of working in an ethnically diverse team. The questions on well-being included questions about how the respondents like their job and the atmosphere in the group and how they fit into the group. Questions on working in an ethnically diverse team asked how respondents like working with colleagues from different countries or cultures, what they think is the effect of ethnic diversity, and whether annoying remarks on ethnic background are made in the group.[2]

The interviews were conducted by the researcher and three trained interviewers from different ethnic backgrounds. The researcher and one of the interviewers were Dutch whites, another interviewer was Surinamese, and the third interviewer had a mixed Dutch and Surinamese background.[3] All three interviewers and the researcher were women.

Analyses

During the interviews, all answers were written down in condensed form. Then, the answers were classified under several themes. This was done because respondents did not stick strictly to the questions asked. Often, they also gave information on themes that related only indirectly to the theme of the question. If this related theme came back later in the interview, not all the information was repeated. Analyzing per question would thus have meant that part of the information would not be included in the analysis because it was given at the "wrong place" in the interview. To prevent this, the analyses were done per theme.

Within the themes, all answers were put into categories, and the number of respondents per category was counted. For the counting, it did not matter whether a respondent referred to the category once or 10 times because in a structured interview such as this, the number of times a theme comes up is influenced by the type of questions and not just by the importance of the theme for the respondent. Part of the categorization was repeated by a second person to test the reliability of the rating system. There was a 74% overlap in the ratings. Considering that the categorization was not per question, but had to be based on the whole interview, we consider this a high enough overlap. Some answers of respondents are quoted in the text as illustrations.

Results

Multicultural = Problems

The first interesting insights this research project produced emerged while we introduced the research and selected teams to be interviewed. At this stage, we noticed clearly how sensitive the topic of interethnic relations is and how people tend to think about it. Apparently, the first thought that came to mind when people were informed of the project was discrimination. This showed in our first contacts with respondents. Quite often, we were greeted as "the persons doing the research on discrimination." We had never introduced the research in these terms. In fact, in our letter of introduction we tried our best to state the topic of the research in neutral terms, making clear that the research was about working in multiethnic groups. Discrimination was not mentioned in the letter.

Another interesting finding at this stage was the reaction of the potential respondents. As we expected, some of the minority officers we approached did not want to cooperate. Among the reasons they gave were that they did not want to be approached as an ethnic minority officer or that they did not think of themselves as belonging to an ethnic minority group. They were also reluctant to get special attention. Other reasons included that they were tired of interviews or that researchers always focus on problems and difficulties of minority workers and they did not want to be seen as a problem.

Although there was some hesitation on the part of the minority officers regarding cooperation in the research, this was completely absent with the majority officers and supervisors. All majority persons who were approached agreed to cooperate. Some of them, however, hesitated during the interview when it became clear that the questions were not only about the minority officers but also about the majority ones. The majority officers had not expected that, even though it was stated both in the letter and when we made appointments with them.

These early findings give an impression of how respondents selectively perceive research on working in intercultural groups—the research focuses on problems (discrimination) and on the position of minority workers. Information that does not fit this description is not easily picked up. We fear that these findings are true not only for how people think about research on intercultural groups but also for how they think about intercultural work; they think of problems and minority workers as the causes of these problems.

Discrimination

The triple jeopardy thesis states that discrimination can be, and all too often is, a major issue in multicultural groups. It is also a topic that is sensitive and difficult to talk about. During the interviews, incidents of discrimination were reported quite often, but most of the time these incidents were not labeled as discrimination by the respondents. Many of them were reluctant even to use the word *discrimination*. This had already surfaced in pilot interviews in which there was an explicit question on experiences with discrimination. Respondents, both of majority and minority background, became very annoyed with this question; therefore, we changed the word *discrimination* to the more neutral *annoying remarks*.

When asked to rate the frequency of annoying remarks, 22 minority officers reported that annoying remarks do occur, although most of them indicated that this seldom happens. Of the majority officers, 14 reported that annoying remarks about the minority officer are made, as did 14 supervisors.

Apparently, annoying remarks were made in most groups (22 of 31), but in some cases majority colleagues did not notice that their minority colleague had to face this burden. This may mean that the remarks were made when the majority person was not present, but it may also mean that the majority respondents had a different definition of what is annoying. In the latter case, this is a potential source of tension. The minority officer will feel offended by certain remarks, and the majority colleague(s) will not understand the reason for this. They may feel the minority officer is oversensitive, as was indeed heard several times.

As mentioned previously, many minority respondents indicated that annoying remarks were made but very seldom. When asked to tell more on the subject, they tended to tell stories that were clearly quite annoying and, in the perception of the interviewers and researchers, indicated clear discrimination. Respondents, however, refused, often explicitly, to use this term. Also, the wording of the stories indicated that these were not exceptional incidents but more or less standard happenings. This raises serious doubts about the truth of the statements that remarks are made seldom.

Minority officer: They make jokes all the time, but it does not bother me. They are not about me personally but about minority persons in general.

Majority officer: Minorities in the police need to have a skin like a rhinoceros. Sometimes remarks are made that make me very angry, and then my minority colleague tells me to forget it, that he hears things like that so often. This was especially so when he first started work.

Many "annoying" (or discriminating) incidents that were reported concerned "jokes." Respondents found it hard to classify these jokes. Are they real jokes or is the undertone hostile, racist? These questions not only make it hard to classify jokes but also make it hard to react to them. By not reacting, the joking will continue. A reaction, however, whether from a minority or majority member, is often met with an accusation; suddenly the complainer is the one being difficult, the one confronting the norm. This is a no-win situation, keeping many people from reacting and thus maintaining a situation that is considered unpleasant (to say the least) by many, both majority and minority members.

Minority officer: They are only jokes, I know who makes them. I learned to live with it. I do not know any other situation than to be called names. It is no use saying anything against it. I am prepared for it, then you take it more easily. It is just a couple of them that are annoying, they do not determine how I feel.

Discrimination comes not only from colleagues but also from civilians. The comments of minority officers suggested, however, that they did not take this very seriously. Remarks by civilians did not harm them because they saw them as not meant for them as a person but for the police in general. The only time minority officers did seem to care was when the remarks were made by people from their own ethnic group—this really hurts.

Minority officer: Sometimes there are annoying remarks of civilians, for example, suspects, but that is because I am an officer, not because I am a minority.

Solo

Previous research has pointed out the difficulties of being in a solo position— of being the only minority in the group. In our research, half of the minority officers were in such a solo position. A comparison between minority officers in a solo position and minority officers who were non-solos did not reveal any consistent differences; they received similar evaluations of their performance and gave similar answers on questions about well-being, experiences in the group, and so on (see de Vries, 1992). This may be explained by the position of many non-solos in the police force. Of the 17 non-solos, only 3 had a colleague who was of the same sex and same ethnic background. Therefore, in practice most of the minority officers in our sample were still in a solo position. Apparently, this position was not different from being a real solo.

Inspired by previous research indicating the dangers of the solo position, we asked our respondents what would be the best way to decide where new minority officers should work. Would our respondents, especially the minority respondents, warn against solo positions? It turned out that eight of them did, as did five supervisors and three majority officers. They said it would be better to place minority officers with two or more together because they have a stronger position that way.

Three minority officers explicitly warned against grouping. They stated that the fact that a colleague belongs to a minority group does not automatically mean that they feel attached to that person. This seems to be the case especially when the colleague belongs to a different minority group than them. Even if they do not feel a special attachment with the other minority officer, others will always see the two of them as belonging together, as the same, and as natural allies. An additional disadvantage of two minority officers in a group was mentioned: They are constantly compared, and people mix them up.

All these answers point to the same problem: Minority officers are easily seen as members of the group labeled "minority" and not as individuals. Grouping minorities makes this mechanism stronger. At the same time, majority officers exaggerate the differences between majority and minority people. In effect, this kind of position may be more difficult than being a real solo.

Minority officer: Spreading is the best. If you place two minority officers together they will be mixed up, their names etc., and they are constantly compared. They will not support each other, for that you have to look at character and not ethnicity.

Minority officer: Working with someone with the same color is difficult, they expect me to be like them, and Dutch people expect me to be different from them [the Dutch].

Most minority officers and a number of majority respondents (officers and supervisors) recommended spreading the minority officers over as many groups as possible. They saw this as the best way to bring as many officers and supervisors as possible in contact with minority officers and to spread the benefits of the presence of minority officers over the groups. Another reason for being in favor of spreading was the fear of minority officers forming a "clique," a group within the group, and apparently they saw that as a threat. This fear of a group within the group and the negative evaluation of it was reported most often by minority officers.

Most majority officers and supervisors and some minority officers thought it best not to treat minority officers differently than majority officers. They were against special strategies and thought it most fair to place minorities where there is a vacancy. This would make it more likely that minority officers would be accepted as "normal."

Minority officer: For the acceptance of minority officers it is better not to differentiate, so majority officers see that it goes "just like it was with us."

Tokens

In this research, we could not compare minorities in a token position and minorities who were not hired under an affirmative action program. Almost all minority officers were hired under this program, and the few that were not (9 of

31) had been on the force longer, making it hard to compare positions. Because many respondents brought up the effects of affirmative action on the position of minority officers, however, we do have information about these perceived effects.

More than half of the minority officers (18) and a considerable number of majority officers (10) and supervisors (6) reported that the affirmative action program had a negative effect on the acceptance of minority officers. They explained that some of the majority officers are jealous because of the special attention given to minority officers. They also mentioned that the changes in the selection procedure and in the training program caused doubts about the quality of the new minority officers. The saying was that the standards had been lowered to get enough minority recruits. This idea of lowered standards fuels the expectation that minority officers will not perform as well as majority officers and thus has a negative effect on acceptance.

Majority officer: They pick up the first black person that walks in, just to reach the quota. They do not care whether the person is capable. Some do not even speak Dutch.

Minority officer: Sometimes I doubt whether they wanted me because I am black or because of my education. My colleagues express this doubt as well.

Minority officer: At the start the atmosphere was bad, people accused me of coming in via the special policy for minorities. Literally they said: "Why do minorities get everything and white men nothing?"

Acceptance

Acceptance is influenced not only by the hiring procedure but also by the idea that minorities are different from majority officers. This is illustrated by reactions to questions about the acceptance of both types of officers. Many respondents found talking about acceptance of majority officers strange: "Of course" they were accepted. With the minority officers this was less evident. Both minority and majority respondents noted that it often took longer before minority officers were accepted by the other group members. Also, several respondents mentioned that group members had negative expectations about the capacities of their new minority colleagues.

Minority officer: I am accepted in the group, but some colleagues do not want to say hello to me. They do not want to know me because of my background.

Minority officer: At the start they found me strange because I am from a minority group, but soon I was seen as normal.

Minority officer: First, I was seen as an intruder; later people were surprised that I could do the work. Now it is OK.

Majority officer: The minority colleague came in as a Turk. Everybody was very skeptical, but once he was here that soon disappeared though people had a wait-and-see attitude.

Effects of Multicultural Groups

All three groups of respondents saw a positive effect of the presence of minority officers. They liked the diversity and found it stimulating and interesting. They also saw positive effects on the quality of the work. The positive effects mentioned with the greatest frequency concerned the variety of cultural backgrounds and language capacities. Differences in cultural background are interesting topics to talk about, and these talks can also have a positive effect on how the work is done. Majority respondents reported that they learned better ways to relate to minority clients and public and had become less prejudiced as a result of working in multiethnic groups. Both minority and majority workers felt that the different viewpoints and experiences in ethnically diverse groups led to productive discussions about how the work should be done. The risk of overlooking certain aspects of a situation is smaller in diverse groups. Furthermore, the different languages in a diverse group can be handy when dealing with clients who do not speak the Dutch language.

Minority officer: Public and police will look differently at minorities. They now see them in positive situations as well. If you only see white officers, you could start thinking that there is something wrong with minorities.

Supervisor: You can have a lot of profit from the presence of minority officers. You get more background information. You get more conscious about it, etc. It is useful that they understand the language and understand what the conflicts are about.

Majority officer: The public sees that there are people from their own background and culture working with the police. They will not be that frightened of the police any longer. In their country, the police are often very different from the police here. The police have to be the mirror image of the society, then it will function better because every group is represented. This prevents problems.

An interesting point is that cultural and language differences, although the most mentioned positive points of multiethnic groups, were also the most often mentioned reasons for negative effects. Not everybody liked the discussions, based on cultural differences, about how to do the work. Having to reconsider all kinds of practices and procedures takes time and energy, and not everybody was prepared or capable of giving that. Cultural difference can also be a source of misunderstanding and miscommunication, as can be said of language differences.

Supervisor: I often have to explain the behavior of minority officers, especially to people from other units.

Summary and Conclusions

In an extensive overview of the literature on minority workers in organizations, Pettigrew and Martin (1987) conclude that these workers are confronted with specific problems. They identify three main problems: discrimination, the solo role, and the special position of affirmative action candidates (the token role). They call these problems the triple jeopardy. In this study, we tried to investigate whether these problems hold for minority officers in the Dutch police force. Furthermore, we were interested in the perceived effects of working in a multiethnic team.

Discrimination, the first factor in the triple jeopardy, was indeed reported by most minority officers in our sample of Dutch police. Supervisors and majority officers also reported that minority officers are discriminated against. Discrimination, however, was not generally seen as a serious problem, perhaps because the situation is not different from that in other organizations.

Minority officer: What difference would it make to leave? Discrimination is everywhere, I can not escape it, wherever I go.

We strongly recommend that organizations combat discrimination. Our research indicates that discrimination is present in most mixed groups and that it is a taboo topic. People find it hard to talk about and to mention it by name. Majority persons often do not recognize it, and minority persons find it hard to react to. Here, training may be helpful. Majority persons can be taught to recognize what discrimination is and to get an idea of the pain it inflicts. Minority persons can be trained to manage racism and their reaction to it. In addition to this, strict norms and effective and credible grievance procedures and sanctions will be necessary to really combat discrimination.

As expected, many minority respondents were the only minority in their workgroup and thus fitted the definition of a solo. Although previous research (e.g., Kanter, 1977; Ott, 1985, 1989; Yoder & Sinnett, 1985) pointed out the negative effects of the solo position, we did not find the expected difference between solos and non-solos. The absence of the solo effect may be explained by our strict definition of a solo. Using this definition, minority workers who have a colleague of another ethnic background are not considered a solo, even though they are the only person of their particular ethnic group. Maybe a more liberal definition of solo position, in which solos are those minority workers who do not have a colleague of the same ethnic group, would fit better with the experiences of minority workers in such positions. From our respondents, we learned that working with a minority colleague who is very different from yourself may be as difficult as being a real solo because now you are constantly compared with someone you do not see as similar.

More research on the solo effect or, more general, the effect of numbers and proportions seems necessary. This research should give more insight as to when someone should be considered a solo (the only minority in a group or the only minority of a specific ethnic background in a group?) and as to the precise effect of being a solo. Until more research has been done, it is hard to give practical recommendations on this topic.

As expected, respondents mentioned negative effects of the token position. Minority officers in general have more difficulties becoming accepted by the group than majority officers but even more so when the minority came in under a policy of affirmative action. Majority colleagues expect that affirmative action candidates are less qualified; they fear that the requirements have been lowered for minorities. This makes it more difficult for them to accept minority officers as equals.

From this, we learn that when introducing affirmative action or multiethnic groups or both, it is important to be clear and explicit about what is being done. It should be absolutely clear that the standards are not being lowered and that the new minority colleagues are fully capable for their job.

As for the effect of working in a multiethnic team, most respondents were positive. They liked the diversity and saw a positive effect on the quality of their work. This does not mean that there are no problems; differences in culture and language cause tensions and misunderstandings. They are, however, outweighed by the positive effects.

The positive evaluations and the positive effects of multiethnic groups should be pointed out more clearly in organizations, especially to groups with little or no experience with minority workers. In these groups, expectations are often negative, with the risk of these negative expectations becoming self-fulfilling prophecies. By focusing more on the positive effects, people may become more open to recognizing the positive points and finding ways to overcome the difficulties.

The overall conclusion of our research on multiethnic teams in the Dutch police force is that the expected problems for minority workers do occur but that on the whole our respondents were positive about working in a multiethnic team. The positive effects seem to override the negative ones.

Notes

1. This procedure, and some of the questions, are taken from Ott (1985). I thank her for her advice.

2. Another part of the research consisted of a comparison of the performance and reported well-being of minority and majority workers. This part of the research will not be discussed in this chapter. A detailed discussion can be found in de Vries (1992) and de Vries and Pettigrew (1994).

3. The ethnic background of the interviewer did not have a statistically significant effect on the answers of the respondents.

References

Bouw, C., & Nelissen, C. (1988). *Gevoelige kwesties: Ervaringen van migranten met discriminatie* [Sensitive matters: Experiences of migrants with discrimination]. Leiden, The Netherlands: Centum voor Onderzoek van Maatschappelijke Tegenstellingen.

de Vries, S. (1992). *Working in multi-ethnic groups: The performance and well-being of minority and majority workers.* Arnhem, The Netherlands: Gouda Quint.

de Vries, S., & Pettigrew, T. F. (1994). A comparative perspective on affirmative action: Positieve aktie in the Netherlands. *Basic and Applied Social Psychology, 15*(1 & 2), 179-199.

Essed, Ph. (1991). *Understanding everyday racism: An interdisciplinary theory* (Sage Series on Race Relations, Vol. 2). Newbury Park, CA: Sage.

Heilman, M. E., & Herlihy, J. M. (1984). Affirmative action, negative reaction? Some moderating conditions. *Organizational Behavior and Human Performance, 33,* 204-213.

Hofstede, W. K. B., Campbell, W. H., Eppink, A., Evers, A., Joe, R. C., Van de Koppel, J. H. M., Zweers, H., Choenni, C. E. S., & Van der Zwan, T. J. (1990). *Toepasbaarheid van psychologische tests bij allochtonen* [Applicability of psychological tests for ethnic minorities]. Utrecht, The Netherlands: Landelijk Bureau Racismebestrijding.

Jussim, L. (1990). Social reality and social problems: The role of expectancies. *Journal of Social Issues, 46*(2), 9-34.

Kanter, R. M. (1977). Some effects of proportions on group life: Skewed sex ratios and responses to token women. *American Journal of Sociology, 82,* 965-991.

Martens, E. P., Roijen, J. H. M., & Veenman, J. (1994). *Minderheden in Nederland: Statistisch vademecum 1993/1994* [Minorites in the Netherlands: Statistical vademecum 1993/1994]. Den Haag, The Netherlands: SDU-uitgeverij.

Morrison, A. M., & Von Glinow, M. A. (1990). Women and minorities in management. *American Psychologist, 45*(2), 200-208.

Ott, E. M. (1985). *Assepoesters en kroonprinsen: Een onderzoek naar de minderheidspositie van agentes en verplegers* [Cinderellas and crown princes: Research on the minority-position of female police officers and male nurses]. Amsterdam: Sua.

Ott, E. M. (1989). Effects of the male-female ratio at work: Policewomen and male nurses. *Psychology of Women Quarterly, 13,* 41-57.

Pettigrew, T. F., & Martin, J. (1987). Shaping the organizational context for black American inclusion. *Journal of Social Issues, 43*(1), 41-78.

Sikking, E., & Brassé, P. (1987). *Waar liggen de grenzen? Een case-study naar rassen-discriminatie op de werkvloer* [What are the boundaries: A case-study on racial discrimination at the workplace]. Utrecht, The Netherlands: Landelijk Bureau Racismebestrijding.

Taylor, S. E., Fiske, S. T., Etcoff, N. L., & Ruderman, A. J. (1978). Categorial and contextual bases of person memory and stereotyping. *Journal of Personality and Social Psychology, 36,* 778-793.

Van Beek, K. W. H. (1993). *To be hired or not to be hired, the employer decides.* Unpublished master's thesis, Universiteit van Amsterdam, Amsterdam.

Veenman, J., & Roelandt, Th. (1990). Allochtonen: Achterstand en achterstelling [Ethnic minorities: Time-lag and subordination]. In J. J. Schippers (Ed.), *Arbeidsmarkt en maatschappelijke ongelijkheid* (pp. 241-265). Groningen, The Netherlands: Wolters-Noordhoff.

Yoder, J. D., & Sinnett, L. M. (1985). Is it all in the numbers? *Psychology of Women Quarterly, 9,* 413-418.

15

Strategic Utilization of Ethnicity in Contemporary Organizations

Willem C. J. Koot

In the past few years, there has been steadily growing criticism on what Martin (1992) has called the integration approach of organizational culture. In this approach, it is taken for granted that we cannot speak of culture before consensus has been achieved and members of a group share values and standards. In addition, there should be consistency in cultural forms, and the group should be reasonably stable. Schein (1985), who may be considered one of the major authors of the integration approach, has observed, "If groups can be defined as stable units with a shared history of experience, they will develop their own cultures" (p. 8). The underlying thought—particularly in management practice—tends to be that unity is better than diversity; unity makes for strength and diversity for failure.

Although in management practice the concept of unity is still the prevailing one, among scientists, as previously mentioned, increasing attention is being paid to the processes of differentiation and fragmentation in organizations (e.g., Alvesson, 1993; Czarniawska-Joerges, 1992; Koot, 1994; Meyerson, 1991; Sackmann, 1992; Van Maanen, 1991). Most of the time, organizations lack such a thing as consensus or consistency in cultural forms or both. Virtually in all cases, differences are found, quite often manifesting themselves as discrepancy in oppositional forces. Apart from this, in certain situations the cultural rules are not clear or one is confronted with contradictory rules, which creates ambiguity. Moreover, several authors (e.g., Mastenbroek, 1991, 1993) have pointed out that differences within organizations do not always impair. Tension between groups, provided it is well managed, can be productive.

This notion of using tensions in productive ways is hardly present in the literature on intercultural management. In the present context, this is referring to managing groups of different ethnic or national and cultural origin inside an organization. Most authors who develop models on organizing international organizations explicitly or implicitly depart from what is called a "one best way strategy." Some authors—for example, Hofstede (1980, 1992) and Laurent (1986)—argue that such a strategy of unity is not feasible because in organization and management models the contingency factor of national cultural differences should be taken into account. They particularly underline the problematic nature of what they call "cultural distance." Collaboration between groups of certain national cultures (e.g., the Belgians and the Dutch, who belong to different cultural clusters) is considered to be troublesome and to be avoided. Other authors, such as Terpstra and David (1985), Adler (1991), and Trompenaars (1993), observe problems in intercultural communication and management but take the view that with some goodwill these can be solved. They advocate the concept of synergy, which means that "the positive of both cultures" should be combined. This message could also be phrased as: try to find each other, work toward an understanding and appreciation of one another, accentuate the communalities, strive for harmony, and steer away from antagonism.

This chapter proposes to dispute and challenge the concepts of both unity and contingency and questions some of the basic assumptions of what I call the synergetic view. In my opinion, the latter lacks a sense of reality and is quite often the product of arrogance and an ethnocentric worldview (those in power are usually in favor of tolerance and the less powerful simply want to have more power). Apart from that, paradoxical as it may sound, such a view of management is not always commendable. After all, ethnic rivalry may produce energy and power, as the result of studies on processes of ethnicity among migrants show (e.g., Glazer & Moynihan, 1963; Koot & Rath, 1987; Roossens, 1986). Ethnicity is a strong organizing principle and a good vehicle for social mobility because it rallies people of all ranks and ages and hence produces solidarity.

In my empirical research, in more than one instance have I have been able to observe the power—in a positive or a negative sense—of ethnic rivalry in organizations. One example represents my research on collaboration between two Philips plants in Austria and on cooperation between Curaçaoans and Venezuelans in a former Shell refinery on Curaçao. Both cases are described in the following section before exploring answers about how to deal with ethnic rivalry from intercultural and interethnic management theory and critically evaluating these answers.

Case 1: The Fighting Spirit and Success of a Philips Plant in the Agrarian District of Carinthia in Austria Fostered by a Rivalry With a Twin Plant in Vienna[1]

The Philips electronic company in Althofen (Carinthia, Austria) is currently one of the few European businesses that can compete in electronics with companies in the Far East. It is situated in an agricultural, somewhat isolated and underdeveloped region. In 1968, a member of the board of the Philips plant in Vienna spotted problems in capacity. Headquarters in Eindhoven, The Netherlands, subsequently issued an order to find a new location to set up a production unit. With the availability of labor, stable social conditions, infrastructure, and a piece of land on offer serving as criteria, the Carinthian town of Althofen was chosen.

It turned out to be an excellent decision. Right from the start, the Carinthians were eager to outstrip the Viennese. At first, the latter were rather stoical in their responses and did not feel threatened at all. The patriarchal and bureaucratic atmosphere hardly encouraged a willingness to innovate. The Viennese looked down on the Carinthians and had done so for a very long time. The Carinthians knew and felt this and accordingly were alert and combative. Their traditional work ethic, tremendous discipline, strong collectivism, and the fact that there were few alternative employment opportunities in the area combined with the presence of a strong leader who wanted to take revenge on the Viennese plant seemed to be their success formula.

The leading man in Althofen was a self-determined economist who had fallen afoul of the crowd of highly trained, inventive engineers in the Viennese plant who entertained very hierarchical notions and had been banished to "the country" to fill the post of managing director. To the Viennese, this was a good solution to their problem. As a matter of fact, they did not think the Carinthian plant would survive anyway. There was no way in which "a bunch of clodhoppers" could compete in the high-tech line of consumer electronics.

As it turned out, they had completely underestimated the enormous fighting spirit in the plant in Althofen. The managing director, a prototypical strong leader, and the Carinthian management struck a pact against the Viennese. Soon they were producing at prices 10% cheaper than the Viennese. Later, this percentage rose to an even higher level. As a result of this fight, the Viennese plant was taken over by the Carinthians with the consent of headquarters.

In 1989, the management of Philips commissioned me to evaluate the process so they could learn from it. We (my assistant and I) conducted a three-month field research study of the organizational culture and the ethnic and economic environment of the plant using different methods of data collection. Semistructured interviews and group discussions were held with key informants from outside the two organizations (staff members of the Philips headquarters; economists, geographers, and sociologists from local universities; and representatives of the local community). My assistant made participant observations for eight weeks in both factories by adopting the role of a research trainee for a business school who was working on his MBA thesis.

The situational, political approach of ethnicity, based on the theoretical notions of Barth (1969), Royce (1982), and Koot and Rath (1987), served as a theoretical framework. These theorists argue that strengthening ethnicity can be a driving force in the emancipation process. In their view, ethnicity is not so much related to external, "objective" differences marking members of an ethnic group but rather it is related to the degree to which the members consider themselves as being different from others. In so doing, it does not matter whether they refer to historically verifiable traits. Ethnicity can vary strongly because of the strategic and selective use of ethnic group members. Barth (1969) observed that they used one cultural trait as an indication of difference, whereas they neglected other features.

In fact, we are dealing with social identity—an identity that is exclusively determined by socially relevant factors. When interpreted in this way, the phenomenon of ethnicity can occur only in situations of mutual contact. Within such a situation, Barth (1969) continues, there must be a minimal competitive struggle concerning benefits, services, and other resources. These conflicts of interest between ethnic groups particularly occur in complex (e.g., industrial) societies. How ethnic groups will develop in such situations depends largely on the choice made by the "agents of change." Barth attaches to the "new elites" a central role in the interest struggle between ethnic groups. Depending on their information, ethnic groups can assimilate, isolate themselves, or ethnicize. The last option is the most interesting one to us. It concerns the use of ethnic identity for the purpose of bettering one's social position. By making ethnic differences organizationally relevant, ethnic groups can present themselves in the interest struggle as pressure groups or as political movements.

From analysis of our data, we concluded that the fighting spirit in the Althofian factory was caused by a coincidence of external and internal factors: pressure on the organization to survive in a very competitive branch; the pressure of a traditional ethnic rival; a regional culture characterized by collectivism, discipline, and work ethic; and a management style in line with this regional culture—directed at revenge, openness, teamwork, and steadiness.

Our main piece of advice to the management team of Philips Consumer Electronics in Eindhoven was to pay more attention in the future to the "fighting spirit" available in areas when setting up new plants, with characteristics such as disfavoring, ethnic rivalry, solidarity, and work ethic serving as significant indicators. As a matter of fact, Philips has become increasingly convinced that this factor should be taken into account in selecting new locations for business. In an interview in *De Volkskrant* (Gray, 1996), Philips' current chairman, Mr. Timmer, on a visit to Indonesia, was quite clear on this:

> Right now we are building plants in the Northwest of England. This is not random. You have to know misery before you can survive. The future is here in Asia. Absolutely. . . . In this part of the world there is a will to win, a will to be on top. Personally I am never satisfied. I will never make the mistake of being self-satisfied. (p. 16)

Case 2: Changing Identities in the Oil Refinery on Curaçao[2]

In the late 1960s, Shell came to Curaçao and started building a refinery to process Venezuelan oil. The advent of this refinery involved a dramatic change in both the social and the economic system. Huge unemployment and poverty vanished and were replaced by prosperity. The infrastructure as well as medical and social services drastically improved. The demand for labor rose to such an extent that foreign workers were attracted from all directions. Curaçao turned into an immigrant society, which is a rare phenomenon in the Caribbean. Also, from The Netherlands countless numbers of people were drawn toward the large offer for employment. The majority of them were higher educated and started to occupy the better jobs in the refinery and within the government. In government functions, they ousted the Dutch who have lived in Curaçao for centuries—the so-called Protestant whites who are descendants of the erstwhile plantation owners. This caused much resentment among the latter. As a consequence, there is growing segregation and segmentation between the European Dutch and the Curaçaoans. The European Dutch did not seek contact with the black population and neither did they come into contact with the other two main groups (the Protestant whites and the Jews). The European Dutch became isolated, materially as well as socially. The Curaçaoans, at first mainly the Protestant and Jewish sections, started explicitly and publicly to point out their affinity with the Latino culture.

In the late 1960s, a movement for more autonomy in Curaçao began. Opposition against Dutch interference and "suppression" grew within this context. Shell was seen as the symbol of suppression and patronage. When Shell then in the late sixties made people redundant by the introduction of automation, a revolt started. Although Dutch marines succeeded in crushing the rebellion, the political and social impact was dramatic. The European Dutch were marginalized and many of them left the island. A strong Antilleanization manifested itself in both the government and the refinery. The openly professed affinity with Latino culture became even more outspoken. Then, the oil crisis emerged accompanied by a worldwide recession.

For Shell, it was increasingly difficult to refine oil for a profit, one of the reasons being that the Venezuelans kept charging higher prices for their crude oil. In 1985, Shell finally decided to leave Curaçao and close the refinery. Closure, however, meant an economic catastrophe to Curaçao and the government decided to call in The Netherlands for help. The Dutch government started negotiations with the governments of The Netherlands Antilles and Curaçao. The negotiations between the three governments resulted in the government of Curaçao taking over the refinery and renting it to the Venezuelan state-owned company PDVSA. This entailed a Venezuelan management and staff along with the introduction of a total quality control (TQC) system that was also operational in the Venezuelan parent company. Reality, however, was totally contradictory to this policy of quality. One of the main pillars of TQC, teamwork and communication, was hardly taken seriously.

The Curaçaoans were getting more exasperated at (in their view) the overbearing Venezuelans and after a while started to resist. As a result, the old Shell culture, with its values of openness, reliability, and involvement, was highly praised and people dissociated themselves from the Latino culture. After some time, ethnicizing of the Curaçaoan part of the organization had set in. Tensions mounted so high that recently the chairman publicly announced he expects to suffer serious losses because of the ethnicizing.

These two cases may seem exceptional and the processes of ethnic rivalry rather accidental and nonmanageable. In my opinion, both assumptions are incorrect. Before stating my view as to how ethnic rivalry can be made productive, I shall explain the ethnic processes with which present-day organizations are confronted and how the theory on intercultural management relates to this.

Contemporary Processes of Globalization[3] and Particularization

The Growing Significance of Ethnicity in a Globalizing World

In the past 15 years, on a global and local level events have become highly intertwined. Local events are being increasingly influenced by events that take place thousands of miles away and vice versa. During this period, literature on the subject has become quite extensive (e.g., Featherstone, Lash, & Robertson, 1995; Friedman, 1994; Giddens, 1990; Lash & Friedman, 1992; Lash & Urray, 1994; Latour, 1994). Intertwining of local and global issues also applies to organizations that can be seen as hybrids that have resulted from the interaction of global and local factors.

Hannerz (1992) draws attention to present-day hybridization, but he mainly concentrates on processes that take place in the periphery (a term he uses for Third World countries). In this connection, he has introduced the phrase of "creolization." By means of extensive and detailed empirical material, Hannerz illustrates that this so-called periphery does not take up all kinds of cultural elements from the center indiscriminately, but that it selects and fits them in with care. The periphery, partly due to the use of technologies and organizational forms identical to those of the center, increasingly "talks" back. In other words, more and more often cultural elements are being supplied to the center and even offered for sale—"commodified" as Giddens (1990) and Appadurai (1986) have phrased it. This applies not only to music, clothing, literature, and art but also to know-how of, for example, organizations. The supremacy of the so-called First World is diminishing and one could imagine that the periphery of today will be the center of tomorrow (Hannerz, 1992, p. 226). In a number of areas—for example, in Southeast Asia—instances of this kind of change can already be found.

Nederveen Pieterse (1995) and Friedman (1995) criticize Hannerz (1992) for his use of the term *creolizing* exclusively for processes occurring in the periphery. Every culture is a mixture of other cultures. Friedman gives a good example. Pasta, considered an Italian product and sundry, was brought back from Asia by Marco Polo. Hardly anybody knows this, including the Italians, and those who know it do not talk about it. Italians are proud of their pasta—it is part of their identity. To the researcher, it is interesting to find out how this process of cultural adaptation and distortion of historical facts and identification has come about in Italy. As far as the "average" Italian is concerned, he or she could not care less. Pasta is Italian and that is all there is to it. It is not important if a cultural element is objectively original or exclusive; the meaning that people themselves attach to cultural forms is what counts. Adoption of Western clothing in West Africa, for instance, may not at all be seen by the local elite as a sign of Westernization but rather as a means of consolidating the local hierarchy.

The worldwide proliferation of knowledge and technology, and also of cultural elements, has in some aspects led to unification, homogenizing, and standardizing in others to differentiation and fragmentation. The latter notably apply to the question of ethnic identities. It is precisely the process of globalization that has made people aware of differences and, extremely important, the historical reason of their existence: not merely differences in opinion but also in status, power, and possession of scarce commodities. This in turn has led to a stronger sense of identity and the significance of it. For affective reasons (a desire for security and safety in the growing massiveness), but also for reasons of strategy and self-interest, people are standing up for their own group or region. Phenomena such as ethnic revitalization, cargo cults, and inventing or reinventing of traditions (Hobsbawm & Ranger, 1983) are frequently occurring in our globalizing world. This concerns not only the periphery but also the center.

These are reasons why globalization does not imply that the world is being homogenized. On the contrary, it is rather likely to lead to more differentiation and contrast. Religion has lost ground on the one hand, but on the other hand it has gained ground with the rise of fundamentalism and spiritualism. Localization is the logical counterpart of globalization. The two processes cannot be seen as separate. Globalization leads to antiglobalization (Van Binsbergen, 1994) and particularization. Therefore, several authors (e.g., Ohmae, 1990; Robertson, 1995) use the term *glocalization.* We shall return to this later.

This worldwide rearranging also manifests itself in quite a different manner. Sometimes new global networks are being formed with new identities, and new symbolic boundaries are drawn between people in various countries on the basis of shared traditions (fictitious or otherwise). Processes of rearranging and trans-formation do not occur exclusively as a result of this interplay of global and local processes. Postmodernism, with its emphasis on values such as openness, flexibil-ity, boundlessness, individual responsibility, and self-control, has also strongly affected processes of attributing meaning and, by means of processes of in- and exclusion, the reshuffling of international relations and networks. Literature as well as art, fashion, and advertising have focused on the development of personal lifestyles for years, whereby fixed roles, hierarchical relationships, bureaucracy, efficiency, mass production, and quantity are out of the question. Everything that seems to hinder the uniqueness of our personalities is apparently rejected. As a consequence, increasingly more often a choice has to be made in compartmental-izing subworlds. As currently happens with so many cultural forms and ideologies, these postmodern values are likewise globalized and creolized—assimilated in local cultures. Sometimes, as I have noticed, they come back in an adapted form to the center, where they were originally developed.

The proliferation of cultural commodities from the center to the periphery and vice versa does not exclusively happen via telecommunication and traveling; it also occurs through the massive inflow of migrants—persons that for various reasons are forced to move to a foreign country for a certain time. This category includes not only political refugees and migrant workers but also students from the periphery as well as the so-called expatriates from the center. The large increase in immigration in the past few decades from Third World countries to Europe and the United States has not merely resulted in a mutual transference of culture; in many cases, it has led to mutual processes of ethnicizing. Migrants who have lost hope of finding a job or housing and natives who feel threatened are drawing ethnic boundaries for protection (Koot & Rath, 1987). Fundamentalism, ethnocentrism, racism, ethnic regionalism, and a general shift to the right are all phenomena that are intertwined.

Thus, in a number of spheres cultural diffusion and ethnic segmentation go hand in hand. Certain cultural forms are exchanged and reintegrated in existing ethnic frameworks and settings. Other cultural forms, however, are being carefully guarded within a particular group as a means of distinction. Mutual cultural assimilation and synergy tend to be the ambition of native Western policymakers. In practice, policy usually differs from the ideal of integration. In the fight for scarce commodities and power, differences in culture and ethnic identity are turned into means for distinction and exclusion. In many cases, migrant workers get too little benefit from assimilation and therefore it is not a powerful instrument for social mobility.

Cultural processes, as I have argued (e.g., Koot & Boessenkool, 1994; Koot & Hogema, 1992), cannot be separated from the attendant oppositions in power. In that respect, the overall growing importance of ethnicity is not a mere coincidence, but rather a derivative of changing world order (cf. Friedman, 1994, 1995). Thus, an important consequence of globalization, localization, and migration from the periphery to the center will be increasing ethnic and national segmentation, identification, and rivalry. According to the theory of ethnicity (see Baud, Koonings, Oostindie, Ouweneel, & Patricio, 1994; Koot & Boessenkool, 1994; Koot & Rath, 1987), cultural differences within and between organizations will be more accentuated.

The question is how internationally operating organizations can deal with this and which strategy for cooperation may be the best option for them. What does the theory of intercultural and interethnic management have to offer with regard to models and strategies?

Theory of Intercultural and Interethnic Management

Three ideal-type strategies for cross-cultural cooperation can be distinguished: the ethnocentric, polycentric, and geocentric approaches (see Fung, 1995).

The ethnocentric approach is characterized by the pursuit of unity, efficiency, monitoring by the parent company or headquarters, and strong appreciation of the values of the home country. Cultural diversity is seen as threatening instead of an "opportunity." In practice, this approach implies that Western managers impose their manner of organizing and managing and that local managers (if appointed at all) are carefully selected. The underlying idea is that the Western way of organizing and managing is the most "logical" (being the most successful) and for this reason universally applicable. The response to culture imposed from above tends to be one of local resistance.

Who are the most important adherents of the ethnocentric approach? Although in recent years cultural diversity has received growing attention, the "one best way" strategy is currently the prevailing approach in management science and no doubt in management practice. Academic literature mainly concentrates on the question of what characterizes successful organizations and how organizations may appropriate such features. Until the early 1980s, effectiveness and efficiency were pre-eminent. Afterwards, largely due to the best-selling authors Peters and Waterman (1980) and Deal and Kennedy (1982), cultural characteristics such as openness, flexibility, client orientation, and decentralization followed—features that derived from research of American business enterprises.

The Japanese success has added hallmarks such as corporate identity, strong culture, long-term employment, total quality control, teamwork, the learning organization, lean production, self-monitoring, and empowerment. There is an increasing mixture of American and Japanese elements, jointly promising ultimate success. An early example of this was Ouchi's (1981) theory Z. A more modern example is provided by Morton (1994), who claims that "World Class Manufacturing Industries" possess the following characteristics: high quality, low cost, and delivery on time. If a company does not have these characteristics, it cannot possibly be a "global competitor" and will not survive in the long run: "Essentially, the issue is one of competitiveness and survival" (p. 5). High quality can be achieved by delegating more responsibilities as well as by operating with self-monitoring and enterprising teams. Morton believes that the essential ideal world-class organization is the right mix of appropriate Eastern and Western values: "The trick is to marry individualism and initiative from the West to 'group-think' from the East" (p. 10). A marriage like this can be made, Morton states, even though "it will take some pains for 'us, British' to make ourselves familiar with the oriental attitude, but arduous training and other management and organizational instruments should make such a union" (p. 10).

Less successful countries copy models and strategies of more successful ones. Smaller businesses concentrate on bigger ones and the nonprofit organizations follow the example of business life. Also, in developing countries American and Japanese best-sellers are circulating. As a matter of fact, to some people this trend amounts to a corroboration of the hypothesis of the rise of a single predominant economic system and one "melting pot" of cultures (Mommaas, 1991).

The polycentric approach begins with the idea that a universal strategy is not possible and that international business enterprises should accommodate to the local situation: "When in Rome, do as the Romans do" (Harris & Moran, 1987). Diversity is allowed and appreciated and monitoring from above is substituted by relative autonomy of local branches. Corporate culture is seen as a melting pot of cultures. Who are the principal adherents of this approach and when was it developed?

As indicated previously, although the majority of management scholars and practitioners do not publicly express their doubts about the intercultural validity of the one best way strategy, various authors even before 1980 have pointed out that such an approach is untenable (Chung, 1978; Crozier, 1964; Gallie, 1978; Kakar, 1971). Only after the IBM data had been processed and published by

Hofstede (1980) did a breakthrough in focusing attention on differences in work attitudes between countries occur (e.g., Adler, 1986; Harris & Moran, 1987; Hofstede, 1992; Laurent, 1986; Terpstra & David, 1985; Trompenaars, 1993). Their conclusion is that standardized, universal management methods (style of leadership and systems of selection and assessment) and organizational forms such as central organization versus decentral organization are not realistic and that (national) cultural differences should be taken into consideration.

This viewpoint from management scholars may be considered a simplified version of the contingency approach (cf. Frissen, 1989). National culture is considered an environment factor with which an organization is confronted and that cannot be ignored. This variable is seen as a restriction, although at times its facilitating nature is underlined. Certain sectors (e.g., services) are deemed to fit in well with national culture. Hofstede (1992), together with various other authors (e.g., Laurent, 1986), holds that collaborations between companies from certain countries are to be avoided, whereas those from other countries are to be stimulated. For Hofstede, this depends on the degree to which countries score equally on his dimensions such as uncertainty avoidance and power distance. Culture in this context is considered to be a more or less fixed system of shared values and standards defining action. Hofstede even boldly uses the phrase collective mental programming. Culture is viewed as having no links with organizational aspects and power.

In previous publications (Koot, 1994; Koot & Boessenkool, 1994), I have criticized this static approach of culture. Between cultural system and "agency," a continuous interaction can be observed (Giddens, 1984; Hannerz, 1992). The theory of ethnicity (e.g., Baud et al., 1994; Royce, 1982) teaches us that differences of power perceived between persons and groups strongly affect the extent to which cultural differences are considered important. From research into Flemish-Dutch collaboration (see Haverkamp & Marcha, 1995) executed under my supervision as well as research into Dutch-German mergers conducted by Olie (1994), we have learned that cultural distance in itself is not indicative for possible successful cooperation. Sometimes, differences are trivialized, and at other times they are accentuated. Those that find themselves in an inferior position or think they belong to a nation that, historically speaking, also finds itself at a disadvantage are more apt to stress cultural differences and cause "problems." This applies to the Flemings in relation to the Dutch and the Dutch in relation to the Germans. The logical consequence of Hofstede's (1992) theory—and one that is often drawn in practice—is that international businesses would do wise not settling in certain countries. If they do so, they should adjust to the local situation to an extreme degree, which involves attracting local managers, decentralizing, and maintaining local organizational cultures and identities.

Adler (1991) and Trompenaars (1993), along with Hofstede (1992) and Laurent (1986), favor the opinion that collaboration between businesses (or units) from certain countries tends to be relatively easy and from others relatively difficult. Thus, Trompenaars distinguishes countries with "guided missile," "Eiffel Tower," "family," and "incubator" cultures, clusters of countries that are marked by differences of opinion about worker relations, attitudes toward authority and conflicts, and ways of changing, learning, motivating, and rewarding. These researchers, however, think that the differences can be bridged and need not be problematic, provided people are tolerant toward one another, show respect, have confidence, and take on a conciliatory attitude. Ethnocentrism and stereotyping are altogether forbidden. Adler warns us that "people from one ethnic group are not inherently any better or worse than those from another group; they are simply different" (p. 97). With some goodwill, synergetic collaboration may be created so that "we can go beyond awareness of our own cultural heritage to produce something greater by cooperation and collaboration" (Harris & Moran, 1987, p. 3).

Exactly how the differences within international organizations and between cooperating international organizations should be organized is not stated clearly by most of the previously cited authors. They do not state what the relation between unity and difference in international businesses should be. Neither do they state the degree of centralization and decentralization, what ought to be decentralized, and for what reason. The main message appears to be that differences are here to stay and should be respected. It would seem that the most ardent supporters of the polycentric approach prefer an extreme decentralization.

Trompenaars (1993) remains an exception. He pays special attention to the matter but does not profess to be in favor of complete decentralization. According to him, a successful business enterprise is one that has created a fair balance between differentiation and integration, with the role of headquarters being one of coordination rather than control. Nevertheless, in his view, differentiation and decentralization still appear to be predominant. Headquarters ought to be no more than a coordinating center. In the long run, he even sees headquarters being broken up into several coordinating centers in various countries. Trompenaars also mentions the importance of central control, however restricted it should be in his opinion. This places him with authors that advocate the geocentric approach.

The supporters of the geocentric approach (e.g., Dekker, 1991; Fung, 1995; Nonaka, 1990; Ohmae, 1990) assume that some central rules are required to achieve "corporate efficiency." The outlook of the local managers is a global one. Diversity is appreciated, but everyone should realize that he or she is part of a global company and identify with it. To Ohmae, the latter notion also implies sharing a number of central values. Regarding the balance between local and central values, Ohmae states,

> A company's ability to serve customers around the globe in ways that are truly responsive to their needs as well as to the global character of its industry depends on the ability to strike a new organizational balance. What is called for is what Akio Morita has termed global localization, a new orientation to look into both directions. What makes this orientation difficult is not so much the organizational complexity it requires. The real difficulty is that the challenge cannot be met by redrawing structural charts, no matter how complex they are. Basically the question is a psychological one, a question of values. (p. 115)

In Fung's (1995) view, corporate culture should not be imposed, but rather constitute an issue of continuous negotiation between headquarters and local branches:

> The corporate culture of a multinational should rather be regarded as a potential, which can be employed to facilitate the process of cross-cultural cooperation. Such corporate culture can never impose any particular mode of conduct, but only facilitate behaviours that enhance cooperation and constrain those that do not. (p. 64)

The ultimate objective of management, according to Fung, should be to achieve a situation of cultural synergy in which both parties (local plant and headquarters) adjust themselves:

> Adaptation to cultural differences becomes a two-way process, which means that western management to some extent adjusts the company's policies and procedures to local circumstances, while locals to some degree accommodate to the requirements of the corporate strategies and procedures. (p. 65)

In his view, mutual adaptation while at the same time preserving personal identity is possible and desirable. He has termed this "a strategy of hybridization."

Another important representative of the federalistic model is Handy (1995). In his opinion, there is no problem in organizing unity and diversity, as long as a so-called Chinese contract and the principle of subsidiarity are taken as starting points. The former implies that there is a readiness to compromise instead of solely aiming at personal interest. Reciprocity is acknowledged and there is a willingness to give up personal interests for the sake of staving off future harm. Self-interest in a Chinese contract is best served by contributing to collective interest. The principle of subsidiarity implies delegating in the opposite direction—that is, delegation from the periphery toward the center. According to Handy, this is a moral principle. It is taken that the periphery possesses power that it can devolve to the center. The periphery may do this because it believes that the center on a collective basis will be able to perform certain tasks better than itself. Subsidiarity is not synonymous with empowerment. In the latter case, the periphery is accorded power and autonomy. Actually, power is being delegated. In the instance of subsidiarity, local autonomy is the starting point and delegation is in the opposite direction. As far as international organizations are concerned, Handy's two principles result in a structure consisting of autonomous local organizations that, out of self-interest, transfer part of their power and authority and tasks to headquarters.

Roosevelt (1991) and Cox (1993) developed their ideas for managing ethnic and other differences (age and gender) within U.S. organizations, but they are also used in learning to deal with ethnic differences in European organizations and international organizational contexts. At the heart of Roosevelt's theory is the idea of "managing diversity." This phrase refers to a form of organization directed at developing and evaluating organizational cultures to improve its skills in managing a diverse workforce. Managing diversity goes beyond and, in a way, is a continuation of affirmative action. In his opinion, enrolling (women and) ethnic minorities is not as essential in modern society as utilizing their talents and possibilities on every level. This is no longer a matter of decency but of professional survival. Eventually, a new organizational culture must come into being that will enable all workers to cooperate in such a way and be open to learning that a synergetic effect will occur resulting in increased productivity. Roosevelt holds that heterogenous organizations, provided they are well controlled, may enlarge creative and innovative potential. This statement is based on a study of Moss Kanter (1989), which shows that highly innovative organizations deliberately create heterogenous work units, thus obtaining a maximum of different perspectives in solving problems. Therefore, groupthink occurs less frequently.

The ideas of Roosevelt (1991) have provided Cox (1993) with a basis for developing a new typology. He distinguishes three types of organizations: monolithic, plural, and multicultural. A monolithic organization has a demographically

and culturally homogenous workforce, the members of which belong to the dominant social group (mostly white and male in the United States and Europe).
If members of minorities are to be found in the organization, they are not in
higher positions and have to adapt to the dominant majority. In short, in monolithic organizations structural and cultural integration are lacking. An advantage
of this type of organization, Cox records, is that intergroup conflicts hardly ever
arise.

Plural organizations are more heterogenous. They are inclined to take steps
toward appointing members of minority groups. Nevertheless, the latter remain
underrepresented in higher functions and participation in informal networks inside
the organization is restricted. The sense of menace on the part of the majority makes
for a high risk in intergroup conflicts. Cultural integration is not complete and hence
problematic.

Integration of this kind, according to Cox (1993), can indeed be found in the
so-called multicultural organization, in which diversity is not only appreciated
but accorded and awarded real value. The minority does not accommodate
here, but the standards and values of the two groups are together. Mutual dependency plays a role here. In the ideal organization, interethnic conflicts are absent,
along with any form of racism and discrimination. The multicultural organization
in Cox's view is an ideal type that few organizations have reached. According to
Cox, the path to this ideal situation harbors a number of pitfalls that he collectively
calls examples of modern racism: dysfunctional accommodation of members of
minorities and condescending behavior, blaming the victim, avoiding contact,
denying and trivializing cultural diversity, or repudiating political significance of
diversity. He also mentions six responses to this type of racism, calling them
expressions of internalized suppression: beating the system, disposing of any form
of criticism as discrimination, blaming the system, avoiding contact, disclaiming
one's cultural background, and trivializing the political consequence of racial
suppression and avoiding political conflicts.

Twuyver (1995), whose work is indebted to Cox (1993) and Roosevelt (1991),
suggests the following instruments to create multicultural organizations: the
introduction of a specific policy of attracting, selecting, and promoting migrants;
and learning to cope with differences through training and multiethnically composed task groups.

How does the theory of intercultural management help to answer the question
stated previously—that is, What is the best way for international businesses to deal
with the (foreseeable) worldwide increase in ethnic segmentation?

Evaluation of the Theory of Intercultural Management in the Light of Foreseeable Processes of Ethnicizing

Many of the authors on intercultural management mentioned previously either explicitly or implicitly employ a one best way approach. In doing so, they take for granted that successful organizational cultures can be universally applied, values and standards of other groups can be imitated, and subsequently culture can be made. This is a type of approach that betrays a limited orientation on organizational models developed in the economically successful parts of the world: the United States, Japan, and the European Community. Globalization of the home-developed model appears, for most of the adherents of this approach, to be the main target. Authors, however, who have a more polycentric or geocentric approach and, as a consequence, underline the importance of the difference in culture almost invariably assume that organizing these differences should and can occur in harmony. Ethnocentrism to them is anathema. The attitude should be one of tolerance and willingness to equally value similarities and differences (Adler, 1991, p. 108). According to these authors, an attitude of this kind will no doubt lead to synergy. Parochialism will eventually vanish and a pluralistic global society will come into being in which the various countries and regions are highly interdependent and internationally oriented. It is imperative that globalization of the synergetic range of ideas be energetically implemented.

In my view, these "academic" expositions on intercultural management bear an ideological stamp and, although perhaps not intended, they have a blind spot with regard to the possible advantages of ethnicizing in situations of deprivation. In nearly every instance, ideals are presented, whereas processes related to culture and ethnicity are left unanalyzed. Issues of power, politics, and economics are rarely addressed. Most of the models, however, are founded on a political and economic basis. There seems to be a wish "to sell" one's own success model or to realize other hidden objectives and to this end the finest rhetoric is employed.

Globalization is often represented as the next step to be welcomed in the internationalization of economics because it makes people give up their prejudices. "The word globalization suggests harmony and appeals to the hope that old rivalries be overcome between different people. In short, the word globalization carries the promise of a better tomorrow" (Ruigrok & Van Tulder, 1993, p. 55).

Under the guise of communality and equality, strategies are presented that are meant to secure personal interests. This is how learned "theories" are made to serve either economic or political interests or both at one time. As early as 1980,

Wallerstein (1980) drew attention to the fact that "the dominant economic forces find it helpful to encourage intellectual and cultural thrusts, movements and ideologies" (p. 38).

What kind of interests could be served by tolerance, harmony, interdependence, and synergy? To tolerate literally means "to bear." It implies putting up with something that one disapproves of at the same time. It was Procée (1991, p. 133) who pointed out that, theoretically, we can distinguish two kinds of "bearing":

1. bearing in a situation in which one is powerless; wanting to do something about the unwanted situation. Resignation is the correct word here; and
2. bearing in a situation of power; this is the case when one is capable of altering the situation. Here we may speak about "real" tolerance.

According to Procée (1991), the first definition is self-explanatory. There is no question of tolerating things—merely of being subjected to them. The second type yields a definition of tolerance: bearing with an idea, action, person, group, or state of affairs that one disapproves of, while being able (or thinking one is) able to counteract them. Being tolerated is the fate of the weak. Hoffman and Arts (as quoted in Essed & Helweg, 1992) state that "tolerance is a one-sided instrument of the dominant majority: A group—or a member of that group—tolerates practices and opinions that they disapprove of or look upon as inferior" (p. 510). Essed and Helweg (1992) also uses a similar phrasing: "The language of tolerance is one of good will, but its practice means that ethnic groups are being examined, categorized, pigeon-holed and judged by the standards of the dominant group" (p. 24).

Harmony is the catchword of those who want to maintain the status quo. Thus, synergy may be considered to be the prevailing concept of current Western postmodernistic society, which is fragmentizing, in danger of losing its political and economic supremacy, and is trying to make overtures and latch on to (what used to be) the periphery. Fear of loss of global supremacy lies at the root of the rhetoric of synergy and interdependence. Ruigrok and Van Tulder (1993) demonstrated quite convincingly that in reality very little indeed is realized by the policy of large American, Japanese, and European multinational concerns to glocalize (e.g., by internationalizing their managerial workers and entering into relations with their local partners). Tennekes (1994) also questions the openly professed sympathy for other cultures on the part of Western business enterprises:

> Members of organizations and companies who try to gain an understanding of each other across cultural boundaries, do not do so because they take such a tremendous interest in each other's culture, but because they personally—as

organizations or individuals—want to benefit from it. That is why intercultural communication will not easily take the shape of an open debate on the positive and negative aspects of one another's culture or of a combined effort to try and find a culture appealing to all concerned. (p. 140)

The question remains to be answered, however, whether the method of harmonizing, chosen to stave off the danger of loss of Western supremacy, is a successful one. As previously noted, nationalism and ethnic regionalizing are rather the rule than the exception in the current globalizing world. Professional literature on circumstances that influence ethnicizing of ethnic minorities tells us that the current conditions are extremely favorable. Factors such as inequality relations as a result of history, ethnocentrism of the dominant group, examples of success by groups that have already been ethnicized, and the presence of minority leaders that are well acquainted with the culture of the majority are frequently considered to be extremely significant (e.g., Koot & Rath, 1987). It is these factors—all of which can be traced back to inequality of power—that in the wake of the migration and globalization discussed previously seem to loom large in many countries.

For this reason, in the years ahead ethnic differences and rivalry will not be on the way out but vice versa. Regarding this subject, John Gray stated,

> The breakthrough of Islamic fundamentalists in Turkey signals that the big conflicts in the world in the next century will not be fought between opposite Western ideologies. The problems we are going to be confronted with will be in the range of religious fanaticism, the fight between ethnic groups and—no less important—the growing pressure of population in combination with a shortage of natural resources. There is no hope of spreading our liberal-democratic values in such a world. As it is, liberal democracies will have a hard time to survive at all. . . . We must prepare ourselves for a future when non-Western nations will treat us with the same respect as we did them in colonial times. (*de Volkskrant,* Literary Supplement, Jan. 10, 1996)

The question remains to be answered as to whether a policy of tolerance toward the increasing ethnic consciousness among immigrants and growing confidence in a number of non-Western countries will works out favorably. Its effect may even be the opposite. Creating distance and accentuating one's ethnic origin tend to be (very strong) weapons in the struggle against the dominant party. These weapons will not be easily surrendered. Realizing this, we would probably do better to take it for granted that in international organizations ethnic oppositions do exist and consequently go about organizing them. In some cases, this may involve an attempt to eliminate the differences; in other cases, however, it may be advisable to leave the rivalry intact or even stimulate it. Adler, Cox, and others want us to believe that it is better to start from differences, to accept these, and thus end up in harmonious collaboration. In my opinion, this point of view is rather idealistic, patronizing, and at times counterproductive. If differences are interrelated with inequality relations, tolerance, as noted previously, boils down to accepting the status quo. If one wants to reduce cultural distance, paradoxically one should not focus mainly on the differences in culture but also concentrate on differences in power and conflicting interests. This is notably the case when groups employ differences in culture in opposing inequality of power.

I have found this more than once in my research of collaboration between Antilleans and Dutch and, as mentioned previously, under my supervision performed research into collaboration between Flemings and Dutch (see Haverkamp & Marcha, 1996). For example, Antilleans on the island of Curaçao feel hard pressed particularly by the direct, confident manner and (to them) superior fluency of the Dutch. They fear they will be outmaneuvered, and that they will be made to go to the wall or lose their jobs and land. In addition, it is pointed out in this study that Curaçao has traditionally been patronized by The Netherlands. By way of protection, the Dutchman has turned into an arrogant character with whom one cannot possibly communicate and nothing is left untried to accentuate the cultural differences. Papiamento, the local tongue, in this respect is an excellent means of distinction. The Dutch are not only being reproached for not speaking Papiamento; they are also given a hard time in learning it. As a rule, an Antillean will answer in Dutch when being addressed by a Dutch person who wishes to speak Papiamento. For their part, the Dutch are far less conscious of their cultural defenses with the Antilleans. They are apt to brush aside insinuations of the kind and on occasion may even facetiously remark on it: "It's a kind of 'Amsterdam-plus' we're having here" (Amsterdam with a Caribbean flavor added). In a situation like this, the working relationship tends to be characterized by tensions. In cases in which Antilleans are in a position of power (i.e., hold higher posts or possess a larger percentage of the shares in a joint venture), however, the cultural difference is played down.

Conclusions

Organizing and managing ethnic rivalries as a form of management strategy in our globalizing world is not just more realistic than aspiring to cultural synergy, it may even release a large amount of energy. How much energy can be set free is illustrated in the two cases described at the beginning of this chapter on collaboration between Philips plants in Austria and between Curaçaoans and Venezuelans in a former Shell refinery in Curaçao.

The two cases on ethnic rivalry in Austria and Curaçao have illustrated the kind of power that, in a positive or negative sense, may be generated by ethnicity in an organization. In the first case, the traditional ethnic rivalry between Carinthia and the Vienna region proved to be the most important factor for the success of the Althofian factory in a sector such as consumer electronics in which it is almost impossible for European factories to compete with Asian companies. Ethnic rivalry produced an enormous fighting spirit and outweighed the disadvantages of the relatively high labor costs in Austria. In the Curaçaoan refinery, however, the discrimination and arrogance from the white Venezuelan top management toward the black Antillean middle managers and workers led to a process of ethnicity among the Antilleans and to an economic failure for the refinery. The Venezuelans were not aware of the risks of ethnic segmentation and had no strategy to cope with it.

Hence, it is important to handle ethnic antagonism with care because it can make for success or failure. On the destructive side, it will most likely boil down to unequal power relations instead of differences in culture. Ethnic rivalry, however, can also release energy. This is why management should know when and how ethnic rivalry can be used strategically. In my opinion, there are some necessary conditions for the strategic utilization of ethnic rivalry in organizations. First, one must separate tasks to create autonomous competing units on an ethnic basis, which can be the case when looking for a location of a new company plant. Here, one should remember the characteristics of the Carinthian region: economic backward position, little alternative employment possibilities, good infrastructure, discipline, and a strong work ethic, but above all the presence of feelings of relative deprivation and ethnic rivalry toward another region where there already exists a successful company plant. A second necessary condition is the presence of a manager who is able to mobilize the ethnic energy in the newly created autonomous unit. Such a person needs a strong identification with the ethnic ideals or should be seen by the group in question as very useful for the realization of their ethnic ambitions.

In some cases, it will be possible to reorganize in such a way that a branch or business unit can operate rather autonomously, which is, however, not always feasible. If units or branches depend on each other, an organizational arrangement will have to be found whereby autonomy and mutual dependency are evenly balanced, creating creative tension (cf. Mastenbroek, 1991, 1993).

Growing ethnic segmentation in the world calls for a vision in which recognition and appreciation of differences and contrasts are central notions. This implies starting from a number of perspectives without singling out any one organizational solution as final. Contradictions should not be seen as problematic but as starting points for a learning process. Overall, confrontations are more productive than harmony.

In our globalizing world, (ethnic) differentiation, fragmentation, and segmentation are bound to increase rather than decrease. In a large organization with varied interests, customs, preferences, and contrasting definitions of reality (cf. Lammers, 1987), a pluralistic vision of management tends to be more realistic than an integrative approach. Because (ethnic) differentiation, fragmentation, and segmentation are bound to increase, managers would do wise to prepare thoroughly for it.

Notes

1. For an extended overview of the research methods and the results, see Koot and Hogema (1992).

2. The data of this case are based on research by Julie McCreedy (1993) executed under my supervision.

3. An appropriate definition of globalization has been given by Giddens (1990): "The intensification of worldwide social relations which link distant localities in such a way that local happenings are shaped by events occurring many miles away and vice versa" (p. 64).

References

Adler, N. (1991). *Organizational behavior.* Belmont, CA: Wadsworth.

Adler, N. J. (1986). Do MBA's want international careers? *International Journal of Intercultural Relations, 10*(3), 277-300.

Alvesson, M. (1993). *Cultural perspectives on organizations.* Cambridge, UK: Cambridge University Press.

Appadurai, A. (1986). *Cultural perspectives on organizations.* Cambridge, UK: Cambridge University Press.

Barth, F. (1969). *Ethnic groups and boundaries: The local organizational of culture difference.* Oslo, Norway: Universitatsforlaget.

Baud, M., Koonings, K., Oostindie, G., Ouweneel, A., & Patricio, S. (1994). *Etniciteit als strategie in Latijns-Amerika en de Caraïben.* Amsterdam: Amsterdam University Press.

Chung, K. H. A. (1978). *A comparative study of managerial characteristics of domestic, international and governmental institutions in Korea.* Paper presented at the Midwest Conference on Asian Affairs, Minneapolis, MN.

Cox, T., Jr. (1993). *Cultural diversity in organizations: Theory, research and practice.* San Francisco: Berett-Koehler.

Crozier, M. (1964). *The bureaucratic phenomenon.* Chicago: University of Chicago Press.

Czarniawska-Joerges, B. (1992). *Exploring complex organizations: A cultural perspective.* London: Sage.

Deal, T. E., & Kennedy, A. A. (1982). *Corporate cultures. The rites and rituals of corporate life.* Reading, MA: Addison-Wesley.

Dekker, R. (1991, October). *Skill sheets.* Rotterdam, The Netherlands: Rotterdam School of Management.

Essed, Ph., & Helweg, L. (1992). *Bij voorbeeld. Multicultureel beleid in de praktijk.* Amsterdam: Stichting FNV-Pers.

Featherstone, M., Lash, S., & Robertson, R. (Eds.). (1995). *Global modernities.* London: Sage.

Friedman, J. (1994). *Cultural identity and global process.* London: Sage.

Friedman, J. (1995). Global system, globalization and the parameters of modernity. In M. Featherstone, S. Lash, & R. Robertson (Eds.), *Global modernities.* London: Sage.

Frissen, P. H. A. (1989). *Bureaucratische cultuur en informatisering.* Den Haag, The Netherlands: SDA.

Fung, R. J. (1995). *Organizational strategies for cross-cultural cooperation.* Delft, The Netherlands: Eburon.

Gallie, D. (1978). *In search of the new working class.* London: Cambridge University Press.

Giddens, A. (1984). *The constitution of society. Outline of the theory of structuration.* Cambridge, MA: Polity.

Giddens, A. (1990). *The consequences of modernity.* Cambridge, MA: Polity.

Glazer, N., & Moynihan, D. P. (1963). *Beyond the melting pot.* Cambridge, UK: Cambridge University Press.

Gray, J. (1996, January 10). De hegemonie van het Westen loopt ten einde. *de Volkskrant,* Literary Supplement, Section Forum, p. 16.

Handy, Ch. (1995). *De paradox van de lege jas.* Amsterdam: Uitgeverij Contact.

Hannerz, U. (1992). *Cultural complexity: Studies in the social organization of meaning.* New York: Colombia University Press.

Harris, P., & Moran, R. (1987). *Managing cultural differences.* Houston, TX: Gulf.

Haverkamp, I., & Marcha, V. (1995). *Gedeeld of Verdeeld? Culturele verschillen en samenwerking van Belgen en Nederlanders in Baarle-Hertog en Baarle-Nassau.* Utrecht, The Netherlands: ISOR/Centrum voor Beleid en Management.

Hobsbawm, E., & Ranger, T. (Eds.). (1983). *The invention of tradition.* Cambridge, UK: Cambridge University Press.

Hofstede, G. (1980). *Culture's consequences. International differences in work related values.* London: Sage.

Hofstede, G. (1992). *Cultural constraints in management theories.* Lecture at the Annual Meeting of the Academy of Management, Las Vegas, NV/Maastricht: International Researchcentre for International Communication/ITIM.

Kakar, S. (1971). The theme of authority in social relations in India. *Journal of Social Psychology, 84,* 93-101.

Kanter, R. M. (1989). *When giants learn to dance.* New York: Simon and Schuster.

Koot, W. C. J. (1994). Ambiguïteit en wisselende identiteiten. *M & O, Tijdschrift voor Organisatiekunde en Sociaal Beleid, 48*(2), 113-129.

Koot, W. C. J., & Boessenkool, J. (1994). De cultuur van een arbeidsorganisatie: Theoretisch uitdagend, voor onderzoekers een ramp! *Antropologische Verkenningen, 13*(2), 54-69.

Koot, W. C. J., & Hogema, I. (1992). *Organisatiecultuur: Fictie en werkelijkheid.* Muiderberg, The Netherlands: Uitgeverij Coutinho BV, tweede druk.

Koot, W. C. J., & Rath, J. (1987). Etnicity and emancipation. *International Migration, 25*(4), 426-440.

Lammers, C. J. (1987). *Organisaties vergelijkenderwijs.* Utrecht, The Netherlands: Het Spectrum BV.

Lash, S., & Friedman, J. (Eds.). (1992). *Modernity and identity.* Oxford, UK: Blackwell.

Lash, S., & Urray, J. (1994). *Economies of signs and space.* London: Sage.

Latour, B. (1994). *Wij zijn nooit modern geweest. Pleidooi voor symmetrische antropologie.* Rotterdam, The Netherlands: Van Gennep.

Laurent, A. (1986) *The cross-cultural puzzle of international human resource management.* Fontainebleau, France: Insead.

Martin, J. (1992). *Cultures in organizations. Three perspectives.* Oxford, UK: Oxford University Press.

Mastenbroek, W. F. G. (1991). *Conflicthantering en Organisatieontwikkeling* (derde herziene editie). Alphen aan den Rijn, The Netherlands: Samsom.

Mastenbroek, W. F. G. (1993). *Macht, organisatie en communicatie.* Heemstede, The Netherlands: Holland.

McCreedy, J. (1993). *Cultures at work. A study of ethnic diversity at Isla oil refinery, Curaçao.* Utrecht, The Netherlands: Centrum voor Beleid en Management.

Meyerson, D. (1991). Normal ambiguity? In P. Frost (Ed.), *Reframing organizational culture* (pp. 131-144). London: Sage.

Mommaas, D. (1991). Mondialisering en culturele identiteit. *Vrije Tijd en Samenleving 3/4,* 11-41.

Morton, C. (1994). *Becoming world class.* London: Macmillan.

Nederveen Pieterse, J. (1995). Globalization as hybridization. In M. Featherstone, S. Lash, & R. Robertson (Eds.), *Global modernities.* London: Sage.

Nonaka, I. (1990). *Managing globalization as a self-renewing process: Experiencies of Japanese MNC's.* In C. Bartlett, Y. Doz, & G. Hedlund (Eds.), *Managing the global firm* (pp. 69-95).

Ohmae, K. (1990). *The borderless world: Power and strategy in the interlinked economy.* London: Fontana.

Olie, R. (1994). Internationale fusies en cultuur. *M & O, Tijdschrift voor Organisatiekunde en Sociaal Beleid, 46*(2), 175-195.

Ouchi, W. (1981). *Theory Z: How American business can meet the Japanese challenge.* Reading, MA: Addison-Wesley.

Peters, T. J., & Waterman, R. H. (1980). *In search of excellence.* San Francisco: Harper & Row.

Procée, H. (1991). *Over de grenzen van culturen.* Meppel, The Netherlands: Boom.

Robertson, R. (1995). Glocalization: Time-space and homogeneity-heterogeneity. In M. Featherstone, S. Lash, & R. Robertson (Eds.), *Global modernities.* London: Sage.

Roosevelt, T., Jr. (1991). *Total quality, managing diversity; Keys to competitive advantage in the 1990's.* New York: AMACOM.

Roossens, E. (1986). *Micronationalisme. Een antropologie van het etnisch reveil.* Leuven, Belgium: Acco.

Royce (1982). *Ethnic identity: Strategies of diversity.* Bloomington: Indiana University Press.

Ruigrok, W. M., & Van Tulder, R. J. M. (1993). *The ideology of interdependence. The link between restructuring, internationalisation and international trade.* Amsterdam: Proefschrift Universiteit van Amsterdam.

Sackmann, S. (1992). *Cultural knowledge in organizations: Exploring the collective mind* (2nd ed.). Newbury Park, CA: Sage.

Schein, E. H. (1985). *Organizational culture and leadership.* San Francisco: Jossey-Bass.

Tennekes, J. (1994). Communicatie en cultuurverschil. *M & O, Tijdschrift voor Organisatiekunde en Sociaal Beleid, 48*(2), 130-143.

Terpstra, V., & David, K. (1985). *The cultural environment of international business.* Cincinnati, OH: South-Western.

Trompenaars, F. (1993). *Zakendoen over de grens.* Amsterdam: Uitgeverij Contact.

Twuyver, M. van (1995). *Culturele diversiteit in organisaties. Een kansrijk perspectief.* Schiedam, The Netherlands: Scriptum.

Van Binsbergen, W. (1994). Dynamiek van cultuur, enige dilemma's van hedendaags Afrika in een context van globalisering. *Antroplogische Verkenningen, 13*(2), 17-34.

Van Maanen, J. (1991). The smile factory: Work at Disneyland. In P. Frost (Ed.), *Reframing organizational culture* (pp. 58-77). London: Sage.

Wallerstein, I. (1980). *The capitalist world-economy. Essays by Immanuel Wallerstein.* Cambridge, UK: Cambridge University Press.

Part V

Social Identity as a Critical Concept in Dealing With Complex Cultural Settings

The two chapters in Part V focus on organizational and social identity, respectively, and answer some of the most critical questions that the perspective of multiple cultures raises, such as how individuals may handle simultaneously existing multiple cultural identities, which kind of cultural identity may become salient in a specific situation, and what might trigger such salience. Both authors take a step beyond the mere description of the complex interplay of multiple cultural identities by indicating ways in which such a complex interplay can be successfully managed, including its inherent contradictions.

Helge Hernes explores social identity in terms of its magnitude and salience by contrasting and comparing prosocial behavior of two different professions (doctors and nurses) within the Norwegian hospital industry.

As such, he addresses issues of handling multiple cultural identities based on profession and industry within the same national (Norwegian) context at the suborganizational level. The results of the study indicate that, within that specific cultural context, professional identity seems to have the strongest explanatory power for prosocial behavior.

Peter Dahler-Larsen explores the issue of multiple cultural identities within the context of a strike that actually should not have occurred because of the highly praised homogenous organizational culture of the organization (the Scandinavian Airline System [SAS]). His investigation of "we typifications" (who are "we" as opposed to "them") includes identities at the suborganizational, organizational (SAS), and national level (Danes vs. Swedes) as well as cross-cutting identities (profession). The findings of his study shed light on the complex dynamics of handling multiple cultural identities: how people can handle multiple cultural identities that may actually be in conflict with each other and how their salience may quickly change depending on the critical issues at hand.

Chapter 16

Cross-Cutting Identifications in Organizations

Helge Hernes

Organizational culture in recent years has gained increasing interest (Alvesson, 1990). Some of the organizational culture theory and empirical research is based on the assumption that the employees have shared values, beliefs, and norms throughout the entire organization, whereas other scholars focus on the cultural differences between subparts, such as departments, divisions, and so on, of the organizations. The issue that employees may be members of more than one group, and thus be inclined to have different and even conflicting cultural norms, is less understood. This chapter provides theoretical and empirical knowledge about this phenomenon.

The basic premise of the chapter is that organizational culture and group membership are related concepts—that is, that the values, beliefs, and norms of people in organizations may be explained by their identifications with the groups in which they are members. Between such groups, certain patterns of intergroup relations evolve. Such intergroup relations are important for several reasons. First, they are important because the previously mentioned groups are perceived as important by their members. Second, the evolving intergroup relations also have major impacts for the entire organization. In many organizations, subgroups interact directly with regard to, for example, task coordination, professional or administrative decisions, or social processes. Management in such a context thus means managing a myriad of intergroup relations. Knowledge about them is necessary for managing them skillfully and hence successfully.

The importance of intergroup relations, however, varies among organization types. In some organizations, such as the machine bureaucracy type (Mintzberg, 1979), they are of minor importance because of the strict division of labor and hierarchical structure. Other organizations can be conceptualized as collections of intergroup relations in organizations. Hierarchal authority is limited and subgroups may have and may need great autonomy.

Cross-Cutting Identifications

Intergroup analyses are particularly useful in the analysis of employees' simultaneous membership in several groups as discussed in Chapter 2 of this volume in the context of the perspective of cultural complexity. In addition to being a member of their organizational unit, employees are also members of a gender, age, professional, ethnic background, and so on.

Multigroup memberships are of special importance in multiprofessional organizations—for example, hospitals. They have departments between which intergroup cooperation or intergroup conflict or both may evolve. The professional dimension is important because of the high level of professionalism. Thus, typical hospital employees are members of at least cross-cutting groups. Therefore, they may categorize themselves and their colleagues into in-/in-groups, in-/out-groups, out-/in-groups, and out-/out-groups according to whether they have none, one, or both of the memberships in the two groups in common with the other ones.

The question of which of the previously mentioned intergroup relations (organizational subunit and profession) is the most important one is reformulated here into "To which of the two groups do hospital employees have the strongest identifications?" Social identity theory (SIT; Hogg & Abrams, 1988; Tajfel & Turner, 1985) and self-categorization theory (SCT; Turner, Hogg, Oakes, Reicher, & Wetherell, 1987) pose the question "Who am I?" from the point of view that identity may be linked to the groups of which the individual is a member (in-group) as opposed to other groups (out-groups). Such identifications to groups are shown to have cognitive as well as behavioral consequences; a depersonalization is occurring that is an antecedent for ethnocentrism and other in-group biases as well as for discrimination toward whom prosocial behavior is directed. Group identifications thus have major impacts on organizational culture and behavior.

This chapter is divided into two sections; in the first section, a framework for understanding multigroup memberships is developed on the basis of social identity theory and self-categorization theory. The second section of the chapter reports the results from an empirical study of intergroup relations at Norwegian hospitals and the discussion and summary follow.

Framework for Understanding Multigroup Membership

Since the early 1970s, when Tajfel, Billig, Bundy, and Flament (1971) conducted minimal group experiments, SIT (Hogg & Abrams, 1988; Tajfel & Turner, 1985) and later SCT (Turner et al., 1987) have been the predominant theoretical approaches for studying intergroup relations. One preceding approach of major importance is that of Sherif (1967), which posited that competition of scarce resources was the major explanation of intergroup relations. According to SIT and SCT, distinct intergroup behavior is possible even in the absence of scarce resources or other manifest conflict dimensions. The one and only necessary condition is that people define themselves and others as members of groups—that they categorize themselves and others into in-groups and out-groups. Tajfel et al.'s experiments demonstrated discriminating behaviors between explicitly randomly assigned groups. In a series of experiments in the mid-1980s, Brewer and Kramer (Brewer & Kramer, 1986; Kramer & Brewer, 1984, 1986) showed the linkages between social identifications and cooperation. By the end of the 1980s, SIT and SCT had become the dominant intergroup relation paradigm; this also applies to organizational behavior (Ashforth & Mael, 1989).

The main proposition of SIT and SCT is that people are answering the question "Who are you?" by referring to one of the groups of which they are a member (in-group) as opposed to other groups (out-groups). By such identification to groups, it is assumed that the individual's "self" is linked to these groups: "Social identification therefore, is the perception of oneness with or belongingness to some human aggregate" (Ashforth & Mael, 1989, p. 21).

Abrams and Hogg (1990) stated, "When social identity is salient, the group is represented in the individual self-concept. Self-conception as a group member, rather than interpersonal relationships within groups or explicit social pressure, is what creates the uniformity of group behavior" (p. 4).

Social identity is different from personal identity (which is a matter of relations to other persons in the same group) and from human identity (which is about relations to other species) (Turner et al., 1987). Social identity may be enhanced or reduced depending on whether the in-group is perceived to be distinct and whether it is perceived as better than out-groups: "Social identity is always attached to some social referent, usually a social group. If your psychological fortunes wax and wane with the fortunes of that social referent, then you identify with the referent" (Augoustionos & Walker, 1995, p. 98).

The previously mentioned "oneness with or belongingness to some human aggregate"—"when I becomes we" (Brewer, 1991, p. 476)—is coined depersonalization: "Depersonalization refers to the process of 'self-stereotyping' whereby people come to perceive themselves more as the interchangeable exemplars of a social category than as unique personalities defined by their individual differences from others" (Turner et al., 1987, p. 50).

This process is assumed to have cognitive as well as behavioral consequences. Even if the cleavage between them may be somewhat arbitrary, it is distinguished here between these two types of consequences.

Cognitive Consequences

Once a social identity has become salient for a person (the processes leading to this are discussed below), there is a tendency to exaggerate the intergroup differences. This accentuation effect (Abrams & Hogg, 1990; Turner et al., 1987) stands in contrast to relative heterogeneity or the out-group homogeneity effect; the in-group members are perceived as being more heterogenous than the out-group members (Brewer, 1991, 1993).

According to SIT and SCT, "people are evaluated positively to the degree that they are perceived as prototypical of the self-category in terms of which they are being compared" (Turner et al., 1987, p. 57). Thus, ethnocentrism may emerge as the "we are better than they" effect. According to Turner et al., this attraction to one's own group as a whole depends on the perceived prototypicality of the in-group compared with relevant out-groups.

In summary, the cognitive consequences of social identifications may be referred to as in-group bias.

Behavioral Consequences

To the degree that the self is depersonalized, according to Turner et al. (1987) so too is self-interest: "the perception of identity between oneself and ingroup members leads to a perceived identity of interests in terms of the needs, goals and motives associated with ingroup membership" (p. 61). This implies what Turner et al. conceptualize as empathic altruism—the goals of other in-group members are perceived as one's own and empathic trust and other in-group members are assumed to share one's own goals: "The self-interested egocentric view of human nature does not explain why individuals risk or sacrifice personal comfort, safety, or social position to promote group benefit. . . . People die for the sake of group distinctions" (Brewer, 1991, p. 475).

Contact between members of groups may change the behavior pattern between them. The traditional approach (Allport as cited by Johnston & Hewstone, 1990) is that such contacts improve the intergroup relations. Johnston and Hewstone have challenged this view: "Contact per se is not sufficient to produce an improvement in intergroup relations" (p. 186). Intergroup contact provides an opportunity for comparisons between groups (Johnston & Hewstone, 1990). Such comparisons may improve the intergroup relations. The possibility of conflict, however, also arises. Johnston and Hewstone offer no complete framework for which of these effects is the strongest one. Therefore, it is an empirical matter in what direction intergroup relations are influenced by intergroup contact.

Multigroup Membership

The previous discussion refers to the simple case in which an individual is a member of one group relative to one or more out-groups. As Allen, Wilder, and Atkinson (1983) state, however, regularly an individual is a member of many groups:

> If a very simple society existed in which only a single group membership were possible, social identity would be predictable on the basis of the groups's attributes and would be highly stable across situations and over temporal periods. . . . An industrialized society produces social fragmentation, division of labor, and a heterogeneity of interests; as a consequence social identity is determined by membership in many different types of groups. (p. 96)

In such multigroup member situations, at least four issues are important:

1. Conceptualization of the multigroup membership—are the groups subgroups of each other or are they groups on the same level?
2. The strength or salience of the potential identification

3. Whether the group memberships are concordant or discordant (in harmony with or at odds with each other)

4. Whether the identifications are stable or varying across specific situations

Conceptualization of Multigroup Membership

Multiple group memberships may be conceptualized along two dimensions. First, it is a level issue; one subgroup of which a person is a member (e.g., a working group) may be a subgroup of another group (e.g., a department) which in turn may be a part of a division or an entire organization. According to Kramer (1991), however, the individual's identification is defined to the primary group in the organization even though the identification level may vary among situations. Kramer states,

> It is postulated here that organizational identification is defined, all else being equal, at the level of the individual's primary group in the organization. By primary group is meant simply the group with which an individual most frequently interacts and in terms of which other members of the organization interact with him or her. (p. 203)

The second issue is about groups that are not subgroups of each other—for example, gender, age, or ethnic groups. Some of these group memberships overlap each other (e.g., gender and occupations such as nurses, oil operators, etc.), and other multigroup memberships are orthogonal (e.g., membership in one group is entirely independent of membership in the other group). This last case can be described as crossed categorizations (Hewstone, Islam, & Judd, 1993). Using two orthogonal dimensions and dichotomous variables, four groups emerge: double in-group, double out-group, in-group/out-group, and out-group/in-group. This may be illustrated as shown in Figure 16.1.

Salience of Identifications

SIT and SCT suggest that in each situation one identification is the salient one: "Turner postulated that an inherent tension or antagonism exists between different psychological identities. When one identity is dominant, he suggested, the impact of the others will be recessive. When one becomes figure, the others become ground" (Kramer, 1993, p. 256).

	X	Y
A	AX	AY
B	BX	BY

Figure 16.1. In-Group/Out-Group Matrix

Which identification is the salient one may vary across situations, as explained by the categorization process (Hogg & McGarty, 1990):

> The basic mechanism is the cognitive process of categorization which accentuates similarities among stimuli (whether they are physical, social or aspects of the self) belonging to the same category and differences among stimuli belonging to different categories on dimensions believed to be correlated with the categorization. (p. 12)

The salient social identification is further assumed to be explained by the interaction between accessibility and fit: "the salience of some ingroup-outgroup categorization in a specific situation is a function of an interaction between the 'relative accessibility' of that categorization for the perceiver and the 'fit' between the stimulus input and category specifications" (Turner et al., 1987, p. ???).

Accessibility is defined by Turner et al. (1987) as

> the readiness with which a stimulus input with given properties will be coded or identified in terms of a category—the more accessible the category the less input required to invoke the relevant categorization, the wider the range of stimulus characteristics that will be perceived as congruent with category specifications and the more likely that other less accessible categories which also fit stimulus input will be masked. Two major determinants of accessibility are past learning of what tends to go with what in the environment, its "redundant structure," and the person's current motives. . . . The idea of fit simply refers to the degree to which reality actually matches the criteria which define the category. (p. 55)

This is in accordance with Bruner (1957), who states,

> The greater the accessibility of a category, (a) the less the input necessary for categorization to occur in terms of this category, (b) the wider the range of input

characteristics that will be "accepted" as fitting the category in question, (c) the more likely that categories that provide a better or equally good fit for the input will be masked. (pp. 129-130)

This mechanism may also be described as "the principle of metacontrast": "The salient category is that which simultaneously minimizes intracategory differences and maximizes intercategory differences within the social frame of reference" (Hogg & McGarty, 1990, p. 14; Turner et al., 1987).

Concordance and Discordance

Tensions or antagonism may exist between identifications or they may be in harmony with each other. This distinction is conceptualized as discordant or concordant identifications: "Social identities associated with two different group memberships are discordant if they are inconsistent or contradictory in a logical or psychological sense" (Allen et al., 1983, p. 97). Thus, the relations between potential identifications are assumed to vary rather than being constant.

As Ashforth and Mael (1989) suggest, individuals are thought to be able to live with discrepancies between discordant identifications:

Individuals have multiple, loosely coupled identities, and inherent conflicts between their demands are typically not resolved by cognitively integrating the identities, but ordering, separating, or buffering them. This compartmentalization of identities suggests the possibility of double standards, apparent hypocrisy, and selective forgetting. (p. 35)

Stability of Social Identifications

According to SIT and SCT, identifications vary across situations. Kramer (1993) states,

Individuals often describe, and presumably experience, identity as a relatively stable entity, reflecting the existence of clearly defined preferences, values, attitudes, and dispositions. . . . They feel, for example, that they know who they are, what they are like, and can predict how they will act in a variety of situations. This phenomenology is deceptive. Identification in organizations is neither stable nor fixed. Rather, it depends largely on the context in which the individual is embedded. A given identity may be highly salient in one context, exerting considerable impact on perception, judgment, and behavior. In another setting, the same identity may have low salience and exert little impacts. (p. 255)

Alternatively, Hewstone et al. (1993), by focusing on the stable aspects of identifications by crossed categorizations, suggest that some identifications are of equal importance to each other, whereas in other cases one may dominate the other(s).

By bringing the previously mentioned issues together, the framework shown in Figure 16.2 can be established for relationships between stable and situational identifications.

In Figure 16.2, the quadrants to the left indicate the stable aspects of social identifications whereas the top right quadrants indicate the corresponding situational identifications.

Situational factors probably strengthen or weaken the previously mentioned stable identifications. The framework suggests that these associations vary according to whether the relation between the stable identifications is that of dominance and whether they are concordant or discordant: In the case of highly discordant identifications, one of them presumably is salient in the specific situations, squeezing the other ones out. In another situation, however, another identification may be salient. In the case of concordant identifications, it seems plausible to assume that two identifications may be salient at the same time. Thus, the degree to which only one or, alternatively, more identifications may be salient in the same situation in this framework is regarded as a variable, rather than a constant, and is explained by whether the identifications are concordant or discordant. Thus, which of two identifications is the dominant one explains which of the two potential identifications will be salient (by discordance) or strongest (by concordance).

This framework is applicable to all multigroup contexts irrespective of whether these are in organizations. For modern organizations, conceptualized as a collection of groups, the framework is particularly useful for understanding the microprocesses that constitute organizational culture.

Intergroup Relations in Hospitals: An Empirical Study

If social identifications are important for explaining cultural processes in organizations, knowledge is needed about the magnitude of these identifications with regard to the existing groups and about their antecedents. In this case, we chose two dimensions—departments and professions in hospitals. Hence, the first research question was to identify the magnitude of these identifications and how profession type (doctors and nurses), hospital type,

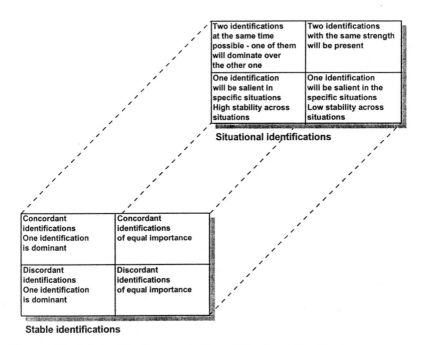

Figure 16.2. Relationships Between Stable and Situational Identification

hospital department type, integrating hospital department leadership, hospital and hospital department conflicts, age, gender, and other demographic characteristics and unusual events (successes and failures) and their attributions effect social identifications to departments and professions in hospitals.

The second research question was based on the previously mentioned predictions of SIT and SCT about discriminating prosocial behavior: To what extent do social identifications predict prosocial behavior toward members of the organizational unit and profession groups, respectively?

By examining these questions, SIT and SCT were applied in a real-life multiprofessional organizational setting to gain knowledge about the microprocesses in such organizations. These processes and relations do not necessarily contribute to good coordination of hospital activities. They may also impede coordination between groups. Knowledge about hospital employees' identifications is important for various reasons, including that it may be beneficial to the development of the relations and coordination within as well as between groups. Many of the managerial challenges in hospital organizations are about how to succeed in getting various groups to interact constructively in a setting in which professionals have complicated patterns of identifications linked to respective cultural norms and loyalties. The circumstances of management of Norwegian hospitals add a specific interest in the study: There is a long-lasting conflict between doctors and nurses in Norway as to whether hospital departments (medical, surgical, etc.) should have one manager (a doctor) or two managers (a doctor and a nurse). The patterns of identification and the behavioral consequences thereof may be an important premise for the choice of managerial model. If the identifications to the organizational units are stronger than those to the professions, the one-manager model presumably is easier to implement than if the opposite is the case. Thus, knowledge about the identification patterns is of interest when designing hospital department management models.

In addition, identification with groups is taken for granted and taken to be unchangeable. Knowledge about identification with groups, their antecedents, and their consequences may be used to design actions to change dysfunctional identification patterns.

Developing a Model: Relevant Variables

Independent Variables

Among all the variables that might explain the social identifications in the setting of the study, some selection had to be done. The main criterion was an assumed influence on a theoretical basis and whether the variables may be manipulated by some form of organizational action. It is managerially interesting to know both which manipulatable variables influence social identifications and which do not.

Profession Type. For the purpose of the study, it was sufficient to include profession type as a variable without specifying further dimensions. The number of professions in the study was restricted to two profession types: doctors and nurses.

Hospital Type. The hospitals vary with regard to size and the tasks they perform. Some of them are local hospitals with only two departments, whereas others are highly differentiated. Some of the hospitals in the study, such as psychiatric hospitals, perform special tasks, whereas others are more universalistic.

The hospitals in the study were grouped into six types, encompassing size as well as the type of hospital tasks they perform.

Hospital Department Type. Hospital department types (medical, surgical, etc.) are quite similar to each other among hospitals. Therefore, because hospital department type may be an explanad for social identifications, it was included in the study as a variable.

Hospital Department Management and Integrating Leadership. Mintzberg (1979) describes the difference between a functional and a market organization and how, in the so-called professional bureaucracies, these principles are collapsing. Therefore, there are less options for organization design variations in professional organizations than in many other organization types in which the choice between market and function as the organizing principle is the most important one. Thus, the composition of work groups in hospitals is relatively similar among hospitals, enabling comparisons between the same type of departments at different hospitals. The hospital department management might affect the relations between occupational groups, thus influencing the social identifications to departments as well as to professions. One important issue here is the design of the hospital department management—whether it is the one-manager or the two-manager model. In addition to these formal aspects of management, it is also important how leadership is actually enacted: The concept of integrating leadership is used here incorporating both the degree to which the hospital department management enhances cooperation between the professions by, for example, emphasizing the belongingness to organizational subunits, and the formal management design.

Conflicts. Conflicts in the hospital, whether they are between departments or professions and what organizational level is concerned, may affect the social identifications in such organizations. Therefore, the hospital and hospital department conflict levels are included in the study as a control variable.

Age and Gender. Because the respondents' age and gender may contribute to explaining their social identifications, they were included in the study.

Other Demographic Factors and Contact With Other Professions. Some factors in the respondents' past may also explain their social identifications. On the basis of managerial considerations, we examined how past work practice influenced current social identifications among employees because such knowledge may be utilized to design career patterns beneficial for the organization.

Successes and Failures. Successes and failures in professions as well as in organizational units were expected to influence the social identifications in the hospitals.

Intermediate Variables: Social Identifications. The social identification concept is based on SIT and SCT expressing the "oneness with or belongingness to some human aggregate" (Ashforth & Mael, 1989). Social identifications are included in the model as two variables: social identifications with organizational subunits and social identifications with professions. Thus, the two identifications are assumed to vary independently of each other.

Outcome Variable: Direction of Prosocial Behavior. According to SIT and SCT, social identifications have both cognitive and behavioral consequences, with cooperation being one of the behavioral variables. Cooperation, however, is a relational construct contingent on a reciprocal response from one or more individuals on an initially cooperative or intended action from an individual. In this study, the direction of behavior is theoretically interesting. Individual behavior, and especially the beneficiaries of such behavior, rather than the relational construct of cooperation was used. Behavior in organizations may be categorized according to a variety of dimensions, including "role prescribed" versus "extra role" behavior, prosocial versus antisocial behavior, and organization functional versus organization dysfunctional behavior. The following concept of prosocial behavior defined by Brief and Motowidlo (1986) is used in this study, including both organizationally functional and dysfunctional role-prescribed and extra-role behavior:

> Pro-social organizational behavior is behavior which is (a) performed by a member of an organization, (b) directed toward an individual, group, or organization with whom he or she interacts while carrying out his or her organizational role, and (c) performed with the intention of promoting the welfare of the individual, group, or organization toward which it is directed. (p. 711)

Brief and Motowidlo (1986) distinguish between the following types of prosocial behavior:

1. assisting coworkers with job-related matters;
2. assisting coworkers with personal matters;

3. showing leniency in personnel decisions;
4. providing services or products to consumers in organizationally consistent ways;
5. providing services or products to consumers in organizationally inconsistent ways;
6. helping consumers with personal matters unrelated to organizational services or products;
7. complying with organizational values, policies, and regulations;
8. suggesting procedural, administrative, or organizational improvements;
9. objecting to improper directives, procedures, or policies;
10. putting forth extra effort on the job;
11. volunteering for additional assignments;
12. staying with the organization despite temporary hardships; and
13. representing the organization favorably to outsiders.

The Model. On the basis of the previously mentioned variables, the model shown in Figure 16.3 was developed.

From the model, the hypothesis is derived that there is an association between profession type and social identifications: On many dimensions, doctors are more professionalized than nurses. Therefore, doctors are assumed to have stronger identifications with professions than nurses. Nurses, however, are hypothesized to have stronger identifications with departments than doctors. The integrating hospital department leadership variable is assumed to be positively associated with identifications with departments and negatively associated with identifications with professions. Successes and failures are assumed to interact with the other variables in that success and externally attributed failure are hypothesized to strengthen these associations, whereas those by internally attributed failures weaken associations.

Social identifications with organizational subunits are hypothesized to positively influence prosocial behaviors of department in-group members, whereas no or negative associations are assumed between department-oriented social identifications and profession in-group members. The same pattern is suggested for identifications with organizational units.

Research Design and Operationalizations

An empirical study was conducted in 48 Norwegian hospitals including 145 hospital departments. In a pilot study, both the stable and the situational identifi-

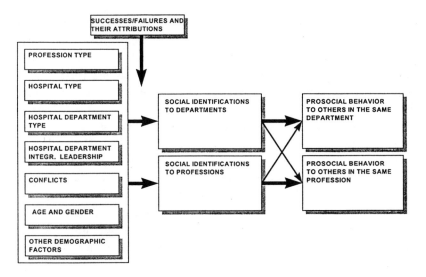

Figure 16.3. The box around the additive independent variables and the two arrows from that box are used to indicate that of all the variables interact with the two intermediate ones. The vertical arrow from the "unusual events and their attributions" variable is an indicator of interactive associations. The large arrows from the intermediate variables to the outcome variables indicate hypothesized positive relationships, whereas the small arrows suggest no or negative associations.

cations were investigated by manipulating salience: Two randomly constituted groups of respondents were asked to list the main differences between professions and departments, respectively, thus enhancing the salience of the groups in question. The results showed, however, no consistent patterns. Therefore, the main study was concentrated on the stable aspects of the model described previously and also including the success and failure variable. The respondents were doctors and nurses without any formal managerial responsibilities.

A 12-page questionnaire was mailed to 1,861 potential respondents; 917 questionnaires were returned, which represents a response rate of 49.3%. There were no systematic response rate differences between the respondent groups constituted by professions, hospitals, hospital type, and hospital department types.

Operationalizations. The integrating hospital department leadership construct was measured by Likert scale items on the cooperation within the departments. According to Hogg (1992), social identity cannot be measured directly. The effects of social identifications, however, may be measured. Hogg emphasizes that one must understand the social content and context of the specific group being studied to measure social identifications properly. Some general measures of social identifications have been developed—for example, by Mael and Tetrick (1992): "When someone criticizes . . . it feels like a personal insult"—and so on. In this study, translations and adjustments of these items were used. Additionally, items for the specific context of the study were developed: Work-related ethnocentrism items, such as "We perform more important/difficult tasks," "We work more seriously," and so on, were used. Effectiveness and quality evaluations were also asked for. Because of the common observation that hospital employees are highly interested in budget allocation issues, budget evaluations were also used as indicators of social identifications. Also, questions about the heterogeneity of groups were included. To a great extent, the same wordings were used by asking about organizational subunits and about professions. In total, 26 social identification items were used in the questionnaire.

Successes and failures were asked for by open-ended questions about unusual events and the respondents' descriptions of why those events had happened.

The direction of prosocial behavior was operationalized by asking the respondents to give some characteristics (number of prosocial behaviors, profession, department, gender, and age group) of the persons to whom they had given help and support during the past 6 months. Thus, data for such behaviors directed to members of in-group/in-group, in-group/out-group, out-group/in-group, and out-group/out-group were obtained. This question was posed in two versions regarding job-related and privately related behaviors.

Results

Data Analysis

Factor analyses of the data resulted in the following five factors:

Belongingness
Ethnocentrism
Effectiveness and quality evaluation
Budget evaluation
Heterogeneity evaluation

Except for the ethnocentrism items, the factor analyses did not discriminate between organizational subunits and professions. Rather, the type of questions posed seems to be the main characteristic to construct the factors. This finding may be interpreted in several ways. One alternative is that the social identifications concept was of little interest and significance to the responding professional groups. Second, the social identification concept is important, but it was not measured properly in this study. The adopted operationalizations as well as those developed for the study may have been less relevant for the Norwegian context or poorly translated into Norwegian. Interestingly, studies up to now have not included more than one dimension; thus, they have not examined whether the operationalizations are discriminating between two or more groups to which people identify. Third, only the ethnocentrism measures are valid because they are the only ones that discriminate between the two groups. Fourth, the concepts are interesting, they are operationalized properly, and multidimensionality exists in the concepts that is properly reflected in the analysis. This alternative would imply that the social identification dimensions are independent of each other and that correlations exists between the identifications to departments and to professions.

For the multiple regression analyses reported below, the last interpretation alternative was chosen. Thus, factor scores have been computed separately for social identifications to organizational subunits and to professions. For professions, the factor analyses produced two distinct belongingness factors. Thus, instead of the two social identification variables in the initial model, 11 distinct factors emerged.

Magnitude of Social Identifications
and Prosocial Behavior

Social Identifications. As shown in Table 16.1, the 26 social identification items were counted and grouped according to the dimensionality of the social identifications reported in the previous section and their mean scores. The scale ranged from –2 to +2, except for the effectiveness and quality evaluation items for which the scale range was from –3 to +3.

The items measured by the –2 to +2 scale had a range from –0.55 to +1.05. Ten of the 26 items had negative mean values, which made it difficult to draw any unequivocal conclusion that any inherent in-group bias exists among respondents.

For some of the belongingness measures, identifications with departments by and large were stronger than with professions. On the ethnocentrism measures,

Table 16.1 Number of Social Identification Items[a]

	Item Mean Scores (Range)					
	-2 through -1	-1 through -0.5	-0.5 through 0	0 through +0.5	+0.5 through +1	+1 through +2
Social Identifications to Organizational Subunits						
Belongingness			1	1	3	1
Ethnocentrism		1	1			
Effectiveness/quality evaluation						2
Budget evaluation			1			
Heterogeneity evaluation				1		
Social Identifications to Professions						
Belongingness			4		2	
Ethnocentrism			2	1		
Effectiveness/quality evaluation						2
Budget evaluation					1	
Heterogeneity evaluation				1	1	

a. Grouped according to their mean.

however, identifications with professions were stronger than with departments on both the comparable measures. Budget allocation evaluations indicated stronger identifications with professions than with departments.

Prosocial Behavior. There are six target groups of prosocial behavior constituted by two department (own and other) and three profession groups (own, opposite, and other), respectively. The means of reported job-related and privately related prosocial behaviors are shown in Figure 16.4.

The main conclusion that can be drawn from Figure 16.4 is that prosocial behavior is to a much higher degree directed toward members of the in-group constituted by department than those in the profession in-group. The double in-group, however, is the primary target for prosocial behaviors. There is a very similar pattern between job-related and privately related prosocial behavior with consistently higher mean values for job-related than for privately related behaviors, except for the small numbers in the double out-group (other department and other profession).

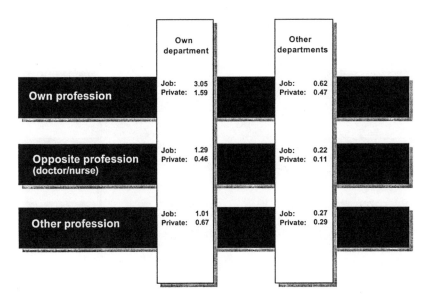

Figure 16.4. Prosocial Behavior to Six Target Groups

The analysis of the differences between the occupational groups reveals that the means are quite similar across professions in three of the six group combinations, whereas the means are somewhat different in the remaining three groups as shown in Figure 16.5.

The results further suggest that the similarity between doctors and nurses with regard to prosocial behaviors toward others in the same profession needs to take into account the numerical differences of professional colleagues in the two occupational groups. There are more nurses than doctors in all hospital departments, which means that doctors direct about the same amount of prosocial behaviors toward their relatively few profession in-group colleagues as nurses do toward their profession colleagues. Profession type, therefore, is a stronger predictor of prosocial behaviors than the first impression of Figure 16.5 may convey.

In addition, a distinct hierarchical pattern emerged: Doctors direct more prosocial behavior to nurses than the other way round. This is true for in-department as well as out-department prosocial behaviors. For prosocial behaviors toward other occupational groups besides doctors and nurses, however, nurses have higher scores than doctors.

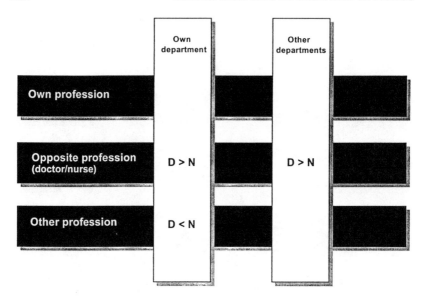

Figure 16.5. Prosocial Behavior—Differences Between Doctors and Nurses

---

Relationships Between Variables

Because of the multidimensionality of the social identification concept, the hypotheses testing became rather complicated. A summary of results is reported in Table 16.2.

The profession type variable had significant effects on some of the social identification dimensions. Nurses had higher scores on the belongingness dimension to departments (beta coefficient = .17) as well as to professions. Doctors had higher scores than nurses on the ethnocentrism to profession dimension (beta coefficient = .52). By and large, the hypothesis about the integrating leadership variable was supported: Positive effects could be observed on two of the social identification to department dimensions and negative effect were observed on the ethnocentrism to profession dimension (beta coefficients range from .07 to .12).

The relationship between the profession type variable and prosocial behavior was the same as reported in Figure 16.5 (beta coefficient = .23). The difference between psychiatric and other departments is probably due to the composition of work groups; psychiatric departments normally encompass more persons from different occupations than in other hospital department types.

Table 16.2 Effects of the Explanatory Variables on Social Identifications and Direction of Prosocial Behavior[a]

	Social Identifications		Prosocial Behavior	
	To Departments	*To Professions*	*Toward Department In-Group Members*	*Toward Profession In-Group Members*
Profession type	The belongingness dimension: nurses > doctors	The belongingness dimension: nurses >doctors; the ethnocentrism dimension: doctors > nurses		Doctors direct more prosocial behaviors to other professions than nurses do
Hospital type				
Hospital department type	Higher effectiveness and quality evaluations for most departments other than psychiatric			More prosocial behavior to other professions in psychiatric departments than in most other department types
Integrating hospital department leadership	Positive effect on the belongingness and the ethnocentrism dimensions	Negative effect on the ethnocentrism dimension; positive effect on the effectiveness and quality evaluation dimension		
Conflicts	Negative effect on the belongingness dimension; positive effect on the ethnocentrism dimension; negative effect on the effectiveness and quality evaluation dimension; positive effect on the budget evaluation dimension	Negative effect on the belongingness dimension; positive effect on the ethnocentrism dimension; negative effect on the effectiveness and quality evaluation dimension; positive effect on the budget evaluation dimension		
Gender				
Other demographic characteristics				

a. Spaces indicate no significant effects.

The social identification dimensions described previously had no significant effects on the direction of prosocial behavior. The explained variances in the multiple-regression analyses were .03 and .04, respectively, thus discarding the hypotheses that social identifications are explanads for prosocial behavior.

The open-ended unusual-event question was answered by only 205 of the 917 respondents. The answers were content analyzed as to whether the unusual events were organizational subunit oriented or profession oriented and how they were attributed. A high degree of intercorrelations resulted between the variables. A comparison between those who answered the open-ended question and those who did not revealed a distinct pattern that the associations between the explanatory variables and the intermediate variables are stronger for the groups that answered the question.

Summary and Discussion

This chapter explored social identifications in multigroup memberships within organizations based on the premise that organizational culture and group memberships are related constructs. A framework for analyzing the stable and situational social identifications was developed and discussed. The stable aspects of social identifications with organizational subunits and professions were analyzed in a large-scale survey study of Norwegian hospital employees.

The phenomenon of cross-cutting identifications is not restricted to hospitals, even if the hospital setting is an ideal one for studying them. Therefore, some of the results of this study may be generalized to other settings with some restrictions due to some special features of the context of this study: Few organizations have so many different professions and organizational units, and the relations between professional groups may be special for hospitals. Additionally, Norwegian hospitals have little competition; organizationally dysfunctional behavior, therefore, may occur to a larger degree than in more market-driven organizations.

The results of the study can be summarized as followed: First, social identifications are a much more multifaceted construct than were treated as in previous studies. Identifications were measured by a variety of items—some of them directly translated from previous social identification studies, whereas other items were developed for the special context of this study. The data analysis revealed that the type of question posed, rather than the two groups in question, is the criterion for the dimensions extracted from the factor analyses. From this finding, it may be interpreted that the social identification concept is not important or was not properly measured in this study. This implies that the multiple-regression analyses of the direct effects from the explanatory variables on the outcome variables are the most interesting ones.

If, however, the measurement analysis is interpreted as an indication of the complexity of the social identification concept in a cross-cutting setting, it is meaningful to analyze the relationships between intermediate and outcome variables. This analysis, however, did not show any associations between these variables, thus disconfirming this hypothesis. This result may indicate that constraints in the daily work settings may overrule the effects of the social identification dimensions. In this case, too, the relationships between the explanatory and the outcome variables in this study are the interesting ones.

Here, profession type seems to be the predominant explanatory variable for the direction of prosocial behavior. The conclusions, therefore, are that it is a complicated task to grasp the cognitive and behavioral patterns in hospitals and that to understand hospital life, one must understand the life within and between the health care professions.

References

Abrams, D., & Hogg, M. A. (1990). *Social identity theory. Constructive and critical advances.* New York: Harvester Wheatsheaf.

Allen, V. L., Wilder, D. A., & Atkinson, M. L. (1983). Multiple group membership and social identity. In T. R. Sarbin & K. E. Scheibe (Eds.), *Studies in social identity.* New York: Praeger.

Alvesson, M. (1990). On the popularity of organizational culture. *Acta Sociologica, 33,* 31-49.

Ashforth, B. E., & Mael, F. (1989). Social identity theory and the organization. *Academy of Management Review, 14,* 20-39.

Augoustionos, M., & Walker, I. (1995). *Social cognition. An integrated introduction.* London: Sage.

Brewer, M. B. (1991). The social self: On being the same and different at the same time. *Personality and Social Psychology Bulletin, 17,* 475-482.

Brewer, M. B. (1993). The role of distinctiveness in social identity and group behavior. In M. A. Hogg & D. Abrams (Eds.), *Group motivation. Social psychological perspectives.* New York: Harvester Wheatsheaf.

Brewer, M. B., & Kramer, R. M. (1986). Choice behavior in social dilemmas: Effects of social identity, group size, and decision framing. *Journal of Personality and Social Psychology, 50,* 543-549.

Brief, A. P., & Motowidlo, S. J. (1986). Prosocial organizational behaviors. *Academy of Management Review, 11,* 710-725.

Bruner, J. S. (1957). On perceptual readiness. *Psychological Review, 64,* 123-152.

Hewstone, M., Islam, M. R., & Judd, C. M. (1993). Models of crossed categorization and intergroup relations. *Journal of Personality and Social Psychology, 64,* 779-793.

Hogg, M. A. (1992). *The social psychology of group cohesiveness: From attraction to social identity.* New York: Harvester Wheatsheaf.

Hogg, M. A., & Abrams, D. (1988). *Social identifications: A social psychology of intergroup relations and group processes.* London: Routledge.

Hogg, M. A., & McGarthy, C. (1990). Self-categorization and social identity. In D. Abrams & M. A. Hogg (Eds.), *Social identity theory. Constructive and critical advances.* New York: Harvester Wheatsheaf.

Johnston, L., & Hewstone, M. (1990). Intergroup contact: Social identity and social cognition. In D. Abrams and M. A. Hogg (Eds.), *Social identity theory. Constructive and critical advances.* New York: Harvester Wheatsheaf.

Kramer, R. M. (1991). Intergroup relations and organizational dilemmas: The role of categorization processes. *Research in Organizational Behavior, 13,* 191-228.

Kramer, R. M. (1993). Cooperation and organizational identification. In J. K. Murnighan (Eds.), *Social psychology in organizations. Advances in theory and research.* Englewood Cliffs, NJ: Prentice Hall.

Kramer, R. M., & Brewer, M. B. (1984). Effects of group identity on resource use in a simulated commons dilemma. *Journal of Personality and Social Psychology, 46,* 1044-1057.

Kramer, R. M., & Brewer, M. B. (1986). Social group identity and the emergence of cooperation in resource conservation dilemmas. In H. Wilke, C. Rutte, & D. M. Messick (Eds.), *Experimental studies of social dilemmas.* Frankfurt, Germany: P. Lang.

Mael, F., & Tetrick, L. E. (1992). Identifying organizational identification. *Educational and Psychological Measurement, 52,* 813-824.

Mintzberg, H. (1979). *The structuring of organizations.* Englewood Cliffs, NJ: Prentice Hall.

Sherif, M. (1967). *Group conflict and co-operation: Their social psychology.* London: Routledge Kegan Paul.

Tajfel, H., Billig, M. G., Bundy, R. P., & Flament, C. (1971). Social categorization and intergroup behaviour. *European Journal of Social Psychology, 1,* 149-178.

Tajfel, H., & Turner, J. C. (1985). The social identity theory of intergroup behavior. In S. Worchel and W. G. Austin (Eds.), *Psychology of intergroup relations* (2nd ed.). Chicago: Nelson-Hall.

Turner, J. C., Hogg, M. A., Oakes, P. J., Reicher, S. D., & Wetherell, M. S. (1987). *Rediscovering the social group. A self-categorization theory.* Oxford, UK: Basil Blackwell.

Chapter 17

Organizational Identity as a "Crowded Category"

A Case of Multiple and Quickly Shifting "We" Typifications

Peter Dahler-Larsen

It is usually essential to the operation of the organization that there should not be the same image of the organization in the minds of the participants.
—Kenneth Boulding

It has been said that among the things that society "is" or "is like," it is or is like identification (Ardener, 1975). Cultural meanings generate patterns of congregation and segregation (Cheney & Tompkins, 1987). They do so by promoting a "consciousness of kind" as well as a "consciousness of difference" (Weber as quoted in Van Maanen & Barley, 1984) that help sustain a shared identity.

A similar line of thinking has been applied to organizations within the past 10 to 15 years. One of the most important propositions in the emergent field of organizational culture is that organizational action is undergirded by a symbolically defined sense of organizational identity (Albert & Whetten, 1985; Broms & Gahmberg, 1983; Czarniawska-Joerges, 1994; Dutton & Dukerich, 1991). Before an organization knows what to do, it must know who it is (Sevon, 1996), and any significant change in the course of action requires a change in organizational identity. As a corollary, it has been one of the dominant ideas in the past 10 to 15 years of managerial research and consultancy that organizational identity, often in the form of a strong organizational culture, is of utmost importance for organizational commitment, productivity, company loyalty, innovation, creativity, effectiveness, excellence, and eventually profitability (Deal & Kennedy, 1982; Peters & Waterman, 1982).

How does "an organization" know what its "identity" is? Reification tends to influence our thinking of both organization and identity. If identity exists at all, it is definitely not a thing. At best, it emerges only as a part of an ongoing, interactive discourse (Gergen, 1992)—an unfinished process that involves constantly renewed codification (Barth, 1969; Bouchet, 1995). Phenomenologically, "members" of organizations may not live the same type of life, may not experience the same organization, and may not even identify themselves as organizational members (Van Maanen & Barley, 1984, 1985). It may be less justified to take organizational identity for granted than to wonder how any identification with a "we" is possible in complex and highly differentiated organizations embedded in an individualistic society. To combine the two orders of organization and "culture" may thus be an interesting heuristic exercise, but it should not be regarded as an easy and remainderless procedure.

The dominant traditions in the field of organizational culture have largely broken down the complexity by focusing on four different dimensions or units of analysis. One at a time, these have been studied as the guiding principles of collective identity in organizations.

First, some of the earliest applications of the concept of culture to organizational studies focused on cross-national comparisons (see Chapter 1, this volume). Other well-known studies such as Hofstede's (1980, 1982) have suggested that national value systems are irreducibly diverse and of utmost importance in organizational life.

In an internationalized world in which multinational corporations and joint ventures proliferate, organized activities are bedeviled by fundamentally different national value systems undergirded by deeply embedded national identities, the incompatibility of which continues to be a main theme in cross-cultural studies. In this context, culture remains an underlying pattern that for all practical purposes must be regarded as an independent variable.

Second, in another generation of research, attempts have been made to transform the concept of culture into something more manageable. The crucial difference here is not one between national cultures but one between excellent and nonexcellent companies (Ebers, 1991). Protagonists of "corporate culture" have argued that organizations, especially successful ones, are themselves characterized by strong and distinct cultures (Deal & Kennedy, 1982; Peters & Waterman, 1982) that require and enhance emotional commitment and identification (Ray, 1986). In this perspective, organization itself is almost synonymous with a sense of we.

Third, others have argued from a phenomenological perspective that organizational affiliation is often less salient than a sense of occupational identity. Occupational communities instill a sense of we that is supported by year-long educational socialization and subsequent intense daily social interaction among cooperating colleagues (Van Maanen & Barley, 1984). Occupational cultures exercise some degree of control not only over how the daily work is done but also over professional and cultural standards and norms, thus enhancing a relative autonomy vis-à-vis organizational and managerial control systems.

Fourth, it is argued that organizations are nevertheless places in which domination is enacted and class conflict is ever present, although sometimes only in a latent form. As a corollary, the contradiction between labor and management tends to surface in terms of corresponding bipolar collective identities—for example, the blue collars versus the white collars (Lysgaard, 1961; Smith & Eisenberg, 1987; Turner, 1971).

Unfortunately, as studies have coalesced around these four principles of collective cultural identity, the field of organizational culture has been segmented accordingly. Different schools of thought and different researchers have specialized in each type of we, and their results have to a large extent been allocated to different journals or, at the very best, to different chapters in the same book. To segregate the components of a larger cultural complexity in intellectual time and space in this way, however, is perhaps not the most fruitful approach.

If a respect for the actors' own definitions of their "we-ness" is applied as a sound principle in cultural analysis, none of the previously described four dimensions should be taken for granted as the generic principle for cultural identity in organizations. Researchers should not choose conceptual models that legislate preordinately about which and how many "we's" occur when and how.

The purpose of this chapter is to present, analyze, and discuss a case study in which identification with different we's emerges along all four of the previously described dimensions. The focus is on how these four manifestations are related, how they change over a short time, and how the findings can be interpreted within an organizational-cultural framework. In this endeavor, bandwidth will be sacrificed for depth. The data give a thick description of dramatic events during nine days in one particular company, Scandinavian Airlines System (SAS).

Organizational Identity as a Problem

In contemporary society, there is a peculiar pressure on organizations to base their activities on the articulation of organizational identity. The thinking of marketing, of organizational ethics, and of "excellent companies" are but a few examples of the expectation that organizational identity exists and should be expressed. It is obviously not easy for the human mind to understand anonymous structures such as organizations. One way to reduce their complexity may be to infuse them with qualities that make them similar to natural persons whose identity we can better grasp. Organizational members may also demand a sense of we to find meaning and orientation in an otherwise complex and confusing organizational life.

A demand for clear identity, however, is not equivalent to a clear identity itself. I provide just two relatively simple sociological observations that motivate skepticism about any image of organizational identity as deep, harmonious, consensual, and taken for granted.

The first observation concerns the modern work organization as a specific form of social relations. The modern work organization is an archetype of the Gesellschaft type of social relations that are based on interest, contract, and exchange and only a partial inclusion of the whole personality, in contradistinction to the Gemeinschaft's more immediate immersion of the total personality in a collective, solidaristic we (Nisbet, 1966).

Albert and Whetten (1985) studied an organization marred by a "double identity" consisting of both a normative and a utilitarian dimension. Perhaps their finding is much more general to the extent that organizations must balance their Gesellschaft properties with desires to connect emotionally to a more Gemeinschaft-oriented collectivity. The picture of the modern work organization I wish to evoke is one in which the attempts to promote a normative and cultural identity on behalf of the whole organization are not easily compatible with the utilitarian constellation of "interests" that emerge as a result of the particular institutionalized type of contract-based Gesellschaft relations that undergird modern work organizations. In any case, the sociohistorical context of technical rationality that characterizes modern work organizations does not disappear merely because the problem of organizational life is formulated in terms of organizational culture (Adams & Ingersoll, 1988).

Another relevant observation is that we live in a time in which the element of choice in cultural identity is becoming more dominant. As the links to tradition are gradually weakened (Beck, Giddens, & Lash, 1994), cultural identity tends to lose its character of givenness. Culture reveals some of its constructed character (Bouchet, 1995). This increases the possibility and the importance of choice, but it also makes it difficult to choose because it is not always clear why one dimension in identity should be more salient than another.

Without this shift in the sociohistorical conditions for cultural identity, the instrumental view on the management of corporate culture could not and would not have emerged. The point is, however, that the element of choice cannot be ignored once it is there (Bouchet, 1995). The lack of obviousness also hits a "constructed" organizational culture. Empirical studies have revealed that corporate cultures are often contested, redefined, played tongue in cheek, or ridiculed (Kunda, 1992; Smircich, 1983; Smith & Eisenberg, 1987; Van Maanen, 1991). In general, the idea of managerially controlled and highly integrated cultures in organizations has been severely criticized on conceptual and normative grounds (Alvesson & Berg, 1992; Gregory, 1983; Kunda, 1992; Turner, 1986; Van Maanen & Barley, 1985; Willmott, 1991).

An interesting attempt to summarize how the whole field of organizational culture has conceptualized and can conceptualize culture in organizations is Martin's (1992) well-known three-perspective framework codified under the headlines of integration, differentiation, and ambiguity/fragmentation. In this framework, a story is told about how the "integration" perspective, with its focus on harmonious, clear, and shared meanings among all members of an organization, has been dethroned. Alternative perspectives have developed such as the "differentiation" perspective with a focus on each subculture in an organization as an island of clarity and on an "ambiguity" or "fragmentation" perspective stipulating shifting and issue-dependent meanings and coalitions. I am indebted to Martin for her framework, but I also attempt to transcend it.

In Martin's (1992) three perspectives, no careful distinction is made between an emic (insider's) understanding of culture and an etic (researcher's) analysis. This leads to a blind spot toward situations in which evidence of these two types does not conform to the same cultural paradigm, such as when members of a highly differentiated and unstable social entity emphasize a constructed and abstract integrative we despite—or to compensate for—a lived practice that sustains internal boundaries and differentiations.

How can one conceptualize organizational identity in organizations so that these complications are respected and perhaps better understood?

We Typifications as a Key to Organizational Identity

Cultural theory suggests that the way things in the world are categorized is an invention (Castoriadis, 1984; Sahlins, 1976). It is arbitrary in the sense that irreducible meaning is added. Human beings live in a symbolic universe, in a "web of significance" they themselves have spun (Geertz, 1975). An important key to cultural categorization systems in general, however, is social organization. Collectivities tend to create conceptualizations of the world in their own image. The general rule—that cultural concepts reflect the organization of society (Douglas as cited in Wuthnow, Hunter, Bergesen, & Kurzweil, 1984)—can be applied to a very special type of categorization, that of identity. It follows that identity should be understood as a product of social organization. A social unit produces images of its typified members and the nature of the social bond between them. These images are, however, at the same time both products of social organization and arbitrary cultural inventions. The image of the we is not a representation, at face value, of the social collectivity. A reflexivity is involved that is not trivial.

A community invents itself by appointing certain characteristics to be essential, distinct, and stable over time (Albert & Whetten, 1985). A community can be based on gender, age, ethnicity, war, or on "any function or purpose imaginable" (Nisbet & Perrin, 1977). As Durkheim (1965) noted (see also Nisbet, 1966; Ray, 1986), it is when certain principles are cathected (i.e., infused with a sacred quality and invested with emotional energy) in a particular way that a social community establishes itself.

Communities are at least partly created from within. Self-categorization plays an indispensable role in the concept of collective identity. This is not to say that identity is not developed, dynamically, between mirrors (Bouchet, 1995) set up and looked at by outsiders as well as insiders. It means, however, that identity cannot be imposed or determined solely from an external viewpoint. Members may see—or not see—something in themselves that nobody else can see, and this may be constitutive of membership and "shared identity."

As a corollary, there is often a discrepancy between emic and etic definitions of identity. Anthropologists have found, for example, that a particular ethnic category is imposed on a group of people, none of whom want to identify with that category. It becomes a "hollow category" (Ardener, 1975). One can also imagine what I call a "crowded category"—that is, a particular etic category that happens to be populated by several competing emic identifications. Organizational identity can be such a crowded category, for example, when several definitions of what it means to belong to the organization are stepping on each other's toes.

It is not easy to study the complications of the concept of identity in practice. In an attempt to do so without sacrificing too much complexity, I have found the concept of *we typifications* to be useful. This concept is inspired by Schutz's (1975) theory of typifications according to which any phenomenon can, in principle, be typified in multiple ways. By "appointing" something to be typical for a group of phenomena, one constitutes a phenomenologically determined essence that is stipulated to represent the phenomenon as such. This is a fundamentally subjective and creative act because a particular typification can be "seen" regardless of observable physical indicators. In addition, typification implies naming and categorization. These processes also imply choices that add meaning.

Consider along the same lines the typifications that actors apply to themselves. A we typification suggests what is essentially distinct and relatively stable over time for those who identify with it. There is never any complete unification between human subjects, however, only certain symbolic connections (Christensen & Cheney, 1994, p. 227). Again, an understanding of the insiders' own identification with their we is essential. The degree of overlap between the emic we typifications among a particular etic category of individuals is therefore an open (empirical) question. For this reason, it may be very difficult to speak on behalf of a we. Strictly speaking, my definition of we is only a suggestion of what we may share, for the time being, until further notice. I may refer to established cultural meanings in the available stock of social knowledge (Berger & Luckmann, 1967) and present these as naturally given, and I may apply rhetorical tricks to my discourse, including integrating your own assumptions into my line of reasoning (Cheney & Tompkins, 1987), but in the end it is only your presence and free right to speak that guarantee that I have not usurped your subjective perspective when typifying our we (Spiegelberg, 1973). In organizations, however, people speak on behalf of others all the time. It is therefore an interesting empirical question of how and under what circumstances members of an organizational we accept, refuse, invent, or reinvent particular we typifications that are claimed to stand for organizational identity as such.

The concept of we typifications is sufficiently open and flexible toward multiple and complex forms of organizational identity because no built-in assumptions are required about the unity and clarity of organizational identity and the specific levels of analysis and categories of actors to which it is linked. We typifications are also attractive keys to an empirical study because in contradistinction to identity, we typifications appear directly in observable lexemes and grammar in case study data.

A Case: Two Strikes in SAS

Within nine days during 1989, two strikes occurred among the Danish flight attendants in SAS. They ought not to have occurred. This is because in Scandinavia, no company has been more intensely studied and promoted as a successful example of an excellent corporate culture than SAS (Busk, 1989; Carlzon, 1985; Christensen, 1984; Edström, 1985; Olaisen & Revang, 1991). Consultants have held SAS in high regard (Røvik, 1992), and Scandinavian research in organizational culture was at a certain time more motivated by the events in SAS than by scientific debate (Alvesson & Berg, 1992, p. 22).

SAS was established in 1946 as a joint Danish-Norwegian-Swedish company headquartered in Stockholm, Sweden. The company has continuously been bedeviled by the difficulties of balancing commercial and public interests as well as the various national interests involved (Edström, Norbäck, & Rendahl, 1989, p. 23). Among the staff, however, employment in SAS has been something special, a belief undergirded by beneficial personnel policies. Turnover has been low and company loyalty high. The "traditional" SAS was challenged, however, by symptoms of crisis in the 1970s that revealed that SAS was not very cost conscious and not very customer oriented (Edström et al., 1989).

In the beginning of the 1980s, a new chief executive officer (CEO), Jan Carlzon, was appointed. Under his leadership, a "New Corporate Identity" was launched, and he became a symbol of cultural themes such as service orientation, antihierarchical values, and a sense of interdependence among all groups of employees (Busk, 1989, p. 127). Carlzon's initiatives, however, also tied into a more deeply rooted traditional company loyalty in SAS. All this was combined with a new business strategy (Christensen, 1984, p. 18ff). Carlzon also introduced a number of young top managers who were trained in crisis management in other business areas (Edström et al., 1989, p. 40).

Economic success followed. During the late 1980s, however, the success story began to fall apart. Competition increased. Management presented new strategic initiatives, including alliances with foreign airlines. This—along with general cost reductions—caused dissatisfaction among the 1,200 Danish cabin attendants who were anxious about their job security. In 1989, the SAS management declared the abolition of the pan-Scandinavian seniority principle according to which pursers had automatically been appointed (a purser is a crew leader among the cabin attendants). This specific event triggered the first strike on November 15, 1989. Almost all the Danish cabin attendants participated. They handed out flyers directly to waiting passengers explaining their dissatisfaction with management. The strikers resumed work after the Stockholm headquarters promised to enter negotiations—phony negotiations, it turned out, according to the striking cabin attendants.

Nine days later, on the morning of November 24, the Danish cabin attendants initiated the second strike to break the deadlock. This time, they were joined by thousands of other airport employees at Copenhagen Airport. The pan-Scandinavian seniority system was no longer on top of the agenda because the frustration and dissatisfaction this time hinged on a more general fear of secret management plans that implied the transferral of jobs from Copenhagen to Stockholm. In addition, there was considerable resentment toward management's "broken promise" to enter negotiations. Total chaos reigned in the airport for several hours until management gave in and promised to reinstall the pan-Scandinavian seniority principle. The Danes resumed work. They felt they had won a small victory, but the whole chain of events had only reinforced their suspicion toward their managers. In the subsequent years, strikes occurred among cabin attendants, pilots, and other groups. In 1995, after problematic investments in hotels, partly failed negotiations about new strategic alliances, and continuous labor unrest, Jan Carlzon left the company.

My question is, how were the strikes possible? Assuming that the excellent culture had not fully disappeared, how does a meaningful cultural universe look in which it is possible to combine the strikes with an excellent culture? Which we typifications exist in this universe of meanings? Is there a "we as SAS members," and if so, how is it possible to identify with the compnay and go on strike at the same time?

Methodology: A Study of We Typifications

To answer these questions, I decided to focus primarily on the emic perspective of a few central actors who organized the strike or were related to the Cabin Attendants's Union, assuming that these key persons would deliver a more articulate and elaborate ideal-typical account than other participants. An intensive four-hour interview was conducted with the members of the strike committee. Interviews were also carried out with the chairman of the trade union, a former trade union official, as well as two ordinary cabin attendants. Fully in line with the spirit of qualitative case studies and data analysis (Lincoln & Denzin, 1994; Stake, 1994), an intensive understanding of the set of typifications that could make the strikes meaningful was emphasized rather than an extensive study of the degree to which these typifications were shared by all participating strikers.

When interviewing the key persons, a free-flowing discourse was encouraged, with continuous probes and with more elaborate questions checking apparent paradoxes or inconsistencies only at the end of each interview. Detailed summaries of the interviews and some initial interpretations were returned to the participants for comments and corrections. The retrospective accounts given during the interviews were also compared to the flyers handed out by the strikers at the time of each strike. Newspaper articles and official company material about the "corporate culture" were used as cross-references.

All the collected interview data were read several times to tune into a generic set of meanings for each interview (Giorgi, 1988) before cross-cutting categorizations were made. Then all pieces of data relevant for we typifications were coded. The coding procedure was less complicated than it sometimes is in qualitative analysis because we typifications surfaced directly in the words of the interviewed actors.

The data revealed that the strikers referred to four different we typifications: we as cabin attendants, we as SAS members, we as employees, and we as Danes. These four dimensions were not determined before data were collected. The introduction to this chapter mentioning the same dimensions was written after the case study was conducted. Other we typifications, such as one based on gender, was checked in the data without success.

It was assumed that each of the occurring we typifications could be described according to the following three simple questions:

1. What is our core value? Presumably, a we is organized on the basis of one theme that is seen as essential and distinct. It is a value that motivates a "consciousness of kind," a cathected principle around which the we is formed.
2. Who are they? Each we typification tends to be based on a "consciousness of difference" vis-à-vis an out-group that helps illustrate and define the we in terms of a negative contrast.

3. How should boundaries and the boundary between us and them be handled properly? If boundary maintenance is a key feature in a we typification, the specific nature of proper boundary handling must be a good analytical key to the nature of the we and its relation to the outside world.

A combination of the four we typifications and the three questions produced an empty 4 × 3 matrix. All data were then checked and data relevant for each cell in the matrix were coded and distributed in the matrix. As a result, there were no empty cells. Within each cell, one or a few key words were selected to summarize the data. At this point, data reduction was not very difficult because data were quite redundant within each cell. The total results of this process are shown in Table 17.1. This decisive condensation of data (along with additional text explaining the meaning of the key words, i.e., an initial version of the text) was fed back to informants in both oral and written form to call forth comments and corrections. This resulted in a minor revision of the key word in only one cell and a general acceptance of the table. There was no difference between the members of the striking committee and the other informants with respect to the general acceptance of the table as a valid summary of their points of view.

The Four We Typifications

Table 17.1 displays the four we typifications and their characteristics. As cabin attendants, the strikers viewed the ability to deliver service to customers as their key characteristic. No other group of employees had a contact with customers comparable in time and intensity to that of cabin attendants, and they saw themselves as indispensable for the overall interdependency among all employees in SAS. What they wanted from other groups in SAS was a recognition of this unique contribution to the functioning of the whole company.

As SAS members, the striking Danes felt they had built up a strong company loyalty through many years of SAS experience. In contradistinction to newcomers (such as Carlzon's young managers), they had learned personally what company loyalty means.

As employees, they demanded respect from management. The proper regulation of management and labor relations was that of negotiation (rather than one-way communication).

Table 17.1　The Four We Typifications and Their Characteristics

	We Typification			
Question	*Cabin Attendants*	*SAS Members*	*Employees*	*Danes*
What is our core value?	Service	SAS experience	Respect	Non-authoritarianism
Who are they?	Other employees	Newcomers	Managers	Swedes
How should boundaries be handled properly?	Recognize value for inter-dependence	Learning	Negotiation	Autonomy

As Danes, the striking staff demanded a certain extent of autonomy vis-à-vis the headquarters, which happened—unfortunately—to be located in Stockholm and staffed mainly by Swedes.

During the first strike, Columns 1 and 2 (Table 17.1) dominated the worldview of the striking flight attendants. The break with the pan-Scandinavian seniority principle symbolized the manager's lack of recognition of the contribution from flight attendants to the overall functioning of SAS. The strike, however, obviously proved that without the cabin attendants SAS cannot fly.

The break with the seniority principle also threatened the privileges of SAS seniors vis-à-vis newcomers. Symbolically, this was important because the traditional members of SAS (Danish cabin attendants have a high average seniority) identified with the company as such. "It is our company, we want to put it back on the track," one member said. Carlzon's new managers were excluded from the quintessence of organizational identity because they had yet to learn what SAS really means and because they do not fly—a perceived necessary prerequisite of status and importance in an airline company. It is these distinctions between genuine SAS members and newcomers that allowed the strikers to declare that they were striking in defense of the company. Symbolically, the strike is a way to teach the newcomers what happens if they attempt to derail the company.

During the second strike, however, Columns 3 and 4 (Table 17.1) entered the symbolic picture in a decisive way. The clash between managers and employees was intensified because of the "broken promise" on the side of managers regarding genuine negotiations. This was seen as a clear violation of the proper handling of the boundary between labor and management.

The conflict between Swedes and Danes was also extraordinarily cathected because of the rumors of the secret transferral of jobs from Copenhagen to

Stockholm and because the management style in handling the whole case was seen as unnecessarily "Swedish"—that is, authoritarian. The seniority principle was no longer on the top of the agenda. The corresponding shift in we typifications, from we as cabin attendants and as SAS members to we as employees and as Danes, was exactly what made it meaningful for thousands of employees who were not cabin attendants and perhaps not even SAS members to join the second strike.

Notice also that the idea of Danish "autonomy" entered the symbolic landscape. This is probably the most troublesome of the four recipes for boundary maintenance because it basically says "leave us alone," whereas the other three principles of boundary maintenance do make certain legitimate types of interaction possible across the boundary between us and them. The shift toward emphasis on the management and labor contradiction and the Danish and Swedish contradiction changed the nature of the conflict qualitatively and quantitatively and eventually rendered it impossible for management to handle.

On the basis of this account of the we typifications in the case, I further elaborate three observations in the following sections. First, quite simply there were several we typifications involved and their mobilization changed over time. Second, elements of the corporate culture (such as service and company loyalty) were given very special meanings on the basis of the we typifications of the strikers. Third, it appears that we typifications evolve in connection to a chain of events. Therefore, I elaborate on the interactive and dynamic character of we typifications.

Several We Typifications Were Cathected Differently Over Time

We as cabin attendants, as SAS members, as employees, and as Danes were relevant typifications in the case but to a different degree at different times. The multiplicity and flexibility of we typifications may be a simple observation, but it is not trivial because so far most of the dominant schools of thought have confined organizational culture to "shared meanings" and assumptions (Schein, 1985), even in case studies in which multiple interpretations of the same phenomenon are reported explicitly (Smircich, 1983).

The findings in the SAS case are more consistent with an image of organizational culture as "multiple, cross-cutting cultural contexts rather than as stable, bounded, homogeneous cultures" (Gregory, 1983, p. 365) and in line with Martin's (1992) "ambiguity perspective" in the sense that the relevance of particular cultural meanings and the appearance of particular coalitions is highly situation dependent.

The case demonstrates that the situational context that nourishes particular we typifications can change dramatically even within a nine-day period. An important question is, of course, what triggers a shift in we typifications?

The multiple we typifications that the striking cabin attendants refer to at different times provide them with a repertoire of discursive options. They use these options in a creative and flexible way as responses to what they see as threats in a particular organizational context. One might therefore speculate about the political function of their we typifications. These constructs can be seen as rhetorical instruments that were helpful in aligning "cabin attendants" with "SAS members" and "employees" and "Danes" at the right time. The we typifications not only defended the interests of the strikers but also helped build a powerful (and victorious) coalition against the Swedish management.

It is problematic, however, to view we typifications in this case as mere derivatives of interests. This is because interests cannot be seen as completely independent of cultural meanings. Interests are culturally and institutionally defined (Dobbin, 1994; Wildavsky, 1987). For instance, as SAS members, the strikers define their interests as maintaining the "traditional and genuine" SAS even at the expense of potentially damaging the company as an economic structure by striking and, perhaps eventually, threatening their own job security. If the strikers have interests, these are also partly interpreted and defined from the perspective of the involved we typifications.

Interests can therefore not merely be viewed as an explanatory variable. In general, I hesitate to attempt to pinpoint "explanatory variables" that "predict" particular we typifications. I believe more can be learned from the case by acknowledging that we typifications are created in part by being made meaningful from within.

A social collectivity may produce several we typifications to sustain itself on several symbolic fronts. This suggests that various diacritica may be cathected differently and may enter the definition of a collectivity differently depending on time and circumstances (Barth, 1969). Boundary-marking diacritica can be moved for particular purposes. Boundary crossing occurs, in principle, in two different situations: Either somebody crosses the boundary or boundaries are moved to catch a boundary crosser on whom sanctions can be exercised (Douglas as cited in Wuthnow et al., 1984). The sanctions that are released in this situation are one of the powerful ways in which the community is symbolically sustained. We-ness may be defined as much by congregation as by segregation (Cheney, 1983), as much by consciousness of difference as by consciousness of kind (Van Maanen & Barley, 1984), and as much by the negative cult as by the positive one (Nisbet,

1966, p. 248). In other words, boundary maintenance rather than cultural "content" may be the best analytical key to we-ness (Barth, 1969, p. 15).

Relatively few diacritica may be cathected to distinguish a we from a "non-we." The point is not any absolute amount of objective differences. Thus, we typifications do not describe precisely the social collectivity from which they originate but rather the normative order in which the collectivity wishes to find itself. Once a particular we has been typified on the basis of this normative order, it favors, legitimizes, and triggers a type of social interaction that illustrates, supports, and enacts this particular set of cultural concepts rather than another (Barth, 1969, p. 16). As a particular chain of events unfolds in the case, the strikers respond flexibly by emphasizing a corresponding boundary maintenance along different we typifications.

How can the normative messages from the strikers be presented as normatively binding for those who are not cabin attendants? The answer to this question is by reference to the "shared culture" in SAS that becomes defined in a very special way.

Elements of the Shared Culture Are Given a Special Meaning From the Perspective of Particular We Typifications

The case shows that elements of the notorious corporate culture in SAS are given a particular meaning from the strikers' perspective. The resulting meaning of "service" and of "SAS loyalty" is far from what might have been the intentions when these constructs occurred as elements of a corporate culture designed by managers.

Meanings are not inherent in signs. Meanings are determined by the relative location of signs in particular meaning systems (de Saussure, 1959). Ambiguity can be regarded as a normal state of affairs in the sense that multiple interpretations are, in principle, always possible to the extent that the "same" sign can find different relative locations in different systems of meaning. Many of the corporate cultures that have been made famous during the past 15 years of interest in organizational culture happen to be relatively vague, unclear, unspecific, and ambiguous.

McGovern and Hope-Hailey (see Chapter 9, this volume) found that the strength of the culture of an excellent company resided not in rigorous indoctrination but rather in a certain ambiguity of the core symbolic creeds. This allowed the culture to be sustained across national and business unit boundaries in recessionary as well as prosperous times. The "light" form of cultural control even promoted a high degree of commitment to the company.

A we formulated with conviction and emotion, but vaguely specified, may be one way, if not the only way, to achieve a "unification of diversity" in culturally complex organizations (Eisenberg, 1984). Vagueness in defining a we and its goals may facilitate creative experimentation (Martin & Meyerson, 1988). Sometimes it may be a necessary precondition for joint organized action among actors with different interpretive systems (Donnellon, Gray, & Bougon, 1986).

For instance, religious communities are sometimes built on the principle of a very ambiguous "via negativa": God can never be defined explicitly, yet his way should be followed. The follower is left with the responsibility of "solving" the paradox by means of imaginations and interpretations of the mysterious. In doing so, the individual achieves connectedness and commitment (Flanagan, 1985; Kesich, 1987) to a community that cannot be made fully explicit.

Organizational identity may rely partly on similar principles. It may be important for members to think and talk about connectedness to a we, although its core is never defined. For instance, corporate art collections (Joy & Baba, 1991) may provide such occasions to talk about a special organizational identity without implying any specific denotations at all. To know what the shared meanings really mean becomes itself a symbol of affiliation, competence, connectedness, and loyalty. This type of maintenance of shared meanings may, under routine conditions, be very functional in the sense that members feel emotionally secure, they reduce tensions, they become integrated, they rely on their leaders and themselves as a group, and so on. After all, who is against such themes as service and company loyalty? Perhaps the broad and vague character of terms such as these help explain their occurrence in "integrative" corporate cultures. In this case, however, we have seen how the same vague cultural themes have been infused with special meanings that justify a strike.

The paradox seems to be that the more ambiguous meanings are to "unify diversity," the more susceptible they are to be redefined from various interpretive perspectives during conflicts. In crisis situations, the ambiguous character of the shared meanings reveals itself. They do not facilitate choices between various alternatives for action. Specific meaning has to be added. Then it becomes obvious that the shared we is far from clearly defined and therefore vulnerable. Various conflicting interpretations of what the we really means surface in practice. The general hypothesis I offer is that these conflicting cultural "redefinitions" of organizational identity are not a coincidence. They may be due to the fact that in sufficiently complex organizations shared meanings are vulnerable because only if they were very vague and ambiguous in the first place could they be candidates for the unification of diversity (temporarily and to some extent) in the organization.

The Interactive Nature of We Typifications

In this case, we have seen how Carlzon recycles the theme of SAS loyalty in his attempt to introduce a new corporate culture for all SAS members. In turn, elements of this corporate culture are recycled by cabin attendants. When the response of the managers to the first strike is fully known, the strikers launch yet another set of we typifications with a particular instructive message to managers.

Thus, each we typification appears to be embedded in an ongoing, evolving exchange of meanings. Perhaps each typification is best understood in terms of its dynamic relation to other we typifications. Each we is related to other we typifications in a double sense; each is both a response to earlier typifications and a stock of meanings that can be recycled in new ways by we typifications to come.

An important feature of the interactive character of we typifications may be the instructions that each we typification tends to communicate to those who are on the boundary or beyond but who should behave as prescribed by the normative order of the we. This is possible because once a certain we is formulated, it is an interpretive filtering device that helps distinguish between legitimate and illegitimate collective actions (Dutton & Dukerich, 1991).

The we that delivers this instruction is, of course, formulated not as a construction but as a given essence to be taken for granted. We have seen, however, that the presence of various interpretation systems renders the shared meanings ambiguous enough to be recycled, dynamically and interactively, with a dramatically different content each time they are referred to. In this case, Carlzon attempts to instruct his employees about proper behavior under the aegis of the "new corporate culture." Later, the strikes instruct Carlzon and his new managers about proper behavior given a certain symbolic order in which traditional SAS loyalty has been attributed a very distinct meaning.

Because we definitions can be understood as mutual normative instructions only within a relative and interactive space, each we definition, in principle, symbolically bears the trace of other we definitions (Gergen, 1992). Each reflects them, compensates for them, instructs them, opposes them, and maybe, paradoxically, enhances them. It is possible then to think of we typifications not as expressions of deeper, underlying essences, but as products of interactive, never-ending discourse concerning the reciprocal maintenance of organizational microidentities within the framework of organizational identity as a crowded category.

Conclusion and Implications

The best understanding of organizational culture emerges if one does not link culture to organization in simple, mechanical ways. It is perhaps only because of the relatively differentiated, fragmented, and complex character of most contemporary organizations that the contemporary desire to explicate a clear identity in organizations—a shared and consensual we—is accentuated. This we, however, is at the same time a compensation for differentiation, fragmentation, and complexity. A we such as the one known from corporate culture has to be formulated instrumentally and sometimes manipulatively exactly because it is embedded in a context that does not spontaneously produce a "we-ness" as a given fact. It is, however, precisely the same conditions that often make the resulting definitions of a shared we vague and ambiguous and vulnerable—that is, open to conflicting redefinitions.

In practice, shared meanings may oscillate between the lack of specificity that is necessary to "unify diversity" in organizations and the specificity necessary to prevent the vague shared cultural themes from becoming meaningless or continuously fragmented when interpreted from various interpretive perspectives.

The less specific a unifying we is formulated, the less likely it is to help the organization make subsequent decisions. When critical decision-making opportunities occur, conflictual we definitions are likely to surface that have very different action implications but all claim to be grounded in the unified we. Due to their vague and ambiguous character, the shared meanings become recycled and redefined.

The case study suggests that an important aspect of such "recycled" cultural elements is the instructions that are delivered to organizational members who happen to be depicted as "outside" or "on the boundary." When a particular we is formed around a particular normative order, a message is sent to organizational members who "ought to" adjust their unacceptable behavior according to the norms that are suggested. This is more than just a struggle between subcultures because only when a particular normative order is formulated to be valid for the organization as such can it be presented as normatively binding for those who happen to be depicted as boundary crossers but who are instructed to comply to the norms defined by a particular organizational we.

When internal factions then attempt to instruct each other differently, organizational identity becomes a crowded category.

The desire to formulate organizational identity can in this light be understood not merely as a functional prerequisite for emotional security or a cognitive reduction of chaos. It is perhaps better understood as a discursive exchange concerning organizational microidentities. It is through their interaction and reciprocity that these microidentities are given life. The Danish cabin attendants of SAS would probably not be who they are if they did not know how to define themselves in contradistinction to the specific combination of other employees, managers, and nonmembers of SAS and Swedes.

One evident implication of this depiction of organization identity is that there is a need for new and more complex models of ways of understanding cultural leadership. Dominant models of cultural leadership have focused on leaders as persons who create and supply shared meanings and assumptions in organizations (Pfeffer, 1981; Schein, 1985; Smircich & Morgan, 1982). Some even endorse "strong cultures" as a management instrument. The underlying ontology here is one in which the interactive character of the attempts to formulate organizational identity cannot be fully understood, as is stated by Hurst (quoted in Ford & Backoff, 1988):

> Management believes that it can (does) stand outside the system and manipulate the processes for its own benefit. Such actions generate perverse reactions because management is not outside the system looking in; it is inside the system looking at itself. (p. 115)

Attempts in practice to define cultural consensus in an organization are often frustrating and perhaps counterproductive because each particular we typification "bears the trace" of other we typifications; it calls forth alternative, sometimes conflicting, definitions of what ought to be the shared normative order.

If managers-to-be leave the business schools with only the dominant models of cultural leadership in mind, they will be equipped with a conceptual apparatus that does not help them understand the consequences that their attempts to control culture may generate in complex and dynamic organizational settings.

In search of a more systematic and general conceptual model in which the interactive nature of we typifications can be framed, Weick's (1979) model of "double interacts" comes to mind. These are fundamental reciprocal interactions that Weick views as the building blocks of all organizing. A minimal double interact consists of self's reaction to other's reaction to self's actions. For example, the more employees enforce a view of organizational relations as family-oriented (because management is seen as business oriented), the more managers emphasize that the organization must also be business oriented because it cannot be too family-oriented (Smith & Eisenberg, 1987).

This type of double interact displays the properties of an organizational "deadlock" (Spencer & Dale, 1979). Each group interprets the unfortunate interaction as caused by the other group, and attempts to unlock the deadlock lead to more of the same. Thus, in a double-interact model, we may see much more paradoxical and counterintentional effects of attempts to instill a strong corporate culture than in a simple model with independent and dependent variables.

Strength is a poor and misplaced metaphor of what it takes to interact cleverly and to unlock a deadlocked interaction because "more of the same" only enforces the ill it seeks to cure. To transcend the poverty of existing cultural models of leadership is possible only if this physical metaphor is dismantled and attempts are made to explore how creativity, sensitivity, systemic thinking, and an ability to bear paradox may create alternative paradigms for cultural management.

As researchers, we must also be careful not to let desires for clear and unambiguous conclusions lead us to overly simplify the organizational identities and cultures we study. It is always dangerous to reduce multidimensional and complex identity to one unidimensional image (Bouchet, 1995). It is perhaps especially unwarranted, however, when it comes to organizational identity. At least this case has shown some remarkable consequences of various attempts to formulate organizational identity in an organizational world marred by complex cultural constellations and paradoxical interaction.

References

Adams, G. B., & Ingersoll, V. H. (1988). Painting over old works: The culture of organization in an age of technical rationality. In B. Turner (Ed.), *Organizational symbolism* (pp. 15-31). Berlin: de Gruyter.

Albert, S., & Whetten, D. (1985). Organizational identity. In L. L. Cummings & B. Staw (Eds.), *Research in organizational behaviour, Vol. 7* (pp. 263-295). Greenwich, CT: JAI.

Alvesson, M., & Berg, P. O. (1992). *Corporate culture and organizational symbolism.* Berlin: de Gruyter.

Ardener, E. (1975). Language, ethnicity, and population. In J. H. M. Beattie & S. Lienhardt (Eds.), *Studies in social anthropology. Essays in memory of E. E. Evans-Pritchard by his former Oxford colleagues* (pp. 343-353). Oxford, UK: Oxford University Press.

Barth, F. (1969). Introduction. In F. Barth (Ed.), *Ethnic groups and boundaries* (pp. 9-38). Oslo, Norway: Universitetsforlaget.

Beck, U., Giddens, A., & Lash, S. (1994). *Reflexive modernization*. Stanford, CA: Stanford University Press.

Berger, P., & Luckmann, T. (1967). *The social construction of reality*. New York: Doubleday.

Bouchet, D. (1995). Marketing and the redefinition of ethnicity. In J. Costa & G. Bamossy (Eds.), *Marketing in a multicultural world* (pp. 68-104). Thousand Oaks, CA: Sage.

Broms, H., & Gahmberg, H. (1983). Communication to self in organizations and cultures. *Administrative Science Quarterly, 28,* 482-495.

Busk, I. (1989). Kvalitet er drivfjederen i et velsmurt serviceforetagende [Quality is the mainspring of a well-run service cooperation]. In B. Larsen (Ed.), *Kvalitet i praksis* (pp. 125-138). Copenhagen: Sporskiftet.

Carlzon, J. (1985). *Riv pyramiderne ned!* [Tear down the pyramids!]. Copenhagen: Gyldendal.

Castoriadis, C. (1984). The imaginary: Creation in the social-historical domain. In P. Livingston (Ed.), *Disorder and order. Proceedings of the Stanford International Symposium (Sept. 14-16, 1981)* (pp. 146-161). Saratoga, FL: Anma Libri.

Cheney, G. (1983). The rhetoric of identification and the study of organizational communication. *Quarterly Journal of Speech, 69,* 143-158.

Cheney, G., & Tompkins, P. (1987). Coming to terms with organizational identification. *Central States Speech Journal, 38,* 1-15.

Christensen, L., & Cheney, G. (1994). Articulating identity in an organizational age. In S. Deetz (Ed.), *Communication yearbook 17* (pp. 221-235). Thousand Oaks, CA: Sage.

Christensen, S. (Ed.). (1984). *Carlzons klister—Kultur og forandring i SAS* [Carlzon's glue—Culture and change in SAS]. Copenhagen: Valmuen.

Czarniawska-Joerges, B. (1994). Narratives of individual and organizational identities. In S. Deetz (Ed.), *Communication yearbook 17* (pp. 193-221). Thousand Oaks, CA: Sage.

Deal, T., & Kennedy, A. (1982). *Corporate cultures. The rites and rituals of corporate life*. Reading, MA: Addison-Wesley.

Dobbin, F. (1994). Cultural models of organization: The social construction of rational organizing principles. In D. Crane (Ed.), *The sociology of culture. Emerging theoretical perspectives* (pp. 117-141). Oxford, UK: Blackwell.

Donnellon, A., Gray, B., & Bougon, M. (1986). Communication, meaning and organized action. *Administrative Science Quarterly, 31*(1), 43-55.

Dutton, J., & Dukerich, J. (1991). Keeping an eye on the mirror: Image and identity in organizational adaptation. *Academy of Management Journal, 34,* 517-554.

Durkheim, E. (1965). *The elementary forms of religious life*. New York: Free Press.

Ebers, M. (1991). Der Aufstieg des Themas "Organisationskultur" in problem- und disziplinge schichtlicher Perspektive [The rise of the theme "organizational culture" in problem- and discipline-historical perspective]. In E. Dülfer (Ed.), *Organisationskultur. Phänomen—Philosophie—Technologie* (2nd ed.). Stuttgart: C. E. Poeschel.

Edström, A. (1985). *Leadership and corporate development. The case of SAS* [Working report]. Stockholm: The Council for Management and Working Life Issues.

Edström, A., Norbäck, L. E., & Rendahl, J. E. (1989). *Förnyelsens lederskap. SAS' utveckling från flybolag til reseföretag* [Management of renewal. The development of SAS from airline cooperation to travel company]. Stockholm: Norstedt.

Eisenberg, E. (1984). Ambiguity as strategy in organizational communication. *Communication Monographs, 51,* 227-242.

Flanagan, K. (1985). Liturgy, ambiguity and silence. The ritual management of real absence. *British Journal of Sociology, 36,* 193-223.

Ford, J. D., & Backoff, R. W. (1988). Organizational change in and out of dualities and paradox. In K. S. Cameron & R. E. Quinn (Eds.), *Paradox and transformation. Toward a theory of change in organization and management* (pp. 80-121). Cambridge, MA: Ballinger.

Geertz, C. (1975). *The interpretation of cultures. Selected essays.* London: Hutchinson.

Gergen, K. J. (1992). Organization theory in the postmodern era. In M. Hughes & M. Reed (Eds.), *Rethinking organization* (pp. 207-225). London: Sage.

Giorgi, A. (1988). Validity and reliability from a phenomenological perspective. In W. J. Baker (Ed.), *Recent trends in theoretical psychology* (pp. 167-176). New York/Berlin: Springer-Verlag.

Gregory, K. (1983). Native view paradigms: Multiple cultures and culture conflicts in organizations. *Administrative Science Quarterly, 28,* 359- 376.

Hofstede, G. (1980). *Culture's consequences. International differences in work related values.* Beverly Hills, CA: Sage.

Hofstede, G. (1982). Ledelsesmetoderne og de nationale kulturforskelle [Management methods and national culture differences]. *Harvard Børsen, 1,* 7-23.

Joy, A., & Baba, V. (1991, June). *Corporate art collections and organizational culture. An ethnographic inquiry.* Paper presented at the 8th SCOS conference, Copenhagen.

Kesich, V. (1987). Via negativa. In M. Eliade (Ed.), *The encyclopedia of religion.* New York: MacMillan.

Kunda, G. (1992). *Engineering culture: Control and commitment in a hi-tech firm.* Philadelphia: Temple University Press.

Lincoln, Y. S., & Denzin, N. K. (1994). *Handbook of qualitative methods.* Thousand Oaks, CA: Sage.

Lysgaard, S. (1961). *Arbeiderkollektivet* [The workers' collective]. Oslo, Norway: Universitetsforlaget.

Martin, J. (1992). *Cultures in organizations. Three perspectives.* New York: Oxford University Press.

Martin, J., & Meyerson, D. (1988). Organizational cultures and the denial, challenging and acknowledgement of. In M. Moch, L. Pondy, & H. Thomas (Eds.), *Managing ambiguity and change.* New York: John Wiley.

Nisbet, R. (1966). *The sociological tradition.* London: Heinemann.

Nisbet, R., & Perrin, R. G. (1977). *The social bond.* New York: Knopf.

Olaisen, J., & Revang, Ø. (1991). *Information management as the main component in the strategy for the 1990s in SAS.* Sandvika, Norway: Handelshøyskolen BI.

Peters, T., & Waterman, R. (1982). *In search of excellence. Lessons from America's best run companies.* New York: Harper & Row.

Pfeffer, J. (1981). Management as symbolic action. In L. L. Cummings & S. Staw (Eds.), *Research on organizational behaviour, Vol. 3.* Greenwich, CT: JAI.

Ray, C. (1986). Corporate culture: The last frontier of control? *Journal of Management Studies, 23*(3), 287-298.

Røvik, K. A. (1992). *Den Syke Stat. Myter og Moter i Omstillingsarbeidet* [The sick state. Myths and fashions in reform activities]. Oslo, Norway: Universitetsforlaget.

Sahlins, M. (1976). *Culture and practical reason.* Chicago: Aldine.

de Saussure, F. (1959). *A course in general linguistics.* New York: McGraw-Hill.

Schein, E. (1985). *Organizational culture and leadership.* San Francisco: Jossey-Bass.

Schutz, A. (1975). *Hverdagslivets Sociologi* [The sociology of everyday life]. Copenhagen: Hans Reitzel.

Sevon, G. (1996). Organizational imitation in identity transformation. In G. Sevon & B. Czarniawska-Joerges (Eds.), *Translating organizational change.* Berlin: de Gruyter.

Smircich, L. (1983). Organizations as shared meanings. In L. R. Pondy, P. J. Frost, G. Morgan, & T. C. Dandridge (Eds.), *Organizational symbolism* (pp. 55-68). Greenwich, CT: JAI.

Smircich, L., & Morgan, G. (1982). Leadership: The management of meaning. *Journal of Applied Behavioral Sciences, 18*(3), 257-273.

Smith, R., & Eisenberg, E. (1987). Conflict at Disneyland: A root-metaphor analysis. *Communication Monographs, 54,* 367-379.

Spencer, L., & Dale, A. (1979). Integration and regulation in organizations: A contextual approach. *Sociological Review, 27*(4), 679-701.

Spiegelberg, H. (1973). On the right to say "we": A linguistic and phenomenological analysis. In G. Psathas (Ed.), *Phenomenological sociology. Issues and applications* (pp. 129-158). New York: John Wiley.

Stake, R. E. (1994). Case studies. In N. K. Denzin & Y. S. Lincoln (Eds.), *Handbook of qualitative research* (pp. 236-247). Thousand Oaks, CA: Sage.

Turner, B. (1971). *Exploring the industrial subculture.* London: MacMillan.

Turner, B. (1986). Sociological aspects on organizational symbolism. *Organization Studies, 7,* 101-116.

Van Maanen, J. (1991). The smile factory: Work at Disneyland. In P. Frost, L. Moore, C. Lundberg, & J. Martin (Eds.), *Reframing organizational culture* (pp. 58-76). Newbury Park, CA: Sage.

Van Maanen, J., & Barley, S. (1984). Occupational communities: Culture and control in organizations. In L. L. Cummings & S. Staw (Eds.), *Research in organizational behaviour, Vol. 6* (pp. 287-365). Greenwich, CT: JAI.

Van Maanen, J., & Barley, S. (1985). Cultural organization: Fragments of a theory. In P. Frost, L. Moore, C. Lundberg, & J. Martin, (Eds.), *Organizational culture* (pp. 31-54). Beverly Hills, CA: Sage.

Weick, K. E. (1979). *The social psychology of organizing.* Reading, MA: Addison-Wesley.

Wildavsky, A. (1987). Choosing preferences by constructing institutions: A cultural theory of preference formation. *American Political Science Review, 81*(1), 3-21.

Willmott, H. (1991, June). *Strength is ignorance; Slavery is freedom: Managing culture in modern organizations.* Paper presented at the 8th International SCOS Conference, Copenhagen.

Wuthnow, R., Hunter, J., Bergesen, A., & Kurzweil, E. (1984). *Cultural analysis.* London: Routledge Kegan Paul.

Epilogue

As we come to the end of the book, it is hoped that the wide variety of contributions included in this book have not confused but rather helped to paint a clearer and more differentiated picture of the "messiness" of cultural complexity in organizations. This very contradiction represented by the two words *clearer* and *messiness* in the previous sentence is one of the issues that this book has addressed. Organizational life is more complex, messy, and inherently paradoxical than most conceptualizations and managerial recommendations may suggest. The concept of cultural complexity advocated here suggests that culture in organizational settings may be several things at the same time: homogenous, differentiated into several subcultures, and composed of multiple cultural identities that create contrasts and contradictions and ambiguity. The reported studies have provided good examples of a richer organizational life that can be researched. Figure 1.1 serves as a map to locate the various issues that were addressed in the different chapters and thus helps create some order amidst the wide variety of issues. It may also have revealed, however, the blank spots—issues that were not addressed, questions that were not raised, or answers that were not given.

As mentioned in the introduction, this volume can be considered a work in progress. It has provided a few answers while opening many new avenues for research. Many more national contexts exist and should be investigated. These nationally based investigations, however, should proceed with a strong focus on their interplay with other cultural levels and groupings, such as region, and organization or cross-cutting cultural identities, such as profession or gender. Many more industries have not yet been well explored in terms of their cultural characteristics. The role of ethnicity as a source of cultural identity and its impact on organizational life warrants further exploration. Also, more research investigating multiple cultural identities and their interactions, impacts, and managerial implications may be a key to a better understanding of cultural dynamics in organizations as well as to many cultural problems.

The creativity in research approaches, with their variety of methods and time dedication, may encourage more researchers to step away from mainstream definitions and expectations about what constitutes "good" research. In the process, they may realize that such a journey of discovery is not just full of hurdles but can also be quite a bit of fun. Finally, it appears that the time has come to enter into a more creative dialogue among researchers whose work may address the same issues and cultural contexts. These researchers come from different cultural backgrounds, such as nation, discipline, and profession, and thus offer varying lenses and different perspectives. Consider the synergies that could come from working together in an appreciating way. Together, let's embark on the further exploration of cultural complexity!

About the Editor

Sonja A. Sackmann, MS (Psychology), PhD (Management), is Professor in the Faculty of Management and Organizational Sciences at the Universität der Bundeswehr München, Germany, and a partner at the MZSG Management Zentrum in St. Gallen, Switzerland. She has taught at the Graduate School of Management at UCLA, the School of Business Administration at the University of Vienna, and the business departments of the University of St. Gallen, the Jiao Tong University in Shanghai, and the University of Konstanz. Prior to her position in Munich, she was head of research and development, project leader, and consultant in the behavioral area at the MZSG (1987-1992). She has consulted the top and middle management of many international firms, such as Ford Motor Company, the VW Group, and Lufthansa, as well as government agencies and hospitals. Her international teaching, research, and consulting include personal, team, management and organizational development and change, communication, leadership, organizational culture in national and international settings, and intercultural issues. Her work has appeared in English in the *Handbook of International Management Research, Administrative Science Quarterly, Human Relations, Communication Yearbook,* and *Personnel Journal,* and books published by Sage (*Cultural Knowledge in Organizations,* 1991) and Dow Jones-Irwin (*Tough Choices: The Decision Making Styles of America's Top 50 CEO's,* 1990; coauthored with

W. Pelton and R. Boguslaw). She has recently published articles on organizational development and culture change in hospitals, human resources management practices in Germany, diagnosing culture at the organizational and national level, and the soft factor in project management (all in German). She is currently on the editorial boards of *Organisation, Management Learning,* and the *Journal for East European Management Studies.* She is a member of the Academy of Management, the Academy of International Business, the Western Academy of Management, the Standing Conference on Organizational Symbolism, and the Schweizer Gesellschaft für Arbeits- und Organisationspsychologie.

About the Contributors

Ceyhan Aldemir, PhD, is Professor of Organization and Management, Faculty of Business, at Dokuz Eylül University, Izmir, Turkey. Since 1975, he has been teaching courses especially in the areas of organization theory, organizational behavior, organizational development, and human resource management. He taught at Cornell University, Rochester Institue of Technology, and St. John Fisher College, Rochester, New York, and in Germany at Troy State University in the European Region's master of public administration program. He served as a chairman of Department of Business. He has published several articles both in Turkey and abroad. His recent research interests include the history of Turkish managerial culture. He also headed and participated in several projects for both public and private sector enterprises in Turkey.

Yasemin Arbak, PhD, is Assistant Professor of Organization and Management, Faculty of Business, at Dokuz Eylül University, Izmir, Turkey. During her 7 years of work experience, she has contributed to and participated in several projects, mainly in the field of organization and management. Currently, she is serving the World Bank, Igeme, agroindustry project as a management consultant. Her current research interests include managerial values and person and culture fit topics.

She recently coauthored (with H. Kabasakal, A. E. Katrinli, Ö. T. Özmen, and I. Zeytinoglu) an article titled "Women Managers in Turkey: The Impact of Personalities and Leaderships Style," which will be published in the *Journal of Management Systems*.

Christophe A. J. J. Boone, PhD, is Research Professor at the University of Maastricht and codirector of the Maastricht Research School of Economics of Technology and Organizations. His research interests focus on the relationship of top management team composition and organizational outcomes and on the dynamics of competition and the structure of industries.

Nakiye A. Boyacigiller, PhD, is Professor of International Management at San Jose State University. Her research on cross-cultural organizational science and international human resource management has appeared in the *Journal of International Business Studies, Academy of Management Review, Organization Studies, Research in Organizational Behavior, Handbook of International Management Research,* and *Advances in International Comparative Management,* among others. She is coauthor (with N. J. Adler, M. B. Teagarden, and M. A. von Glinow) of *Organizational Behavior and Human Resource Management: A Resource Guide for Internationalizing the Business School Curriculum.* She serves on the editorial boards of the *Journal of Management Inquiry, Asia Pacific HRM,* and the *Bogazici Journal* (published in Turkey). She is chair-elect of the International Management Division of the Academy of Management and is active in the Academy of International Business and the Western Academy of Management. At San Jose State University, she received the dean's Faculty Excellence Award (1989) and the Meritorious Performance College of Business Teacher-Scholar (for 1995-1996). She has taught at the Anderson Graduate School of Management (UCLA), the Stockholm School of Economics' Institute of International Business, Bilkent University (Ankara), and Bogazici University (Istanbul).

Katrina Burrus, PhD, is founder and principal of MKB Conseil, an organizational development consulting firm located in Geneva, Switzerland. She teaches at the Open University and Thunderbilt's campus in Geneva. In addition, she consults in the United States and in Europe and specializes in the areas of managing system change efforts, implementing quality initiatives and organizational assessments, and executive development. Previously, she was responsible for all U.S. start-up functions of a prestigious line of sportswear manufactured in Italy with the authorized Ferrari label from Enzo Ferrari. She has 7 years of experience working for Swiss banks that included devising client segmentation, packaging financial products to customers' needs, controlling sales results of the mutual funds department, and interfacing with quality improvement teams.

Myung-Ho Chung, PhD, is Chief Researcher at Samsung Economic Research Institute (SERI) in Seoul, Korea. He works in the area of management innovation at SERI and his current research interests include paradox and contradiction and organizational change, organizational learning, and new product system.

Peter Dahler-Larsen, PhD, is Associate Professor in the Department of Political Science and Public Management of Odense University in Denmark. With a starting point in qualitative studies of organizational culture, he has remained interested in cultural and institutional perspectives on organizations. In his recent publications, he has applied these perspectives to such thematic areas as organizational ethics, leadership studies, and evaluation research.

Sjiera de Vries, PhD, is Assistant Professor of Organizational Psychology at the University of Leiden, The Netherlands. She has been working in the field of interethnic relations for the past 10 years in several academic and nonacademic settings. Currently, her research focuses on the quality of products of interethnic work teams and attitudes concerning working in ethnically diverse organizations. She serves as secretary of the Society of Interethnic Education, Training, and Research (SIETAR), The Netherlands. SIETAR is an international organization of professionals with branches in different countries.

Thomas S. Eberle, PhD, teaches sociology at the University of St. Gallen, Switzerland. He is a former vice president of the Swiss Sociological Association and served as an editor of the association's newsletter and of its publishing company, SEISMO. His research areas include the sociology of culture, organization, communication, work, and methodology. His predominant perspective is a phenomenologically founded sociology of knowledge. His recent publications include "A New Paradigm for the Sociology of Knowledge: The Social Construction of Reality After 25 Years" in *Schweizerische Zeitschrift für Soziologie (1992);* "Psicología Social y Sociología del Conocimiento" (Social Psychology and the Sociology of Knowledge) in *Revista de Psicología Social* (1993); "Relational Knowledge in Organizational Theory: An Exploration in Some of Its Implications" in D.- M. Hosking, H. Peter Dachler, & K. J. Gergen (Eds.), *Management and Organization: Relational Alternatives to Individualism* (1995); and "Dislocation Policies in Western Europe: Past, Present, and Future" in *Annals of the American Academy of Political and Social Science* (1996).

Tatjana Globokar, PhD, is a researcher at the French National Center for Scientific Research [Centre National de Recherche Scientifique (CNRS)] and works in Paris with a research group, Gestion et Société, that studies the influence of national cultures on management. A former specialist of the economies of Eastern Europe, she focuses currently on cultural management models of Central and Eastern European countries. She is secretary general of the Ecole de Paris of Management, an international debate forum founded in 1993. She is author of many publications on Eastern European economies and on cultural management models.

Helge Hernes is a researcher at Agder Research Foundation, Kristiansand, Norway, with a wide range of research interests, predominantly in the public sector. He recently completed his PhD at The Norwegian School of Economics and Business Administration in Bergen, Norway. Prior to his doctoral studies, he worked for approximately 12 years in hospital administration, an occupational practice that has shaped his interest in research in a hospital setting.

Veronica Hope-Hailey, PhD, UMIST, is Lecturer in Human Resource Management at the Cranfield School of Management. From 1993 to 1995, she was a research fellow on the Leading Edge project based at the Judge Institute of Management, University of Cambridge. She has published papers on cultural change in organizations, career management, and human resource management.

Gülem Atabay Ishakoglu is Research Assistant in Organization and Management, Faculty of Business, Dokuz Eylül University, Izmir, Turkey. Currently, she is completing her PhD dissertation on person-organization fit. She is working with Ceyhan Aldemir and Jülide Kesken on the topic of cultural background. Her current research interest is the plateau stage of career planning of employees in private sector organizations.

Seungkwon Jang, PhD, is Chief Researcher at Samsung Economic Research Institute in Seoul, Korea. He is currently interested in poststructuralism, chaos theory, and East Asian management practices.

Alev Ergenç Katrinli, PhD, is Professor of Organization and Management, Faculty of Business, at Dokuz Eylül University, Izmir, Turkey. She has taught at St. Fisher University, Rochester, New York, as a visiting associate professor. Her recent research interests include service quality and organizational involvement and cultural systems of organizations in Turkey. She is coauthor (with Ö. T. Özmen) of "Women Managers in Turkey," published in *Women in Management* (1994), and of "Women Managers in Turkey: The Impact of Personalities and Leadership Styles" (with H. Kabasakal, Ö. T. Özmen, I. Zeytinoglu, and Y. Arbak), forthcoming in the *Journal of Management Systems.*

Jülide Kesken is Research Assistant in Organization and Management, Faculty of Business, at Dokuz Eylül University, Izmir, Turkey. Currently, she is completing her PhD dissertation on organizational politics. Her recent research interest is in the cultural background of Turkish managerial systems.

M. Jill Kleinberg, PhD, is Associate Professor of Organizational Behavior and International Management in the School of Business and Management, University of Kansas, Lawrence, where she teaches courses in organizational behavior, comparative and cross-cultural management, and organizational ethnography. She has done extensive field research on Japanese firms operating in the United States that focuses on cross-cultural management issues. Her recent publications examine emergent cultures in Japan-U.S. binational organizational settings and Japan-U.S. business negotiation as a context for negotiated culture.

Bas A. Koene, PhD, works as a management consultant for the Holland Consulting Group in Amsterdam.

Willem C. J. Koot, PhD, is Professor of Organizational Anthropology at the Free University of Amsterdam, The Netherlands. His main research topics are ethnicity, cultural change in organizations, minority studies, and intercultural management. His regional specialization is the Caribbean and the coasts of Latin America. Until recently, he worked as a consultant for companies such as Philips and Sony. With some colleagues, he is currently writing a book on paradoxes in organizations (e.g., globalization vs. localization and control vs. participation). Previous articles on ethnicity and organization culture include (among others) "Ambiguity and Changing Identities: On the Dynamics of Organizational Culture" in W. Shadid and P. J. M. Nas (Eds.), *Culture Development and Communication. Essays in Honour of J. D. Speckmann* (1993).

Juha Laurila, PhD, is Research Fellow of the Academy of Finland at the Helsinki School of Economics and Business Administration. He is author of *Social Movements in Management* (1995) and his articles have appeared in *Finnish Administrative Studies* and the *Finnish Journal of Business Economics*. His current research interests include the actor-focused approach to management in general and in the management of technology in the paper industry context in particular. He grew up in the context of a Finnish industrial locality that has fostered his interest in the long-term development of capital-intensive industries and the managers and other social communities within and around them.

Patrick McGovern, DPh, is Lecturer in Sociology at the London School of Economics and Political Science, London, England. He previously was employed as a researcher at the London Business School and, more recently, as Lecturer in Sociology at Aston University. His research interests include the sociology of employment and economic life. He has published papers on employers' labor market practices, human resource management, and the employment practices of multinational firms.

Ömür Timurcanday Özmen, PhD, is Professor of Organization and Management, Faculty of Business, at Dokuz Eylül University, Izmir, Turkey. She has taught at St. John Fisher University, Rochester, New York, and the University of Pennsylvania. Her recent research interests include business ethics and organizational commitment and cultural systems of organizations in Turkey. She has written many articles on organization and management and organizational behavior. She is coauthor (with A. E. Katrinli) of "Women Managers in Turkey," published in *Women in Management* (1994), and of "Women Managers in Turkey: The Impact of Personalities and Leadership Styles" (with H. Kabasakal, A. E. Katrinli, I. Zeytinoglu, and Y. Arbak), forthcoming in the *Journal of Management Systems*.

Margaret E. Phillips, MS, PhD, is Assistant Professor of Organization and Management in the School of Business and Management at Pepperdine University, Malibu, California. She has worked with multi-institutional consortia in California and New York, within the U.S. federal government, and in both line and staff positions in various public sector organizations. In her teaching, research, and consulting in the United States, Jamaica, and Italy, she focuses on cultural influences on behavior in and of organizations, management development in multicultural contexts, qualitative research methods, and the management of the arts. She is coauthor (with S. A. Sackmann, N. A. Boyacigiller, and M. J. Kleinberg) of "Conceptualizing Culture," a chapter in the first *Handbook for International Management Research* (1996). Her article, "Industry Mindsets," originally published in *Organization Science,* will be published in the forthcoming book *Cognition Within and Between Organizations* (Sage).

Terry Schumacher, PhD, is a Research Fellow in Multimedia at The Open University, Milton Keynes, UK. He is currently developing a training simulation addressing the organizational issues in innovation. The description of Camelot in this book was drawn from his dissertation project, which produced a simulation that described Camelot's culture. His research interests include organizational culture and culture change, cognitive maps, the design and use of training simulations, strategy and scenario planning, technology management, and futures research.

Diana Rosemary Sharpe, PhD, is Lecturer in Organizational Management at Birmingham University, England and a Doctoral Programme Researcher at Manchester Business School, England. Her research interests include cross-cultural management and comparative studies of the nature of shop floor work organization and its relation to shop floor practices. She is also exploring these interests in the context of the quality of working life and the experience of work. She has a strong interest in ethnographic approaches to research. Time spent living and working outside her native country has influenced her commitment to learning about cultures by immersing herself in the culture being studied. In research terms, this has meant primarily working in factories on the shop floor for extended periods of time.

Joseph L. Soeters, PhD, teaches sociology at the Royal Netherlands Military Academy. He has published extensively on organizational issues in health care, industrial organizations, accounting firms, and police departments. His current research interests focus on the internationalization of military life—for example, the formation of the first German and Dutch army and the performance of military men and women in U.N. operations.

Sierk B. Ybema, PhD, is Lecturer in the Department of Cultural Anthropology, Section Culture, Organization and Management, at the Vrije Universiteit (Free

University) in Amsterdam, The Netherlands. His research focuses on cultural and political order and disorder in organizations. He is coeditor (with W. C. J. Koot and I. Sabelis) of a book on paradoxes in organizations titled *Contradictions in Context.*